Psychedelics Encyclopedia

☆ **psy·che·del·ic** (sī′kə del′ik) *adj.* [< PSYCHE + Gr. *delein*, to make manifest] **1.** of or causing extreme changes in the conscious mind, as hallucinations, delusions, intensification of awareness and sensory perception, etc. **2.** of or associated with psychedelic drugs; specif., simulating the auditory or visual effects of the psychedelic state —*n.* a psychedelic drug —**psy′che·del′i·cal·ly** *adv.*

Psychedelics Encyclopedia

REVISED EDITION

by Peter Stafford
Technical Editor Jeremy Bigwood

J. P. TARCHER, INC.
Los Angeles
Distributed by Houghton Mifflin Co.
Boston

Editors: Karl Stull, Nona Sanford, Bruce Eisner

Illustration consultant: Bob Barker,
Curator, Fitz Hugh Ludlow Memorial Library

Molecular diagrams: Alexander Shulgin & Marlyn Amann
Design and layout: Flack Studios and Michael Bass

This book is derived from experiences and observations
of many dear friends. Extra special thanks to—
Bonnie Golightly, Richard Evans Schultes, Kat McKenna,
Michael Horowitz, Timothy Leary, the Santa Cruz *Express*,
Michael Starks, Chester Anderson, Illis Casteel,
R. Gordon Wasson, Stanislav Grof, Albert Hofmann,
Sigrid Radulovic, Paul Williams, David Luttrell,
Michael Aldrich, John Beresford, Humphry Osmond,
Robert Connell Clarke, Sam Selgnij, Jonathan Ott,
Sebastian Orfali, Derek Gallagher, Oscar Janiger,
John Patterson, Wayne and Margaret.

Library of Congress Cataloging in Publication Data

Stafford, Peter
  Psychedelics encyclopedia.

  Bibliography: p. 407
Includes index.
  1. Hallucinogenic drugs. 2. Drugs—Physiological
effect. 3. Drug abuse—United States—History.
4. Drugs—Psychological aspects. I. Bigwood,
Jeremy, 1951-   II. Title
HV5822.H25S74   1982   362.2'93   82-10482
ISBN 0-87477-231-1

Manufactured in the United States of America
V 10 9 8 7 6 5 4 3 2 1

Second Edition

To Sasha,
for future reference.

Keith Graves

The author has made every effort to trace the ownership of all copyright and quoted material presented. In the event of any question arising as to the use of a selection, he offers his apologies for any errors or omissions that may inadvertently have occurred, and will be pleased to make the necessary corrections in future editions of this book.

Acknowledgment and thanks are due the following authors, photographers, illustrators, agents and publishers for permission to use their materials:

Crawdaddy!	Lou Watts
Psychedelic Review	Harlan Reiders
Journal of Psychedelic Drugs	Claudio Naranjo
Jack Call	PharmChem
Berkeley Bonaparte	Carmen Helisten
Allen Ginsberg	NORML
R. Cobb	David Hoye
Steve Gladstone	Humphry Osmond
B. Madden	Arthur Brack
Frank Siteman	Jonathan Ott
Mel Frank	Paul Stamets
And/Or Press	

Burns & MacEachern, Ltd., *Psychedelic Ecstasy,* © 1967 by William Marshall & Gilbert W. Taylor

His Highness, Art Kleps, Chief Boo Hoo, The Neo-American Church

"Pot Could Save His Sight," reprinted with permission from *The National Observer,* © Dow Jones & Company, Inc. 1976

Michael Valentine Smith, *Psychedelic Chemistry,* © Rip Off Press 1973

United Native Americans and the Print Mint

Church of the Tree of Life

Claudio Naranjo, *The Healing Journey: New Approaches to Consciousness,* © 1973. Reprinted by permission of Pantheon Books, a Division of Random House, Inc. and of Hutchinson Publishing Group Limited, the British publishers

Peter T. Furst, *Flesh of the Gods: The Ritual Use of Hallucinogens,* © 1972 by Praeger Publishers, Inc., New York. Reprinted by permission of Praeger Publishers, Inc., a Division of Holt, Rinehart and Winston

Richard Lingemann, *Drugs From A to Z,* © 1974. Used by permission of McGraw-Hill Book Co.

Vera Rubin and Lambros Comitas, *Ganja in Jamaica,* © Mouton and Company, The Hague/Paris

Gary Menser, *Hallucinogenic and Poisonous Mushroom Field Guide*

Richard Evans Schultes, Professor of Natural Sciences; Director Botanical Museum, Harvard University, Oxford St., Cambridge, Mass. 02138

R.E.L. Masters and Jean Houston, *The Varieties of Psychedelic Experience.* By permission of Holt, Rinehart and Winston

Richard Heffern, *Secrets of the Mind-Altering Plants of Mexico,* Pyramid Books

Marlene Dobkin de Rios, *Visionary Vine*

Ginsberg and Burroughs, *the YAGE letters,* City Lights Books

Grieve, *A Modern Herbal*

D. Wallechinski, S. Salyer & M. Shedlin, *Laughing Gas*

CONTENTS

FOREWORD

by Dr. Andrew Weil, page x

PREVIEW

CHAPTER ONE

The LSD Family (the archetype) 34-101

CHAPTER TWO

Peyote, Mescaline and San Pedro 102-155

CHAPTER THREE

Marijuana and Hashish 156-221

Foreword

When Peter Stafford's *Psychedelics Encyclopedia* first appeared in 1977, it was a major addition to the literature on an important group of drugs affecting the mind. It provided detailed and straightforward accounts of LSD, mescaline, marijuana, and a host of other chemicals and plants. Stafford's information was accurate, balanced and uncontaminated by polemic. Clearly, he was sympathetic to intelligent experimentation with these agents, and, clearly, he was experienced with them personally, but his purpose was to present a logical selection of facts rather than to push his own views.

This new edition of the book, with its many revisions, additions and refinements, is a welcome appearance. *Psychedelics Encyclopedia* should be in the collection of everyone interested in psychoactive drugs, in the experiences they can release, and in the controversies they have stirred in science, the media, government and the public at large. This is a fine reference book, always engaging and easy to read.

Stafford discusses a number of substances I do not consider psychedelics. In my view, the true psychedelics are the indoles (LSD, psilocybin, the tryptamines, harmaline, etc.) and the phenethylamines (mescaline, MDA, DOM, etc.). These drugs and the plants they come from constitute a distinct pharmacological group, all of which stimulate the central and sympathetic nervous systems and all of which affect serotonin or dopamine pathways (or both) in the brain. These drugs are also distinguished by great medical safety, particularly the indoles. They do not kill, injure or produce any serious physical toxicity even in large overdoses or chronic use over lifetimes. Despite much desire and activity on the part of some scientists, reporters and governmental agencies to come up with damning evidence of harm, the true psychedelics still look like the safest drugs known to medicine.

I refer to medical safety only. There are dangers of psychedelic plants and chemicals having to do with acute psychological toxicity—that is, bad trips. These reactions are more the products of set and setting than of pharmacology. Their probability of occurrence can be reduced to a minimum by careful attention to the purity of the substances, dosage, time and place of use, and availability of experienced guides. Employed intelligently, they are not only safe but sometimes highly beneficial, since they have the potential to produce dramatic cures of both mental and physical problems as well as to provide experiences of great personal value to some persons. Finally, the abuse potential of the true psychedelics is quite low. They are almost never associated with dependence, and very few people use them in destructive ways. Stafford explains them fully and gives a good description of their positive potential.

The other drugs he includes are generally more toxic, less useful to most people, and more easily abused. Marijuana is somewhat more irritating than LSD or mescaline, capable of causing respiratory problems in those who smoke it excessively. I have yet to see good evidence of other ill effects on the body, but I have seen no end of cases of marijuana dependence. Compared to the true psychedelics, pot is insidious in lending itself to regular and frequent use, a pattern that easily turns into an unproductive and stubborn habit, providing few of the interesting effects that novice smokers experience.

The belladonna alkaloids are very much more toxic than the indoles and phenethylamines. Furthermore, they are just plain dangerous, and the experiences they give are, at best, difficult to integrate with ordinary consciousness. Kava-kava seems to me more like alcohol than like the psychedelics, as does nitrous oxide, a general anesthetic with similar depressant qualities. PCP and ketamine are pharmacological curiosities, not related to other recreational drugs. Many users like the "dissociative" states they provide, but few find them truly psychedelic. Their toxicity and abuse potential are significant.

Yet all of these drugs can be mind-manifesting for some individuals. That is the literal meaning of "psychedelic," and I suppose Peter Stafford has included them for that reason. Certainly, marijuana deserves a place here, both because it is commonly mind expanding for those who first try it or are new to it or who use it only infrequently, and also because it moves in the same circles as the true psychedelics.

I know that Stafford is most interested in the indoles and phenethylamines. He devotes much more space and attention to them than to the others and rightly makes them the focus of his encyclopedia. Like me, he finds them totally fascinating from many different perspectives, including those of botany, chemistry, psychology, anthropology, sociology, religion, politics and the law. More than most substances in our world, psychedelics touch on many vital areas of human life and so can teach us much about ourselves, whether we use them or not, promote them or crusade against them, study them or just like to read about them.

I am pleased to have a chance to write the foreword to this new edition of *Psychedelics Encyclopedia*. It is a good book. I have no hesitation in recommending it as a source of interesting and reliable information.

—Andrew Weil
Big Sur, California

Glenn T. Perry

Preview

*. . . a psychedelic drug is one which, without causing
physical addiction, craving, major psyiological disturbances,
delirium, disorientation, or amnesia, more or less reliably
produces thought, mood, and perceptual changes otherwise
rarely experienced except in dreams, contemplative and
religious exaltation, flashes of vivid involuntary memory,
and acute psychoses.*

—Lester Grinspoon and James B. Bakalar,
Psychedelic Drugs Reconsidered

Mind-altering substances have been used in all societies except among the Eskimos and some Polynesians, and thus many of the plants discussed in this book have long and exotic histories. Much of the history, including early New World native use, is undocumented, and much is veiled in legend. We may never know whether Buddha's last meal was of mushrooms ("pig's food"). However, many scholars have now accepted the identification of Fly Agaric mushrooms as the inspirational "Soma" in the world's earliest religious text, the *Rig-Veda*, and evidence seems strong that ergot, an LSD-like substance, was the mysterious *kykeon*, used for more than 2,000 years in the annual ancient Greek Eleusinian Mysteries.

The anthropologist Weston La Barre characterized the use of mind-altering plants as being the source and mainstay of "the world's *oldest* profession"—that of the shaman or medicine man. He adds that such a specialist was "ancestor not only to both the modern medicine man or doctor and the religionist priest or divine, but also ancestor in direct lineage to a host of other professional types." Shamanism in the New World was fostered by indigenous psychedelics that are powerful and quite safe. The Old World had to rely on less dependable, more erratic substances, such as hashish, belladonna, thorn apple and Fly Agaric mushrooms. It is now evident that the prescriptions of specific plants in the recipes in witches' brews of the Middle Ages was not as superstitious or random as earlier supposed.

After accompanying Columbus on his second voyage, Ramón Paul brought back word of *cohoba* sniffing among natives in Haiti. The earliest account of peyote was set down in 1560 in Bernardino de Sahágun's *History of the Things of New Spain*. In 1615, botanical notes made by the Spanish physician Francisco Hernández about the mind-changing effects of morning glory seeds were published.

The first report on use of *Amanita muscaria* mushrooms among Siberian tribesmen didn't appear until 1730. Forty-one years later, a Swedish botanist accompanying Captain James Cook on his first voyage to the

1

Hawaiian Islands described kava-kava and the natives' ceremonial use of this substance. One year later, Sir Joseph Priestly, who first isolated oxygen, produced nitrous oxide (N₂O). At the beginning of the nineteenth century, Baron Alexander von Humboldt, after whom the Pacific current is named, gathered together the first "scientific" report on the use of *yopo* snuff in the Amazonian region.

Around the middle of the nineteenth century, the pace of knowledge of psychoactive substances greatly quickened. In 1839, W. B. O'Shaughnessy introduced *Cannabis indica* into the Western pharmacopoeia, and five years later Theophile Guautier established *Le Club des Haschischins* in Paris. In 1851, the British explorer Richard Spruce first observed *ayahuasca* practices among the South American natives; four years later, Ernst Freiherr von Bibra published an account of seventeen plants capable of affecting the mind. Urging others to study this field, he described it as "promising for research and fraught with enigmas."

In 1864, the earliest description of psychoactive effects from the African bush *Tabernantha iboga* appeared. It wouldn't be until near the end of the nineteenth century, however, that peyote investigations eventually produced

Ernst Friherr von Bibra laid the foundation for modern pharmacological studies in his 1855 Die narkotischen Genussmittel und der Mensch (Narcotic Inebriants ["mediums of enjoyment"] and Humanity).

the world's first psychedelic compound in crystalline form. Louis Lewin, another German important in the development of modern psychopharmacology, traveled to the southwestern United States and brought peyote back to laboratories in Berlin. Eight years later, Lewin's rival, Arthur Heffter, isolated "mezcalin" from Lewin's specimens. After fractionating the alkaloids, or nitrogen-containing compounds, from this cactus, Heffter was able to locate the source of peyote's psychoactivity only by trying the various fractions himself.

The first account of the peyote experience from someone who had actually tried it appeared in 1896. This came from a distinguished author and Philadelphia physician, S. Weir Mitchell, who then forwarded "peyote buttons" to the prominent psychologists William James and Havelock Ellis. After ingesting them in his flat in London, Ellis called the resulting experiences "an orgy of visions" and "a new artificial paradise" (from the titles of his two reports). James, however, got a severe stomachache after eating only one, declaring that he would "take the visions on trust."

Scientific curiosity about peyote dimmed shortly after the turn of the century but was revived in 1927 by the French pharmacologist Alexandre Rouhier, who gave an extraction from the cactus to several students and published accounts of their "exotic" visions. A year later, Kurt Beringer published his 315-page study *Der Meskalinrausch (Mescaline Inebriation)*. A year after that, an English monograph that attempted to catalog the elements of "mescal visions" was published. By this time, a continuing interest in what we now call psychedelic states was emerging. However, there was little indication yet that psychedelics would eventually affect and enchant a great many people.

That eventuality began to take shape in 1938, when the Swiss chemist Albert Hofmann synthesized d-lysergic acid diethylamide tartrate—LSD-25. In mid-April 1943, Hofmann apparently absorbed some of this compound through the skin of his hands and thus learned what animal tests had failed to show: that this substance was a mind-altering drug that had about 4,000 times the potency of mescaline.

In 1947, Werner A. Stoll, the son of Hofmann's superior, broadcast news of this discovery in scientific literature. Within two years, Drs. Nicholas Bercel of Los Angeles and Max Rinkel of Boston brought LSD to the United States.

The change that would take place in our thinking about molecules and their ability to affect the mind was catalyzed during the mid-1950s. In a slender, much noted book, Aldous Huxley described how his "doors of perception" had been cleansed by 500 milligrams of mescaline sulfate. In May 1957, *Life* magazine published the third part of a "great adventures" series with ten pages of color photographs: R. Gordon Wasson described how he had become one of the first two white men to be "bemushroomed." Since then, knowledge about psychedelics has grown steadily, as have the numbers of people interested in them.

Origin of the Word Psychedelic

In the early 1950s, researchers Humphry Osmond and John Smythies wrote a paper about the mental effects of mescaline that came to the attention of Aldous Huxley, who invited Osmond to visit him if he should be in the Los Angeles area. Huxley's wife, Maria, was initially apprehensive about such a meeting, fearing that Osmond "might wear a beard." When Osmond did go to L.A. for a psychological conference, Maria was satisfied that he was not a Bohemian or a mad scientist (he didn't have a beard), and he stayed with the Huxleys. Maria, ironically, finally asked about getting some mescaline for Aldous. Osmond's reaction to the proposal was favorable, with one reservation:

> The setting could hardly have been better, Aldous seemed an ideal subject, Maria eminently sensible, and we had all taken to each other, which was very important for a good experience, but I did not relish the possibility, however remote, of being the man who drove Aldous Huxley mad.

In the literature then available about what we now call psychedelic drugs, the term most commonly used to describe the effects was *psychotomimetic* (meaning psychosis-mimicking). Yet it is evident from Huxley's description in *The Doors of Perception* that when he tried mescaline sulfate he was not going through some kind of "imitation psychosis." Huxley believed he had experienced something akin to mystical experience. He was considered an authority on the subject, being the author of one of the classics in this field, *The Perennial Philosophy.*

Osmond was already sensitive to the lack of an adequate term for the mental state induced by mescaline and LSD. He and his colleague Abram Hoffer had been observing LSD's effects in the treatment of acute alcoholism, and the states produced in their subjects were not as expected. Having read in the literature that LSD produced temporary psychosis, they had reasoned that such a substance could be used to touch off a kind of artificial and controllable *delirium tremens.* About 10 percent of those who experience *d.t.*'s *never drink again.*

Osmond and Hoffer tried LSD on two patients—one recovered, the other remained an alcoholic. They began to use LSD as regular treatment for their worst alcoholic cases, and it gradually became clear that recovery seemed to occur most commonly when the *d.t.*'s hypothesis was forgotten altogether. Hoffer has since commented:

> . . . by 1957 it was apparent that even though many of our patients were helped by LSD, it was not its psychotomimetic activity which was responsible. In spite of our best efforts to produce such an experience, some of our subjects escaped into a psychedelic experience.

The new term came out of a regular correspondence that developed between Osmond and Huxley. *Psychedelic*—coming from the Greek *psyche*

Humphry Osmond, an early LSD, mescaline, morning glory seed and adrenolutin researcher, proposed the word psychedelic.

(soul) and *delein*, to make manifest, or *deloun*, to show, reveal—was first proposed in 1956 by Osmond.

Huxley took the lead, proposing words derived from roots relating to "spirit" or "soul." He invented the word *phanerothyme* and encased it in a couplet for Osmond's consideration:

To make this trivial world sublime,
Take half a gramme of phanerothyme.

Osmond has since remarked that the word Huxley selected was *too* beautiful. He replied:

To fathom hell or soar angelic,
Just take a pinch of psychedelic.

Especially noteworthy about *psychedelic* is the presence of the first *e*—which varies from the ordinary way of combining Greek roots and thus dissociates this word from the misleading connotations of *psychotic*. *Soul-manifesting* belongs to the category of meanings that make sense in terms of contrast: just as *empty* implies *full*, as *child* implies *adult*, so *soul-manifesting* implies an enlargement or actualization of consciousness. This point about psychedelics is often hard to get across.

For better or worse, Osmond's *psychedelic* has been largely accepted as a description of the state produced by the substances to be discussed in this book.

PSYCHEDELIC REVIEW

Issue Number 1
SUMMER 1963
$1.50

This journal, mainly edited by the psychologist Ralph Metzner, promoted the adjective and noun that eventually came to be most closely associated with LSD, mescaline and similar substances.

Other Terms Proposed

The word *intoxication* is said to have more synonyms than any other word in English, but none of them conveys the essense of a psychedelic mental state. To be psychedelicized is not at all the same as being drunk.

Intoxication by alcohol may hint at the experience that is characteristic of psychedelics. Hermann Hesse speaks of alcohol in *Steppenwolf* as being capable of "lighting the golden trail." William James wrote about the impulse it gives to mystical feeling and "Yea-saying." However, it cannot approach the revelatory power of psychedelics, and its well known drawbacks—loss of lucidity and sometimes of memory—put it in an altogether different category from LSD or mescaline. If any of the *intoxication* synonyms are to be used to describe soul-manifested states, the best is probably *inebriation*, because it lacks the connotation of poisoning contained in *toxi-*.

Hallucinogen is another word commonly used for substances producing a psychedelic experience. There is some truth in the characterization, for users often see "visions," especially with the eyes closed. However, most users consider the hallucinatory effect to be only one part of the experience— often a minor part. Even so, the man who formulated the word *psychedelic* used *hallucinogen* in the title of a book he wrote later with Abram Hoffer. Richard Evans Schultes and Albert Hofmann in their books about the botany and chemistry of these substances weight the various descriptive terms and settle on *hallucinogenic* and *hallucinogen*, while pointing out how inaccurate they are. The chemist Alexander Shulgin, after explaining that most MDA-like compounds evoke no visual imagery at all, labeled them "hallucinogenic" substances in his writings.

Even in the second edition of his book on the botany of psychedelics, the ethnobotanist William Emboden retained the title *Narcotic Plants*. These psychedelic plants and related compounds are quite the opposite of narcotics: unlike opiates, they are basically stimulating, and they are non-addictive. (Psychedelics also differ from true stimulants; they increase lucidity but not, as with amphetamine, at the expense of psychological warmth.)

The most common psychiatric term for these botanicals and compounds has been *psychotomimetic*, stemming from a concept proposed in the late nineteenth century by the French doctor J.J. Moreau de Tours. He was the first to raise the hope that chemicals could produce insights toward the alleviation of mental illness. The hope was only partially realized. While the psychedelic state may have some similarities to psychotic ones, the differences are more numerous and more significant, a main difference being that the induced state is known to last only a short while. By the 1960s, few of the therapeutic projects using psychedelics were attempting to bring about psychotic mental states. Yet the term still lingers, with papers describing blissful, beneficial results ascribed to some "psychosis-mimicking" drug.

Another psychotherapeutic term that has much currency, especially in Europe, is *psycholytic*, which has been specifically limited to refer only to low dosage use of psychedelics in conjunction with therapeutic sessions. Shulgin has compiled several more from the prominent psychotherapeutic literature: *delirients, delusionogens, dysleptics, misperceptionogens, mysticomimetics, phantasticants, pharmakons, psychotaraxics, psychoticants, psychotogens* and *schizogens.* Many observers have favored Louis Lewin's suggestion of *phantastica,* but this early formulation never caught on.

Several writers have turned to German or Sanskrit to find more appropriate words, but these have largely been ignored. More notable terms are *peak experiences,* a term popularized by the psychologist Abraham Maslow; *altered states,* popularized by the psychologist Charles Tart; *alternative states,* coined by Norman Zinberg; and *cosmic experience,* popularized in William James' *The Varieties of Religious Experience.*

The latest term proposed comes from the team of Ruck, Bigwood, Staples, Ott and Wasson, writing in the January-June 1979 *Journal of Psychedelic Drugs.* They feel strongly that "not only is 'psychedelic' an incorrect verbal formulation, but it has become so invested with connotations of the pop-culture of the 1960s that it is incongruous to speak of a shaman's taking a 'psychedelic' drug." They offer *entheogen,* calling it

> a new term that would be appropriate for describing states of shamanic and ecstatic possession induced by ingestion of mind-altering drugs. In Greek the word *entheos* means literally "god (*theos*) within," and was used to describe the condition that follows when one is inspired and possessed by the god that has entered one's body. It was applied to prophetic seizures, erotic passion and artistic creation, as well as to those religious rites in which mystical states were experienced through the ingestion of substances that were transsubstantial with the deity.

Combining this Greek root with *gen,* "which denotes the action of 'becoming,' " they argue further for the suitability of *entheogen:*

> Our word sits easily on the tongue and seems quite natural in English. We could speak of *entheogens* or, in an adjectival form, of *entheogenic* plants or substances. In a strict sense, only those vision-producing drugs that can be shown to have figured in shamanic or religious rites would be designated entheogens, but in a looser sense, the term could also be applied to other drugs, both natural and artificial, that induce alterations of consciousness similar to those documented for ritual ingestion of traditional entheogens.

After being around for a couple of years, the term *entheogen* has entered the ethnobotanical literature and is about to be included in the *Oxford English Dictionary.* So far as popular usage is concerned, it doesn't seem to sit as easily on the tongue as orginally claimed. For now, the term *psychedelic,* even if a little shabby and cheapened by overuse, will have to do. It is commonly understood, and since 1976 it has been included in the Addenda to *Webster's Third International Dictionary.* Here, with illustrations, is Webster's perception of this book's theme:

¹**psy·che·del·ic** \ˌsīkəˈdelik, -dēl-\ *adj* [Gk *psychē* soul + *dēloun* to show, reveal (fr. *dēlos* evident) + E *-ic* — more at PSYCHE, ADEL-] **1 a :** of, relating to, or causing an exposure of normally repressed psychic elements ⟨~ drugs⟩ **b :** of, relating to, involving, or resulting from the use of psychedelic drugs ⟨~ indulgences⟩ ⟨a ~ experience⟩ ⟨experimental ~ therapy⟩ **c :** of, relating to, or concerned with psychedelics ⟨hippies escaping to their ~ lairs —T.E. Mullaney⟩ ⟨~ medicine designed to help LSD users⟩ **2 a :** imitating or reproducing the effects (as distorted or heightened sense perception) of psychedelic drugs ⟨~ light show⟩ ⟨~ art⟩ **b** (1) **:** brightly colored ⟨ferryboats soon will take on a ~ look, with an overall coat of international orange and touches of red and yellow — *N.Y. Times*⟩ (2) *of colors* **:** FLUORESCENT **c :** making use of electronically distorted sounds ⟨~ rock⟩ **3 :** of, relating to, dealing in, or being the culture associated with psychedelic drugs ⟨~ shops⟩ — **psy-che·del·i·cal·ly** \-lək(ə)lē\ *adv*

Varieties of "Psychedelics"

Inspired by LSD and mescaline, the term *psychedelic* has since been used for many plants and synthetic compounds that produce similar changes in the ordinary functioning of consciousness. Exactly which substances should be included in this category and which should not has been a subject of considerable controversy for several reasons. Andrew Weil has discussed some of these considerations in the foreword to this book. The main difficulty is that there are several components to the psychedelic experience, appearing in different combinations and intensities with each drug. If one tries to index psychoactivity according to response to color, for example, then the MDA and marijuana compound-clusters would be excluded by some. (Many people would exclude marijuana because it has a different chemistry than most of the others and acts more subtly. However, for some people its use can be "inspiring" and it has widened "the scope of the mind" for many. Aside from the variations among mind-altering compounds, there are variations among users to consider. Some people seem especially sensitive to a very wide range of substances. Jean Cocteau felt quickening, mind- and soul-manifesting effects from opiates. The creative response he showed to those drugs is rare.

Well over a hundred compounds and plants are discussed throughout this book. Most are "indoles," a very small part of the world of chemical compounds. The non-indole psychedelics also tend to "cluster" together in chemical families, though the dissimilarity among the various families is too great to make chemical composition a defining characteristic of a psychedelic substance. Botanical considerations are similarly confounding. Researchers in related fields have had equal difficulty in trying to delineate the action of psychedelics—after decades of intensive investigation. Albert Hofmann, reacting to being known as the father of LSD, said: "It started off in chemistry, and went into art and mysticism."

Generally speaking, the psychedelics considered in this volume touch a spiritual core in their users, have exhibited physical healing qualities, have been used ritualistically, facilitate creative problem-solving and change the sense of time and spatial relationships. They are neither addictive nor toxic. Because their most significant action is mental, and thus fairly non-specific, Andrew Weil has characterized a psychedelic as being like "an especially active placebo," meaning that the user's response depends very much on his or her expectations. Art Kleps, much experienced with psychedelics, was once asked, "What are the side-effects of LSD?" He said, forthrightly, "There are nothing but side-effects." The same could also be said about most of the substances to be discussed in this book.

Perhaps the easiest way to distinguish a compound as psychedelic is by means of two primary mental criteria: (1) that it induces enlargements in the scope of the mind, and (2) that these enlargements or new perceptions are influenced and focused by the user's "mind set" and by the "session setting." Osmond has provided a broad but usable definition of "enlargements," saying that "the brain . . . acts more subtly and complexly than when it is normal." "Mind set," usually shortened to *set*, refers to the user's attitudes, preparations, preoccupations and feelings toward the drug and toward other people in attendance at a psychedelic session; *setting* is a word for the complex set of things in a session's immediate surroundings: time of day, weather, sounds or music and other environmental factors. If results don't vary considerably with sets and settings, the compound almost certainly isn't a "psychedelic."

Most psychedelic substances fall into one of nine main compound-clusters. Each of the compounds in each cluster is unique. Many will be discussed ahead, but for the sake of conciseness emphasis will be put on just a few representatives from each group. The nine clusters will be presented in the order of importance to regular users. Here is a listing of these clusters and their representatives:

Cluster 1: **The LSD Family**, the major catalyst opening "the psychedelic age" and the archetype

Cluster 2: **Peyote, Mescaline and San Pedro**, a cluster once considered the most powerful, the "door opener" for psychedelics in the 1950s

Cluster 3: **Marijuana and Hashish**, the earliest recorded psychedelics, which exhibit synergistic action with all of the others

Cluster 4: **Psilocybian Mushrooms**, the easily identified, gently persuasive and yet powerfully mind-changing fungi containing psilocybin and/or psilocin that re-introduced an appreciation of psychedelic effects in the late 1970s

Cluster 5: **Nutmeg and MDA**, the empathic compounds that create few "visuals," stimulating research into discrete psychedelic effects

Cluster 6: **DMT, DET, DPT and Other Short-Acting Tryptamines**, a family of varying intensities but including the psychedelic that's the most impressive visually

Cluster 7: **Ayahuasca, Yage and Harmaline**, the "visionary vine" complex from the Amazon that is a "telepathic" healer

Cluster 8: **Iboga and Ibogaine**, the bush from Africa used in initiatory rites and by hunters to produce extended stillness, and its principal alkaloid that produces vivid imagery and stimulation

Cluster 9: **Fly Agaric, Panther Caps and "Soma,"** the colorful, fascinating, sometimes frightful, legendary mushrooms that have been used shamanically and may, as "Soma," have provoked "the religious idea in *homo sapiens*" (R. Gordon Wasson)

What are the Common Effects?

Some of these substances cause nausea or giddiness upon ingestion, but the usual course for users is to reach an initial "high plateau" shortly after the onset of action; this plateau constitutes the first quarter or third of the experience. After that, there is often a build-up of intensity to the "peak" of the experience, usually occurring about halfway through the session. During the second half of the experience, the effects gradually diminish, although mental stimulation may last in a more subdued fashion for some time. Memory of the experience is generally sharp and detailed, and physical after-effects are minimal. Feelings of elation are not uncommon and may continue for a day or longer after the experience has ended.

Whatever its duration, the experience widens the scope of awareness. One is transported internally to what Huxley called "The Other World"—a locale experienced spiritually, esthetical and intellectually. The environment perceived during ordinary states of mind isn't altered, but the perception of it is. This perceptual transformation of the external world is temporary, but the insights provided by it are often significant and lasting. The quality of psychedelic recognition can be compared crudely to seeing the same glass as half empty and then seeing it half full.

A CIA agent illustrates such a switch-over in awareness resulting from his LSD experience. As he told it to John Marks, the agent began

> seeing all the colors of the rainbow growing out of cracks in the sidewalk. He had always disliked cracks as signs of imperfection, but suddenly the cracks became natural stress lines that measured the vibrations of the universe. He saw people with blemished faces, which he had previously found slightly repulsive. "I had a change of values about faces," he says. "Hooked noses or crooked teeth would become beautiful for that person. Something had turned loose in me, and all I had done was shift my attitude. Reality hadn't changed, but I had. That was all the difference in the world between seeing something ugly and seeing truth and beauty."

Generally, an initiate's first comment focuses on heightened awareness of internal and external sensations and on alterations in "unalterable reality." Dr. Oscar Janiger, an early LSD researcher, listed these as "an un-usual wealth of associations and images, the sharpening of color perception, the synesthesias, the remarkable attention to detail, the accessibility of past impressions and memories, the heightened emotional excitement, the sense of direct and intrinsic awareness, and the propensity for the environment 'to compose itself' into perfect tableaus and harmonious compositions . . . ."

Thoughts often seem to occur simultaneously on several "levels"—a dramatic demonstration of the mind's ability to resonate at different frequencies. The linear nature of ordinary thought is replaced with a more intuitive, holistic and "holographic" approach to understanding reality. Many investigators have compared the logic of this "Other World" to that of dreams and other functions often associated with the right hemisphere of the brain.

Description of the psychedelic experience as a kind of dream state where one is wide awake and remembering or as a state in which right hemispheric brain functions are amplified is consistent with most experiential reports. These are usually full of comments about enhanced sensitivity to rhythm as well as new appreciations of music and dance.

Many observers feel that the rhythmic aspect of this experience marks a progression into deeper "stages." Robert Masters and Jean Houston describe four stages of deepening awareness in their *The Varieties of Psychedelic Experience*.

Walter Houston Clark, another LSD pioneer, is among those who speak of psychedelics as mainly "catalysts" to feelings, understandings and thinking. A psychedelic "adds nothing to our consciousness, but it brings to the surface many parts of our consciousness that had been lying dormant most of our lives." Recently Clark gave out 140 questionnaires asking users about the nature of their experiences. He noted that "there wasn't a single one" of those responding who didn't mention at least one—and most mentioned several—of the characteristics in "the universal core" of mysticism, as compiled by a leading religious scholar. Clark's conclusion from his own observations and from those of the respondents

> has been that the typical person, wherever he's found, turns out to be a mystic when you go right down to the bottom of his personality. What I'm saying is that all of us here in this room are potential mystics. As William James said in his chapter on mysticism, "Given the appropriate stimuli, mysticism will come to the surface."

Aldous Huxley had a similar point of view. After writing about how use of psychedelics had deepened his feeling for the spiritual, he received a letter from Thomas Merton, a Trappist monk and noted poet. Questioning the validity of drug-induced mystical experience. Merton asked about distinctions that might be drawn between mystical and aesthetic aspects. In January 1959, Huxley responded with his evaluation of the "deeper" aspects

FUNCTIONS OFTEN ASCRIBED
TO THE BRAIN'S

RIGHT
LOBE

the craftsman   the dancer

feminine

the artist   mysterious

light   relational

intuitive

oblivious to time and space

passion   artistic endeavor

spatial awareness   balance

non-linear, non-analytical

awareness of one's own body

musical ability   the "dark" side

the dreamer

passive

recognition of faces   holistic mentation

language tone & accent

of the psychedelic experience (reprinted in his *Moksha* writings, edited by Horowitz and Palmer). He stated that

> there are those whose experience seems to be much more than aesthetic and may be labeled as pre-mystical, or even, I believe, mystical. I have taken mescaline twice and lysergic acid three or four times. My first experience was mainly aesthetic. Later experiences were of another nature and helped me to understand many of the obscure utterances to be found in the writings of the mystics, Christian and Oriental. An unspeakable sense of gratitude for the privilege of being born into this universe. ("Gratitude is heaven itself," says Blake—and I know now exactly what he was talking about.) A transcendence of the ordinary subject-object relationship. A transcendence of the fear of death. A sense of solidarity with the world and its spiritual principle and the conviction that, in spite of pain, evil and the rest, everything is somehow all right . . . .
>
> Finally, an understanding, not intellectual, but in some sort total, an understanding with the entire organism, of the affirmation that God is Love. The experiences are transient, of course; but the memory of them, and the inchoate revivals of them which tend to recur spontaneously or during meditation, continue to exercise a profound effect upon one's mind . . . . There is a feeling—I speak from personal experience and from word-of-mouth reports given me by others—that the experience is so transcendently important that it is in no circumstances a thing to be entered upon light-heartedly or for enjoyment. (In some respects, it is not enjoyable; for it entails a temporary death of the ego, a going-beyond.)

Some have criticized this and similar descriptions from Huxley on the ground that most people don't have the intellectual and imaginative resources that he brought to this experience; his response, they claim, was atypical. This objection has some validity, but Walter Clark has indicated that most users do have experiences along similar lines. What individual users make of them is influenced by their knowledge, religious feeling, willingness to accept new perceptions as valid, circumstances under which the psychedelic was taken, and the amount of attention subsequently paid to the insights or feelings aroused.

Almost no one who has taken a powerful psychedelic has come away unimpressed. Psychologist Ralph Metzner observed over a period of years that people awakened by psychedelics to the myriad possibilities for human consciousness often go on to pursue other ways and methods of increasing awareness. Osmond, writing in the *Annals of the New York Society of Medicine*, described the awe that is a frequent sustained effect:

> Most subjects find the experience valuable, some find it frightening, and many say that it is uniquely lovely. All, from [anthropologist J.S.] Slotkin's

unsophisticated Indians to men of great learning, agree that much of it is beyond verbal description. Our subjects, who include many who have drunk deep of life, including authors, artists, a junior cabinet minister, scientists, a hero, philosophers, and businessmen, are nearly all in agreement in this respect. For myself, my experiences with these substances have been the most strange, most awesome, and among the most beautiful things in a varied and fortunate life. These are not escapes from but enlargements, burgeonings of reality . . . . .

Andrew Weil, who has sought out and tried most of the psychedelics, recently told a gathering that their greatest impact for him—and he hopes for society—has been the elimination of limitations. Here are some of his comments:

> I had begun to do hatha yoga. I was experimenting with being a vegetarian and I had never done any body-work before, and, for me, yoga was very discouraging. I found that there were a number of postures that not only could I not get in, but there seemed to be no hope of getting in. There was one in particular that was really a great stumbling block to me, and that was "The Plough." I would lie on the floor and get my feet over my head, and when my toes were about a foot from the floor I would get an excruciating pain in my neck. I felt so bad I could hardly get out of the position I was in. I tried for at least four or five weeks to work at that every day, but there was no progress. I made a little progress at first, and then hit what seemed to be an absolute limit defined by this pain in my neck. I was really on the verge of giving up. I thought that I was too old (I think I must have been twenty-eight then) and stiff. I thought I had waited too long to do yoga; it was just an impossibility.
>
> Well, we all took acid on this perfect day. There were puffy clouds, butterflies and all the usual things on a wonderful spring day. I was feeling so good that at some point I thought, "Well, gee, I ought to try doing some yoga postures." And I lay down, and I tried The Plough. When I thought I had about a foot to go, my toes touched the ground—and I couldn't believe it! I raised my legs and lowered them, and kept raising them and lowering them, and not only was there no pain in my neck, it felt great!
>
> I burst out laughing, it was so wonderful—and suddenly I had this feeling that nothing was impossible, that all the limits I had imagined just weren't there suddenly. And, "If I could do that, why couldn't I do all these other things that I never thought I could do?" In fact, I began doing some of them.
>
> The next day, still elated from this experience, I tried to get into The Plough. And, a foot from the floor, there was that excruciating pain in my neck again. But there was a difference. I knew I could do it now, and the fact that I knew it was possible motivated me to keep working at it. If I had not had that experience, I would have given up. There was no reason to think that I would have continued in that direction. Having had that experience changed what that meant for me.

Jeremy Bigwood

Andrew Weil, author of The Natural Mind *and* The Marriage of the Sun and Moon *and President of the Beneficial Plant Research Society.*

What are the Benefits to Humanity?

Many benefits are conferred upon humanity by these extraordinary substances that affect thinking and feeling; illustrations abound for nearly every psychedelic.

The first crest of the psychedelic movement, in the 1960s, coincided with a general recovery of the religious impulse, seen especially in the revival of interest in Eastern religions. A new flexibility in religious belief and spirituality came about at a time when influences such as existentialism had convinced many that "God is dead." The psychologist Stanley Krippner has suggested that the psychedelics were "the single most important factor in bringing back dedication to this country."

A sense of harmony spread with the use of psychedelics, along with a new appreciation of non-violence. However, these religious feelings weren't organized; they occurred spontaneously within individuals and were accepted largely as recognitions common to people who had seen beyond ordinary states of consciousness. A large percentage of users became vegetarians after an eight- or ten-hour experience made them feel that they couldn't eat flesh any more.

Mary Bernard raised the question of the possible religious origins and consequences of psychedelics in *The American Scholar:*

> When we consider the origin of the mythologies and cults related to drug plants, we should surely ask ourselves which, after all, was more likely to happen first: the spontaneously generated idea of an afterlife in which the disembodied soul, liberated from the restrictions of time and space, experiences eternal bliss, or the accidental discovery of hallucinogenic plants that give a sense of euphoria, dislocate the center of consciousness, and distort time and space, making them balloon outward in greatly expanded vistas?
>
> Perhaps the old theories are right, but we have to remember that the drug plants were there, waiting to give men a new idea based on a new experience. The experience might have had, I should think, an almost explosive effect on the largely dormant minds of men, causing them to think of things they had never thought of before. This, if you like, is divine revelation . . . .
>
> Looking at the matter coldly, unintoxicated and unentranced, I am willing to prophesy that fifty theobotanists working for fifty years would make the current theories concerning the origins of much mythology and theology as out-of-date as pre-Copernican astronomy.

Psychedelics have brought us closer to an understanding of the human mind, as is evidenced by new directions in formal studies of the brain. Krippner, who has visited many investigators in fields dealing with "alternative realities," has remarked that the main impact of psychedelics from a scientific point of view was to get people interested in research into consciousness:

> not only with psychedelics, but with sleep, dreams, biofeedback, hypnosis, meditation, etc. Many of the very prominent consciousness researchers today, though few will admit it, were turned on to this whole experience by their early acid trips back in the 1960s.

Krippner described the magnitude of these effects while introducing a panel discussion in July 1981 on the social and cultural implications of consciousness research:

> I think it would be no exaggeration to compare the discovery of LSD, and the use of LSD, by such pioneers as Dr. [Stanislav] Grof, whom you heard last night, to the Copernican revolution, the Darwinian revolution, and the Freudian revolution.
>
> The Copernican revolution took the human being's planet out of the center of the universe and out of the center of its own solar system and put it on the periphery. The Darwinian revolution placed the human being in direct descent from lower animals. The Freudian revolution pointed out that much of human motivation is unconscious, rather than conscious. Human beings were still holding on to that little bit of conscious motivation that they had until Albert Hofmann came along with LSD, suggesting to us that what little conscious motivation we have is chemical in nature and that it can be influenced very radically by chemicals.
>
> This was premature, because within the last few years there have been many experiments with endorphans and other neural transmitters which support this view. The chemical basis of behavior, of memory, of cognition and of perception is now taken for granted more than it was back at that time.

For individuals, psychedelics have facilitated problem-solving and creativity, encouraging many users to take more responsibility for their destiny. Duncan Blewett, an early Canadian researcher, has described the effect of psychedelics on personality as akin to "the development of self-awareness," but which is the beginning of a progression or "move from being a self-aware organism to a state of being where an individual responds spontaneously in Zen terms." These drugs often encourage the conviction that reality is self-determined rather than predestined. Many aspects of this change in attitude are discussed in Timothy Leary's books, particularly his *Neurologic, Exo-Psychology* and *Changing My Mind, Among Others.* Many users agree with his notion that these substances promote "self-actualization" and that their use facilitates "re-imprinting" of more desirable attitudes.

Many of the medical benefits from psychedelics haven't been explored very fully, but even the limited work to date has given us a new understanding of the psychosomatic aspects of ill health. As will be pointed out ahead, most of these substances have extensive healing histories that are worthy of further study. A model for such study may be found in the approach taken by the recently formed Beneficial Plant Research Association in Carmel, California, which is especially interested in the tonic and other benefits ascribed to the use of coca leaves. This group's "Coca Project" has gone through the red tape to get approval for a comprehensive investigation of coca's efficacy as: (a) treatment for painful and spasmodic conditions of the gastrointestinal tract, including gastritis and peptic ulcers; (b) a topical anesthetic in dentistry; (c) a treatment for acute motion sickness; (d) a treatment for laryngitis; (e) a substitute stimulant for coffee in patients who are dependent on coffee but cannot tolerate its irritant effects on the gastrointestinal or urinary systems; (f) a regulator of carbohydrate metabolism in cases of hypoglycemia and diabetes; (g) an adjunctive therapy in programs of weight reduction and physical fitness; and (h) a rapid-acting antidepressant.

As a result of their mental experiences, many users have become more aware of what the body's needs are and how to take care of them, and these people have given impetus to the renaissance in organic farming, herbal lore, health foods and many other nature-inspired practices for improving the functioning of the human body.

Psychedelics, which once helped create a "generation gap," have also had the effect of improving family relationships, as happened for psychologist Richard Alpert. After taking a large dose of LSD one night, he went to a family reunion the next day. His brother asked, "How's the nut business?" This "digging at each other" was typical of his family; it "was our form of love. It was a Jewish, middle-class tradition."

Still affected by his psychedelic state, Alpert saw an arrow coming out of his brother's mouth, slowly crossing the table. In his mind, Alpert reached up, took this arrow and put it next to his spoon. Then he "picked up a heart and blew this over" to his brother and said, "Gee, your kids are getting so incredibly big and handsome." A look of confusion crossed his brother's face, because Richard wasn't playing the family game. After some silence, his brother sent over another arrow: "Well, you're certainly not growing much hair, are you?" Alpert's response was to reach up for this arrow and set it down on the table. He sent back another heart shape: "Boy, your wife is getting more beautiful all the time."

Alpert says that by mid-afternoon all of the family—husbands and wives and kids gathered in the living room—were experiencing the family bond in a new way, enjoying just being together. "There was this incredible love feast." Nobody wanted to leave. When it was time to break up, everybody stood outside in the street, "and for a long time nobody could get into their car to go. Nobody wanted to break the love bond that had been formed." The gathering, by all reports, "in fact had been a totally unique experience in everybody's life."

His experience and reports of similar effects from many other users caused Alpert to become interested in the nature of "contact highs," where one person conscious in a special way can bring about changes in consciousness of other people. This phenomenon suggests that psychedelic mind expansion is not solely the result of chemical stimulation.

Countercultural Influences

The development in the 1960s of an "alternative culture" was the result of many influences, chiefly the Vietnam war, the availability of psychedelic drugs, and the prosperity that enabled "war babies" to become "flower children." Thousands and then millions of people began to experiment with psychedelics, ending the earlier phase when the population of users was limited mainly to Native Americans and experimental subjects. Several important consequences were to flow from this change.

For many people, taking a psychedelic became something of a political act. Experimenting with marijuana, for instance, was a "statement" that the government's case against it was exaggerated. Benevolent experiences with marijuana led many users to question authority in other areas as well; if the government misinformed people about marijuana, what about our role in the Vietnam war? What else might be in error? Use of stronger psychedelics, no doubt, also contributed to people's skepticism.

Psychedelic festivals called "Be-ins" were the natural outgrowth of the feelings of unity experienced by early users, as were many efforts at communal living. Whereas previously psychedelics were usually taken by only one person, often in a clinical setting, the new emphasis was on open, uncontrolled, large-scale enjoyment of expanded consciousness. Consequently, much of the public became frightened at the massiveness of this "movement," fearing that some alien force was stealing its children away. Alpert, viewed by many at the time as a leading psychedelic "Pied Piper," blames the over-exuberance of early LSD missionaries for triggering a general hysteria about psychedelics, especially Ken Kesey and the Merry Pranksters, who conducted "Acid Tests" where LSD was available in a punch.

> We thought we had a few more years of sneaking under the wire with legitimacy before the whistle got blown. But Ken made them blow the whistle. I mean, the day after the San Jose "Acid Test," the big headline in the paper was about a "Drug Orgy." Then the legislators had to act. Their hand had been forced.

Once legal restrictions were enacted, promising scientific studies were curtailed. James Goddard, head of the Food and Drug Administration at the time, declared that alleged creative and other benefits from psychedelics were "pure bunk." Janiger, reflecting on the stigma suddenly thrust on LSD researchers, said that he had come to be perceived as

> a villain who was, you know, trying to seduce people into taking it. It was absolutely bizarre! From the heroes, we were suddenly some creatures who were seducing people into changing their consciousness.

The use of psychedelics on a mass scale released enormous creative impulses that continue to affect us all. Whether or not one uses these substances, they have permeated society down to the grass roots. Many had hopes that these powerful compounds could be absorbed in society in legitimate ways, thereby changing the character of use and avoiding unnecessary paranoia. Ivan Tors, probably best known as the producer of the "Flipper" TV series, was one who gave up LSD once the laws banning psychedelics went into effect:

My upbringing was such that the thought of doing something illegal would put me in a negative state, and thus interfere with my LSD experiences. I feel this is true of others as well, and may account for many of the untoward reactions of those who use LSD in the underground.

Questions about Impurity and Other Complications

By the beginning of the 1960s, four powerful psychedelic agents were available, though not yet widespread: peyote, mescaline sulfate, psilocybin and LSD-25. Marijuana and hashish were more widely available. Most of those who swallowed the stronger substances up until about this time probably ingested pure psychedelics. Sandoz Pharmaceuticals spent about $3 million in sending out samples of LSD and psilocybin for investigative purposes. Mescaline was available from a variety of chemical houses, and in most states peyote could be ordered through the mail.

Were there any negative results? Surprisingly few. In 1960, Dr. Sidney Cohen, attached professionally to UCLA and the Veterans Hospital in L.A., wrote sixty-two doctors who had published papers on use of LSD and mescaline/peyote, asking about dangers of such psychedelic treatment. Forty-four replied with detailed comments, covering more than 5,000 patients and volunteers given psychedelics in more than 25,000 sessions. The dosage range in the case of LSD went from 25 mcg. (millionths of a gram) to 1,500 mcg.; 200 mg. to 1,200 mg. was the range for mescaline.

In this survey, not a single physical complication was reported—even when psychedelics were given to alcoholics with generally impaired health. This result was somewhat unexpected, because it had been assumed previously that a diseased liver would produce an adverse reaction. There was also a surprisingly low incidence of major mental disturbances. Despite the profound psychic changes that occur when a person is under the influence of LSD or mescaline, psychotic and other adverse reactions lasting longer than forty-eight hours developed in fewer than 0.2 percent of the cases reported. The attempted suicide rate was just over 0.1 percent. Not one case of addiction was reported, nor any deaths from toxic effects.

If this sampling of 5,000 early psychedelic users is divided into two classes—mentally sound volunteers and people who were mentally unstable—the findings seem even more encouraging. Among those who volunteered for LSD or mescaline experiments, a major or prolonged psychological complication almost never occurred. In this group, only one instance of a psychotic reaction lasting longer than two days was reported, and there were no suicides. Among the mentally ill, however, prolonged psychotic states were induced in "one out of every 550 patients." In this group, "one in 830 attempted suicide," and one carried the attempt through.

In evaluating these statistics, it should be pointed out that at the time of this survey (1960) the proper uses of these substances for therapy were not

well understood. Some of the negative reactions, furthermore, were deliberately brought about, since many of the doctors were trying to produce
"model psychoses" in their patients, and some even gave the drugs in conjunction with electroshock treatment. Nevertheless, such statistics clearly
demonstrated that the dangers in using these powerful drugs were far less
than had been expected.

Since this 1960 survey, new and more appropriate techniques have
been introduced, and the methods of administering psychedelics have been
refined. These advances have resulted in the reduction of potential hazards.
Dr. Hanscarl Leuner, an outstanding European expert on psycholytic therapy,
has since had this to say about Cohen's findings:

> Cohen . . . showed very well how low the relative risk of the therapy is, if it is
> carried out responsibly by qualified doctors. Thus, we actually are threatened
> less by adverse results, or severe complications, than we had to assume at the
> start. Our experience has shown that this risk can be reduced to practically
> zero in a well-institutionalized therapy, as in our clinic. This holds for the
> activation of depressions and schizophrenic psychoses, as well as attempted or
> successful suicides.

As a result of psychiatric and psychological experiments, many mental
patients and volunteers (an example of the latter is the novelist Ken Kesey)
were exposed to the effects of LSD and other psychedelics. Sandoz deserves
most of the credit for this, because it distributed LSD and psilocybin to licensed
researchers all over the world, mostly free of charge. This was done with
hopes that a researcher somewhere would find a medical use for these novel
compounds.

But then the picture changed. Books like Huxley's, first-person
accounts from a number of others (like the nutritionist Adelle Davis, writing
about *Exploring Inner Space* under the name Jane Dunlap), and additional
research such as that with psilocybin by the psychologist Timothy Leary and
associates at the Concord, Massachusetts prison system, led before long to
heightened expectations. Many millions of people developed a desire to
experience a "psychedelic trip"—in contrast to a "psychotomimetic" one,
which appealed to few. Many people, who lacked access to certified dispensing
physicians, soon determined that they would get some one way or another.

As psychiatric experimentation expanded into personal experimentation and interest in psychedelics spread, the supply of pure drugs manufactured by pharmaceutical houses ran short of demand. The underground
chemists went to work. The first underground lab to attract public attention
belonged to two partners, Bernard Roseman and Bernard Copely, who were
arrested in 1962 for "smuggling" 62,000 doses of LSD because of a story they
told to misdirect attention from the fact that they themselves had made this.
(Production of LSD at this time, however, was still legal.) The disturbing
part about Roseman's account of this affair—in his book *LSD: The Age of
Mind*—was his mention that their LSD turned into a blackish, slimy

material. He tried it anyway and was impressed by the effects, and so the two of them packaged it for sale. The purity of psychedelics on the black market has been an issue ever since.

By 1965, the first massive manufacturing and distributing operation had come into being—Owsley's marvelous "tabs." Yet Stanley Owsley came from a background of interest in amphetamine, and some users soon raised questions as to whether he liked to add "speed" to the product. Bruce Eisner, who has written much about the question of psychedelic purity, talked with Owsley's lab assistant, Tim Scully, and believes that speed was never added.

October 16, 1966 is an important date in psychedelic history—it was the day when California outlawed LSD (an action soon to be repeated by the federal government), and the day of the first "Be-ins," occurring both in San Francisco and New York City. Soon after, Sandoz—the only legitimate source of LSD and psilocybin—stopped supplying these chemical agents to American investigators. Sandoz turned over the remainder of its stockpile in its New Jersey facility to the National Institute of Mental Health, which in turn soon curtailed research programs using psychedelic drugs in human subjects from more than a hundred down to a grand total of six. The chances of anyone getting "pharmaceutically pure" LSD rapidly dwindled.

In 1967, DOM—also called STP—was introduced to the counterculture but soon withdrawn amid controversy over excessive dosages and impurities. It still appears on rare occasions, sometimes sold as STP but often disguised by a less stigmatized name. "Orange Wedge" appeared in early 1968, in strong dosages and available internationally; it was followed in early 1969 by another massive psychedelic production effort—the "Sunshine" trip. In both cases, allegations sprang up that these products had been adulterated with speed, STP, strychnine, etc.

By the early 1970s, doubts about the purity of underground products were common—and for good reason. There were weak 'blotters' of LSD, requiring four or five to "get a buzz." At about this time, nearly a hundred drug analysis organizations, the most prominent being PharmChem in Palo Alto, began to examine the quality of underground psychedelic products. What they found was not reassuring. Quality control was non-existent. A summary from PharmChem for the year 1973 showed the following:

Of 405 samples said to be *LSD,* 91.6% were as alleged, 3.4% had no drug at all, 3% were actually DOM, PCP and others, and 2% had DOM, PCP and methamphetamine in addition to LSD.

Of 127 samples said to be *marijuana,* 89.7% were as alleged, 6.3% had no drug at all, 1.6% was nicotine, and 2.4% had PCP and cocaine in addition to marijuana.

Of 64 samples said to be *THC,* none were as alleged, 95.3% were PCP, and the rest were LSD and other substances.

Of 185 samples said to be *mescaline*, 17.3% were as alleged, 7.6% had no drug at all, 61.6% were LSD, 11.4% were LSD + PCP, and there were three that were PCP and two others as well.

A single sample of *DMT* was as alleged.

Of 59 samples said to be *MDA*, 71.2% were as alleged, with the rest (28.8%) composed of DOB, DOM, 2,5-DMA, PMA, PCP and LSD + PCP.

A single sample said to be *MMDA* was found to be LSD.

A single sample of *ibogaine* was as alleged.

Of 33 samples said to be *PCP*, 84.9% were as alleged, 12.1% had no drug at all, 3% were marijuana.

If marijuana products are excluded, just over 55 percent of so-called "psychedelics" tested out as claimed (501 out of 906 samples). More than 9 percent contained no psychoactive substance at all; a full 34.5 percent were assayed as some entirely different mind-altering chemical. Although many of these samples may have been sent in for testing because there was already some question about their content, this rundown indicates a serious problem with the purity of black market psychedelics from that era.

The early 1970s was the worst period of misrepresentation. Siva Sankar recorded findings that were even worse when better analytical equipment was used:

Marshman and Gibbins tested 519 samples of street drugs for which the vendor's claimed composition was available. Of the samples alleged to be LSD, 44% contained LSD with 2 or more contaminants, or even were mixtures of intermediate chemicals resulting from unsuccessful attempts to synthesize LSD. None of the drugs alleged to be mescaline contained mescaline. Lundberg, Gupta and Montgomery analyzed several alleged street drugs, mostly from the California area. Of 96 samples sold as psilocybin, only 5 contained psilocybin. The rest were either LSD or mixtures of LSD and phencyclidine.

It's unfortunate that underground manufacturing and distribution of psychedelics developed this way. The purity of a complex chemical is difficult to test, and doubts about the purity of an untested chemical can create paranoia, multiplied easily while in a psychedelic state. Furthermore, an impure dose may well encourage fundamental misinterpretations by the novice as to the nature of the psychedelic experience.

All the results I have ever seen indicated that "Sunshine" (as an example of a suspect psychedelic) was pure LSD-25. The PharmChem listings above show virtually all the *acid* examined to have been pure, though the matter of contaminants may not have been examined very thoroughly. PharmChem found a quantitative average for acid during 1973 of 67.25 mcg.; during 1974, 96 mcg. It was mescaline and psilocybin that were generally found to be misrepresented. This situation has since improved, but there is still good cause for being wary.

While most attention has focused on purity to account for the bummers experienced by many using black market acid, it should be noted that the psychedelic molecules are delicate and should be handled gently in transport. Also, most oxidize fairly easily and should be kept away from light, heat and water.

Use and Misuse

The question of *use* and *misuse* has always been a difficult one in regard to psychedelics, and it can never be answered satisfactorily because the experience depends so much upon circumstances, attitudes and the presence or absence of a ritual. These points will be emphasized throughout this book: the traditions of shamanistic use, the "Good Friday experiment" and the work at Spring Grove Hospital will be given as examples for setting up good rituals. If users think of the psychedelic experiences as sacramental, as a special event to be prepared for, the results are bound to be better than if they're viewed as "recreational," as a way to stave off boredom.

Timothy Leary goes to the heart of this matter in an essay entitled "After the Sober, Serious, Safe and Sane '70s, Let Us Welcome the Return of LSD." He restates a controversy that raged among the pioneers of the psychedelic age as to whether these substances should be reserved for use by only a few or whether they were appropriate for "democratization, even socialization." In any event, the choice was probably beyond the control of the early users. Summing up what he sees as the results from "seven million Americans" having used LSD, Leary concludes:

> Our current knowledge of the brain and current patterns of LSD usage suggest that the Huxley-Heard-Barron elitist position was ethologically correct and that the Ginsberg-Leary activism was naively democratic. Our error in 1963 was to overestimate the effect of psychological set and environmental setting. We failed to understand the enormous genetic variation in human neurology . . . .
>
> LSD and psilocybin *did* seem to be fool-proof intelligence-increase (I^2) drugs *because our experiments were so successful!* In thousands of ingestions we never had an enduring "bad trip" or a scandalous "freak-out." Sure, there were moments of terror and confusion aloft, but confident guidance and calm ground-control navigation routinely worked. Our mistake, and it was a grave one, was that we failed to understand the aristocratic, elite, virtuous self-confidence that pervaded our group . . . .
>
> It was the Heisenberg Determinacy once again. We produced wonderful, insightful, funny, life-enhancing sessions because we were a highly selected group dedicated to the scientific method. We were tolerantly acceptant of ambiguity, relatively secure, good-looking, irresistibly hopeful and romantic. So we fabricated the realities which we expected to create. *We made our sessions wonderful because we were wonderful and expected nothing but wonder and merry discovery!*

Psychedelic usage can be life-changing, particularly in terms of one's relationships with others. The spiritual insights achieved may make it difficult to live in the same way one has in the past. Leary's guidance as to who is most likely to gain from the experience is worth keeping in mind (it is put with his characteristic flamboyance):

ACID IS NOT FOR EVERY BRAIN.... ONLY THE HEALTHY, HAPPY, WHOLESOME, HANDSOME, HOPEFUL, HUMOROUS HIGH-VELOCITY SHOULD SEEK THESE EXPERIENCES. THIS ELITISM IS TOTALLY SELF-DETERMINED. UNLESS YOU ARE SELF-CONFIDENT, SELF-DIRECTED, SELF-SELECTED, PLEASE ABSTAIN.

Dealing with Difficulties

Dr. Stanislav Grof provides a useful start in evaluating the possibility and meaning of a turbulent experience with a psychedelic:

The problem is the definition of a "bummer." Difficult experiences can be the most productive if properly handled and integrated.

The best set and setting and quality of LSD cannot guarantee a "good" trip, if this means easy, pleasant, uncomplicated. The problem is more management of the experience than the experience itself. We can increase the productiveness of sessions.

Although this book isn't designed as a session guide for tripping, it is appropriate here to provide some background on minimizing tight moments that may develop. The management of a session and the role of "guides" are treated in Masters and Houston's *The Varieties of Psychedelic Experience*, in Leary, Metzner and Alpert's *The Psychedelic Experience* and in Cohen and Alpert's *LSD*.

John Beresford, a psychiatrist who has had much experience with psychedelics since the early 1960s, outlines a basic strategy:

Confrontation is precisely what should be avoided when a person who has taken LSD shows signs of agitation or depression or in some other way is manifesting resistance to the natural flow of the experience. What the person helping can do then is search for and suggest an image or idea which complements the image or idea which acted as the springboard of resistance. The resistance is undone and the normal flow of the session can proceed.

Art Kleps, with more than two decades of interest in psychedelics, makes many suggestions in his *Boo Hoo Bible* about the often crucial role played by the guide:

As long as there are complaints about or fears of loss of ego the ego is not lost, nor is it diminished in any simple way. You are not, in this situation, dealing with a six year old child, who can easily be put off or led down the garden path. The ego at bay is a mobilized ego, alert to all danger, suspicious of your every move and word. *Always* assume that the [user] can "see right through you," no matter how bizarre his behavior. Be honest. If you honestly think distraction is called for, then say so. For example, "Well, if questions like that are bothering you, why not look at some of these pictures instead?" Don't pretend a sudden interest in something you are not really interested in at all. As for saying, "Try not to think about it" or something of the sort, well, try not to think of a purple cow yourself and see how much luck you have . . . .

Let's come right out with it: unless you are enlightened, don't bother trying to guide Ivory Sessions—sit by if requested to do so, but make no pretense of being anything more than a servant, "ground control" or whatever the hell you want to call it. The fact of the matter is that fakery is impossible in this situation anyway; there are no standards; there is no third party, no precedents, no law. It all depends, and it depends on nothing constructible. Circumstances, and circumstances only.

Finally, here is a list of some "do's" and "don't's" that Bonnie Golightly and I compiled in our *LSD—The Problem-Solving Psychedelic:*

1) *User is in control and can change directions.* Under the influence of such substances, the user is not simply adrift, a tourist cast off at the mercy of the elements and in the grip of forces that cannot be influenced. He or she is, instead, yet in control and can change directions. Because of the overwhelming nature of what occurs, however, this may not be easy to remember.

The user under the influence of a psychedelic can function normally and can also alter the experience. This should be fully grasped before taking this type of drug. Once into a session, the user should take time out and practice "reversing" sensations. Water may taste like wine just by thinking it; a light object can be made to feel heavy; or another's glistening tears can be turned into a dry-eyed expression of joy. When sufficiently skilled, the user will be able to "select hallucinations" at will.

2) *Preparing for "take-off."* For the initiate, some difficulty may be encountered in "take-off," since the transition is comparable to a jet thrust. Care should therefore be taken to reduce rigidity and awkwardness. The best approach for entering "inner space" gently is made with the aid of a "fluid," not-too-highly structured selection of music and simple breathing exercises, or possibly a massage, since a tense, tight attitude may grow out of "waiting for something to happen."

3) *"Going with" negative states.* During the eight or ten hours of altered reality under the influence of most psychedelics, much that is shocking or distasteful may occur within the user, especially unpleasant fantasies of a physical nature. Cardiac specialists as well as other doctors often direct their heightened psychedelic sensitivity to their bodies and witness in surgical detail the actions of internal organs. These physical scrutinies also preoccupy the layperson, of course, and birth experiences—being born or giving birth—are within the ordinary line of psychedelic events. As mentioned previously, disorientation with regard to time may terrorize the most valiant.

Many frightening "hallucinations" are mainly subjective experiences with little basis in everyday fact. If the user wants them to "go away," the best remedy is to dispense with the natural impulse to "fight them." "Going with them" or "giving one's self over" disperses the unwanted vision and the "screen" is cleared for something else.

Facing terrifying psychedelic events may call for courage and stamina in early sessions.

4) *Boosting the experience.* If resistance remains high, the experience may become repetitious, leading up to a crucial point but without a breakthrough. The user vacillates—hot and cold, back and forth, endlessly affixed to the same treadmill. He or she cannot make decisions, and has been through all this many times before.

In such instances, "boosting" may be called for. An additional dosage is usually enough to "break the set" and move the user off his or her plateau. Dr. Duncan Blewett gives the rationale:

> One of the things we discovered is that if you don't give a large enough dose of the drug, a person gets into a sort of interim position, with one foot in the camp of the usual frame of reference and the other in the camp of unhabitual perception. The user finds it impossible to make a break between these two . . . . But if a large enough dose of the drug is used, so that the person is propelled rapidly out of the old context and cannot maintain the self-context as previously, then—rather than becoming more uncomfortable as you would think—he or she becomes much more comfortable and able to accept as valid this new and novel way of seeing the world.

A reason for the occasional vortex-like recurrence of the same material seems to lie in the fact that the drug effects come in waves, and if the user is allowed to persist in one area too long, he or she may be caught in an undertow. The favored method for breaking through this "hang-up" is to change the subject matter completely—with the intention of returning to it later if it seems worthwhile. If the recurrent material is deliberately brought up again after some time has passed, the subconscious will have had a chance to devise other approaches and the insight level will probably be more acute. A good technique in such instances, borrowed from hypnosis, is to suggest that in a specified length of time the user will return to the problem and then be able to resolve it.

5) *Recognizing physical symptoms.* The development of physical symptoms (such as coldness, nausea, pressure on the spine, restlessness, tingling, tremors or "a pain in the kidneys") is often the body's way of evading psychedelic effects. With peyote, and to a lesser extent with sacred mushrooms or morning glory seeds, these effects may be attributed to the drug, but with LSD and most other synthetics such symptoms are most frequently a sign of resistance. The guide should in such cases recognize these symptoms as an indication that the drug is about to take effect, and should reassure the user that these physical symptoms will soon pass, with "the psychedelic experience" taking their place.

6) *Reacting to verbal stimuli.* Another evasion of the full psychedelic experience may involve over-intellectualizing what happens and talking on and on throughout the session. Because language depends upon familiar ways of thinking, reliance on words keeps much that is non-verbal from developing and restricts the psychedelic experience. To carry on a lengthy conversation confines "psychedelia" even further, since the user when questioned or spoken

to is somewhere "out in orbit" and must then come back and touch down before replying. For the average person, a period of verbalization may not develop into a problem, but a rigidly defensive person, on the other hand, may use words to avoid the experience, and as time passes may become increasingly desperate, or even aggressive, reacting with hostility towards the guide. A variety of menacing motivations may be imputed to the guide. In such a situation the guide should refuse these various "ploys," gently reminding the user what he or she is there for.

7) *Physical comfort.* If terror grips the user continuously during the session, physical comforting may lend the needed reassurance. But as pointed out previously, this is a delicate matter unless the guide is certain that the user will not misinterpret the gesture. Because attendant psychedelic distortions may seem too vile or alien to be shared, the user who has lodged in a crevasse can most successfully be brought out, if other means have not been satisfactory, by the guide's taking him or her into the arms and soothing the frightened tripper.

8) *Counter-diversion.* If "reversing" any disturbing "hallucinatory" material has not dispelled anxiety, counter-diversion should be attempted. The user should be encouraged to try some appropriate physical activity such as dancing, keeping time to music, playing the piano or even gardening! Taking deep breaths and paying attention to the lungs as they expand and contract is quite effective. Such diversionary efforts will in all probability become the new focus of attention.

9) *Extra resources.* The skilled guide always has extra resources up the sleeve or is capable of fast, imaginative thinking. One example, which can serve as a pattern for the latter, occurred when a user decided she was made of metal and was unable to move. "Oh, you're the friendly robot in that TV serial," the guide remarked genially, and as the user was familiar with the program referred to, she immediately "recognized herself" and began moving gaily in a deliberate parody of an automaton's gyrations.

Leary had an amusing and instructive episode to recount along these lines. An electronics engineer had taken psilocybin and was reacting with great anxiety.

> . . . his traveling companion was unable to calm him down. The psychologist in charge happened to be in the bathroom. He called to his wife, who was drying the dishes in the kitchen: "Straighten him out, will you?" She dried her hands and went into the living room. The distressed engineer cried out: "I want my wife!" and she put her arms around him, murmuring: "Your wife is a river, a river, a river!" "Ah!" he said more quietly. "I want my mother!" "Your mother is a river, a river, a river!" "Ah, yes," sighed the engineer, and gave up his fight, and drifted off happily, and the psychologist's wife went back to her dishes.

10) *Eliminating unpleasant "hallucinations."* Pinpointing the source of an unpleasant "hallucination" can eliminate it rapidly. One user, for instance, convinced that the house was on fire, said he could actually see his "charred limbs" in the ruins. He was set straight when he was shown a burned-out candle in an ashtray, still smoking because the wax had been set afire by cigarette butts. Another person was able to deal with distasteful psychic material when

told that he was "merely a visitor passing through a slum" and that "a better neighborhood would soon emerge."

11) *"Game-playing."* Crises do sometimes arise even in well planned sessions. If the user is unable to cope with them in a sober manner, the guide may suggest "game-playing." The user should be instructed to think of himself or herself as a versatile actor who must portray a character in a serious role, stand aside and let the play begin.

12) *Getting home.* If the user has insisted upon taking a stroll through heavy traffic, wants to drive a car or undertakes some other ill-advised pursuit, and if the guide has been outwitted or lost contact, the user should remind himself or herself that what is happening is due to the psychedelic taken and that its effects will, in time, wear off. Finding the way home is not an impossible feat, and the user should try to recall, step by step, how it was done the day before. Since evaluating distance may be difficult, it is important to obey all traffic signals rigorously in crossing streets, taking a cue from the surge of the crowd. Any inclinations towards bizarre behavior should be curbed, bearing in mind that the mission is simply to get home.

If the user has been driving a car, upon realization of the situation it's important to park as soon as possible, and take a cab, a bus or proceed on foot. Although the user may not believe it, most people will have no idea of his or her condition, either through their own preoccupations or the simple fact that it is not always easy to detect psychedelic drug behavior.

In point of fact, "runaway" and out-of-control sessions are extremely unusual. Once a psychedelic experience has been completed, the carry-over depends on where the stepping stones have been placed or if the desired bridge has been reached. Ideally, time should be allowed for relaxation in "normal reality" to let the subconscious integrate its new insights. This is the time to put the "psychic house" in order, to speculate about what has been resolved and what remains to be resolved.

Drawbacks to Psychedelic Usage

Most users of psychedelics claim that the effects from these substances on their lives have been beneficial. Many, in fact, state that they have been influential in producing the most meaningful and positive experiences of their lives. On the other hand, a small number of people who have used psychedelics have had what they consider to be long-term negative effects.

In the days when these drugs were taken with less awareness of the psychedelic experience's potentials, there were undoubtedly drug abuse tragedies. Much of the bad press for psychedelic drugs originated from these occurrences. The illegal status of LSD, psilocybin and MDA came about as a result of the dangers inherent in self-experimentation during the 1960s.

A variety of psychedelic substances are now widely used throughout our society, even though it is usually illegal to buy, sell or even possess them. Although this author believes that their dangers have been vastly exaggerated (and are much less than the dangers of alcohol), abuse of these substances can and has occurred. Almost all of this at present can be characterized as involving unintelligent use.

Because alterations in consciousness produced in psychedelic states can possibly lead to impairment, care in choosing the circumstances, dosage, quality of drugs, companionship and related matters should always be exercised. Thoughtless and reckless use of these compounds is a violation of their positive, indeed sacred, characteristics.

The best psychedelic experiences are life-changing and life-enhancing. Throughout this book appear both a) enthusiastic statements in regard to the benefits, and b) warnings where appropriate about dangers. Attention paid to these matters will help bring the time when psychedelics will be more widely appreciated in our society for their medical, therapeutic, creative, religious, insightful and relationship-enhancing capabilities.

Future Directions

In the future, psychedelic users are mostly likely to be self-selected. They will have an opportunity to experiment with an array of compounds that can provide wide variations on the basic LSD experience. In an *Omni* magazine article about "Future Drugs," Alexander Shulgin notes the implications of synthesizing drug analogues of known psychedelics:

> The time will come when we'll separate all our senses and capabilities—the visual from the auditory, the tactile from the sense of smell as well as wit, intellectual capability, creativity—and [be able] to enhance them with drugs.

Being able to choose psychoactive compounds with more specific effects than LSD, mescaline and psilocybin has already resulted in more subtle possibilities, along with giant strides in our understanding of how alterations in psychoactive molecular structures affect their duration, as well as empathetic, visual and other qualities. New psychedelic substances may have some surprising effects. In the future, we may have psychedelics that go beyond LSD for power and interest.

Related to these developments have been interest and experimentation in the synergistic effects derived from ingesting different psychedelics within a relatively close timespan. Use of MDMA to induce a relaxed mental set prior to taking LSD, or employment of DMT together with another psychedelic, qualitatively alter the consequences that would ordinarily come about from taking just a single compound. Synergism—"the simultaneous action of separate agencies which, together, have greater total effect than the sum of their individual effects"—is a well recognized quality of drugs and seems especially characteristic of psychedelics. L.M. Boyd, who writes a syndicated newspaper column about oddities called "Grab Bag," once gave an analogy in terms of food:

> You don't get out of beans what you get out of meat. You don't get out of rice what you get out of meat. But although the vegetable proteins are incomplete separately, they're complementary. So you do get out of beans and rice together what you get out of meat. Curious.

Impressive breakthroughs have been made recently in mapping "receptor-sites" for chemicals entering the brain, in photographing neural activity, and in improving analytical equipment. Evidence is confirming that several psychedelics are normally present in people's heads. Harmala alkaloids appear in the pineal gland, possibly in greater concentrations among yogis (see Chapter Seven). DMT, discussed in Chapter Six, has been located in the brain and in cerebrospinal fluid (see the *Medical Tribune*, October 5, 1977 for an early report).

Moreover, it's now clear that many of the substances outlawed by drug legislation are actually important neurotransmitters. Shulgin, in a 1977 talk in San Francisco, commented on the federal prohibitions against peyote which proscribe "every compound" of this plant:

> ... if this were pushed into a point of legal absurdity, since dopamine is a compound of the plant, and since it's a mandatory neurotransmitter in our normal functions, it would mean in a very humorous way we would possibly all be possessors and carriers of a Schedule I drug in our normal, healthy state.

A related finding from other recent analyses is that opium-like substances are concentrated about twenty times as strongly as normal in the milk of mammals. Because such compounds appear in lettuce and many of the grasses that cows commonly graze upon, some nursing babies must be starting life "getting stoned."

Along with greater sophistication about the many roles played by psychoactive compounds in people's lives and the possibility of exposure to a wider variety of psychedelics, users in the future will also be beneficiaries of recent techniques that (1) aim at realizing the "peaks" of the psychedelic experience through nondrug means, and/or (2) are designed to enhance the productiveness of sessions. Bruce Eisner, writing about such contemporary research, sketched some examples:

> ... we see such practices as Stan Grof placing a blindfold on the experiencer in a quiet room, putting on music and telling him or her to go with the flow, and Salvador Roquet, who takes groups of twenty or more and bombards them with light, sound and other means of sensory overload. John Lilly tells us that a sensory isolation tank is best, while Jean Millay would take her dose connected to a biofeedback device. And then there is Jay Hippie, merging with the light on a secluded beach.

Concepts and traditions from Eastern religions and shamanic procedures will continue to be assimilated into Western culture and they will alter our sense of human potentialities. Dr. Stanislav Grof has illustrated this point by describing how he tried to fit his observations from LSD experiences into the Freudian outlook about psychological functioning for several years. Eventually, he had to give this up, since this hardly took into account "ancestral, racial, evolutionary, past incarnation, precognition and telepathy, planetary and extra-planetary, and time and space travel" phenomena, as Michael Horowitz summed up Grof's findings, that regularly crop up in such sessions.

Huxley described his expectation about the major influence from psychedelics as essentially producing "an everyday mysticism underlying and giving significance to everyday rationality, everyday tasks and duties, everyday human relationships." That, no doubt, is occurring now and will in the future. This is but one of the prominent areas catalyzed by these drugs, however, and their eventual impact upon society involves much more.

That experiences caused by psychedelics have now become much more manageable is evidenced by the closing of "psychedelic rescue services" and by a decline in users seeking help at hospitals. We can anticipate that future usage will make significant contributions to psychological and physical health, to creative innovation and to an understanding of some of the stranger aspects of human behavior.

The fact is that, as the science fiction writer Norman Spinrad says, "psychochemistry [has] created states of consciousness *that had never existed before.*" Taking a psychedelic dramatically changes the traditional notions of "free will." Spinrad's view is that "psycho-chemicals are a declaration of independence from the minds we were born with," and that hence "we will no longer be able to count on our 'naturally evolved' brain chemistry as a benchmark of sanity."

Even though many psychedelic experiences do not have much resonance, others have consequences all out of proportion, especially when people apply the heightened sensitivity prompted by these substances to disciplines that they have pursued for years. Shulgin, again, provides a good example. He has described in a book entitled *Mind Drugs* how he has been able, under the influence of MDA-like compounds, to twist molecular arrangements around in his head, and thus could view them differently and from unusual angles. That ability has turned out to be unusually productive. A more disquieting example, to emphasize the "amorality" of science, is that of a futurist associated with a think tank on the East Coast who spent much time during his first psychedelic session considering bombing patterns over China.

As these examples suggest, the consequences from the experiences of psychedelic trips might come to have great significance. It should be emphasized that even if all psychedelic substances were to be wiped off the face of the earth, tremendous effects they have already catalyzed would nonetheless continue on by themselves. This aspect of psychedelic consequences was perhaps most clearly stated when a physician remarked to a medical gathering that although he hadn't actually ever taken a psychedelic, LSD had "changed my life completely."

The future impact of psychedelics will be the sum of changes produced in millions of individual sessions. Most will be considered beneficial by their users, a very small number will not. May it be, as Alan Watts hoped, that by the end of this century we will have accepted the opportunities offered and be "swimming in the ocean of relativity as joyously as dolphins in the water."

An ampule of Sandoz LSD.

Jeremy Bigwood

CHAPTER ONE

The LSD Family
(the archetype)

April 19, 1943: Preparation of an 0.05% aqueous solution of d-lysergic acid diethylamide tartrate.

4:20 P.M.: 0.05 cc (0.25 mg LSD) [250 micrograms] ingested orally. The solution is tasteless.

4:50 P.M.: no trace of any effect.

5:00 P.M.: slight dizziness, unrest, difficulty in concentration, visual disturbances, marked desire to laugh . . . .

—Albert Hofmann

HISTORY

Of all substances that excite the visionary powers of the mind, LSD is the most potent. It belongs to a class of substances that can be divided into two groups. One group occurs naturally, in the fungus ergot and in members of the woodrose and morning glory families. The other group is produced semi-synthetically, the most important member being LSD. Both groups exhibit a four-ring crystalline chemical structure. Unlike most of the psychoactive molecules dealt with in this book, which are called amines, these LSD-type compounds are all amides.

In a curious circle of coincidence, knowledge about the psychoactivity of the natural group came along only after the synthesis of LSD by Dr. Albert Hofmann. He wrote the lab notes quoted at the beginning of this section. Unlike most chemists, who even today work mainly with synthetics, Hofmann was drawn toward study of natural substances at the end of the 1920s. Under the supervision of Dr. Arthur Stoll, who isolated the first ergot alkaloid in a pure chemical form, Hofmann later synthesized a number of ergot analogues (closely related compounds) at Sandoz Pharmaceuticals in Basel, Switzerland.

The First LSD Experiences

Hofmann's laboratory syntheses of ergot analogues resulted in the construction of many new lysergic acid derivatives. Several turned out to be useful in medicine—especially in obstetrics, geriatrics and the treatment of migraine headaches. The twenty-fifth compound in the series his team produced—lab coded LSD-25—was expected on the basis of its molecular

Dr. Albert Hofmann, discoverer of LSD (photo taken in 1981).

structure to be a circulatory and respiratory stimulant. Tested on experimental animals in 1938, it made them restless and caused them to display strong "uterine-constricting" effects. These results were not of sufficient interest to the Sandoz staff; further testing ceased.

In the spring of 1943, Hofmann received "a peculiar presentiment." He felt that LSD-25 might possess properties other than those observed in Sandoz' initial investigation. He therefore set about resynthesizing this substance, intending to resubmit it to Sandoz' pharmacological department for further examination. That was "in a way uncommon," he wrote in his autobiography, "for experimental substances were as a rule definitely stricken from the research program, if they were once found uninteresting from the pharmacological aspect."

In the course of recrystallizing "only a few centigrams" (hundredths of a gram) for analysis, a strange thing happened to Dr. Hofmann.

> I suddenly became strangely inebriated. The external world became changed as in a dream. Objects appeared to gain in relief; they assumed unusual dimensions; and colors became more glowing. Even self-perception and the sense of time were changed. When the eyes were closed, there surged upon me an uninterrupted stream of fantastic images of extraordinary plasticity and vividness and accompanied by an intense, kaleidoscope-like play of colors. After about two hours, the not unpleasant inebriation, which had been experienced whilst I was fully conscious, disappeared.

Hofmann's was the first human experience of LSD, an accident that would never have occurred under careful laboratory conditions. "It was possible that a drop had fallen on my fingers and had been absorbed by the skin." One drop.

The most powerful psychedelic agent known at that time was mescaline. To receive a psychedelic effect, the average human body has to absorb a third of a gram or more of mescaline. However, LSD is about four thousand times as strong as mescaline. A drop on his skin was enough—perhaps 20-50 micrograms (millionths of a gram, abbreviated mcg.)—to give Hofmann a light trip lasting noticeably for two hours. If LSD were only a thousand times as strong as mescaline, Hofmann would probably not have felt its mental effects.

But he did notice. Three days later he resolved to apply methodical analysis to his accidental discovery.

A cautious man, Hofmann started by ingesting a quarter of a milligram (250 mcg.), intending to increase the dosage as necessary to complete a full description of the effects of the drug. That at least was his intention.

Forty minutes after administration of the conservative first dose, less than fifty words along in his efforts to record observations, came a far more powerful reaction: the first intentional human experience of LSD. Hofmann was unable to continue his description in the lab notebook as "the last words could only be written with great difficulty":

> I asked my laboratory assistant to accompany me home as I believed that my condition would be a repetition of the disturbance of the previous Friday. While we were still cycling home, however, it became clear that the symptoms were much stronger than the first time. I had great difficulty in speaking coherently, my field of vision swayed before me, and objects appeared distorted like the images in curved mirrors. I had the impression of being unable to move from the spot, although my assistant told me afterwards that we had cycled at a good pace . . . .

Expecting another short, "not unpleasant inebriation," Hofmann found the extremely small quantity he had ingested "to be a substantial overdose," causing a profound disruption of ordinary perception.

> The faces of those present appeared like grotesque colored masks; strong agitation alternating with paresis; the head, body and extremities sometimes cold and numb; a metallic taste on the tongue; throat dry and shriveled; a feeling of suffocation; confusion alternating with a clear appreciation of the situation.
>
> I lost all control of time; space and time became more and more disorganized and I was overcome with fears that I was going crazy. The worst part of it was that I was clearly aware of my condition though I was incapable of stopping it. Occasionally I felt as being outside my body. I thought I had died. My "Ego" was suspended somewhere in space and I saw my body lying dead on the sofa. I observed and registered clearly that my "alter ego" was moving around the room, moaning.

A doctor arrived after Hofmann reached "the height of the crisis" and found a somewhat weak pulse but normal circulation. Six hours after he began the test of *d*-lysergic acid diethylamide tartrate for mental effects, Hofmann's condition "improved definitely," though

> the perceptual distortions were still present. Everything seemed to undulate and their proportions were distorted like the reflections on a choppy water surface. Everything was changing with unpleasant, predominantly poisonous green and blue color tones. With closed eyes multihued, metamorphosizing fantastic images overwhelmed me. Especially noteworthy was the fact that sounds were transposed into visual sensations so that from every tone or noise a comparable colored picture was evoked, changing in form and color kaleidoscopically.

Fearing he had poisoned himself with a substance he himself had made, Hofmann was particularly concerned that he hadn't made a proper "leave-taking" from his wife and family, who had traveled earlier that morning to nearby Lucerne. After a night of frightening visions, he felt relieved the next morning and curiously rejuvenated.

> What I found further surprising about LSD was its ability to produce such a far-reaching, powerful, inebriated condition without leaving a hangover. Completely to the contrary, on the day after the LSD experiment I felt myself to be in excellent physical and mental condition . . . .
>
> A sensation of well-being and renewed life flowed through me. Breakfast tasted delicious and was an extraordinary pleasure. When I later walked out into the garden, in which the sun shown now after a spring rain, everything glistened and sparkled in a fresh light. The world was as if newly created. All my senses vibrated in a condition of highest sensitivity that persisted for the entire day . . . . It also appeared to me to be of great significance that I could remember the experience of LSD inebriation in every detail.

Early Distribution of LSD

With this eye-opening, frightening experience, Hofmann entered a world largely unknown to Westerners but long familiar to tribal users of sacred, mind-altering plants. LSD was something genuinely new in two important ways. First was the extreme potency of this compound—which figures out at 100,000-300,000 substantial doses to the ounce. Second, LSD was the first psychedelic that does not occur in nature. Mescaline had been synthesized after analysis of peyote, but it was the same drug as in the plant. LSD never existed before Dr. Hofmann synthesized it.

When his superior, Arthur Stoll, read the report, he telephoned immediately to ask, "Are you certain that you have made no mistake in the weighing? Is the stated dose really correct?" Professor Ernst Rothlin, director of the pharmacology department at Sandoz, and two of his colleagues then repeated the experiment using only a third of what Hofmann had tried. Even with this reduction, the effects were "extremely impressive and fantastic." As Hofmann has put it since, "All doubts in the statements of my report were eliminated."

Subsequent studies were carried out by Werner Stoll, the son of Arthur Stoll, involving forty-nine administrations to twenty-two people at the University of Zurich. In 1947, he published the first article on LSD's mental effects in the pages of the *Swiss Archives of Neurology*. This was followed in 1949 by his second communique on LSD to this journal, entitled "A New Hallucinatory Agent, Active in Very Small Amounts." Two further studies on clinical experiences with LSD were issued that same year.

Six years after Hofmann's discovery, LSD made its way to the United States. It was taken to Los Angeles by Nicholas Bercel, a psychiatrist now specializing in the electroencephalograph (EEG), who had been handed some casually by Werner Stoll with a request that he try it. LSD was requested and received through the mail at Boston's Psychopathic Hospital, where it was first given to Dr. Robert Hyde, the Assistant Director. After swallowing 100 mcg., he became paranoiac but claimed that there was no effect and that the hospital had been cheated. He even insisted on making his hospital rounds. An associate commenting later said, "That was not Dr. Hyde's normal behavior; he is a very pleasant man."

The psychiatrists A.K. Busch and W.C. Johnson also sent for LSD, looking for "a good delirient" for use in therapy. They thought LSD "might shake up things," as Busch later remarked. By August 1950, they were discussing the drug's role as a possible aid in psychotherapy in an American journal, *Diseases of the Nervous System:*

> We believe that L.S.D.-25 is a drug which induces a controllable toxic state within the nervous system, that reactivates anxiety and fear with apparently just enough euphoria to permit recall of the provoking experiences. It does this without the sluggishness or speech difficulties so frequently encountered during I.S.T. [Insulin Shock Therapy] and following E.C.T. [Electroconvulsive Therapy].
>
> On the basis of the preliminary investigation, L.S.D.-25 may offer a means for more readily gaining access to the chronically withdrawn patients. It may also serve as a tool for shortening psychotherapy. We hope further investigation justifies our present impression.

The history of LSD until 1966, when curbs were placed upon further experimentation, can be seen in microcosm in Dr. Hofmann's first two experiences of the drug: initially there was keen interest and optimism; as the power of LSD came to be understood, there was panic. On the basis of Hofmann's light first experience, Sandoz hoped that it might be marketed generally, like barbiturates and tranquilizers. Sandoz thus distributed LSD at cost to many investigators, trying to find a standard use for it.

Sandoz was understandably nervous about some of the wilder aspects of Hofmann's second trip, such as the "out of the body" experience, not to mention other aspects which Hofmann has since described as deeply religious. Nevertheless, the people at Sandoz saw a potential for the drug as a "psychotomimetic" or "schizogen." In the literature distributed with LSD, Sandoz recommended it as an agent for producing a "model schizophrenia" that could be used by psychiatrists and psychologists to explore their patients' states of mind. Sandoz urged that this new substance be tried in only minimal amounts. The earliest studies used miniscule dosages of 20-50 mcgs.

Thanks to the successes of Freudian and Jungian psychology and to discoveries about mood alteration, researchers in many fields were poised to make a frontal assault on the disordered mind and regarded LSD as very promising. On the basis of an analogy with malaria and yellow fever, it was thought that duplicating psychosis or schizophrenia using LSD for an eight- or ten-hour period might well produce insights leading to an eventual cure.

Little of this work panned out as hoped, since there are significant differences between the LSD state and the various psychoses, in which hallucinations, for instance, are usually auditory rather than visual. The analogy was wrong, but it launched LSD into a new decade.

A Decade of Clinical Use

At the start of the 1950s there were only handfuls of papers discussing LSD; by the end of that decade more than five hundred had appeared. This output is a good measure of how fascinated psychotherapists were with the many possibilities LSD opened up. Recently it has come to light that much of this work was encouraged and supported by the CIA and later by Army, Air Force and Navy intelligence. In effect, these agencies triggered an explosion of interest in and use of LSD during the 1960s. In the meantime, more and more research scientists entered this new field, fascinated by its possibilities.

In 1953, Dr. Ronald Sandison established the first LSD clinic open to the public at a small mental hospital in England. Before long, additional centers sprang up in Germany, Italy, France, Holland, Czechoslovakia, several Scandinavian countries, Canada and the U.S. Nearly all used low dosages in a variety of therapeutic approaches. Slowly they changed the image of this "psychosis-mimicking" drug.

Samples of LSD along with a batch of Sandoz tranquilizers scheduled for study were sent in 1954 to the Psychiatric Research Institute in Prague,

Czechoslovakia. The package was opened by a medical student, Stanislav Grof, who was intrigued by the informational leaflet's description of LSD as an agent capable of producing a temporary "model psychosis." Grof tried the LSD in conjunction with a strong flashing light.

> We were doing all kinds of experiments. My preceptor, who gave me LSD, was interested in the EEG among other things, and also in something that's called "driving the brainwaves"—which you can do either using a stroboscopic light or an acoustic input. And then you study whether the corresponding brainwaves would pick up the frequencies that you are feeding into the system.
>
> So when I was "peaking" on LSD, a nurse would come and say, "It's EEG time." She would take me to this little cell. I would lie down and she would take my regular EEG tracing.
>
> And then came the time to "drive my brainwaves." And so she brought the strobe light which we were using, asked me to close my eyes, put the thing above my head—and turned it on.
>
> And this incredible blast of white light came. And the next thing that I knew was that my consciousness was leaving my body. Then I lost the clinic. Then I lost Prague. Then I lost the planet. Then I had a feeling of existing in a totally disembodied state and literally becoming the universe—experiencing it. There was "big bang," there were sort of "white holes," "black holes."
>
> While this was happening, the nurse very carefully was following the instructions—and started at about three cycles, took it up to sixty and back and forth, and put it carefully in the middle of the "alpha" range, and then the "theta" range and "delta" range, and then ended the experiment.
>
> And then I somehow found my body again—and ended up *very impressed.* So what I did, I joined a group of people who had access to psychedelic substances.

Dr. Grof went on to manage LSD observations on human subjects at the Psychiatric Research Institute in Prague and later did similar work at Spring Grove Mental Hospital near Baltimore. Eventually observing more than 3,500 sessions, he introduced views about the LSD experience quite different from those appearing in the early literature. On the basis of his research, he came to believe that psychiatric concepts were inadequate, and he saw the LSD-induced "psychotomimetic" reaction as potentially healing—when, for example, a disruptive experience was allowed to continue to resolution.

In Los Angeles, Dr. Nicholas Bercel was active in "psychophysiological investigations," publishing articles about LSD in scientific journals and introducing this drug to research and medical scientists.

In 1954, Dr. Oscar Janiger, who had been interested in LSD since reading Stoll's first account, was given a chance to try the drug at a mountain retreat: "From that moment on my mind didn't stop for one minute." He wrote Sandoz requesting LSD for a "naturalistic study" and received a "materials grant" (an ample supply).

Janiger set about his study in 1955. His third subject was an artist who claimed the experience was the equivalent of "four years in art school" and entreated Janiger to give it to other artists. Janiger wasn't expecting this development, but he eventually gave in and started a subproject in which one hundred artists drew a Kachina doll before, during and after LSD ingestion. By the end of his investigations in 1962, Janiger had given several thousand administrations of LSD to 875 individuals, many from the creative community in Los Angeles, as well as "plumbers, carpenters, and housewives—whatever that means—and people from different educational and ethnic backgrounds."

Another important figure during the 1950s was the enigmatic, flamboyant Al Hubbard, who bought 4,000 vials of Sandoz LSD and became an early "Johnny Appleseed," repeating a circuit across Canada, down the West Coast to L.A. and back. He gave LSD to many luminaries, including Aldous Huxley and Gerald Heard, and helped establish a long-running LSD clinic in Vancouver, B.C. While most LSD investigators at this time were very cautious, Hubbard saw value in using what were thought to be "massive doses," a practice that became common during the 1960s.

Toward the end of the 1950s, Dr. Sidney Cohen, a psychiatrist affiliated with the Veterans Hospital at UCLA, procured large supplies of this novel drug. He became interested when he heard that this substance was a "superior delirient." After self-experimentation, he told his colleagues that although LSD was not a "true delirient," it was worth intensive study. An account of Cohen's first trip can be found in his *The Beyond Within* (p. 106), which he wrote but attributed to an anonymous doctor.

As Janiger recalls, it was from Cohen's group that social (non-experimental) use of LSD might conceivably have arisen in the United States:

> These people had first taken it experimentally, because that was the only way it was given at all. Then it was just a short step for people who had taken it to say, "Let's try it [again]" and to make up some circumstance which would justify it. At the beginning, nobody would dare say, "Let's just take it." . . . .
>
> So in somebody's home there would be six or eight people, and they would take the drug. I was at one or two of those, and Huxley would be there, and Heard, and you would meet this strata of people. It was here that you met those people who were a mixture of the investigators, plus those people who were some of their subjects—who had shown a special affinity toward or interest in the drug.

Other distribution routes to the general population were developing. From about 1957, a leak sprang up at Sandoz' Hanover, New Jersey plant. Chester Anderson, author of *The Butterfly Kid* and several other books about this period, says that large amounts of LSD and psilocybin with the Sandoz label were being conveyed into "beatnik" Greenwich Village and being taken by musicians, theater people and many others living Bohemian lifestyles.

A fair amount of peyote had also become available as interest in psychedelics spread. Many people had read Aldous Huxley's *Doors of*

Dr. Stanislav Grof, who received LSD in 1954 and subsequently observed more than 3,500 sessions.

Dr. Oscar Janiger, who supervised several thousand administrations of LSD to 875 people.

Al Hubbard, left, an evangelical distributor of LSD during the 1950s, encouraged use of large doses.

Perception, in which he describes mystical feelings evoked by mescaline sulfate, and R. Gordon Wasson's *Life* magazine account of the discovery of "sacred mushrooms" and their ceremonial use in Mexico. The newcomers attracted to LSD were not looking for a psychotic-type experience, nor were they interested in basic research. However, they also weren't taking it just for fun or to get high. The drug had acquired a mystical aura. Although it was used less solemnly and with less forethought than before, its use incorporated overtones of spiritual or artistic value. Many were using it to enhance creative behavior.

In Palo Alto, California, LSD was being studied both at the Veterans Administration Hospital and at Stanford University. At Stanford, the anthropologist Gregory Bateson—who had been introduced to LSD by Dr. Harold Abramson, one of LSD's pioneers—arranged in 1959 for the poet Allen Ginsberg to take it as part of a research program that was secretly sponsored by the military. The novelist Ken Kesey also received LSD in Palo Alto, using his experiences as the basis for his *One Flew Over the Cuckoo's Nest*. Kesey's further adventures with LSD are celebrated in Tom Wolfe's *The Electric Kool-Aid Acid Test*. From Palo Alto LSD began seeping into San Francisco.

Abbie Hoffman, whose first LSD was supplied by the Army, relates how interest in the drug burgeoned along the West Coast toward the end of the 1950's:

> Aldous Huxley had told me about LSD back in 1957. And I *tried* to get it in 1959. I stood in line in a clinic in San Francisco, after Herb Caen had run an announcement in his column in the *Chronicle* that if anybody wanted to take a new experimental drug called LSD-25, he would be paid $150 for his effort. Jesus, that emptied Berkeley! I got up about six in the morning, but I was about 1,500 in line . . . so I didn't get it until 1965.

With the closing of the decade of clinical use came perhaps the most important discovery since Dr. Hofmann first synthesized LSD. Late in the summer of 1959, Hofmann received a parcel of seeds from a researcher he had made contact with while investigating the sacred Mexican fungi. The seeds were of what was then called *Rivea corymbosa*, otherwise known as *ololiuqui*, a Mexican morning glory. In the summer of 1960, Hofmann isolated the active principles and identified them chemically. They were ergot alkaloids. "From the phytochemical point of view," commented Hofmann when disclosing these results, "this finding was unexpected and of particular interest, because lysergic acid alkaloids, which had hitherto been found only in lower fungi in the genus *Claviceps*, were now, for the first time, indicated for the higher plants, in the phanerogamic family *Convolvulaceae*." First synthesized in a laboratory, LSD was now found to have a counterpart in nature.

Richard Evans Schultes: *Harvard Botanical Museum Leaflet*

Turbina *(formerly considered*
Rivea*)* corymbosa, *a Mexican
morning glory found to contain
lysergic acid amides.*

A Decade and a Half of Covert Use

The CIA became aware of LSD in the very early 1950s. That 1/100,000ths of an ounce could derange an individual for eight to ten hours was a matter of great concern to people there. They sought to find out more about its potential than could be gleaned from a few journal articles. They wanted to know how it could be used as a weapon, and whether it would work as a truth serum. Learning about "psychotomimetics" such as LSD became still more important to the CIA in 1951 when military intelligence reported, erroneously, that Sandoz had sent fifty million doses to the Soviets.

In 1953, a military operative in Switzerland indicated that Sandoz wanted to sell 10 kilograms—22 pounds, or about 100 million doses—on the open market. A secret coordinating committee that included CIA and Pentagon officials recommended unanimously that the CIA should buy it all for just over a quarter million dollars in order to keep it "out of the hands of the Russians or other possible buyers." CIA chief Allen Dulles approved, and soon two Agency representatives were sent to Sandoz to negotiate.

As it turned out, their informant had mistaken a milligram for a kilogram, miscalculating by a factor of a million. The president of Sandoz told the visitors that all production until then amounted to less than 40 grams—under 1½ ounces. The ergot used by Sandoz as a starting material had taken many years to find. As a result, it seemed likely that the world supply of LSD would always remain small.

Nonetheless the Swiss company indicated a willingness to step up its efforts and produce as much LSD as the CIA wished. It further agreed to keep the CIA informed about all future production as well as requests for purchases coming in from other parts of the world.

The CIA established a research team in the Chemical Division of its Technical Services staff. Richard Helms, then heading Clandestine Services, recommended the project in early April, 1953; a week and a half later—almost exactly a decade after Hofmann's first trip—Allen Dulles approved. The project was dubbed "MKULTRA" (superseding "Project ARTICHOKE," mentioned in the Psilocybian Mushrooms chapter) and given an initial budget of $300,000. The goal: "to investigate whether and how it was possible to modify an individual's behavior by covert means." Heading the group of about half a dozen was a protégé of Helms, Dr. Sidney Gottlieb, who was authorized to draw on the Agency's account.

This group was interested in determining the effects of LSD and other drugs in diverse situations. Unlike Sandoz, which was seeking therapeutic applications, the CIA was providing grants through front organizations to encourage *any* research. Gottlieb and his associates soon became sponsors of LSD studies conducted at a number of prestigious institutions: Boston Psychopathic Hospital, Mount Sinai Hospital and Columbia University, the Addiction Research Center of the National Institute of Mental Health, the University of Oklahoma and the University of Rochester. "Suddenly there was a huge new market for grants in academica," wrote John Marks in his *The Search for the "Manchurian Candidate,"* currently the best description of these activities. Academics collaborating with the CIA in LSD investigations—some wittingly, many unwittingly—issued a multitude of articles in the scientific literature. These reports hardly reveal what a few of the "witting" were trying to find out for the CIA.

An outstanding example is Dr. Harold Abramson, a New York immunologist who apparently delighted in administering the drug to intellectuals—one instance being Frank Fremont-Smith, who later chaired one of the Josiah Macy, Jr. Foundation conferences that brought together early LSD researchers. Abramson wrote prominently about LSD in scientific publications, mainly about such things as the effect of the drug on Siamese fighting fish (they float at an angle with their noses nearly out of the water, and their color darkens) and the use of low dosages in aiding psychotherapeutic "transference." It wasn't publicly known until the late 1970s that the CIA furnished him with $85,000 in 1953 to provide—as Gottlieb put it—"operationally pertinent materials along the following lines: a. Disturbance of Memory; b. Discrediting by Aberrant Behavior; c. Alteration of Sex Patterns; d. Eliciting of Information; e. Suggestibility; f. Creation of Dependence." Abramson kept in touch with many who had begun to investigate clinical uses of LSD, reporting his findings and theirs to the CIA.

Gottlieb hired Abramson and others and funded academics as a relatively inexpensive way to acquire a broad range of information about LSD and similar substances when used in more or less ordinary settings. The CIA also wanted information on how LSD could be used for its own special ends, information that professors were hardly likely to provide. Only a month after its establishment, the Gottlieb group set up a safehouse in Greenwich Village where people could be observed after they had been given the drug without "informed awareness." The person in charge was George White, a New York narcotics agent who had carried out experiments with *Cannabis* derivatives in search of a truth serum for the OSS (a forerunner of the CIA). The CIA paid the rent and provided White with money to hire prostitutes. Their job was to see whether individuals could be led under the influence of LSD to disclose closely-held secrets.

Desiring control of LSD as a policy objective, the CIA was worried about its dependency on a foreign supplier. In 1953, the Gottlieb group therefore approached Eli Lilly & Co., which had already been working on a process for fully synthesizing LSD. The next year Lilly's chemists made a breakthrough, manufacturing small amounts of LSD from chemicals rather than ergot. An Agency memo to Allen Dulles proclaimed that the government could now buy LSD in "tonnage quantities."

Each member of the Gottlieb group took LSD several times and even dosed each other during the summer of 1953. Scarcely half a year after the establishment of MKULTRA came an unexpected blow that threatened to end all the goings-on. One of their university sources had told Gottlieb's group that LSD might be dangerous in some cases, mentioning a Swiss doctor who had become depressed after she took the drug and who was rumored to have committed suicide. Gottlieb had furthermore been warned twice by his superiors not to turn on outsiders. He was to see first-hand how traumatic uninformed administration could be.

The Technical Services branch of the CIA, which funded the Gottlieb group, was also paying $200,000 a year to scientists with the Army Chemical Corps at Fort Detrick for investigations relating to chemical warfare. In November 1953, Gottlieb's staff gathered with their Army associates for a three-day brainstorming retreat at an isolated lodge in the Maryland woods. During the second evening Gottlieb passed around a glass of Cointreau which—unknown to the others—he had spiked with LSD. All but two tried the Cointreau. Among those who partook from Gottlieb's glass was Dr. Frank Olson, a specialist in airborne delivery of chemical weapons, who came to believe that he had revealed important secrets during his subsequent

LSD trip. He became depressed and was sent, accompanied by Gottlieb's assistant, to see Dr. Harold Abramson. Reluctantly, Olson agreed to enter a mental hospital. The night before commitment, he died after crashing through a window on the tenth floor of the New York Statler-Hilton Hotel.

Any CIA involvement with LSD was quickly covered up, only coming to light in 1976 —twenty-one years later—as a result of the Rockefeller Commission's review of illegal CIA domestic activities. In 1977, Olson's family was invited to the White House for an apology, and Congress passed a bill to pay Mrs. Olson and her three children $750,000 in compensation.

Gottlieb was reprimanded by his superiors. For a short while his supply of LSD was taken from him. CIA outposts in Manila and Atsugi, Japan were told not to use the LSD that had been shipped to them.

Richard Helms persisted in advocating that the "dirty tricks" branch of the CIA continue to experiment with LSD, and soon Gottlieb resumed distributing the drug. George White, promoted to Regional Narcotics Chief, moved his safehouse operation to San Francisco two years later, where he continued dosing people until 1966.

Military intelligence in each branch of the armed services also heard about LSD, and they were fascinated. By the mid-1950s, they too were funding LSD studies. This secret CIA and military involvement is carefully documented by John Marks (1979). The Chemical Warfare Service at the Army's Edgewood Arsenal stockpiled enormous quantities of LSD and other psychoactive compounds, synthesizing known psychedelics like LSD and others that may still be unknown to the outside world. For example, MDM (see Chapter Five), which has only recently been recognized as a psychedelic agent, is identical to Edgewood's "EA [Experimental Agent]-1475."

Army spokesmen began talking publicly about large-scale use of LSD in war. In contrast to the emphasis on individualized administration favored by the CIA, Army officials were showing Congressmen and the press films of soldiers who were unable to march in formation after being dosed with LSD in their morning coffee. LSD was advocated as a way to conduct "humane warfare" against an enemy. Dr. Albert Hofmann later revealed that the Army was contacting him "every two years or so" to request Sandoz' active participation in its efforts. The requests were denied.

The Army engaged in covert "field operations" overseas. A notorious example is the torture of James Thornwell, a black American soldier in France, who was suspected of having stolen classified documents in 1961. We will probably never know the full story on at least nine others, referred to as "foreign nationals," who were subjected to the Army's LSD interrogation project, "Operation THIRD CHANCE."

Thornwell, then twenty-two, was first exposed to extreme stress, which included beatings, solitary confinement, denial of water, food and sanitary facilities and steady verbal abuse. After six weeks, he was given LSD without his knowledge. The interrogators threatened "to extend [his shattered] state indefinitely," according to an Army document dug up later, "even to a permanent condition of insanity." In the late 1970s, Thornwell sued the U.S. government for $10 million; the U.S. House of Representatives approved a compromise settlement of $650,000 in 1980.

The Big Wave Hits

Just after the election of John Kennedy to the presidency, a pediatrician of English extraction working in New York City wrote Sandoz on New York Hospital letterhead requesting a gram of LSD. A package came by return mail to Dr. John Beresford, with a bill for $285 (the approximate cost of manufacture at the time). Beresford had tried other psychedelics, was impressed by the mind/body questions they posed, and was eager to test this new product. Results were clear. He therefore gave part of his gram — over time — to a few associates, including an acquaintance known as Michael Hollingshead.

Hollingshead is important to this chronicle because he managed before long to give some of this gram to Donovan, Paul McCartney, Keith Richard, Paul Krassner, Frank Barron, Houston Smith, Paul Lee, Richard Katz, Pete La Roca, Charlie Mingus, Saul Steinberg, Timothy Leary, Richard Alpert, Ralph Metzner, Alan Watts and many others who contributed to the coming international awareness of LSD. "There is some possibility," wrote Hollingshead later, "that my friends and I have illuminated more people than anyone else in history." His memoir bears the publisher's title, *The Man Who Turned On the World*.

With his part of gram "H-00047," Beresford, with Jean Houston and Michael Corner, opened an LSD foundation in Manhattan in 1962, the Agora Scientific Trust. The impressive, valuable work carried out there is

John Beresford, who received a gram of Sandoz LSD and tried to describe its psychoactive effects scientifically.

Frank Siteman

Michael Hollingshead, who distributed part of Beresford's gram to Timothy Leary, Paul McCartney, Donovan, Keith Richard and many others.

described in Robert Masters and Jean Houston's book entitled *The Varieties of Psychedelic Experience.*

That same year Myron Stolaroff and associates established another important LSD study center, the International Foundation for Advanced Study in Menlo Park. This institution was set up to examine the effects of LSD and mescaline upon carefully selected subjects. The results from several hundred administrations were significant, especially in regard to "learning-enhancement" and "creativity."

By 1962, the number of people who knew about LSD had increased geometrically. Some were enthusiastic about trying the drug but had no access to LSD psychotherapists, the original "gate-keepers." In response to the demand for LSD, the first generation of "acid chemists" arose.

A notable early effort was a batch of 62,000 tablets of questionable content synthesized in 1962 by Bernard Roseman and Bernard Copely. These tabs figured in the first "LSD bust," when Food and Drug Administration agents charged the two with "smuggling" (manufacturing of LSD was then perfectly legal).

Stanley Owsley entered the trade after having been frustrated in his efforts to obtain pure LSD. His trademarks—"White Lightning," "Purple Haze"—and others such as "Batman," "Purple Double-Domes" and "Midnight Hour"—were associated with "tabs" of high quality. An enormous amount of this production was given away, yet Owsley became perhaps the first LSD millionaire. When he was captured in 1967, 200 fresh grams—a million substantial doses—were confiscated.

The first big wave of popular interest was gathering momentum. In 1962, the Gamblers issued the first record including a song about LSD. Many folk musicians were getting "cerebrally electrified." Talk of LSD spread beyond Bohemian and university circles; even Henry Luce, publisher of *Time* and *Life* magazines, and his wife tried the drug. Luce, wandering out into his garden in Arizona, heard a symphony in his head that impressed him greatly because he had previously considered himself tone-deaf. He also acquired affectionate feelings for the cacti there. This may not sound like much, but he claimed it was important personally because he previously "had hated them."

To centerstage came Dr. Timothy Leary.

Already engaged in psilocybin research at Harvard, Leary was one of those who partook of "Lot No. H-00047." He took a tablespoon and a half from Hollingshead's mayonnaise jar of LSD cut with sugar-icing—and didn't talk for five days. Richard Alpert, his close associate, "told everybody not to touch the stuff—we had just lost Timothy." When Leary came back, Alpert remembers him as saying, "Wow!"

Leary's LSD experience, coming after more than a hundred psilocybin trips, changed his life. "I have never recovered from that shattering ontological confrontation," he wrote later. "From the date of this session it was inevitable that we would leave Harvard . . . ." The break was not long in

Norman Seeff

Timothy Leary, who was the first to proclaim LSD as "ecstatic," "fun."

coming. "LSD is more important than Harvard," proclaimed Leary in 1962. Before Timothy Leary, the academics had never quite come clean about their experimenting with LSD. Leary alone emphasized publicly that the drug was "ecstatic," "sensual" and "fun." "It gives you levity and altitude," was his explanation once, "where you see the implausibilities and you see the incongruities and the ridiculousness of what you had taken so seriously before." He gave the media a clear and emotionally charged image to transmit. Before long Leary's name was tied inextricably to the compound now known simply as "LSD."

Leary and associates tried in many ways to train people in the use of this drug, which they saw as a key to the "new age." Even before leaving Harvard, they established an off-campus organization known as IFIF (the International Federation for Internal Freedom) and laid plans for an experiential LSD center on the beach at Zihuatanejo, Mexico. When they advertised this opportunity the next summer, IFIF received more than 1,500 applications. Leary requested 100 grams of LSD, about a million doses, and 25 kilograms of psilocybin, about 2½ million doses, from Sandoz, and sent a check for $10,000 as a deposit. Sandoz returned the check when Leary couldn't provide proper import licenses. The Mexican center lasted only a short while, because of hyped media attention after an American whom they wouldn't allow to participate caused trouble and after an unrelated murder in the vicinity. Leary and his colleagues tried to set up an experiential center on the Caribbean island of Dominica but their visas were canceled the day the main group arrived.

Finding haven at last on a 2,500-acre estate in Millbrook, N.Y., they announced formation of the Castalia Foundation. Here they began turning on many influential people as well as conducting advertised "nondrug workshops" in consciousness change. They started their *Psychedelic Review* in the summer of 1963 and traveled around the United States lecturing about LSD. They pioneered in the presentation of "light shows." Leary eventually set up a religion—the League for Spiritual Discovery. This was not intended as a mass organization, but was limited to a hundred people centered around the Millbrook estate who were dedicated to showing others how they themselves could "help recreate every man as God and every woman as Goddess." Leary emphasized that it would "*not* repeat the injunction classically used by religious prophets: Follow *me*, sign up in *my* flock. It imposes no dogmas except one: Live out your own highest vision."

The Monterey, California Pop Festival of 1963 (four years before the film *Monterey Pop*) marked a new relationship between LSD and music.

The fifty-one room "Big House" at Millbrook, N.Y., a psychedelic
center where the Castalia Foundation experimented with LSD
training.

Many there took LSD to celebrate and enhance their appreciation of this festival. Musicians and artists soon began wide-scale experimentation with ways to perform that would complement, direct and heighten the effects of LSD, or present a "flash" of the experience for the uninitiated. Within a year, the Beatles were singing to everyone, "Turn off your mind, relax and float downstream/This is not dying" (words taken directly from *The Psychedelic Experience,* a book issued by Leary and associates).

By the middle of the 1960s, an important shift in avant-garde energies took place in San Francisco that was to reverberate powerfully throughout the Western world. This shift involved a geographical move of only a few miles—from North Beach to a vicinity near the crossing of Haight Street and Ashbury Avenue (close to Golden Gate Park). Here LSD users banded together, soon signaling the dawning of the new age.

North Beach had served for years as home ground for beatnik activities and had become a center for cultural ferment in America. The beats generally favored stark contrasts of black and white, in their dress and in their thinking. They emphasized the role of the Artist and the Bohemian, celebrated blacks as culture heroes, and were politically active against the Bomb. Their style found expression in after-hours poetry and jazz in coffeehouses. Their taste in drugs inclined to pot, speed and heroin.

The Haight-Ashbury community, catalyzed by LSD, wore the colors of a rainbow and was not emphatically male dominated. It celebrated not the agonies and triumphs of the Individual Artist but rather was "into" communal living and a new "Bay Area" style of music and dancing. Its approach was softer. If it emulated anyone, it was the tribal American Indian.

By 1966, Haight-Ashbury was rife with new energies provided by LSD-using musical groups such as the Jefferson Airplane, the Grateful Dead, Big Brother and the Holding Company and Country Joe and the Fish; by artists such as Mouse, who with his colleagues re-established the powerful appeal once accorded posters; and by the Diggers, who gave away food and clothing. That year, the brothers Ron and Jay Thelin opened the nation's first "headshop" and helped launch the first "psychedelic newspaper," *The San Francisco Oracle.*

Similar but less conspicuous developments took place in East Greenwich Village at about the same time—and half a year later the new style was evident in the low-rent centers of most large U.S. cities. The participants were mainly whites in their teens to thirties, the "baby boom" sons and daughters of people who were secure financially.

An LSD or "flower-child" lifestyle was further encouraged through other "Be-ins," rock music performed with light shows, dozens of psychedelic newspapers and communal living. This proselytizing occurred throughout the U.S. and to a lesser extent in Western Europe, radiating especially from London, Hamburg and Amsterdam.

Announcement for the most impressive "Be-in," January 14, 1967, in San Francisco's Golden Gate Park.

The movement was proclaimed at the time as a second Renaissance. Seen in retrospect, it was at the very least life-altering for millions. Some three or four years of social experimentation, touched off by mass use of LSD, can be credited with having sparked a host of liberation movements. This period changed American attitudes toward work, toward the police and the military, and toward such groups as women and gays. It began our now-established concern with consciousness-raising and personal growth.

Artifacts reflecting the creative ferment during this time are best displayed in *Psychedelic Art* with commentary by Robert Masters, Jean

This "Better Living Thru Chemistry" poster from 1967 San Francisco
typifies the "hippie" attitude: non-threatening, welcoming—everyone
"doing their own thing"—and clear also about the importance of
psychedelic chemicals to the scene. The tone of such an appeal
contrasted sharply with establishment preoccupations as reflected
in the media: ghetto riots and the war in Vietnam.

S.F. Oracle #8, 1967

An example of the "visionary" artwork featured in the tabloid San Francisco Oracle, *this nation's first and, in the opinion of many people, best "psychedelic newspaper."*

Houston and Stanley Krippner. Lester Grinspoon and James Bakalar from Harvard have compiled a list of LSD's contributions—largely missing before then—to our popular language:

> turned on, straight, freak, freaked out, stoned, tripping, tripped out, spaced out, far out, flower power, ego trip, hit, into, mike, plastic [meaning "rigid"],

Movement cartoonist R. Cobb here reflects the hippies'
conviction that their alternative was both obvious and compelling.

going with the flow, laying [a] trip on someone, game-playing, mind-blowing, mind games, bringdown, energy, centering, acid, acidhead, good trip, bum trip, horror show, drop a cap or tab, karma, samsara, mantra, groovy, rapping, crash, downer, flash, scene, vibes, great white light, doing your thing, going through changes, uptight, getting into spaces, wiped out, where it's at, high, ball, zap, rush, and so on . . . .

The big LSD wave crested during "the summer of love," 1967. "Wearing flowers in their hair," several hundred thousand people came to San Francisco. "Gonzo journalist" Hunter Thompson recalls the atmospherics of this period:

> San Francisco in the middle sixties was a very special time and place to be a part of. Maybe it *meant something*. Maybe not, in the long run . . . but no explanation, no mix of words or music or memories can touch that sense of knowing that you were there and alive in that corner of time and the world . . . You could strike sparks anywhere. There was a fantastic universal sense that whatever we were doing was *right*, that we were winning . . . . Our energy would simply *prevail*. There was no point in fighting—on our side or theirs. We had all the momentum; we were riding the crest of a high and beautiful wave.

LSD Becomes Illegal

With the LSD wave came a wave of establishment panic. The federal ban on LSD and related drugs was the first bill proposed by President Johnson in 1967.

A clash between traditional American mores and the values adopted by users of Hofmann's crystal had been on its way ever since Harvard University sent Dick Alpert and Leary packing over the issue. The media hurried the conflict to its moment of crisis: for a while it seemed there wasn't a nationally distributed magazine that didn't have an LSD article, usually sensational. *Time* was the first to jump in with a series of articles appearing in late 1965 and early 1966 in its Psychiatry section. These articles railed against LSD with dire warnings about hordes of "acid heads," some of whom were taking "walloping overdoses." *Time* declared that the "disease" was striking everywhere: "By best estimates, 10,000 students in the University of California system have tried LSD (though not all have suffered detectable ill effects). No one can guess how many more self-styled 'acid heads' there are among oddball cult groups . . . ." (March 11, 1966).

Dr. Huston Smith of M.I.T. wasn't far from the mark when he told an LSD conference in 1966 that the confusion about this drug was so great and our knowledge about it so small "that there is no hope of telling the truth about it at this point." All efforts to arrive at a deliberate and informed evaluation of the drug were swept aside by the headlines of that year:

• On March 26th, Timothy Leary was arrested in Laredo after less than half an ounce of marijuana was found on his daughter. The sentence was thirty years. Leary was suddenly transformed into the LSD movement's first martyr.

• On April 6th, a five-year-old girl in Brooklyn swallowed a sugar cube impregnated with LSD that her uncle had left in the family refrigerator. She was rushed to the hospital where her stomach was pumped. She got the scare of her life through this procedure, and remained on the critical list for two days. Published reports of her being examined later indicated that she made a full recovery.

• On April 11th, Stephen Kessler, a thirty-year-old ex-medical student was charged with the murder of his mother-in-law, having stabbed her 105 times. When taken in, he muttered, "What happened? Man, I've been flying for three days on LSD. Did I kill my wife? Did I rape anybody?" At the Brooklyn police station, he kept insisting, "I'm high, I'm really high," and when asked if he were "high" on drugs, he replied, "Only on LSD" (*New York Times* and *New York Herald-Tribune*, April 12, 1966).

• On April 16th, G. Gordon Liddy, then assistant prosecuting attorney in Dutchess County, N.Y., broke into national prominence by leading a raid on Leary's Millbrook estate, where, at a cost of $60 per weekend, nondrug techniques were being used to teach people how to get "high." Liddy since has said that he liked Leary from the moment he first set eyes on him at 2 am, but that he was "acting under orders." A small amount of marijuana was found in the room of a visiting journalist, and Rosemary Woodruff, who was to become Leary's wife, was held in jail for a month for refusing to testify before a grand jury about activities on the estate.

The headlines prompted an appetite for still more coverage. Special interviews with district attorneys, college presidents, narcotics agents, doctors, biochemists and others who might be considered authorities appeared, creating an atmosphere of national emergency.

The chairman of the New York County Medical Society's Subcommittee on Narcotics Addiction said that LSD was "more dangerous than heroin." The FDA and Federal Narcotics Bureau launched new "drug education" programs. Three Senate subcommittees investigated LSD use. Bills that made possession of LSD and other psychedelic drugs a felony were introduced into state legislatures throughout the nation. New York State Assembly Speaker Anthony J. Travia, pushing legislation that called for a minimum sentence of seven years, declared that he would defer public hearings on the law until after it passed because "the problem is so urgent."

Walter Winchell issued an item reading, "Warning to LSD Users: You may go blind."

Bill Trent, writing in the Canadian *Evening Telegram* about an architect's serious and successful attempt to solve a design problem by taking LSD, titled his story "The Demented World of Kyo Izumi."

The mass-market *Confidential Flash* asserted in a full-page cover headline, "LSD KILLS SEX DRIVE FOREVER." *The Police Gazette* reprinted a report from *The Journal of the American Medical Association* with a new title: "LSD and Sex Madness."

In one of the Senate LSD hearings, Senator Robert Kennedy repeatedly asked why the studies conducted by the National Institute of Mental Health, which had been so valuable a month earlier, "no longer were considered so?" It was a question almost nobody wanted to hear or have answered. In short order, existing programs were drastically cut back. Before long, there were new, tighter regulations. Any investigator who had ever experienced the drug personally was now forbidden to conduct LSD research of any kind whatsoever.

And yet, as the Consumers Union's book on *Licit and Illicit Drugs* notes, "by shutting off the relative trickle of Sandoz LSD into informal channels, Congress and the Food and Drug Administration had unwittingly opened the sluices to a veritable LSD flood. By 1970 it was estimated that between 1,000,000 and 2,000,000 Americans had taken an LSD trip." The Consumers Union noted further that driving the drug and its users underground augmented certain of its hazards, listing them under the following headings:

1. Increased expectations of adverse effects.
2. Unknown dosages.
3. Contamination.

4. Adulteration.
5. Mistaken attribution.
6. Side effects of law enforcement.
7. Lack of supervision.
8. Mishandling of panic reactions.
9. Misinterpretation of reactions.
10. Flashbacks.
11. Preexisting pathology.
12. Unwitting use.

For a more careful accounting of "LSD casualties," see "Adverse Effects and Their Treatment," pp. 157-191 in *Psychedelic Drugs Reconsidered.*

In 1967, Dr. Maimon Cohen, a geneticist from Buffalo, N.Y., made an announcement that significantly prejudiced the public's view of LSD. Returning from a visit to the Haight-Ashbury area, Cohen decided to examine chromosomes from a fifty-seven-year-old man who had been given LSD on four occasions during a fifteen-year hospitalization. The patient was found to have more chromosomal breaks than usual. Dr. Cohen also spilled LSD into a test tube containing human cells and observed damage to the chromosomes. Later it was pointed out that similar results could be achieved with the same amount of milk and that Cohen's patient had received regular treatments of Librium and Thorazine, now proven chromosome-breakers.

A drug bust at Tompkins Square, New York City, 1967.

East Village Other

Nonetheless, on the basis of his examination of a single patient and his cell-spilling experiment, Cohen published his conclusions in *Science*. By evening, the charge that LSD could break chromosomes was in all the nation's media.

Shortly thereafter, two doctors in Portland, Oregon reported that they had found an excess of chromosomal breaks in users of street acid. The chart they provided revealed that extra breakage occurred only among users of acid who were also users of amphetamine, which has since been established as a chromosome-breaker. Once again the papers had a field day. A full-page ad for a *McCall's* article on LSD featured a baby broken into parts. Ironically, the article itself cast doubts on the charge of chromosome damage.

Retractions of mistaken opinions and findings about the use and effects of LSD are quiet and very rare, and so it was in regard to the chromosome charge. Even though studies conducted by the National Institute of Mental Health and others disproved the allegation, even though Timothy Leary's chromosomes were examined and showed no abnormal breakage, even though other drugs have now clearly been established to be chromosome-breakers while LSD has not, the media took little if any notice of the new evidence.

Apologia for Timothy Leary (Michael Horowitz)

"Timothy Leary, much to our surprise, showed, in 200 cells, only two with chromosome aberrations, one in each cell. This finding is about as spectacular as must be the amount of LSD that he probably has taken in the past 8 years. I am at a loss to understand or explain this negative finding." —*Hermann Lisco, M.D., Cancer Research Institute, New England Deaconess Hospital, Boston, Mass.*

As a footnote it should be pointed out that at the trial of Stephen Kessler (the "MAD LSD SLAYER" of the April headlines) it was learned that he had taken LSD five times in minimal doses (10-50 mcgs.) between the summer of 1964 and March 1966 (a month before the murder of his mother-in-law). Other drugs may have been influential in the slaying:

> The defendant made no mention of having taken LSD just before the kill-ing of Mrs. Cooper, but said that on April 8, a Saturday, "I felt funny, I had an indescribable feeling and took one-and-a-half grains of pentabarbital" and could recall nothing more until after the murder, the following Monday . . . .
> —*N.Y. Times,* October 10, 1967

> Both doctors . . . told the jury of eleven men and one woman that Kessler had told them he had drunk three quarts of lab alcohol, cut with water, and taken more sleeping pills on the days in question . . . .
> —*N.Y. Post,* October 18, 1967

Ebb and Resurgence

In 1977, the National Institute on Drug Abuse (NIDA) issued a *National Survey on Drug Abuse* based on a sampling of 4,594 people. The report estimated that about ten million Americans (6 percent of the population over the age of twelve) had by then used a strong psychedelic, mostly LSD, with somewhat over a million falling into the category of "reg-ular users."

The peak years were from 1965 to 1968, followed by a substantial decline in LSD use. Many were frightened by the chromosome-damage charge or by experience with adulterated or badly made LSD. Others were put off by the overwhelming nature of "high-dose tripping" or by its illegal status, fearing that the need to act furtively would interfere with and badly taint the LSD experience. Large numbers of previous users turned to meditation to get high.

Some of the leading underground chemists had been arrested. The LSD available was generally weaker and less pure, though there were excep-tions—tabs known as "Mighty Quinn," "Blue Cheer," "Pink Swirls" and the red, white and blue "Peace Sign." Appearing in 1968, "Sunshine" acid (an orange tablet less than a quarter of an inch across) was the first large opera-tion after LSD possession was made illegal. Tim Scully, a prominent second-generation chemist, made some but said that most "Sunshine" came by way of Ronald Stark, who brought approximately thirty-five million doses over from Europe.

LSD use seems to have reached its lowest ebb in the early 1970s and manufacturing shrank to a small scale. Those seeking LSD could find pink, blue and purple "microdots" but very little else.

Then came "computer acid" (one hundred dots in rows of twenty by five on a sheet of blotter paper the size of a dollar bill), which was of pretty good quality and very convenient for distribution. At about the same time arrived "Windowpane" (also known as "Clearlight"), which contained LSD inside a thin gelatin square a quarter of an inch across. Both showed improvement in potency and purity, giving impetus to the flowing in of another LSD wave.

By the end of the 1970s, it was evident that a general reassessment of the earlier, massive LSD experimentation had taken place and that a less flamboyant reacquaintance with LSD had begun. The quality of the products soon available, coming from many different sources, was no longer so seriously in question. Of great importance to this resurgence of interest was the widespread home-production of psychedelic mushrooms. LSD came back into limited public discourse as a sidelight in conferences on the effects of psychoactive mushrooms.

Throughout the 1960s and early 1970s, very few people actually experienced sacred mushrooms. The bulk of mushrooms examined at testing facilities during this period were shown to be almost entirely non-psychoactive, and many had LSD or PCP added (usually in small amounts). In 1976, successful methods for growing the *Stropharia* (often called *Psilocybe) cubensis* mushroom species were published with clearly identifying photographs. Nearly a quarter million of these instruction books and booklets were sold over the next few years, allowing great numbers of people to experience—or re-experience—psychedelic effects from a natural source.

Many who feared synthetic products because of the uncertainties of quality and identification were willing to give natural psychedelics a try. They had been used for millenia, and nothing had been charged against them in terms of chromosomal or other damage. Thanks to the gentle psychoagents in the *Stropharia cubensis* mushroom species, many people discovered or renewed an interest in LSD.

Several convenings of "psychedelic activists" were initiated by Weston La Barre and especially R. Gordon Wasson, and their call for a re-examination of mushrooms was generalized gradually to other psychedelics, including LSD. In 1977, Dr. Albert Hofmann and his wife Anita flew to the Olympic Peninsula in Washington State for a Mushroom Conference. Wasson, Hofmann, Carl Ruck and Danny Staples presented evidence that the famous Eleusinian mysteries were catalyzed by lysergic acid amides extracted from grasses on the nearby Rarian Plain. Their thesis has since been published as *The Road to Eleusis*.

Similar gatherings occurred in Santa Cruz (October 1977), in San Francisco (September 1978), in Los Angeles (January 1979), in Santa Cruz (July 1981) and in Santa Barbara (March 1982).

Another generation of young LSD chemists seems to have taken over from those who were active in the 1960s. At the time of this writing (mid-1982), acid is widely available in myriad forms. Almost all current products contain considerably less LSD than Owsley once thought proper but appear to be good quality. Though available in crystalline or liquid form, most LSD is still distributed on blotter paper, which is convenient but exposes the drug to almost the greatest possible oxidation and damage from light.

Jeremy Bigwood: *Journal of Psychedelic Drugs*

Carl Ruck, Albert Hofmann, R. Gordon Wasson and Danny
Staples at the Second International Conference on Hallucinogenic
Mushrooms, held in October 1977 near Port Townsend, Washington.

Recent blotters range in appearance from graph paper (containing fifty times fifty, or twenty-five hundred, "hits") to fancy color imprints on separated half-inch squares. These are often intricately designed, featuring a four-color Mickey Mouse as the Sorcerer's Apprentice in *Fantasia*, Rosicrucian symbols, a phoenix, a dragon or an Eye of Horus. Some users of LSD object to the more flippant symbols—Plutos or Snoopys; they argue that such designs in combination with the usually low dosages encourage an LSD experience that is little more than recreational.

LSD has recently appeared in a hardened gel in the shape of a tiny pyramid. This is convenient for distribution, yet the hardened surface reduces potential for oxidation. Tablets with LSD spread throughout offer a similar advantage in stability over blotters, one example being the "Om" tab. An appropriate direction in the packaging of LSD would be to emphasize known dosage and purity, as was the case with the original Sandoz ampules which contained one milligram per milliliter of water in a resealable glass container. That kind of quantitative and qualitative care has not appeared as yet.

The course of LSD history over the past few years has been influenced by the establishment of several publications and institutions, including *High Times* and similar magazines, the Fitz Hugh Ludlow Memorial Library in San Francisco, NORML (the National Organization to Reform Marijuana Laws), PharmChem in Palo Alto and other drug-testing facilities and the tradition of annual Rainbow Gatherings in various parts of the U.S. Also

Steve Gladstone

From left, Bonnie Golightly, Ram Dass (Richard Alpert), Allen Ginsberg, Albert Hofmann and Ralph Metzner gathered for a colloquium entitled "LSD—A Generation Later" at the University of California, Santa Cruz in October 1977. More than 4,000 people came to hear Dr. Hofmann's talk.

notable are books from Stanislav Grof, Albert Hofmann, Carlos Castaneda, Timothy Leary and many others.

Dosage is down, causing less potential for panic, along with less spectacular results. The number of people interested seems on the rise. Charlie Haas summed up a decade's change in his "Notes on the Acid Renaissance" for *New West* magazine (August 13, 1979):

> LSD—the scariest and most tantalizing thing you can buy without a prescription, the white hope for instant psychotherapy that became a CIA toy and a bazooka in the Bohemian arsenal, the portable Lourdes that oiled the transition of American youth from Elvis to Elvish and made all those honor students start dressing funny and printing up those unreadable purple-and-aqua posters—*that* LSD—is as nationally popular now as it was ten years ago, despite the fact that the same media which then could speak of nothing else are now virtually silent on the subject. Among people who swallow it or sell it, or who monitor its use from the vantage point of drug-abuse counseling, there is some sporting disagreement as to whether acid has been enjoying a renaissance for about two years or never went away in the first place, with the former view in the majority. But there is a consensus on at least two points: The bad trips and mental casualties that made such hot copy in the '60s seem to have diminished radically, and the volume of acid changing hands suggests that there are actually more users now than there were a decade ago . . . .

CHEMISTRY
Resemblances and Differences Between LSD and Other Substances
LSD-25 is a crystalline molecule that shares, along with many other psychedelics, a two-ring "indole" nucleus—composed of one atom of nitrogen, eight of carbon and seven of hydrogen—in its chemical structure (a drawing of indole appears on page 262). This basic structure is common to the short-acting tryptamines, ibogaine, psilocybin, harmaline and other psychedelics, and it bears considerable resemblance to the chemical structure of serotonin and dopamine, neurotransmitters that carry electrical impulses across synapses in the brain. Mescaline and MDA-like compounds contain only one of these rings. Nitrous oxide (N_2O) and the THCs in marijuana have considerably different chemical structures.

On top of the indolic nucleus, there are two additional rings in the structure of the LSD molecule. These are typical of the LSD family of chemicals: to synthesize LSD and its analogues, one has to obtain the preformed lysergic acid "skeleton" first and then manipulate its chemistry through quite difficult processes. Such is not the case with the one- and two-ring psychedelic compounds, which can be synthesized more readily and altered to a much greater extent.

Lysergic acid, usually appearing as a metabolic product of the fungus *Claviceps purpurea* (growing on rye or barley), has an unusual chemical structure with what might be considered two asymmetric centers. Dependence of pharmacological action on the asymmetry of such compounds has been widely observed. Researchers have shown that psychedelic agents such as LSD interact with serotonin in synapses throughout the brain. Related drugs that are not psychedelic almost always lack such action.

Other Psychoactive Lysergic Acid Derivatives
Through the systematic production undertaken by Sandoz, a great many lysergic acid derivatives have been created and studied. Originally produced for medicinal purposes, these derivatives were re-examined after discovery of LSD's psychoactive effects. Some are psychically inactive, while others have varying psychoactive potentials. The most powerful is LSD-25.

Among the many known lysergic acid amides, a slight change in the four-ring structure has considerable consequences in terms of psychic effects. For example, LSD-25 turns a beam of polarized light clockwise (this is represented by the *d* for *dextro* at the beginning of its chemical name). The *l* or "levo-rotary" form, its mirror image, turns such a beam counterclockwise and has virtually no psychoactive effect.

Comparing the structure of LSD-25 to that of the two most active ingredients in related botanicals—the baby Hawaiian woodrose and certain morning glories to be discussed at the end of this chapter—you'll see that these sources of LSD-like effects have different chemical structures.

| **d-lysergic acid diethylamide (LSD-25)** | **d-lysergic acid amide (ergine) (LA-111)** | **d-isolysergic acid amide (isoergine)** |

LSD (left), and the two major psychoactive agents (middle and right) produced in baby Hawaiian woodroses and some morning glories.

LA-111 and isoergine, which were synthesized in the laboratory before they were known to occur in nature, are significant members of the LSD family. Others have such names as MLD-41, ALD-52, OML-632, LAE-32, BOL-148, MLA-74, ALA-10, LPD-824, LSM-775, DAM-57, LME, LMP, LAMP and LEP. Of these, the acetylated (ALD-52) and methylated (MLD-41) analogues are the next most potent to LSD, possibly because they are quickly converted to LSD upon ingestion. Four others have about a third of LSD's strength, four about a tenth, with the others being much milder.

| *N-acetyl-d-lysergic acid diethylamide (ALD-52)* | *2-bromo-d-lysergic acid diethylamide (BOL-148)* |

ALD-52 is the LSD analogue that's been most often represented as acid on the psychedelic market in the last few years ("Sunshine" was allegedly ALD-52, though this has been disputed). It has slightly over 90 percent of LSD's potency and is transformed into LSD-25 upon contact with water. The resulting trip is generally said to be smoother than one with LSD-25.

    BOL-148 is of special interest because it played a considerable role in psychedelic history. BOL-148 differs from LSD-25 by a single bromine atom, which renders it inactive in terms of mental function. Yet it is capable of producing more anti-serotonin activity than LSD, and it also produces some cross-tolerance with LSD. This compound seems to contradict the simple model that the effects of psychedelics are mediated by serotonin.

    The fact that it blocks, or is cross-tolerant, with LSD was one reason for the spread of interest in LSD as a psychotomimetic: the theory was that if psychosis had a chemical cause, and a similarly cross-tolerant substance could be found, then it would nullify psychosis just as BOL-148 nullifies the psycho-activity of LSD-25.

    It is still possible that serotonin and dopamine have something to do with LSD's effects, but after almost four decades of investigation of this compound, there's still no clear and accepted explanation for LSD's action. Speculating on the mystery surrounding the psychoactive agent he discovered, Albert Hofmann wrote:

> It is perhaps no coincidence but of deeper biological significance that of the four possible isomers of LSD, only one, which corresponds to natural lysergic acid, causes pronounced mental effects. Evidently the mental functions of the human organism, like its bodily functions, are particularly sensitive to those substances which possess the same configurations as naturally occurring compounds of the vegetable kingdom.

    LSD is generally considered cross-tolerant with mescaline but not with psilocybin—meaning that use of LSD a day before taking mescaline will reduce the impact of the mescaline (less tolerance develops if the order of the compounds is reversed). It is well established that LSD is cross-tolerant with itself—self-limiting, in the sense that if a second dose is taken a day later the effects will be considerably diminished. This tolerance endures significantly for three days and does not fully dissipate for a week. Abram Hoffer has remarked that LSD is its own greatest enemy. This feature acts as a control on human abuse of this drug.

PHYSICAL EFFECTS

    LSD can be swallowed, taken on the tongue (producing perhaps the most rapid effects), or absorbed through the skin (particularly with DMSO). It has been ingested in the form of eye-drops and baked in cookies or cake frosting. It has been ingested by almost every means except smoking. LSD taken by mouth has effects almost as rapidly as by intramuscular injection.

    Anywhere from twenty minutes to an hour after being swallowed, this chemical—which often produces an immediate "metallic taste"—may cause one or a few of the following physical sensations: slight chill, dilation of the pupils, vague physical unease concentrated in the muscles or throat, tenseness, queasy stomach, tingling in the extremities, drowsiness. When a novice is asked, "How do you feel?" the answer is likely to be "I don't know" or "Different." If asked about feeling all right, the experiencer will probably not be very sure.

The physical sensations which accompany LSD are usually minor. Often they cannot accurately be likened to sensations ever felt before. As time passes, such physical effects usually disappear. In a few instances, however, they persist throughout much of the experience.

The effect of a particular dosage varies greatly from person to person. Body weight is certainly a factor, but time of day, use of other drugs, mental set and physical setting all play important roles. Generally, 100-250 mcg. is considered a good initial dose, and this can be adjusted at the time of the next session to suit the individual.

Another consideration is the extent of other drug usage. Chronic alcoholics and heavy narcotics users who are on maintenance doses usually need about twice the ordinary amount of LSD to arrive at comparable effects. (Narcotics users who have been free of opiates for less than a year are often hypersensitive, and their dosage must be adjusted with great care. Pretreatment with a minor tranquilizer may be indicated.)

Distribution of LSD throughout the Body

LSD is a very curious chemical. When given by injection, it disappears rapidly from the blood. It can be observed when tagged with Carbon 14 in all the tissues, particularly the liver, spleen, kidneys and adrenal glands. The concentration found in the brain is lower than in any other organ—being only about 0.01 percent of the administered dose. Sidney Cohen, in *The Beyond Within* (p. 380), has estimated that an average dose results in only some 3,700,000 molecules of LSD (about 2/100ths of a microgram) crossing the blood-brain barrier to interact with the billions of cells that make up the average-size brain—"and then for only a very few minutes."

LSD is highly active when administered orally, absorbed through mucous membranes or through the skin, and is almost completely absorbed by the gastrointestinal tract. Concentrations in the organs reach peak values after only ten to fifteen minutes; then they decrease very rapidly. An exception to this rapid decrease has been observed in studies with mice, which show activity in the small intestine increasing over a period of a few hours. Some 80 percent of injested LSD is excreted via the liver, bile system and intestinal tract, with only about 8 percent appearing in urine. After two hours, only 1 to 10 percent is still present in the form of unchanged LSD; the rest consists of water-soluble metabolites—such as 2-oxo-2,3-dihydro-LSD—which do not possess any LSD-type influence on the central nervous system.

Psychic effects of LSD reach their peak about one to three hours following ingestion, when much of the substance has disappeared from the body's major organs, including the brain, though measurable amounts persist in the blood and brain for about eight hours.

It is not at all uncommon to find users experiencing alarming symptoms or sensations, especially during the early phases—the impression of giving birth, melting into the floor, being born, and so on. A few feel that their heart has stopped beating or that their lungs aren't operating regularly any more. These symptoms should also be taken as a sign of altered perception.

No one is on record, for instance, as ever having suffered an LSD-provoked heart attack. However odd it may seem at the time, the body carries on without problems.

For those concerned about immediate medical hazards in ingesting LSD, short references might be in order, just for the record: Abram Hoffer has estimated, on the basis of animal studies, that the half-lethal human dose— meaning half would die (a standard measure for drugs)—would be about 14,000 mcg. But one person who took 40 mg. (40,000 mcg.) survived. In the only case of death reportedly caused by overdose (*Journal of the Kentucky Medical Association* 75:172-173), the quantity of LSD in the blood indicated that 320 mg. (320,000 mcg.) had been injected intravenously. Those concerned about this might also look up "Coma, Hypertension, and Bleeding Associated with Massive LSD Overdose: A Report of Eight Cases," by J.C. Klock, U. Boerner and C.E. Becker in *Clinical Toxicology*, Vol. 8, No. 2, 1975. Large amounts were taken on the assumption that the LSD was cocaine; no one died.

Worries about whether the body under ordinary amounts of LSD will operate all right are only mental illusions. Whatever the mental effects induced by this drug, a physician might notice only:

A slight increase in blood pressure
A slight increase in pulse rate
An increase in salivation, and in lactation in women
A slight rise in temperature
Dilation of the pupils

Pupil dilation occurs more markedly as a result of oral administration than from injection. (Dr. Grof thought pupil dilation the only invariable effect of LSD for quite a while, but then observed an instance in which this oscillated with "pinning.") LSD doesn't affect respiration, though anticipation of such an effect may, on a few occasions, cause small alterations.

Measurable Effects on the Brain

LSD produces slight changes in the EEG, usually with decreased amplitude and increased frequency of brainwaves. Generally, there is a decrease in the alpha rhythm—though, in some cases, there is an increase. Many chemical changes occur in the brain—most of them in the midbrain, which regulates awareness and modulates emotional responsiveness. Recent attention has focused on substantial concentrations found in the brain-stem and in the dopamine receptor system, both responsible for more complex experiences. Hoffer and Osmond's *The Hallucinogens* discusses quite a number of reactions that can be seen regularly when LSD affects the mind's functions. No one really knows, however, which of these alterations are most important, because all occur simultaneously. Much of the metabolizing of LSD takes place in the *liver*, where peyote also lodges. Perhaps it's as the Egyptians used to think: that the liver is "the seat of the soul."

As suggested above, our understanding of how LSD works physiologically and neurologically is still rudimentary, at best speculative. By the beginning of the 1970s, the most intensively examined hypothesis dealing with this interface of mind and body—regarding the displacement of serotonin at the synapses—came to be regarded as a "red herring." Other theories, such as those emphasizing specific "receptor sites," have not really been verified.

Brimblecombe and Pinder summarize the controversies in their *Hallucinogenic Agents* (1975):

> . . . most of the evidence which has emerged since 1966 lends support to the mode of action of LSD proposed that year by Freedman and Aghajanian, that is that interactions with the 5-HT [serotonin] receptor are the primary action of the drug and that the observed changes in metabolism of brain amines are secondary phenomena. Other biochemical changes attributed to the action of hallucinogens, particularly LSD, such as the effects on brain pseudocholinesterase levels (Thompson, Tickner, and Webster, 1955), are so contradictory that they appear to offer little insight into the mode of action of the drugs (Giarman and Freedman, 1965; Hoffer and Osmond, 1967; Brown, 1972; *see* Chapter 4). Nevertheless, a large number of questions remain unanswered. It is still not clear whether LSD is acting as an agonist or as an antagonist, neither is it clear whether the drug has direct or indirect presynaptic actions, and, most important of all, the ways in which the drug-receptor interaction and the biochemical changes are translated into neurological and behavioural phenomenà are very uncertain.

One discovery that may seem particularly relevant is the "complete reversal of amplitude laterality," described by Goldstein, Stolzfus and associates in 1972 after they made chronograms of the electrical activity of left and right occipital EEGs of right-handed volunteers before and after administration of several psychedelics. They found a "progressive narrowing of interhemispheric EEG amplitude differences with eventually complete reversal (to the right) of their relationships." In simpler language, data processing in the brain's cerebral cortex was preferentially shifted under the influence of LSD from the more analytical left hemisphere to the visuo-spatial right hemisphere. This seems an economic and fairly satisfactory explanation of how a psychedelic like LSD increases the "scope" of the mind, brings artistic, creative, rhythmic and problem-solving abilities to the fore and evokes phenomena that Freud referred to as manifestations of "the unconscious."

One often hears that much of the brain is usually dormant. Depending on dosage, LSD may increase mental power perhaps by activating the visuo-spatial centers. In this sense, LSD and other psychedelics could be considered *deliberate and unconscious agents of the right lobe.* For a full discussion of the implications of this theory, consult Roland Fischer's "Cartography of Inner Space" in the Drug Abuse Council, Inc.'s 1975 book entitled *Altered States of Consciousness.*

R. Cobb's cartoon view of the physical
consequences of psychedelic and nicotine use.

Effects upon Chromosomes

It has now been well established that the pure LSD molecule doesn't affect chromosomes at all. This is evident from repeated tests made before and after administration of up to 2,000 mcg. quantities. A summary of the first sixty-eight studies and case reports—the bulk conducted by NIMH—can be found in *Science* magazine (April 30, 1971). The article concludes that "pure LSD ingested in moderate doses does not damage chromosomes in vivo, does not cause detectable genetic damage, and is not a teratogen or carcinogen in man."

LSD and Physical Health

The preceding sections give some idea of how the body reacts during the ten to twelve hours of the LSD experience. In some cases, there are also long-lasting physical effects that should be mentioned. Many doctors have reported, often with pleased surprise, that their patients have achieved spontaneous relief from organic ailments after using LSD. Dr. T.T. Peck, Jr., for instance, at the Josiah Macy, Jr. Conference on LSD, remarked:

> In treating patients for various and sundry psychological complaints, we found that some would come back a week or two later and say, "The headache is gone." We asked, "What headache?" They replied, "Oh, the headache I've had for 10 or 15 years."

A substantial number of cases entered in medical records have now established LSD as a competent agent in the cure of such physical ailments as arthritis, partial paralysis, migraine headaches, hysterical deafness, skin rashes, and so on.

Dr. Peck reported on his study of 216 mentally disturbed patients who were given LSD. Forty-six of these patients suffered also from some physical illness—including various forms of arthritis, asthmas that did not respond to hypnosis, migraine headaches and lasting rashes. Thirty-one of the forty-six made an "excellent" recovery from their symptoms, while five others found marked relief. Other doctors who have treated similar problems with LSD have found that such stubborn conditions can often be eradicated in the course of a few sessions. In their book on the use of LSD in the treatment of neurosis, Drs. Ling and Buckman list five case histories of successful migraine cures—all of which had previously been considered hopeless. They also give a full-length account of LSD's use in treating a severe case of psoriasis, with impressive photographs showing the patient before and after treatment (again, the condition had previously been adjudged hopeless). S. Kuromaru and co-workers in Japan have shown that this multi-functional substance can be used with good results even in the treatment of phantom limb pain.

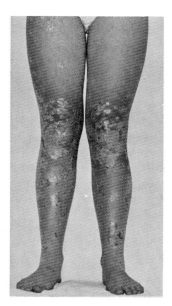 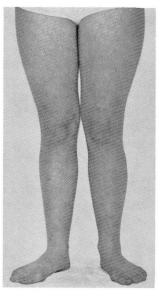

R. Soc. Med.: *Lysergic Acid (LSD-25) and Ritalin in the Treatment of Neurosis*

These photographs were taken before and after treatment of severe psoriasis with LSD and Ritalin.

Pain Reduction

The most enraptured "acid heads" are aware that LSD is not—and never can be—a panacea, a solution to all of this planet's problems. This most powerful psychoactive compound hasn't been demonstrated to keep us from aging or to reverse the course of fatal diseases. However, it does without doubt offer important benefits for people confronted with terminal illness. This is an area in which research, particularly at the Veterans Hospital in L.A., the Menninger Clinic in Topeka and Spring Grove Hospital near Baltimore, has impressed skeptics.

Aldous Huxley deserves special credit as the inspiration for this research, because he wrote about its possibilities in his last novel, *Island*. He took LSD on his deathbed. The medical world became aware of LSD's ability to change the perceptions of death in the mid-1960s when the American Medical Association published a report on fifty dying patients who had been given the drug in a Chicago hospital. In this preliminary study conducted by a noted psychiatrist, Dr. Eric Kast, LSD was shown to be more effective as an analgesic or pain reliever than any of the frequently used morphine derivatives:

> In . . . 50 patients, most with advanced cancer and some with gangrene, LSD relieved pain for considerably longer periods than such powerful drugs as meperidine and dihydro-morphinone . . . . On the average, freedom from pain lasted two hours with 100 mg. meperidine, three hours with 2 mg. dihydro-morphinone and *92 hours with 100 mcg. LSD* [italics added].

To the amazement of observers, terminal patients given LSD changed in their attitudes from depression, apathy and anguish to sensitivity, poignancy and deep feeling for people. They movingly expressed gratitude for life itself. LSD seemed to enable many to face death with equanimity.

Instead of denial or fright, these patients generally experienced a feeling of being "at one with the universe" and looked upon dying as merely another event in eternal existence. "It was a common experience," wrote Dr. Kast, "for the patient to remark casually on his deadly disease and then comment on the beauty of a certain sensory impression." Such desirable emotional balance lasted long after LSD's pain-killing action wore off, for up to two weeks in some cases. Later studies have confirmed how impressive the short but profound impact of LSD can be for the dying.

MENTAL EFFECTS

A few pages can only hint at the range and variety that LSD has caused. Here are a couple of greatly condensed paragraphs attempting definition.

The paragraph on the left is taken from *The Varieties of Psychedelic Experience* by Robert Masters and Jean Houston; the one on the right is part of the definition of LSD-25 in Robert R. Lingeman's revised and updated edition of *Drugs From A to Z*. These summaries, distilled from many descriptions of the drug's mental effects, are comprehensive and yet incomplete in conveying the quality of the LSD experience.

Even the briefest summation of the psychological effects . . . would have to include the following: Changes in visual, auditory, tactile, olfactory, gustatory, and kinesthetic perception; changes in experiencing time and space; changes in the rate and content of thought; body image changes; hallucinations; vivid images—eidetic images—seen with the eyes closed; greatly heightened awareness of color; abrupt and frequent mood and affect changes; heightened suggestibility; enhanced recall or memory; depersonalization and ego dissolution; dual, multiple, and fragmentized consciousness; seeming awareness of internal organs and processes of the body; upsurge of unconscious materials; enhanced awareness of linguistic nuances; increased sensitivity to non-verbal cues; sense of capacity to communicate much better by nonverbal means, sometimes including the telepathic; feelings of empathy; regression and "primitivization"; apparently heightened capacity for concentration; magnification of character traits and psychodynamic processes; an apparent nakedness of psychodynamic processes that makes evident the interaction of ideation, emotion, and perception with one another and with inferred unconscious processes; concern with philosophical, cosmological, and religious questions; and, in general, apprehension of a world that has slipped the chains of normal categorical ordering, leading to an intensified interest in self and world and also to a range of responses moving from extremes of anxiety to extremes of pleasure . . . .

The drug's subjective effects are spectacular if taken in large doses. They are similar to those produced by other hallucinogenic drugs but on a grander scale (if a large dose is taken) and include stimulation of the central and autonomic nervous systems; changes in mood (sometimes euphoric and megalomaniac, sometimes fearful, panicky, and anxiety-ridden); a sense of threat to the ego; an intensification of colors so that they seem brighter; intensification of the other senses so that inaudible sounds become magnified or food tastes better or normally unnoticed aspects of things (such as the pores in concrete) become strikingly vivid; merging of senses (synesthesia) so that sounds are seen as color patterns; a wave-like sense of time so that seconds seem like an eternity; distortions in the perception of space so that surrounding objects seem fluid and shifting; a sense of depersonalization, of being simultaneously both within and without oneself; a closely related feeling of merger (dissolving) with the external world and a loss of personality; a perception of ordinary things as if seen for the first time unstructured by perceptual "sets"; hallucinations of flowers, snakes, animals, other people, etc., which subjects usually know to be hallucinations though they are powerless to stop them; a sense of closeness to, or merger with, other persons in the room as if barriers between individuals had been dissolved; enhanced sensuousness and sexual stimulation (the drug is neither an aphrodisiac nor an anaphrodisiac, but its overpowering mental effects tend to make it more of the latter) . . . .

General Effects

If the experience is all it is said to be, how can anyone go "through this kind of thing without turning into a terrorized blob of babbling jelly?" Art Kleps might have just finished reading either of the above descriptions when he asked this question.

The state is difficult to describe because it is akin to mystical experience, which is . . . ineffable!

"How to describe it!" exclaimed Henri Michaux, the French poet and painter, speaking of this psychedelic experience. "It would require a picturesque style which I do not possess, made up of surprises, of nonsense, of sudden flashes, of bounds and rebounds, an unstable style, tobogganing and prankish."

However, I must now turn around and add that in many ways LSD can also be viewed as a relaxant, as a means to mental calm and to centering. It frequently puts the user in a serene state of mind, at ease. Many users describe it as bringing on the feeling, perhaps for the first time, that they are . . . home.

If that sounds like a contradiction, so be it. The states of consciousness brought about are often paradoxical. This might be expected from a catalyst that channels the brain from a dualistic to a unitary way of looking at things.

Here's what Allen Ginsberg had to say when *Playboy* magazine asked what LSD does:

'What does a trip feel like? A creeping sensation comes over your body, a change in the planetary nature of your mammal eyeballs and hearing orifices. Then comes realization that you're a spirit inhabiting a vast animal body containing giant apertures, holes, circulatory systems, interior canals and mysterious back alleys of the mind. Any one of these back alleys can be explored for a long, long way, like going back into recollections of childhood or going forward into the future, imagining all sorts of changes in the body, in the mind or in the world outside, inventing imaginary universes or recalling ones that existed, like Egypt.

Then you realize that all these exist in your mind simultaneously. Slowly you approach the mysterious feeling that if all these histories and universes exist in your mind at the same time, then what about this one you're "really" in—or *think* you are? Does that also exist only in your mind? Then comes a realization that it *does* exist only in your mind; the mind created it. Then you begin to wonder, Who is this mind? At the height of the acid experience, you realize that your mind's the same mind that's always existed in all people at all times in all places: This is the Great Mind—the very mind men call God. Then comes a fascinating suspicion: Is this mind what they call God or what they used to call the Devil? Here's where a bum trip may begin—if you decide it's a demonic Creator. You get hung up wondering whether he *should* exist or not.

To get off that train of thought: You might open your eyes and see you're sitting on a sofa in a living room with green plants flowering on the mantelpiece. Outside the window, wind is moving through the street in all of its forms—people walking under windy trees—all in one rhythm. And the more you observe the synchronous, animal, sentient details around you, the more you realize that *everything* is alive. You become aware that there's a plant with giant cellular leaves hanging over the fireplace, like a huge unnoticed creature, and you might feel a sudden, sympathetic and intimate relationship with that poor big leaf, wondering: What kind of an experience of bending and falling down over the fireplace has that stalk-blossom been having for several weeks now? And you realize that everything alive is experiencing on its own level a suchness existence as enormous to it as your existence is to you. Suddenly you get sympathetic, and feel a dear brotherly-sisterly relationship to all these selves. And humorous, for your own life experiences are no more or less absurd or weird than the life experience of that plant; you realize that you and plant are both here together in this strange existence where trees in the sunroom are blossoming and pawing toward the sky. Finally you find out that if you play them music, they grow better.

So, the widening area of consciousness on acid consists in your becoming aware of what's going on inside your own head cosmos—all those corridors leading into dreams, memories, fantasies—and also what's happening outside you. But if you go deep enough inside, you may find yourself confronted with the final problem: Is this all a dream-nature? Great ancient question: What *is* this existence we're in? Who are we? Then can come what Timothy Leary terms the "clear light" experience or, as they call it in South America, "looking into the eyes of the Veiled Lady"—looking to see who it is, doing or being all this. What's the self-nature of it all? This is the part of the acid experience that's supposed to be indescribable, and I'm not sure I've had the proper experience to describe it.

Steve Gladstone

Allen Ginsberg, "turned on" to LSD by the U.S. Army, became the poet laureate of the psychedelic movement.

Dosage Considerations

The action of LSD is difficult to classify because it isn't specific, like
aspirin or Miltown. More confusing, it also has variable effects at different
dosages. Dosages estimated by weight result in widely fluctuating reactions
in different animals. Furthermore, within a given species there may be idio-
syncratic responses—even when subjects are all of the same age, weight and
sex. Dosage can be one of the most important determining factors.

Most users are affected by dosages above about 20 mcg. Amounts just
above this produce effects somewhat like a long-lasting "hash high"; Hofmann's initial trip is a fair example. From about 75 mcg. up to about 125
mcg., the amount usually taken, LSD can emphasize internal phenomena,
although it is frequently used at this level for interpersonal matters, problem-
solving or for the enhancement of sensations (for example, at a rock concert).
A heavy dose—on the order of 200-250 mcg.—produces a predominantly
interior, revelatory experience. Higher doses tend to intensify the trip rather
than lengthen it; above 400-500 mcg., there seems to be a "saturation point,"
beyond which increases make little difference.

Therapy and Everyday Problems

From the beginning of its history, LSD has been used as an aid to psychotherapy. The first report in the literature, which stressed low oral dosages
(20-30 mcg.), gave an account of how the compound was administered to
sixteen normal subjects and to six schizophrenics.

Until the time research with LSD was dramatically curbed in 1966
more than 40,000 mental patients had received it in dosages running from
20 mcg. to upwards of 2,500 mcg. It was administered privately in some
instances, and in others it was given to whole hospital wards. Some people
received only one dose; others had as many as 120. In most instances, LSD
was used in small amounts as an adjunct to psychotherapy. Other patients
took it as a one-time, high-dosage treatment.

Many early investigators screened out psychotics and schizophrenics,
but some did not and often claimed surprising success with such cases. Patients
usually received this treatment from only one therapist, but several researchers
came to believe that better results could be obtained when the compound
was given by several persons.

Among many varied techniques, hypnotism was sometimes used in
conjunction with LSD. Other people installed nurses as "parent surrogates"
for their patients. Still others encouraged their patients to "act out" aggres-
sions during the LSD session, giving them objects to tear up or hit. Some
therapists depended primarily upon symbolic interpretation of familiar
objects and universal insignia. Others concentrated on dream materials.
Some used only LSD; some combined it with Ritalin, Librium, Dramamine
or amphetamine. Others added one or another of the mind-altering drugs,
such as CZ-74 (a psilocin derivative).

Almost from the beginning, psychiatrists and psychologists realized that many effects of this drug had implications relevant to personal growth. R.A. Sandison was one of the earliest practitioners to recognize the potentials of LSD:

> There are good reasons for believing that the LSD experience is a manifestation of the psychic unconscious, and that its material can be used in psychotherapy in the same way that dreams, phantasies and paintings can be used by the psychoanalysts.

A characteristic of the LSD experience particularly fascinating to Freudian analysts has been its power to cause the patient to regress to early traumas, which could then be relieved. This chemical is still used as an aid in "transference." Dr. Gordon Johnsen, of Modum Bads Nervesantorium in Norway elaborates:

> If we get sexual perverts, for example, we may question what kind of treatment to give them; we want to find out a little more about them. We could use three or four weeks finding out, but we shorten that and say we will try if we can find out more with one or two LSD sessions. We use small doses then. We find that the symptoms are clearer; they are willing to speak more openly to us; we can get a clearer picture of the diagnosis. We have used it in that way to save time.

By the time of the Josiah Macy, Jr. Foundation conference on LSD at the end of the 1950s, it had become clear that this semi-synthetic drug seemed to affirm the concepts of most of the psychological "schools." The Freudians were using LSD to abreact their patients and to explore Oedipal and other notions. The Jungians found that this drug manifested mandalas and rebirth experiences in their patients. A fascinating account of an extended Freudian treatment appears in *My Self and I*, written by the Kirlian researcher and parapsychologist Thelma Moss (under the name Constance Newland). Dr. Donald Blair, an English consulting psychiatrist, summed up his view of LSD's results:

> People who have had psychotherapy or psychoanalysis for some time, as much as eight years, and haven't gotten anywhere, do so with the drug; it does break resistance . . . . You get neurotic patients who have been to numerous therapists, analysts, and they don't get better. Then they come to one of us who are using LSD and thanks to the effect of the drug, they do get better.

Experimentation with large, "single-shot" LSD doses began in the late 1950s. A great many therapists using this approach started to see in their patients what Sherwood, Stolaroff and Harman later termed "the stage of immediate perception":

> . . . he comes to experience himself in a totally new way and finds that the age-old question "who am I?" does have a significant answer. He experiences himself as a far greater being than he had ever imagined, with his conscious self a far smaller fraction of the whole than he had realized. Furthermore, he

sees that his own self is by no means so separate from other selves and the universe about him as he might have thought. Nor is the existence of this newly experienced self so intimately related to his corporeal existence.

These realizations, while not new to mankind, and possibly not new to the subject in the intellectual sense, are very new in an experiential sense. That is, they are new in the sense that makes for altered behavior. The individual sees clearly that some of his actions are not in line with his new knowledge and that changes are obviously called for.

Records kept of alcoholic recovery rates following ingestion of LSD constitute the firmest quantitative data so far on the effects of this substance. They are especially impressive when one considers that independent studies using different methods achieved substantially identical results. In most instances, the patients were chosen from the worst cases that could be found. (Some studies using different procedures have not been as successful.)

Abram Hoffer had this to say when he published statistics relating to more than 800 hardcore alcoholics who had been treated in the Canadian LSD program:

> When psychedelic therapy is given to alcoholics using methods described in the literature about one-third will remain sober after the therapy is completed, and one-third will be benefitted. If schizophrenics and malvarians [those showing a particularly purplish component of urine] are excluded from LSD therapy the results should be better by about 30 per cent. There are no published papers using psychedelic therapy which show it does not help about 50 per cent of the treated group . . . .
>
> Our conclusion after 13 years of research is that properly used LSD therapy can convert a large number of alcoholics into sober members of society . . . . Even more important is the fact that this can be done very quickly and therefore very economically. Whereas with standard therapy one bed might be used to treat about 4 to 6 patients per year, with LSD one can easily treat up to 36 patients per bed per year.

The majority of LSD therapists had agreed just before being denied access to LSD that this drug is superior to other forms of treatment in its effect on the whole range of neuroses and disorders that ordinarily respond to psychoanalysis. Typical reports indicate that even with severe problems only 10 to 15 percent of patients failed to achieve any improvement. When Hollywood Hospital in Vancouver, B.C., Canada, followed up eighty-nine patients for an average of fifty-five months, it found that 55 percent had a total remission of their problem, 34 percent were improved and 11 percent were unchanged. At the University of Göttingen's Psychiatric Hospital, Dr. Hanscarl Leuner's results, independently rated, showed 76 percent of the patients with character neuroses, depressive reactions, anxiety, phobias or conversion-hysteria were "greatly improved" or "recovered." In an evaluation of his work at Marborough Day Hospital in London, Dr. Ling states:

> An analysis of 43 patients treated privately . . . shows that 34 are completely well and socially well-adjusted. Six are improved, one abandoned treatment,

one had to leave for Africa before treatment was finished, and one failed to respond satisfactorily, so treatment was abandoned.

So far, most of the successful reports on the treatment of mental patients with LSD deal with neurotic patients who have been motivated to get well. There seems to be tacit agreement among therapists that LSD is not effective in dealing with psychoses. Practitioners who have undertaken LSD treatment of schizophrenics have been regarded as brave or reckless. (Schizophrenia is a term so vague that even the American Psychological Association has eliminated it from their list of disorders.)

LSD does not work very well with patients whose mental derangements are seriously advanced. It may precipitate a worsening of the condition. Nevertheless, a large body of evidence indicates that those who have administered LSD in such cases have often obtained positive reactions that are worthy of broader consideration.

Dr. Fred F. Langner used LSD effectively with a number of severely disturbed persons, mainly "schizophrenics." After he used LSD in over 2,000 patient sessions, he concluded that pseudo-neurotics and paranoid schizophrenics do not respond favorably and may, in fact, suffer clinical setbacks. However, he observed that schizoid personalities, whose egos are not too brittle, may through LSD have their first experience with "feeling." One of his patients said, "I know now that I never knew what people were talking about when they talked about feelings till I took LSD. I didn't know till toward the end of my second year in therapy that feelings could be good as well as bad."

LSD has been described by Aldous Huxley as a means of insight into the "Other World." As an instrument of therapy, it has brought many back into contact with reality. Here is another paradox, another example of the unifying action of LSD. Consider a comment by Norma McDonald, a recovered schizophrenic:

> One of the most encouraging things which has happened to me in recent years was the discovery that I could talk to normal people who had had the experience of taking mescaline or lysergic acid, and they would accept the things I told them about my adventures in mind without asking stupid questions or withdrawing into a safe smug world of disbelief. Schizophrenia is a lonely illness and friends are of great importance. I have needed true friends to help me to believe in myself when I doubted my own mind, to encourage me with their praise, jolt me out of unrealistic ideas with their honesty and teach me by their example how to work and play. The discovery of LSD-25 by those who work in the field of psychiatry has widened my circle of friends.

The best accounts of "acid therapy" in English are Stanislav Grof's *LSD Psychotherapy* (1980) and Milan Hausner and Erna Segal's *The Highway to Mental Health: LSD Psychotherapy* (1979). The latter details Hausner's use of LSD as an adjunct to psychotherapy for more than twenty years in Czechoslovakia. In reviewing this volume, John C. Rhead, who participated in LSD experiments as a doctor at Spring Grove Hospital, wholeheartedly welcomed it "as an encouraging sign that good work with psychedelics is still go-

ing on somewhere in the world." Pointing to its "constant theme . . . of correc-
tive/healing experience emerging from the patient's own subconscious,"
Rhead added these comments:

> The fundamental belief in the capacity of the human psyche to be self-healing
> under the proper circumstances is but one of the many striking parallels
> between Dr. Hausner's conclusions and those of the group at the Maryland
> Psychiatric Research Center . . . . Many passages of Dr. Hausner's book sound
> very much like the things that my colleagues/friends in Maryland and I have
> thought, said and/or written . . . .
>
> Examples of these similarities are found in the following areas: the critical
> importance of interpersonal trust in conducting successful psychotherapy
> with psychedelics, the use of music, the importance of having the therapist/
> guide experience LSD as part of an ethically adequate training to do this type
> of work, the unique value of artistic productions by the patient for both assess-
> ment of functioning as well as integration of emerging subconscious material,
> the presentation during the LSD session of significant objects from the patient's
> life (e.g., photographs) in order to stimulate associations and fresh insights
> and perspectives, the need to include the concepts of many diverse schools of
> psychotherapeutic thought in order to understand and utilize LSD, the im-
> portance of working through and integrating the experiences that emerge
> during LSD sessions and the fundamental value or reality of the mystic or
> peak experiences that frequently occur . . . .
>
> I believe that these similarities are the result of two groups of relatively
> blind but curious and well-intentioned investigators independently having
> taken the time to grope rather thoroughly over the entire elephant. As is
> commonly noted in the literature of comparative religion, there really does
> appear to be only one elephant.

Even though a decade and a half has passed since the panic of the mid-
1960s, federal regulations and hospital "Human Rights" committees
continue to block requests to use psychedelics on humans. They are afraid of
negative publicity and lawsuits. When Walter Houston Clark inserted a
questionnaire addressed to research professionals in *Behavior Today* and the
Newsletter of the Association for Humanistic Psychology, nearly all who
replied stated that they would like to do psychedelic research.

Of the first hundred people who responded to Clark's request, half had
been associated at one time with controlled drug studies. Asked why they
weren't engaged in such work any more, eighty-one mentioned governmental
red tape, sixty cited other bureaucratic obstruction, seventy-eight wrote that
they weren't able to secure clearance and fifty-three indicated lack of funding
as "large reasons." Asked to rate the promise of psychedelics in the mental
health area, "assuming opportunity for controlled experimentation," none
called it negative, one thought it might be neutral, seven perceived it as meager,
fifteen felt it was moderate, thirty-four considered it high and thirty-six
believed that investigation of psychedelics held out "breakthrough" possibilities (another seven didn't answer this question).

"Do I feel any patients are being denied an experience of significant value as a result of non-acceptance of LSD as a therapeutic tool?" Dr. Langner asks. "Yes, I do."

Creative Stimulus

A large number of testimonials indicates that LSD can dissolve creative blockage. Many examples are presented in Robert Masters and Jean Houston's *Psychedelic Art* and in Ralph Metzner's *The Ecstatic Adventure*, which contains full reports from participants in the Menlo Park creativity studies (including two architects and an engineer-physicist who was working on a model for a "photon"). A general presentation of that creativity research can be found in Charles Tart's *Altered States of Consciousness*. In the Fall 1980 *Humanistic Psychology Institute Review*, Stanley Krippner summarized the findings of nine major studies in this area.

A notable early example was architect Kyoshi Izumi's design of a psychiatric hospital in Canada. He was given LSD by Humphry Osmond before he made several visits to traditionally designed mental institutions in order to evaluate the effects of their design upon people in altered states of consciousness. Izumi found that tiles on walls glistened eerily and recessed closets yawned like huge, dark caverns. He noticed that raised hospital beds were too high for patients to sit on and still touch the floor with their feet and a sense of time was lost because of the lack of clocks and calendars. Worst of all were the long corridors. (Osmond called the thousands of square feet of polished tiles in these institutions "illusion-producing machines *par excellence*, and very expensive ones at that. If your perception is a little unstable, you may see your dear old father peering out at you from the walls . . . .")

These insights, which were made clear through his use of LSD, resulted in Izumi's design for "the ideal mental hospital," which was commended for outstanding architectural advancement by the Joint Information Service of the American Psychiatric Association. The first hospital on his plan was built in Yorkton, Saskatchewan and was imitated soon after in Haverford, Pennsylvania. The prototype has been reproduced several times since, mainly in Canada. Bonnie Golightly and I summarized distinguishing features:

> The Yorkton hospital consists of small, cottage-like clusters of rooms, thirty to a unit, joined together by underground passageways . . . . There are many windows, low and unbarred, eliminating the old, dismal barnlike aspect of mental hospitals. The walls are painted in pleasant, flat colors, and each patient has his own room in one or another of the clusters, rather than a bed in an austere, nearly bare ward. The beds are low to the floor, and the rooms are furnished with regard to making it easier to define the floor as a mere floor, not a pit. Also, the furniture is comfortable and not unlike that with which the patient is familiar at home. The closet problem has been solved by installing large, movable cabinets which the patient can clearly see possess both a back and a front. Clocks and calendars abound, while floor tiles are sparingly used. The emphasis throughout puts patient needs foremost, without sacrificing utility.

In 1955, Berlin, Guthrie, Weider, Goodell and Wolff reported on four prominent graphic artists who made paintings during an LSD experience. A panel of art critics judged the paintings as having greater value than the artists' usual work—noting that use of color was more vivid and lines were bolder, though the technical execution was somewhat poorer. Similar results were reported by Frank Barron in his *Creativity and Psychological Health* and by Oscar Janiger, who gave LSD to a hundred artists and had them draw an Indian Kachina doll before, during and after their experience (July-August 1959 issue of *The California Clinician*).

By way of contrast, studies made with volunteers who were not particularly interested in LSD's creative potential reflected no significant changes in creativity. William McGlothlin, Sidney Cohen and others, and then the team of Zegans, Pollard and Brown, reported these findings in the *Journal of Nervous and Mental Diseases* (1964) and in the *Archives of General Psychiatry* (1967) respectively. Six months after three 200-mcg. LSD sessions, the McGlothlin team found only one major distinction: 62 percent of their subjects reported "a greater appreciation of music." An increase in the number of records bought, time spent in museums and number of musical events attended was also significantly greater than for two control groups, who were given either 25 mcg. of LSD or 20 mg. of amphetamine per session. Cohen wrote in 1965: "All that can be said at this time about the effect of LSD on the creative process is that a strong subjective feeling of creativeness accompanies many of the experiences." The Zegans group concluded that "the administration of LSD-25 to a relatively unselected group of people, for the purpose of enhancing their creative ability, is not likely to be successful."

On the other hand, the Institute for Psychedelic Research at San Francisco State College, headed by Fadiman, Harman, McKim, Mogar and Stolaroff, came to remarkably positive findings when they gave LSD and mescaline to professionals who were faced with technical problems that they had been unable to solve. Hypothesizing that "through carefully structured regimen, a learning experience with lingering creative increases could result," this group administered psychedelics to twenty-two volunteers. By the time of their report in November 1965, six had already seen concrete benefits in their work. At this point, the Institute's access to psychedelics was terminated. Comments made by some of the people taking part in this project indicate something of the way LSD affected their thinking:

> Looking at the same problem with (psychedelic) materials, I was able to consider it in a much more basic way, because I could form and keep in mind a much broader picture.

> I had great visual (mental) perceptibility; I could imagine what was wanted, needed, or not possible with almost no effort.

> Ideas came up with a speed that was breathtaking.

> I dismissed the original idea entirely, and started to approach the graphic problem in a radically different way. That was when things began to happen. All kinds of different possibilities came to mind.

Diminished fear of making mistakes or being embarrassed.

I was impressed with the intensity of concentration, the forcefulness and exuberance with which I could proceed toward the problem.

In what seemed like 10 minutes, I had completed the problem, having what I considered (and still consider) a classic solution.

... brought about almost total recall of a course that I had had in thermodynamics, something that I had never given any thought about in years.

In 1969, Stanley Krippner surveyed 180 professional artists reported to have had at least one psychedelic experience (eighteen, as it turned out, had never taken a psychoactive chemical). These included "two award-winning film-makers, a Guggenheim Fellow in poetry, a recipient of Ford, Fulbright, and Rockefeller study grants in painting, several college faculty members, and numerous musicians, actors, and writers," mainly from the New York area but with a significant proportion from around the world.

When asked how psychedelic experiences influenced their art, none said his or her work had suffered, "although some admitted that their friends might disagree with this judgment." Five stated that their psychedelic experiences had not influenced their work one way or the other, but most were enthusiastic about the effects. The painter Arlene Sklar-Weinstein, who had gone through only one LSD experience is representative: "It opened thousands of doors for me and dramatically changed the content, intent, and style of my work."

Of the 180 artists surveyed, 114 said that their psychedelic experiences had affected the content of their work; they mainly cited their use of eidetic, or closed-eyes, imagery as a source of subject matter. Fully 131 responded that there had been "a noticeable improvement in their artistic technique," most often mentioning a greater ability to use colors. In addition, 142 attributed a change in creative approach to the psychedelics. Many indicated that dormant interests in art and music had been activated by psychedelic sessions.

LSD has helped to end writer's block. Ling and Buckman's *The Use of LSD and Ritalin in the Treatment of Neurosis* cites the example of a "well-known European writer" whose major work, translated into twelve languages, was written subsequent to LSD usage. Previously, he had had a "burning desire" to write but had been unable to finish a single manuscript. Under the influence of LSD, he was confronted with a sudden awareness that he could die. "With this horror of death realized, I started to experience a most fantastic happiness with the realization that after all I do not have to die now." It freed him as an artist: he no longer felt he was writing "with my neck under the guillotine."

I am no longer afraid of putting one letter after the other to say what I want and this is linked with an enormous number of things, such as speechlessness and inarticulateness. The feeling of being dumb, not being able to express myself, was probably one of my most unpleasant inner feelings . . . .

I [now] seem capable of expressing what many people would love to express but for which they cannot find the words. I did not find the words before because I tried to avoid saying the essential things.

Krippner quotes the Dutch writer Ronny van den Eerenbeemt as having responded similarly:

> When very young, I started writing stories and poems. The older I got, the more I had a feeling of not being able to find something really worthwhile to write about. My psychedelic experiences taught me that what I used to do was no more than scratch the surface of life. After having seen and felt the center of life, through the psychedelics, I now think I do have something worthwhile to write about.

At the conclusion of his survey of the effects from LSD and similar psychedelics, Krippner writes:

> Little scientific research has been undertaken with psychedelic drugs since advances in information theory, brain physiology, and the study of consciousness . . . have revolutionized our understanding of those areas. This increase in knowledge and theoretical sophistication affords science a unique opportunity to study the creative act. Creativity has been a perpetual enigma; now, at last, it may be prepared to divulge its secrets.

A final point about the creative process: it does not seem to have too much to do with conventional I.Q., as measured by existing tests. Frank Barron, while a Research Psychologist at the University of California Institute of Personality Assessment, compared more than 5,000 productive and creative individuals with others in their field who had similar I.Q. but limited productivity:

> The thing that *was* important was something that might be called a cosmological commitment. It was a powerful motive to create meaning and to leave a testament of the meaning which that individual found in the world, and in himself in relation to the world. This motive emerged in many ways, but we came across it over and over again when we compared highly creative individuals with those of equal intellectual ability as measured by I.Q. tests, but of less actual creative ability. The intense motivation having to do with this making of meaning—or finding meaning and communicating it in one form or another—was the most important difference between our criterion and control groups . . . .
>
> I think that as a result of the psychedelic experience there's a heightened sense of the drama of life, including its brevity, and a realization both of the importance of one's individual life and of the fact that a sacred task has been given to the individual in the development of the self.

Religious Considerations

At the core, LSD enables the users to transcend ordinary reality and feel religious effects. Aldous Huxley described the experience with a term from Catholic theology, "gratuitous grace." He wrote Father Thomas Merton about similarities perceived by one user to spontaneous mystical experience:

> A friend of mine, saved from alcoholism, during the last fatal phase of the disease, by a spontaneous theophany, which changed his life as completely as St.

Paul's was changed by his theophany on the road to Damascus, has taken lysergic acid two or three times and affirms that his experience under the drug is identical with the spontaneous experience which changed his life—the only difference being that the spontaneous experience did not last so long as the chemically induced one.

Alan Watts, philosopher and Zen master, had a bad first impression, characterizing his LSD experience as "mysticism with water wings." During two later experiments conducted by associates of the Langley-Porter Clinic in San Francisco, he quickly changed his mind:

> I was amazed and somewhat embarrassed to find myself going through states of consciousness that corresponded precisely with every description of major mystical experiences that I had ever read. Furthermore, they exceeded both in depth and in a peculiar quality of unexpectedness the three "natural and spontaneous" experiences of this kind that had happened to me in previous years.

The religious aspect of LSD ingestion registered strongly among the group at Harvard running the Psilocybin Research Project. Shortly after the project had begun, Michael Hollingshead showed up with a jar filled with LSD; it was given to third-year Ph.D. students in behaviorism. Hollingshead reflected in 1981 on that small class of students and their instructors:

> Al Cohen—he runs the Meher Baba group. He got his Ph.D. in behaviorism.
> Alpert already had his Ph.D. He's a Hindu saint.
> Leary already had his Ph.D. He became the "High Priest."
> Ralph Metzner—he got his Ph.D. He is now running healing work and wholistic therapeutic groups in San Francisco and Berkeley, the total opposite of behaviorism. Ralph accepts that within each person there's a spiritual entity which can be moved if it's once awakened and allowed not only to see but also to be.
> Gunther Weil is now the director of the Media Center of the University of Massachusetts, but he's also been running the Gurdjieff group in Boston. He is closely identified with the Gurdjieffian work. He has put out records, he has tried to create art movies, he's lectured on the acculturation of the psychedelic experience.
> Al Alschuler—well, he's still at Harvard in the School of Education as far as I know. He has moved away from strict behaviorism into creative educational techniques, but through the system.
> Paul Lee—who, when I first met him, wasn't one of the students. He was Paul Tillich's right-hand man. And he had a very profound experience. He's now teaching herbs in Santa Cruz.
> Rolf von Eckartsberg—he's in Philadelphia, running the Open House System, where certain houses are always open to ex-prison inmates.

Hollingshead concludes that for these people LSD was instrumental in realization of the importance of their religious nature:

> To use Aldous Huxley's expression, "the doors of perception" were opened, and they saw inside the house—this house of many mansions which is also

the Self. And then the doors closed at midnight and they were back in the old humdrum again—*but* vouchsaved a glimpse of the other. And then, bit by bit, they began to discover Eastern writings, the *Tao Te Ching*, the *I Ching*, the *Vedas*, the Upanishads, Sufi masters, various forms of music that are designed for people who are in the house to dance. And they began to move off into different areas, which accounts for why they are where they are now.

Houston Smith, Professor of Philosophy at MIT, similarly described this most important aspect of psychedelics (based mainly on his observation of effects from LSD):

> . . . given the right set and setting, the drugs can induce religious experiences indistinguishable from ones that occur spontaneously. Nor need set and setting be exceptional. The way the statistics are currently running, it looks as if from one-fourth to one-third of the general population will have religious experiences if they take the drugs under naturalistic conditions, meaning by this conditions in which the researcher supports the subject but doesn't try to influence the direction his experience will take. Among subjects who have strong religious inclinations to begin with, the proportion of those having religious experiences jumps to three-quarters. If they take them in settings which are religious too, the ratio soars to nine out of ten.

Dr. Smith has given a useful definition of "a religious experience," calling it an experience that elicits from the experiencer a centered response, a response from the core of his or her being.

> As his being includes thoughts, feelings, and will . . . a religious experience triggers in the experiencer a triple movement: of the mind in belief, of the emotions in awe, and of the will in obedience. A religious experience is awesome, convinces the experiencer that its noetic disclosures are true, and lays upon him obligations he acknowledges as binding.

In various LSD studies, episodes of a religious nature have often been manifested even when the intent of the study had nothing to do with religious consciousness. "Cure for dipsomania," William James once said, "is religiomania," a proposition confirmed in the LSD alcoholism studies.

For the 206 psychedelic sessions guided or observed by Masters and Houston—112 with LSD—the statistical breakdown on the following page (rounded to the nearest percentage) indicates the type and frequency of religious images that arose among their subjects.

The Masters and Houston report on mystical experiences is especially interesting because they have taken pains to be more exacting than most in terms of religious criteria. In their *The Varieties of Psychedelic Experience*, they certify only one subject reaching the profoundest depth and only six as attaining the "introvertive mystical" experience. About the latter, they comment:

> It is of interest to observe that those few subjects who attain to this level of mystical apprehension have in the course of their lives either actively sought the mystical experience in meditation and other spiritual disciplines or have

RELIGIOUS IMAGERY

N = 206 subjects
Percent

Religious imagery of some kind:	96
Religious architecture, temples and churches:	91
Religious sculpture, painting, stained glass windows:	43
Religious symbols: cross, yin yang, Star of David, etc.:	34
Mandalas:	26
Religious figures: Christ, Buddha, Saints, godly figures, William Blake-type figures:	58
Devils, demons:	49
Angels:	7
Miraculous and numinous visions, pillars of light, burning bushes, God in the whirlwind:	60
Cosmological imagery: galaxies, heavenly bodies, creation of the universe, of the solar system, of the earth (experienced as religious):	14
Religious Rituals	
Scenes of contemporary Christian, Jewish or Muslim Rites:	8
Contemporary Oriental rites:	10
Ancient Greek, Roman, Egyptian, Mesopotamian and similar rites:	67
Primitive rites:	31

for many years demonstrated a considerable interest in integral levels of consciousness. It should also be noted that all of these subjects were over forty years of age, were of superior intelligence, and were well-adjusted and creative personalities.

When the historical scarcity of mysticism is kept in mind, these limited claims by Masters and Houston are all the more impressive. They may yet substantiate the comment from Ram Dass' guru that religion would come to America by way of a pill.

A number of commentators—notably the sociologist Richard Bunce and the psychiatrist Norman Zinberg—have recently argued that LSD's effects are essentially in line with "recreational drug use." However, most of these observers became interested in this compound in the 1970s, when the usual dosage had dropped to 50 to 100 mcg., far below dosages taken in the 1960s, which frequently exceeded 250 mcg. Dosage is a primary factor in the emergence of religious impulses. Lesser amounts generally have lesser effects, although small doses on occasion have induced psychically powerful results. If "recreation" is the user's only aim, LSD is riskier than most other drugs: the soul may manifest itself anyway.

BOTANICAL SOURCES OF LYSERGIC ACID AMIDES AND THEIR HISTORIES AND EFFECTS

Rye and Other Grasses

The lysergic acid used for the synthesis of LSD was originally obtained from a rye-attacking fungus called *Claviceps purpurea*. The sclerotium, or fruiting body, of this filamentous fungus is known as ergot and contains the "skeleton" for making the psychoactive molecule. Many times during the Middle Ages, and on other occasions up until the first quarter of this century, it was baked inadvertently into bread. Those who ate it felt the terrifying, sometimes deadly, consequences of ergot poisoning, which appeared in gangrenous and convulsive forms and was often called "St. Anthony's fire." People thus affected often experienced ecstasies, but frequently they went into "St. Vitus' dance." Sometimes bodily extremities blackened and fell off. Thousands died.

Raven, Evert and Curtis in their *Biology of Plants* note that in one such epidemic in 994 A.D., "more than 40,000 died. In 1722, ergotism struck down the calvary of Czar Peter the Great on the eve of battle for the conquest of Turkey, and thus changed the course of history." When it was realized in the seventeenth century that ergot-infected rye baked into bread was the cause of these outbreaks, they became less frequent and less extensive. The last ergot epidemic occurred in southern Russia during 1926-1927. (A popular book and many writers have erroneously described a mass poisoning in 1951 in the southern French city of Pont-St. Esprit as the result of ergotism. Thirty people felt that they were being pursued by demons and snakes, and five died. The cause, however, was actually an organic mercury compound that had been used to disinfect seeds.)

At least thirty alkaloids appear in different kinds of ergot, varying in strength and chemical arrangements with the host medium, the weather and other local circumstances. The most common are "peptide alkaloids" of an ergotamine-ergotoxine grouping (not soluble in water) and these have been responsible for the two forms of ergotism. The other alkaloids are lysergic acid amides (which are water soluble), the most important being ergine (*d*-lysergic acid amide) and ergonovine (*d*-lysergic acid-1-2-propanolamide). The latter was isolated independently by four groups of researchers in the 1930s and thus was variously known as ergometrine, ergobasin, ergotocine or ergostetrine.

These distinctions of botanical chemistry are important to this story because of a challenging question R. Gordon Wasson posed to Albert Hofmann in July 1975: "whether Early Man in ancient Greece could have hit on a method to isolate an hallucinogen from ergot that would have given him an experience comparable to LSD or psilocybin?"

Hofmann's response a year later was yes, such effects could have occurred with ergot grown on wheat or barley (rye wasn't known in ancient Greece), and an even "easier way would have been to use the ergot growing on the common wild grass Paspalum." On April 1, 1976, Hofmann confirmed such a possibility when he took an oral dose of 2 mg. of ergonovine maleate, equivalent to about 1.5 mg. of the ergonovine base, which is about six times the normal dose used in medicine for postpartum hemorrhaging. He found that this dose produced mild psychedelic activity that lasted more than five hours.

Arthur Brack: *Sandoz 75 Jahre*

Ergot, the dark parasitic fungus shown here growing on rye, may have provided the ancient Athenians for 2,000 years with "kykeon," the psychedelic used in the Eleusinian mysteries. It has been used by modern chemists as the precursor for synthesizing LSD. The word "ergot," meaning a rooster's spur, comes from the French.

Evidence marshalled for this thesis by Wasson, Hofmann and the Greek scholar Carl A.P. Ruck, along with a new translation of the "Homeric Hymn to Demeter," appears in their *The Road to Eleusis: Unveiling the Secret of*

Germinating sclerotium of ergot of rye (x 8).

Later stage (x 4).

Fully-developed capitula (x 7).

Dr. M. Wilson: *Ergot & Ergotism* (George Barger)

the Mysteries (1978). They demonstrate that the potion used for more than 2,000 years in these annual "mysteries" (mysterious to the uninitiated because the penalty for revealing the ceremony was death) involved water infusions of infected barley and the sclerotium of *Claviceps paspali* growing on the wild grass *Paspalum distichum*, which flourished throughout the area and particularly on the Rarian plain. The complex historical reconstruction of these events, in the words of Jonathan Ott, "for the first time places the sacred mushroom [of ergot] in our own cultural past."

Hofmann wrote in his autobiography, "The cultural-historical meaning of the Eleusinian Mysteries, their influence on European intellectual
history, can scarcely be overestimated. Here suffering humankind found a
cure for its rational, objective, cleft intellect, in a mystical totality experience,
that let it believe in immortality, in an ever-lasting existence."

Up to three thousand people annually were initiated "in a perfect way"
for two millenia, until the suppression of these rites under Christianity in the
fourth century A.D. Anyone who could speak Greek and who hadn't committed murder could present themselves once for this initiation. Half a year
of preparatory rituals began in the spring, culminating in September in a
procession lasting several days from Athens to the temple at Eleusis. The
ceremony occurred at night; ancient writers hint that important things were
seen—in a room "totally unsuited for theatrical performances" (as Ruck described the temple). Among those initiated were Aristotle, Sophocles, Plato,
Aeschylus, Cicero, Pindar and possibly even Homer, plus many Roman em-
perors (such as Hadrian and Marcus Arelius).

Aristides the Rhetor in the second century A.D. called the experience
"new, astonishing, inaccessible to rational cognition." The "Homeric Hymn
to Demeter," which tells us most about what occurred, states "Blissful is he
among men on Earth who has beheld that! He who has not been initiated
into the holy Mysteries, who has had no part therein, remains a corpse in

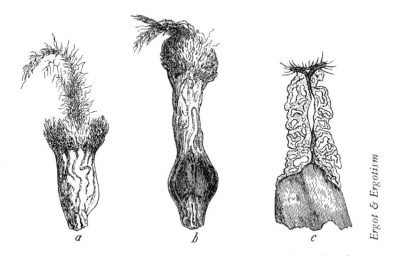

*Claviceps purpurea: (a) a very young ovary of rye in the Sphacelia stage;
(b) older ovary, with the Sphacelia in its upper part, while the sclerotium
is being formed in the lower; (c) longitudinal section through the same
stage as (b). All figures are enlarged—(a) about eight times, and (b)
and (c) about five times.*

gloomy darkness." Pindar remarked "Blissful is he who after having beheld this enters on the way beneath the Earth. He knows the end of life as well as its divinely granted beginning." Cicero said of Eleusis: "Not only have we received the reason there, that we may live in joy, but also, besides, that we may die with better hope." Aristotle revealed only that these Mysteries were *an experience* rather than something learned.

The Road to Eleusis appeared in 1978; so far as I know, nobody since then has tried an aqueous solution of ergot, which is understandable, given the history of ergotism. On the other hand, *Paspalum distichum*, as described by Hofmann, contains "only alkaloids that are hallucinogenic and which could even have been used directly in powder form."

In the January-June 1979 issue of the *Journal of Psychedelic Drugs*, Jeremy Bigwood, Jonathan Ott, Catherine Thompson and Patricia Neely report on their attempt to replicate Hofmann's finding in three experiments with ergonovine maleate, each time in one pastoral setting. They were following up Wasson and Ruck, who tried the same amount as Hofmann but "did not experience distinct entheogenic effects."

With Thompson acting as a guide, three of them took 3 mg. of ergonovine maleate, which appeared as a slightly phosphorescent bluish solution in water. Fifteen minutes later they felt like lying down and looking at the sky; then there were "very mild visual alterations, characterized by perception of an 'alive' quality in inanimate objects." Most of this effect passed within an hour; walking along the beach, they experienced mild leg cramps. Bigwood saw eidetic imagery before going to bed, and the three "slept easily ... awakening refreshed in the morning."

The three experimenters were "convinced that ergonovine was psychoactive, but only J.B. was persuaded the drug was entheogenic." They decided to try it again two weeks later in an increased dosage of 5 mg., but Neely took only 3.75 mg. "Again, we experienced lassitude and leg cramps, more pronounced than in the earlier experiment." The psychic effects were more intense than previously, particularly eidetic imagery. "Now it was clear to all of us that ergonovine was entheogenic .... The entheogenic effects, however, were very mild, while the somatic effects were quite strong. We had none of the euphoria characteristic of LSD and psilocybin experiences."

To determine if higher consciousness alteration was possible, they tried larger oral doses of ergonovine maleate a week later. This time, Neely took a dose of 7.5 mg. and the others took 10 mg.:

> One of us (J.O.) described "flashes in periphery, ringing in ears, inner restlessness" 40 minutes after ingestion, and later noted "mild hallucinosis, cramps in legs" [and] felt the cramping in the legs as painful and debilitating. The psychic effects did not increase with the same magnitude as the somatic effects .... For what seemed like hours, we lay on our backs atop a small pumphouse, watching fluffy cumulus clouds pass silently above us. The effects were still quite intense six hours after ingestion. One of us experienced abundant

eidetic imagery, rapidly-changing, colorful geometric patterns, undulating, never still. We all had a slight hangover the following morning.

Morning Glories

When the Conquistadores subdued the Aztecs, early chroniclers recorded that the Indians made religious and medicinal use of peyote, another psychoactive plant named *tlitliltzin*, and a small lentil-like seed called *ololiuqui*. The third, alleged to have been used also for purposes of divination, came from a vine known in the Náhuatl language as *coaxihuitl* (or "snakeplant").

*An American psychedelic morning glory (*Ipomoea violacea*). This species includes plants popularly known as "Heavenly Blue," "Pearly Gates," "Wedding Bells," "Summer Skies" and "Blue Star"—all of which contain LSD-like compounds.*

When he published some botanical notes by the Spanish physician Hernández, Ximénez stated in 1615 in regard to *ololiuqui*: "It matters little that this plant be here described or that Spaniards be made acquainted with it." He expressed the generally negative Spanish attitude. Hernández and others had described the plant, indicating that it was held in great veneration, and illustrations—as in the *Florentine Codex*—suggested that it was a member of the familiar bindweed or morning glory family (*Convolvulaceae*), but knowledge of this species and its seed was lost to all but a few Zapotec, Chinantec, Mazatec and Mixtec tribes, dwelling mostly in Oaxaca in southern Mexico for more than four centuries.

The ethnobotanist Richard Evans Schultes sent samples of a cultivated Mexican morning glory to Hofmann in 1959, when it was still called *Rivea corymbosa*. He had seen it employed in divination by a Zapotec shaman in Oaxaca. *Corymbosa* is now considered one of five *Turbina* species—the only one appearing in the Americas. Though there are more than 500 species of *Convolvulaceae* widely scattered around the globe, they seem to have been used for their psychoactive properties only by tribes in the New World.

In 1960, Hofmann analyzed the constituents of these seeds and declared that *Rivea (Turbina) corymbosa* contained ergot alkaloids. This information was hard for the scientific world to accept because: (a) previous chemical analysis, recommended in 1955 by Humphry Osmond after self-experimentation with morning glory seeds, had shown no psychoactive principles, and (b) until that time ergot alkaloids had been found only in the rye fungus *Claviceps purpurea*, which belonged in an entirely unrelated wing of the plant kingdom. "Chemotaxonomically," said Schultes, commenting on the unexpected discovery of lysergic acid amides in morning glories, "such an occurrence would be highly unlikely." Hence, many researchers suspected that spores from fungi already in Hofmann's lab had somehow invaded the tissues of the morning glories examined. Later, however, chemical analyses substantiated Hofmann's claim.

The principle agent in this plant was found to be *d*-lysergic acid amide, which had already been synthesized and was known as both ergine and LA-111. Other alkaloids of lesser importance found to be psychoactively influential in *Turbina corymbosa* were *d*-isolysergic acid amide (isoergine), chanoclavine, elymoclavine and lysergol.

In 1960, Don Thomás MacDougall reported that seeds of *Ipomoea violacea* were used as sacraments by certain Zapotecs, sometimes in conjunction with *ololiuqui* and sometimes not. These morning glory seeds, called *badoh negro*, come from the same botanical family—but are jet black rather than brown and are long and angular rather than round. When analyzed, the *badoh negro* seeds were found to have the same mentally-affecting amides as *Turbina (Rivea) corymbosa*, except that ergometrine—a strong uterotonic—showed up in place of lysergol.

Some people believe that *badoh negro* is the seed the early Spanish

Seed contained herein is for planting purposes only

"The most popular Morning Glory," reads the back of this "Heavenly Blue" seed package. "Huge, gorgeous flowers bloom profusely on lush vines. Particularly effective in combination with the pure white of Pearly Gates."

records referred to as *tlitliltzin* (the Náhuatl word for "black," slightly altered by a reverential suffix). These seeds turned out to be stronger in psychoactivity than *ololiuqui*. The total alkaloid content of the *Rivea (Turbina)* is 0.012 percent, while that of *Ipomoea* is about 0.06 percent. American varieties of *Ipomoea violacea* containing *d*-lysergic acid amides are: Heavenly Blue, Pearly Gates, Flying Saucers, Blue Star, Summer Skies and Wedding Bells.

If you compare LSD-25 and the main ingredient of *ololiuqui*—the first and second drawing on page 67—you'll see that the only difference is substitution of two hydrogens in the amide group for two ethyl radicals. This slight change in the molecule makes LSD 50 to 100 times more active than the central ingredient in morning glories. *The First Book of Sacraments* of the Church of the Tree of Life compares the experiential differences between the seeds and LSD:

> The effect of these alkaloids in combination is similar to LSD and other hallucinogens, but more tranquil. Some people experience nausea during the first hour. Large doses are not recommended. After the major effects have worn off one usually feels very soft and relaxed . . . .
>
> It is not advisable for people with a history of hepatitis, jaundice, or other serious liver disease to take [these] lysergic acid amides. Because several of the alkaloids in this family of sacraments have powerful uterus-stimulating properties we recommend that they not be taken by pregnant women.

Hawaiian Woodroses

Chemical investigations have confirmed the appearance of ergot alkaloids in other *Convolvulaceae* (bindweed or morning glory) species, notably in the *Argyreia* genus (in at least eleven species), the large Hawaiian woodrose and in *Stictocardia tilafolia* (which contains six amides of lysergic acid in its seed).

Of these plants, the one that has been most used as a psychedelic is the baby Hawaiian woodrose. This actually isn't a rose, but rather a woody climbing vine or liana with silvery foliage and violet flowers. When dried, the leaves turn tan on the outside and a light, warm saddle brown on the inside. The pod has the color of caramel. This beautiful arrangement has resulted in its use in floral displays and corsages. Native to India, it is now cultivated throughout the world's tropical regions.

Otto Degener in his monumental *Flora Hawaiiensis* in the 1930s described the baby Hawaiian woodrose as thriving in the Islands in drier regions at lower elevations, flowering during August and early September and then becoming "a prolific seeder, the ground under a large vine often being crowded with erect, bud-covered seedlings." According to William Emboden, this has been used as an inebriant by poorer Hawaiians. It has been only occasionally taken by those in the American drug subculture, though advertised in *High Times*. At art fairs in California, a mixture of five of these baby seeds ground up together with ginseng, damiana, gotu kola and bee pollen and pressed into a date has been sold under the name "Utopian Bliss Balls."

Lysergic acid amides are quite concentrated in the seeds of this ornamental, much more so than in psychedelic morning glories. Four to six seeds (the contents of one or two pods) are the equivalent of 100 to 150 *Ipomoea* morning glory seeds and will produce a full-blown experience. The result is generally more tranquil than what is induced by LSD. While LSD is perceived by most users as having stimulant effects, to which a few people are particularly sensitive, the botanical sources have more of a slowing or depressant effect. Some users complain that they have had a hangover, which

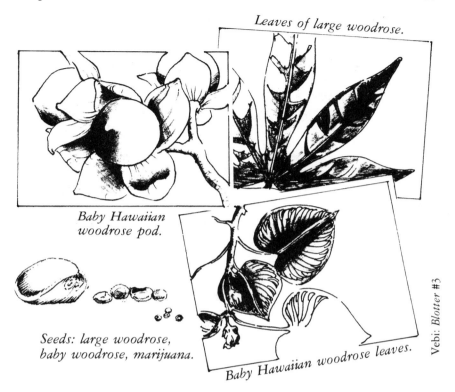

Leaves of large woodrose.

Baby Hawaiian woodrose pod.

Seeds: large woodrose, baby woodrose, marijuana.

Baby Hawaiian woodrose leaves.

Vebi: Blotter #3

has been characterized by Emboden as possibly involving "nausea, constipation, vertigo, blurred vision and physical inertia." More often, however, these seeds have invigorated their users, leaving them feeling as though they had been on vacation afterwards.

Lysergic acid amides including chanoclavine, ergine, isoergine and ergonovine are present in the psychoactive *Argyreia* species—*speciosa, acuta, bernesii, capitata, osyrensis, wallichii, splendens, hainanensis, obtusifolia* and *pseudorubicunda*, mainly concentrated in the seeds. The larger Hawaiian woodrose (*Merremia tuberosa*) also produces such amides, but like the others is not nearly as potent as the baby Hawaiian woodrose. A recent thesis at Harvard illustrates the interest so far: it lists more than 250 references to *Argyreia nervosa*.

FORMS AND PREPARATIONS

The plant sources of lysergic acid amides contain not just one psychoactive molecule but several: variations in effect are possible due to growing seasons and other environmental influences on the chemistry of the plant. Again, I should mention that in the American varieties of psychedelic *Ipomoea* there is a uterotonic effect—hence these should not be used by pregnant women. It's a good idea to check as well to see if the seed company has added anything toxic to the seeds. This should be indicated on the package.

In the case of the proper *Ipomoea* morning glories, each seed is the equivalent of about 1 mcg. LSD; the usual dose lies between 100 and 200 seeds. Many early investigators failed to get any reactions at all. The reason in almost every instance was found to be that they had failed to grind the seeds first. The seeds should be ground to a flour before use; it's also a good idea to soak them in water—the psychoactive components are soluble—and then to strain the liquid through cheesecloth. The amides of value are in the liquid, which is ready for consumption.

As for the baby Hawaiian woodrose, the dose usually taken is four to eight seeds, although some users advise that no more than two or three should probably be taken the first time. With Hawaiian woodroses or morning glories, high dosages are not advisable—beyond a certain level, experience so far has shown a tendency for limbs to get bluish. (From reports I've seen, it's not clear whether the seeds had been dissolved and the amides strained out before ingestion.)

Albert Hofmann has remarked that when he produced ALD-52, it had to be kept in solution and cold because it was quite unstable. Most of the other analogues have been tried by only a few people in research studies and have never appeared on the black market. A methylated form that produces LSD-type effects lasting only four to six hours has recently been distributed in Europe.

LSD appears in crystalline, liquid and many other forms. As a crystal, a substantial dose can barely be seen by the naked eye. Usually, it is dissolved in ethyl alcohol or another solvent and then dropped onto a carrier, usually blotter paper.

When Sandoz distributed LSD, it delivered it in sealed vials or in bottles of calibrated dosage from which precise amounts could be removed by syringe. Such quantitative, not to mention qualitative, care hasn't appeared yet in the black market. More than a few users have discovered considerable differences in the dosage of blotters on the same sheet of paper. Some acid is strong enough to provide four trips from a single tab or blotter, while in other instances the amounts are in the range of 25 to 50 mcg. per blotter.

Ergot was the starting material used until the early 1960s. At the beginning of that decade, the Farmitalia Company of Milan, Italy developed a method for growing this fungus in vats on *Claviceps paspali*. It offered this for sale at $10,000 per kilogram until well past the mid-1960s, when such work was suspended.

In *The Psychedelic Reader*, Gary Fisher described dosage levels for psychotherapeutic sessions as being quite high (generally over 250 mcg.) He also touches on the use of other drugs in conjunction with LSD, particularly small amounts of amphetamine and psilocybin as initial pretreatment.

LSD deteriorates slowly over time, oxidizing into iso-LSD. In about a decade, potency decreases by about half. Some writers have exaggerated the deterioration involved. It does, however, disintegrate rapidly in the presence of light, oxygen and moisture.

Determining the purity of an "acid" sample is not easy for most users. In the first appendix to this book, some of the techniques are detailed; Bruce Eisner discussed many of the relevant issues in the January 1977 *High Times* in an article entitled "LSD Purity: Cleanliness is Next to Godheadliness." Analyses of LSD quality can, however, be obtained by sending a sample to PharmChem, 3925 Bohannon Dr., Menlo Park, CA 94025, along with $15 and a random five digit and single letter code. Mark the outside of the envelope "Hand Cancel" and then call (415) 328-6200 two or three days after you suspect they have received it for results.

PharmChem's analyses are based on thin-layer and gas chromatography. It had been criticized for not taking into much account some of the possible by-products, such as "lumi-LSD," that may be present, but it currently checks for 350 psychoactive compounds and a large number of impurities. Until 1976, this and other testing stations were allowed to make quantitative assays, but this has now been curtailed by federal regulations except for those having the proper licenses. "It doesn't make sense for LSD users not to be able to know what they are using," Jeremy Bigwood comments about the current situation, "even if the state believes it to be illegal at the time."

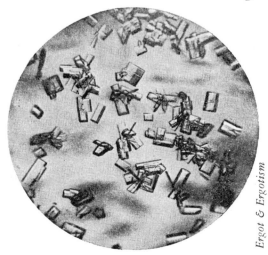

Ergot & Ergotism

Crystals of ergotamine ("E.T."), the precursor usually used in the manufacture of LSD after extraction from ergot fungus.

Smithsonian Report, 1916 (William E. Safford)

CHAPTER TWO

Peyote, Mescaline and San Pedro

The white man goes into his church house and talks about Jesus; the Indian goes into his tepee and talks to Jesus.

—Quanah Parker

HISTORY

Peyote, a slow-growing, unobtrusive and acrid-tasting cactus, appears to be native to two areas of northern Mexico, each with its own species. The yellow-green *Lophophora diffusa* grows in a high desert in the state of Querétaro, some three hundred miles south of Laredo, Texas. The green-blue *Lophophora williamsii* inhabits approximately one hundred thousand square miles south of the Rio Grande.

In *Lophophora diffusa,* 90 percent of its alkaloids are in the form of "pellotine" and there are only trace amounts of mescaline (the first synthesized psychedelic compound). It has larger and whiter flowers than its more familiar relative *L. williamsii* and appears to be an earlier evolutionary form. Its growing range is less than fifty miles in diameter, and it is relatively little-known and unavailable to most people.

Lophophora williamsii contains a substantial amount of mescaline. Its rangeland, shaped something like a mushroom, extends as far south as Zacatecas, but the cactus is most plentiful in the central desert of northern Mexico.

Mesoamerican Accounts

Many people writing about the discovery of peyote suggest that someone lost and starving in the desert came upon this plant and ate it. Native accounts emphasize that the starving wayfarer heard *a voice* saying that this plant should be eaten. The plant was carried back as a divine gift to bring courage and peace to the user's tribe.

Archaeological evidence discovered recently in caves in Texas, including stores of still-psychoactive cacti, indicates that peyote was used ceremonially 3,000 or more years ago. When the Conquistadores wrote about its widespread use, they remarked mainly on the Chichimeca, Toltec and Aztec regions. However, many anthropologists think it was first used by the Tarahumaris, who live closer to its growing area.

In his *History of the Things of New Spain*, also known as the *Florentine Codex* (circa 1560), the Spanish priest Bernardino de Sahagún estimated from events in Indian chronologies that peyote had been used at least 1,800 years earlier. Most Aztec records were destroyed by Cortez and his successors —especially Juan de Zumarraga, the first archbishop of Mexico. In the words of Edward F. Anderson, Zumarraga "searched throughout the former Aztec empire for manuscripts and other pieces of information about their civilization and, in an orgy of unparalleled destruction, burned thousands of Aztec documents and other items." Sahagún tried to recover and record the medical knowledge of Aztec and other priests.

Sahagún, a Jew converted to Catholicism, probably under duress, spent most of his adult life in Mexico and became a great collector of pre-Columbian cultural data. His informants, Aztec noblemen who also had been converted to Catholicism under threat of death, left us our best information about native life prior to the Conquest of the New World. Their manuscripts, filled with hundreds of drawings, are available now in an English translation of the Spanish by Arthur Anderson and Charles Dibble alongside the original Náhuatl language of the Aztecs in a twelve-volume set; a final 1982 volume offers background material and Sahagún's prologues and interpolations.

The Spaniards "discovered" such things as chocolate, potatoes, corn and tobacco in the New World, along with three psychoactive agents: mushrooms, morning glories and peyote. Peyote was associated by the Spanish with the bloody sacrificial rites of the Aztecs and condemned shortly thereafter as "*Raiz diabolica*" (the devil's root). An observation from 1591 (like many others) reported that under the influence of peyote the Indians would "lose their senses, see visions of terrifying sights like the devil and were able to prophesy the future." Once European notions of witchcraft came into play, the Holy Office of the Inquisition enacted the first drug laws in the New World. In 1620, use of peyote was formally denounced as an act of superstition because it was for "purposes of detecting thefts, of divining other happenings and foretelling future events." As late as 1760, peyote was equated with cannibalism in a Catholic text.

The Spaniards made *very* determined efforts to stamp out peyote practices. Over a period of two centuries, a great many Indians were flogged and sometimes killed when they persisted in using it. In one instance, an Accaxee's eyeballs were said to be gouged out after three days of torture; "then the Spaniards cut a crucifix pattern in his belly and turned ravenous dogs loose on his innards." With the breakup of the Mesoamerican civilizations and their extensive transportation and communication routes, peyote distribution was interrupted, and familiarity with the cactus receded to the Chihuahuan Desert.

Use of peyote continued among the rural Indians of north Mexico. Anthropologists believe that the peyote rites practiced today among the Huichol, Cora, Tepecano, Yaqui and Tarahumara tribes are close to those that existed in pre-Columbian times. In this tradition, peyote has been used for divination in shamanic rituals, in the treatment of ailments, in festivals and even in games (among the Tarahumaras, it has been used for endurance in twenty- and forty-mile foot races).

Among the Huichols, an annual pilgrimage for gathering peyote still occurs at the end of the rainy season in October or November. Representatives of the tribe—now numbering approximately 25,000 people—undertake a sacred journey of over 300 miles to the desert regions where the peyote grows. In the past, the gatherers often used to be gone for over a month.

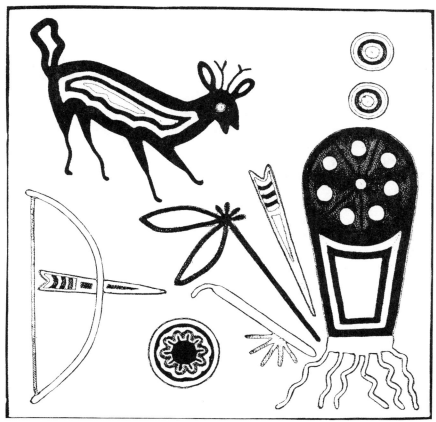

Blotter #4

An example of Huichol "yarn paintings," made of brightly colored "day-glo" yarns attached to a backing with beeswax. The symbols in this representation of the hunt for peyote reveal its association with the deer, which is believed to have left the plants in its tracks after it first appeared in peyote country.

Today they are accompanied by automobiles and usually return in much less time. Reverence for the "hunt" remains unchanged and is marked by vows of fasting, of celibacy, and quite often of silence. The hunt involves certain purification rituals, such as a "confessional" the first night out, during which the pilgrims in turn recount their sexual history. Prayers offered during the search culminate in special ceremonies when the first plant is sighted. Upon their return to the tribe, the pilgrims are greeted with dancing and many expressions of happiness. Preparations for drying the peyote begin, and fresh buttons are consumed. Peter Furst comments in his *Hallucinogens and Culture* on the intensity of the religious exuberance in the peyote country and in the Sierras: "Huichols will literally saturate themselves with peyote, chewing it incessantly for days and nights on end, getting little sleep and eating little normal food, until the entire social and natural environment and the individual's relationship to it take on a wholly mystical dimension."

Peyote Passes to the U.S.
Up until the time of the Civil War, there were few recorded instances of peyote use north of the Rio Grande. During the war, some white soldiers experienced the effects of this cactus, and several U.S. marshals, who were jailed once Texas went Confederate, got inebriated on this "green whiskey." After the war ended, contact between Indians north and south of the border increased. By the beginning of the 1870s, peyote had definitely begun to spread northward.

A peyote religion eventually developed throughout the entire United States as a result of proselytizing by Bert Crowlance, Mary Buffalo, Jack Bear Track, Elk Hair, John Rave and many others. The Plains Indians especially valued "visions."

Much of the subsequent history of peyote in the U.S. was influenced by three exceptional men who were active at the time of crisis among Indians, when they were being herded onto reservations. The Indians had lost their buffalo and all hope that their lands would be restored by the Ghost Dance. This was the time of the Wounded Knee massacre.

The first of the three was a Caddo-Delaware-French individual named John Wilson, who had been renowned as a Ghost Dance leader. Having learned of peyote from a Comanche, Wilson went with his wife into the forest, where he consumed about fifteen buttons a day for two weeks. As Francis Speck described the effect in his "Notes on the Life of John Wilson, the Revealer of Peyote, as Recalled by his Nephew, George Anderson" (1933), "Wilson was continually translated in spirit to the sky realm where he was conducted by Peyote." He was shown the "road" that led "from Christ's grave to the Moon in the Sky which Christ had taken in his ascent." He was told to walk in this path for the rest of his life and to remain faithful to peyote's teachings. He was taught ceremonial details, such as how the face should be painted. He was also instructed on how to sing the songs that were to form a principal part of the worship ceremony (he knew more than two hundred of these). Wilson introduced many Christian elements into subsequent peyote practices.

A second figure influential in the spread of a Christian peyotism was the half-Comanche Quanah Parker, a chief who in 1884 became deathly ill.

Print Mint

Quanah Parker (1839-1911) contributed greatly to spread of the highly ritualized Christian practices associated with peyote. He insisted that women not be restricted from these ceremonies.

When he failed to recover under the care of at least one white doctor, his aunt finally took Parker to a *curandera*, thought to have been a Tarahumara, who revived him with peyote tea in only a few days. That experience changed Parker's life. A militant before, he decided to turn his back on violence and to help spread *peyotyl* as a unifying force for a "pan-Indian movement."

The third man was James Mooney, an anthropologist from the Smithsonian Institution. In 1891, he traveled into the still-dangerous Oklahoma territory, where he became a participant in peyote practices. He became convinced that the Indians ought to unite in a Native American Church (the name is thought to have been his suggestion) to protect their right to use peyote. Mooney called for a meeting of "Roadmen," peyotist representatives of the Great Spirit. In 1918 they incorporated and wrote the charter of the Native American Church.

The "peyote cult" had already developed among some Apaches and Tonkawas and then among the Comanches and Kiowas by the turn of the twentieth century. As time passed, use of this plant became common in more than fifty American tribes, including the Cheyenne, Shawnee, Pawnee, Arapaho, Chippewa, Blackfoot, Crow, Delaware and Sioux. Instead of the shamanism in the Mexican practices, these tribes emphasized a communal ceremony of chanting, meditation and prayer, blending Christian elements into their theology in most instances.

John Wilson and others emphasized that this form of Christianity did not include guilt for the crucifixion of Christ. In Wilson's view, Christ was given to the whites and they crucified Him. Indians were thus exempt on this score; they could receive religious influences directly and in person from God through "the Peyote Spirit." Many accounts exist of peyotists who have had visions relating to Christ. The anthropologist Weston La Barre has argued, however, that Christian elements—of great importance to many— are usually little more than an overlay on the pan-Indian elements, or at least have been subordinate.

By 1922, the number of ceremonial peyote users had grown to about 13,000. It has been said that at present more than half of all North American Indians belong to the Native American Church (about a quarter of a million peyotists altogether). Although there is a good deal of individual and group variation, peyote meetings regularly begin at sundown on Saturday night. Remarkably, there are few church buildings in this religion. Some wooden chapels have been built, and some groups have constructed cement altars, but ordinarily, peyote ceremonies are conducted at a hogan or in a tepee set up for the occasion. Most often, fewer than a score of people participate, gathering around a fire that lights a crescent-moon altar to "Father Peyote." They stay together until some time after sunrise. Then they join others in a large communal meal.

The experience is presided over by a Roadman or Road Chief, who represents the Great Spirit and shows "the peyote road." At least three others officiate: the Fire Chief, who represents the Angelic Host, guards the door, tends the sick, and builds and stokes the fire; the Cedar Chief, representative of the Holy Ghost, who brings any disoriented participants back into communion with the others by waving cedar incense; and the Drum Chief, who represents Jesus and keeps up a beat all night long.

Usually, each participant in turn sings four peyote songs. A point of transition leading to a kind of "second wind" for the experience is reached at midnight, when the Roadman goes out of the tepee and blows a whistle "in the directions of the four corners of the earth." Another shift in mood occurs at the arrival of false dawn, when a woman representing "Peyote Woman" enters the tepee bearing water and simple food. Many observers agree with anthropologist J.S. Slotkin, who testified in congressional hearings in the late 1930s that he had "never been in any white man's house of worship where there is either as much religious feeling or decorum." John Wilson and others emphasized sobriety and the creation of better family lives in their teachings, and many testimonials since indicate that Indians have used this powerful mental drug in socially acceptable ways. "It is the only holy thing that I have become aware of in all my life," said the Winnebago Crashing Thunder when he was converted to peyotism by an experience with the cactus at age forty-five.

From the beginning of this century, zealous whites—and a few Indians— have attempted to outlaw use of this sacred cactus (generally in the name of "protecting" the peyotists). The first case seems to have been brought against three Kickapoos in 1907 in Oklahoma (who were found guilty and fined $25 each and court costs), and it was followed by many other efforts to ban the practice.

Legislation against peyote has been introduced at the federal level a number of times, succeeding only recently. But earlier laws banning peyote were passed in eleven states, mainly in the Southwest. In 1960, Judge Yale McFate of Arizona handed down a definitive opinion overturning the state law and sanctioning peyote use by Native Americans under the Fourteenth and First Amendments' protection ensuring religious freedom. Since then, Indian peyotists appear to have had no further trouble with law enforcement agencies. The federal legislation banning the use or possession of peyote and mescaline contains a special exemption for the "nondrug use of peyote in bona fide religious ceremonies of the Native American Church."

Scientific Scrutiny and Diffusion among Non-Indians

Some people claim that Mrs. Anna B. Nickels, a resident of Laredo, initiated modern pharmacological and scientific studies of peyote in the early 1880s by sending samples to Parke, Davis and Co. and to other investigators in North America and Europe. The records are lost, however, and other historians declare that it wasn't until 1887 that Parke, Davis and Co. began distributing dried peyote, obtained from Dr. John Briggs of Dallas (who obtained it from his brother in Mexico).

Dr. Louis Lewin, a scientist and artist often called the "father of modern psychopharmacology," received some of this material, labeled "Muscale Button," in Germany in 1887. The next year, he traveled throughout the southwestern United States and took dried specimens back to Europe, where he soon isolated numerous alkaloids from peyote. He gave some of his samples to the botanist Paul Hennings of the Royal Botanical Museum in Berlin for study. In 1888, he stimulated other pharmacological investigations by publishing the first report on the cactus' chemistry.

The first account (by a white) of "peyote inebriation" was published in 1897 by the distinguished Philadelphia physician and novelist Weir Mitchell. Soon after, he sent "peyote buttons"—the part of the plant growing above-ground—to Havelock Ellis, a pioneer in psychological and sexual studies. Ellis had read Mitchell's narrative and soon published two influential accounts of his own experiments under the influence of peyote in the *British Journal of Medicine.*

The scientific examination of peyote stimulated by Lewin's enthusiasm resulted in the isolation of the principal psychoactive component in 1897. Arthur Heffter, Lewin's colleague and rival, made this identification by systematically ingesting a number of alkaloid "fractions" made from peyote; as in the case of psilocybin later, animal testing had been inconclusive as to their various psychoactivities. Heffter named the isolate compound "mezcalin" (which soon became "mescaline") and reported that "mescaline hydrochloride, 0.15 g, produces a pattern of symptoms which differs in only a few respects from the one obtained with the drug (peyote)."

Over time, scientific interest in mescaline—first synthesized in 1919 by Ernst Späth—supplanted further investigations of peyote. The last extensive study in this period of the cactus' mental effects was reported in 1927 by the French psychologist Alexandre Rouhier, who caused a stir with his accounts of the exotic "visions" experienced by his subjects.

Also in 1927, Lewin's colleague Dr. Kurt Beringer, a friend of Hermann Hesse and Carl Jung, issued a 315-page description of the effects of mescaline entitled *Der Meskalinrausch (The Mescaline Inebriation).* At the same time a short book by Heinrich Klüver took issue with Ellis' earlier opinion that the chief feature of mescaline "visions" was that they were "indescribable." Klüver tried to catalogue the visual forms of the "hallucinatory constants" induced by this mysterious substance as basically gridwork, spirals, cobwebs and tunnels.

Through the first half of the twentieth century, peyote aroused very little interest in North America among non-Indians, aside from a few isolated instances. A "peyote meeting" held in an apartment in New York City in 1912, for example, was described by Mabel Dodge Luhan in her *Movers and Shakers.*

Louis Lewin (1850-1929) took peyote to Europe and initiated scientific investigations into its properties in the late 1880s.

Annals of Medical History (1922)

S. Weir Mitchell, a Philadelphia physician and novelist, published the first description of peyote's mental effects. He sent the cactus to Havelock Ellis, pioneer in sexual studies, who tried it in London; he also sent it to the psychologist William James, who ingested one button, got "violently sick" and wrote his brother that he would "take the visions on trust."

Ethnopharmacological Search for Psychoactive Drugs

Kurt Beringer (1893-1949), an associate of Carl Jung and Hermann Hesse, published a description of his mescaline studies in 1927—Der Meskalinrausch (The Mescaline Inebriation). *One of his subjects became fascinated with trying to put the "furious succession" of mescaline images on film; later, Walt Disney hired him as the chief visualist for* Fantasia.

Awareness of peyote was slow to develop even among the anthropologists studying native practices. Most of them were mainly interested in recording earlier Indian traditions and thus failed to notice the burgeoning religion of their time. Contemporary Indian practices began to draw attention only after a series of papers on Winnebago peyote rites were published by Paul Radin starting in 1914.

Weston La Barre's *The Peyote Cult*—a book that became something of a bible among members of the Native American Church—was based on field work undertaken during the summers of 1935 and 1936. *The Peyote Religion* by J.S. Slotkin—the next major anthropological study—wasn't published until 1956. Slotkin spent a good deal of time among the Menomini and other Indian tribes; thanks to his defense of peyote in lawsuits, he became known affectionately as the "national secretary" of the Native American Church. David Aberle's *The Peyote Religion Among the Navajo* (1966) is an exhaustive study of how peyote spread to a tribe opposed to its use. The Navajos had had many objections to peyote; they didn't feel it was traditional. However, federal interference with their traditional but "unecological" methods of sheep grazing eventually brought many of the tribe into the pan-Indian movement and then into the Native American Church.

A Decade Opening the "Psychedelic Doors"

In the early 1950s, the story took a significant turn. The British psychiatrist Humphry Osmond—along with Canadian associates John Smythies and Abram Hoffer—began to examine the properties of mescaline in connection with their research on psychosis and schizophrenia. In 1952, Osmond and Smythies published a six-page article about their findings in the *Journal of Mental Science*. Their provocative theories about the actions of brain chemicals attracted the attention of the novelist Aldous Huxley, who soon offered himself as a guinea pig for further experimentation. Thus it was that on a lovely May morning in 1953, in the Los Angeles hills, Huxley took mescaline sulfate—the first of ten psychedelic experiences. This event was to change the way many people look at the world today.

Being the center of controversy was nothing new to Huxley, a renowned author whose ideas expressed in thirty-nine previous books had been discussed at practically all levels in Western society. He had been honored for decades by the literary world after a series of novels whose "cynical" and "immoral" characters had shocked the sensibilities of many people. Still, he must have been surprised by the intensity of the enthusiasm and the antagonism with which his *The Doors of Perception* (1954) was received.

In this book of less than one hundred pages, written in a month, Huxley reported on his initial mescaline sulfate experience and speculated on the nature of such radical mental transformations. Many readers were outraged by his apparent embracing of an experience so alien to our culture— so "pagan" and "mystical." The book shone as an unexpected bright light through the gray complacency of technological civilization. Some of his literary followers didn't at all like his lead this time; they claimed that his thinking had become "mushy." R.C. Zaehner, a professor at Oxford specializing in the study of Eastern religions, took mescaline sulfate with the intention of testing Huxley's assertion that a profound "mystical state" had been induced by a *drug*. In *Mysticism: Sacred and Profane*, Zaehner described his experience as a minor "pre-mysticism" that reminded him mainly of *Alice in Wonderland*.

The interest in mescaline and peyote awakened by Huxley's book was greatly augmented by Robert DeRopp's popular *Drugs and the Mind* (1957)

Humphry Osmond

Aldous Huxley surveying Los Angeles from the Hollywood Hills on that May morning in 1953 when his "doors of perception" were cleansed with 400 mg. of mescaline sulfate. His experience became a turning point in the history of psychedelics.

and by David Ebin's *The Drug Experience* (1961). Both provided lengthy accounts of "classic" peyote and mescaline experiences. By the early 1960s, the media were definitely fascinated by these substances. Alice Marriott wrote about peyote in *The New Yorker*, John Wilcock in the newly established *Village Voice* and Allen Ginsberg in *Birth*. (Ginsberg's poem *Howl* was composed following a night on peyote walking through the streets of San Francisco.) Here is the text of a signed letter, to give another instance, sent to *Life* magazine after it published an account of the "sacred mushrooms" of Mexico in 1957:

> Sirs: I've been having hallucinatory visions accompanied by space suspension and time destruction in my New York apartment for the past three years ... produced by eating American-grown peyote cactus plants. I got my peyote from a company in Texas which makes C.O.D. shipments all over the country for $8 per 100 "buttons."

Peyote could then be acquired by mail from Laredo and nearby areas simply by requesting it, and it soon became a fairly familiar object on many college campuses and in beatnik and artistic circles. In 1960, one of the first peyote busts among whites occurred at the Dollar Sign Coffee House, an East Greenwich Village cafe that sold the ground up cactus over the counter in capsules. The proprietor, Barron Bruchlos, had mail ordered 310 lbs. of this cactus, certified by the Agriculture Department to be without pests. His supply was confiscated, but he was never charged.

Huxley's book opened an era when a number of pioneers of the psychedelic movement first turned on. Robert Masters, who published the earliest account of its effects in the sexual realm in his *Forbidden Sexual Behavior and Morality* (Julian Press, 1962), had his first experience with peyote during the 1950s in Louisiana. In 1960, Arthur Kleps wrote to Delta Chemicals Co. in New York for mescaline sulfate and tried 500 mg. The experience resulted in his leaving his job as a state prison psychologist, in addition to other considerable changes in his life. Here is how he described what occurred:

> At that point I retired to the bedroom and closed my eyes (it having occurred to me that if I kept them open a monstrous gobbler from outer space might come around the corner any moment) and found myself watching a 3-dimensional color movie on the inside of whatever it is one looks at when there isn't anything there. All night, I alternated between eyes open terror and eyes closed astonishment. With eyelids shut I saw a succession of elaborate scenes which lasted a few seconds each before being replaced by the next in line. Extra-terrestrial civilizations. Jungles. Organic computer interiors. Animated cartoons. Abstract light shows. Temples and palaces of a decidedly pre-Colombian American type. There was no obvious narrative connection between scenes or aesthetic coherence to the whole. The most awesome and sublimely well executed spectacles, things that compared quite well with the best in Western art, alternated with gross caricatures. There was never any hint of a "technical" breakdown though—if something merely silly was being presented it was always dressed with all the slick perfection of a Walt Disney feature, plus all kinds of extra touches Disney could never have afforded. Let's say that "despair" was being depicted in the form of the conventional cartoon castaway on a cartoon raft—a two-second thrownaway flash. Well, just for kicks why not add a transparent ocean, perfectly and variously tinted, in which bob a billion seahorses, singing and playing perfect tiny musical instruments? Certainly. Coming right up. That was the spirit of the thing. No job too large, no job too small. The difficult we do right away, and the impossible ... we do right away too.

Art Kleps is Chief Boo Hoo of the Neo-American Church. Author of The Boo Hoo Bible *and* Millbrook, *he first experimented with mescaline sulfate in 1960.*

But I have exposed the conclusions I arrived at later in the terms of my description. What I was seeing was a kind of language of the gods, the ultimate vocabulary of the mind, which was, naturally, much more than just a collection of nouns. I didn't think it through until later, but at the time the tip-off was a radio discussion I turned on in a vain attempt to make the visions stop. Every single word emanated from the radio got a magnificent image to go with it, as if the trivia being spoken had been the life's work of generations of media technicians on planets given over to the production of such artistic wonders— all for the purpose of this one showing in Art Kleps' one man screening room....

Discovery of Mescaline in Other Cacti

The scientific discovery of mescaline and related molecules in cacti other than peyote began in 1945 with the first report that the San Pedro cactus (*Trichocerus pachanoi*) was used in rituals by the Indians of Andean Ecuador. These shamanic practices were quite similar to rituals developed in Mexico for peyote. By 1950, it was established that mescaline constitutes about 1-2 percent of the San Pedro cactus when dried, about 0.12 percent of the fresh plant.

The San Pedro cactus (Trichocerus pachanoi) *contains mescaline and has been used shamanically for divination and healing in the Andes for more than 3,000 years. In the U.S., it is generally a small plant, but it can attain a height of twenty feet. Its flowers are large and fragrant. Their smell is reminiscent of "Beach Nut" chewing gum and is very attractive to bees.*

This columnar cactus attains from nine to twenty feet in height in part of Ecuador, Peru and Bolivia, mainly at elevations between 6,000 and 9,000 feet but occasionally as low as sea level. Some U.S. commercial cactus outlets carry it for sale, and it seems to grow easily anywhere if given plenty of sunlight.

Archaeological evidence relating to the San Pedro cactus goes back well over 3,000 years. A Chavin stone carving from a temple in northern Peru, which shows the principal diety holding the San Pedro, dates from 1,300 B.C.; almost equally ancient textiles from this region depict the cactus with jaguar and hummingbird figures. Ceramics made between 1,000 and 700 B.C. show the plant associated with deer. Other pottery of a somewhat later date exhibits the plant in conjunction with the jaguar again and with spirals, thought to represent the cactus' mental effects.

After the discovery of mescaline in the San Pedro cactus, it was soon found in other tall, columnar *Trichoceri* as well as in a *Stetsonia* species from South America, in *Cereus jamacaru* from Brazil, and in the giant *Pachycereus pecten-aboriginum* of Mexico. (The Mexican cactus contains another psychoactive compound—pectenine—which also appears in the *Carnegiea gigantea* of the U.S. Southwest, where it is called "carnegine."

In 1972, mescaline was identified in a cactus native to the U.S.— *Pelecyphora aselliformis*. This "hatchet cactus" has traditionally been used in native rituals but has been assayed for mescaline content at less than 0.00002 percent of the dried cactus' weight. Alexander Shulgin calculated that one would "need about 100,000 cacti to achieve an effective dose of mescaline."

The San Pedro cactus in the fresh form has about 0.01 percent mescaline, which is a fairly typical percentage for nine of the ten *Trichoceri* known to contain mescaline. *Trichocerus peruvianus*, however, is at least ten times as potent as the others. This branching, candelabra type of cactus, originally collected in Peru, has a mescaline content equal or superior to that in peyote. Jeremy Bigwood comments that it would not be all that surprising to find that this cactus has been used in Andean shamanistic rituals, although no archeological evidence has been presented to date.

Mescaline and Peyote Go "Underground"

Throughout the 1950s and 1960s, mescaline could be purchased from several chemical supply houses in the form of sulfate or hydrochloride crystals. In 1970, mescaline and peyote were "scheduled" as part of a Comprehensive Drug Abuse Prevention and Control Act, which established penalties for possession, manufacture or distribution: "a term of imprisonment of not more than 15 years, a fine of not more than $25,000, or both." Title 21 proscribes possession of "all parts of the plant presently classified as *Lophophora williamsii,* whether growing or not, the seeds thereof, any extract from any part of such a plant, every compound, salt, derivative, mixture or preparation of such a plant, its seeds or extracts."

Various forms of mescaline have continued to appear over the last dozen years but generally only in small amounts made for a few people in the counterculture. Other U.S. citizens wishing to have a mescaline experience have therefore traveled to the Chihuahua Desert of northern Mexico to get peyote. Many of these have taken large quantities back home with them. Because of the law against possession of peyote and its constituents, recent mescaline use has been mostly sporadic and thus unritualized, exploratory and recreational.

Indian peyotists provide the main contemporary example of mescaline and peyote used as a means of psychic exploration. A quarter million practitioners have taken this potent psychedelic—often quite frequently, often for years, often in large amounts without significant physical, psychological or social problems. The exemption provided in the law for members of the Native American Church has in fact fostered a tradition of spiritual growth and communal interaction.

The Church of the Tree of Life, centered in the San Francisco Bay area, tried for years to develop a ritual somewhere between that of the Native American Church and that followed by the Huichol Indians of Mexico. Some members felt that the Native American example was too constricted and focused; they desired a non-denominational ritual encompassing greater possibilities for expression and introspection. ("The NAC," commented one, "hasn't produced the marvelous, artistic, creative explosion seen among the Huichols.") Although the attempt to find a middle ground was pursued seriously, the results were unsatisfactory—or "somewhat hokey."

Native and Non-Native Use under The Bill of Rights

The Church of the Tree of Life attempted to obtain the legal exemption allowed to Indian practitioners. So did the Church of the Awakening, an Arizona-based group founded by John and Louisa Aiken after the deaths of their two sons in the 1950s. Claiming peyote as one of its sacraments, the Church of the Awakening took its case up to the Supreme Court. Years later, the justices refused to hear the appeal. Only in regulations relating to the use of peyote does the government curtail religious freedom and actively discriminate on the basis of skin color.

A recent case testing this law involves the Native American Church of New York, which has met regularly and openly in East Greenwich Village since the early 1970s. This group is particularly interesting because of the legal conundrums that have resulted from its religious use of psychedelics.

In the mid-1970s, this church was granted legal status under the authority of the New York State Health Commissioner's discretionary power to grant exemptions to the drug laws. The group then wrote the Drug Enforcement Administration requesting federal certification as bona fide peyotists. Exemption from the law banning peyote was denied. An appeal went to the 2nd District Court.

Meanwhile, the church went on buying and selling peyote, in many instances from vendors licensed by the government who weren't themselves peyotists. Receipts went to the DEA and to the Department of Public Safety in Texas. Alan Birnbaum, a leader in this church, began a correspondence with the Commissioner of the Department of Narcotics in Albany, New York. He asked to be licensed as a distributor of peyote and made the commissioner aware that he had been receiving shipments of peyote for several years.

The results of the 2nd District Court trial were perplexing. Judge Milton Pollack ruled that the church was not bona fide because it was *selling* peyote. On the other hand, he declared that Birnbaum—although he, too, was selling peyote—was bona fide because he sincerely believed that "peyote was God."

New York state police came to the church on a separate matter, and Birnbaum showed them receipts of purchase for the 20,000 peyote buttons on the premises. Remarkably, the police left without confiscating any. However, new "Rockefeller drug laws," which limited the Health Commissioner's power to grant exemptions to Schedule III drugs, soon brought the police back. They said they didn't want to arrest Birnbaum. But they did want to take the 20,000 peyote buttons, and the only way they could do that was by arresting him.

Judge Pollack's ruling that the church was not bona fide was appealed on constitutional grounds and denied because in the opinion of the new judge *Birnbaum* hadn't been found bona fide! He also declared that if anyone were to be accepted as bona fide, then peyote could be used in worship by everyone in the jurisdiction of the 2nd District Court, which includes Vermont, Connecticut and New York.

An appeal that the Birnbaum case be dismissed "in the interest of justice" has been denied. Birnbaum is now facing a sentence of fifteen years to life.

While generating all these complications, the judicial system has lost sight of the principle at issue, articulated very simply by Alice Marriott and Carol Rachlin in a comment on the NAC as a whole: "That the Bill of Rights of the United States Constitution grants each man his right to worship God in his own fashion is incontrovertible." `

Trekking Back to Peyote Country

Several books—such as Fernando Benitz's *In the Magic Land of Peyote,* Barbara Myerhoff's *Peyote Hunt* and Joan Halifax's *Shamanic Voices*—along with shorter accounts from Peter Furst, Michael Harner and others describe the Huichol Indians' annual trip to gather peyote. These reports have encouraged many Americans to make similar journeys.

Prem Das, a white who apprenticed himself for five years to Huichol shamans Ramón Medina Silva and Matsúwa recently led a group from the Esalen Institute in Big Sur to peyote's native area. The Mexican doctor

Flesh of the Gods (Peter Furst)

Peyote seekers line up by the highway near the city of Zacatecas for a blindfolding ceremony that precedes symbolic passage through the mythic "cloud gates" and entrance into the sacred country.

Salvador Roquet is another who has taken people to the home of *hikuli* (peyote). An author from the Harvard Divinity School has even written an account of experiencing peyote sixty paces from the Huichols. Not being Huichols, he explains, whites don't go to exactly the sacred spots. After ingesting peyote, they may "learn how to be a Huichol" by watching them from a respectful distance.

Much of the peyote growing in the more accessible parts of the Chihuahua Desert has been picked by people without the sense to leave the root. It can still be found in remote areas but is in danger of extinction.

BOTANY

In their four-volume *The Cactaceae,* written at the turn of the century, Britten and Rose describe 1,235 species of cacti; the number of clearly identified species has since gone well beyond 3,000. Peyote is unusual among cacti, displaying spines only as a seedling. It has been found to produce more than sixty separate alkaloids and is thus, as Richard Evans Schultes described the plant, "a veritable chemical factory." In *Peyote—The Divine Cactus,* Edward

Jeremy Bigwood

When Indians collect peyote, they generally use a wooden knife and take only the part that grows above ground so that the root, which contains mescaline, will then produce a cluster of "buttons." These clusters, which have been known to spread to as much as four or five feet across, are regarded by the Huichols as especially sacred and powerful.

Anderson presented the results of twenty-five years of study of its botanical aspects, concluding that "*Lophophora* seems to stand by itself in possessing a particular combination of morphological characters unlike any other group of cacti."

The root of peyote, which is quite large in relation to the portion above ground, looks like a turnip or carrot and is topped by the "button," which resembles a dull bluish- or grayish-green pincushion with a bit of fluff in its center. This wool-like fluff may have given peyote its name, which is thought to be derived from a word in the Náhuatl language meaning "cocoon-silk" or "caterpillar's cocoon." The flowers and the black, "warty" seeds emerge from this fluffy center.

Richard Heffern, in his *Secrets of the Mind-Altering Plants of Mexico*, describes some characteristics of this plant:

> Instead of thorns, the peyote cactus has small, short tufts of a cottonlike material. Buried in the center of each tuft is a tiny, thin-walled, fleshy pod containing several very tiny black seeds. The plant grows outward and downward from

the center. Each tuft was originally at the top center of the cactus. Each time a flower appears at the top of the plant, it is fertilized and is followed by the appearance of the furry tuft encasing the seeds. The furry tuft then moves outward and downward; another flower appears and begins the cycle all over again.

It is interesting to note that peyote is one of the slowest-growing plants in existence. The period from the time a seed germinates until the plant is large enough to bloom for the first time is approximately thirteen years. When peyote was sold in the United States cactus nurseries up until a few years ago, the problem of slow growth was partially overcome by grafting the peyote cactus to the root of a very fast-growing *Opuntia* cactus. This technique greatly accelerated the growth of the peyote cactus. Regardless of what method is used, however, the plant will never grow to more than about four inches in diameter. Instead, new plants appear at the base of the old ones, forming the characteristic peyote clusters.

There are problems of nomenclature confusion that are worth sorting out. Much of the muddle stems from confusion of the name *mescaline* (which Heffter derived from the Mescalero Indians) with the *mescal bean*, which is highly toxic, or with the *mescal plant*, which is a maguey and the source of a famous Mexican fermented liquor known as "pulque." Confusion with the bean is particularly interesting in that the tree it comes from—*Sophora secundiflora*—is often found together with peyote. About the only thing aside from cacti that blooms on the desert, growing up to thirty-five

Jeremy Bigwood

Peyote produces delicate flowers that vary in color from white to reddish-pink and usually appear between March and September.

feet with flamboyant, large violet-blue and scarlet, highly fragrant flowers somewhat reminiscent of wisteria, the presence of the mescal been tree is often taken as a clue to peyote's location. There is evidence that its bean was used as an oracular medium as far back as 10,000 years ago. It is still honored

Peyote was first described in 1560. The first person publishing a binomial name for it was the French botanist Charles Lemaire, who in 1845 called it Echinocactus williamsii *in a horticultural catalog. He didn't describe it, however. The description validating the binomial soon came from another European botanist, Prince Salm-Dyck, who didn't provide an illustration. Above is the first published image of peyote, appearing in* Curtis' Botanical Magazine *in 1847.*

and worn by peyotists. The mescal bean, however, is highly poisonous and can produce death, reportedly even if as little as a half of a single seed is ingested.

A great deal of botanical pother about the peyote plant results from its having been classified first by Lemaire in 1845 as *Echinocactus williamsii*, then by Voss in 1872 as *Anhalonium williamsii* and then by Coulter in 1891 as belonging to the *Mammillaria* genus. By the end of the nineteenth century, botanists had placed it in five separate genera. It was only in 1894 that it began to be known by its present name *Lophophora*. The name *Lophophora* derives from that tuft in the center; it means "crest-bearer."

The Lophophora *Genus*

For a long time after the adoption of the designation of *Lophophora*, debate continued as to whether there were actually two variants—the *williamsii* and the *lewinii*. This controversy was ended in the late 1930s when Richard Evans Schultes displayed a photo of a single plant bearing the characteristics of both. Since then, *L. williamsii* has become the standard designation. Those who saw a difference between the *williamsii* and *lewinii* types were actually seeing a difference between an early stage of the plant and a later stage. A greater concentration of mescaline appears as the plant gets older. The oldest plants are revered by the Indians and kept as personal amulets or placed on the crescent altar to represent "Father Peyote."

In 1967, a botanical description of another *Lophophora* species was proposed: *Lophophora diffusa*. The plant in question appears to be restricted to a tiny area in the state of Querétaro in central Mexico. Yellow-green rather than blue-green in color and lacking ribs, *L. diffusa* seems to have a considerably different chemical makeup, and some botanists now think it is an earlier evolutionary form of the more familiar *L. williamsii*.

Since the designation and acceptance of the *L. diffusa* species, Swedish investigators have re-examined the plant material used in Germany by Lewin and his associates. They found that it was composed of both *L. williamsii* and *L. diffusa* species, which look somewhat similar. However, 90 percent of the alkaloids in *L. diffusa* are in the form of a sedative called "pellotine," with only trace amounts of mescaline present, so it's understandable that the initial studies came to different, contradictory conclusions. (Anderson recounts the complexities wrought by this error on page 136 of his authoritative *Peyote—The Divine Cactus*.)

In the mid-1970s, two Czechoslovakian botanists proposed two more species in the *Lophophora* genus. *L. fricii* was reported to have been first collected in 1931 and then again in 1974 from the vicinity of San Pedro in Coahuila, Mexico. It was to be differentiated from *L. williamsii* by a grayer skin, by the shape of its ribs and seeds, and by its "carmine-red flowers." *L. jourdaniana* was described in 1975 as having come from an unknown location in Mexico; it was said to differ from other *Lophophora* in having

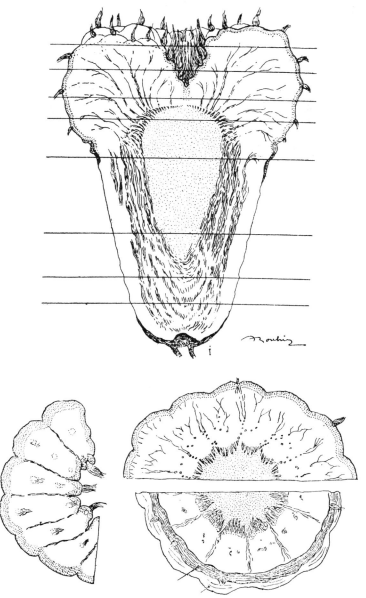

These drawings of the cross-sectioned interior of peyote and of its ribbed exterior appeared in Alexandre Rouhier's 1927 study. The number of ribs and their arrangement vary with age and environment; the number of ribs can range from four when very young to fourteen in maturity.

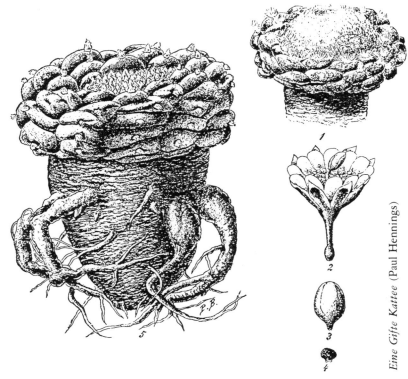

*The first peyote to be scientifically examined came to the
laboratory in Germany in dried form. When dried, the succulent
part of the cactus shrivels greatly, while the center tufts remain
much the same. Boiling the specimens only partially restored
their original appearance, as indicated by this drawing from 1888.*

"rose-violet" flowers and in being impossible to fertilize with the pollen of
the other species. The specimens chosen to typify these proposed species—
the "holotypes"—reside in an herbarium at a university in Pilzen, Czechoslovakia.

More than five years have passed since division of the *Lophophora*
genus to include these possibly new species was proposed (detailed morphological descriptions can be found in *The Journal of Ethnopharmacology #1*
and in Anderson's book). To date, botanists seem skeptical, although few
have done relevant field work. Schultes comments that he hasn't seen the
plants in question but doubts that there are significant differences. Anderson
severely criticizes the descriptions provided by the collectors and says about
the chemical reports issued in 1977 and 1978 that they "do not clarify the
status of these taxa, especially when *L. fricii* from Coahuila and within the

center of distribution of *L. williamsii* is reported to have an alkaloid constitution similar to that of *L. diffusa* from Querétaro."

High Times has on occasion run ads offering *Ariocarpus fissuratus*—often called "living rock" or "peyote cimarrón" cactus—and *Ariocarpus retusus* for sale as a kind of "peyote." These horny, triangular-leafed cacti are known among the Tarahumaris and Huichols as *tsuwiri* and *sunami*, "false peyote." Although they contain alkaloids similar to mescaline, the Indians regard them as "an evil," dangerous because they are somewhat stronger than peyote and "will drive people mad" when ingested. They are not recommended.

Trichoceri

Ten species of *Trichoceri* are known to contain mescaline: *T. pachanoi, T. bridgesii, T. macrogonus, T. terscheckii, T. werdermannianus, T. cuzcoensis, T. fulvinanus, T. taquimbalensis, T. validus* and *T. peruvianus.* These

Plants of the Gods

San Pedro cactus is sometimes stacked high for sale by South American herb vendors.

cacti are the next richest botanical source of mescaline after *Lophophora williamsii*—*T. peruvianus* containing about equal concentrations, the other nine with less than a tenth of peyote's psychoactive strength.

Trichoceri grow much faster than peyote—which may take five years when grown from seeds to reach a ¾-inch diameter—and they contain only a few alkaloids in addition to mescaline. When planted in shallow soil, half-inch slices from the cactus root easily. A two-foot-high San Pedro grows an additional four inches or so in about half a year.

CHEMISTRY

β -Phenethylamines and Tetrahydroisoquinolines

The sixty or so alkaloids in *Lophophora williamsii* fall mainly into two groups: the *β -phenethylamines*, to which mescaline belongs, and a larger assortment of *tetrahydroisoquinolines*. Both kinds differ from LSD and most other compounds regarded as psychedelics in that they don't have a full indole structure.

Most of the alkaloids found in peyote have never been tried on humans in pure form. Only four of these besides mescaline have been described sub-jectively. Much of this work was done by Arthur Heffter, who identified mescaline back in 1897. In 1977, Alexander Shulgin summarized the human tests at a conference in San Francisco:

Anhalonodine leads to sedation at levels of 100-250 mg. in man—a slightly quieted state, but absolutely no central [nervous system] effects of any type whatsoever.

Pellotine has actually been the most explored, and has actually been intro-duced as a drug—in Germany in the 1920s, as a possible sedative. And, indeed, in 15-30 mg. doses in man taken orally, there is a sedation, a quieting. At levels of 50 mg. subcutaneously, a person is led very gently into a quiet sleep, with no after-effects and no hangover. It appears to be a very effective sedative. Heffter ran it up to 240 mg.—at which point, he achieved a state of dizziness, a state of gastric upset, but apparently nothing beyond sedation as being some direct effect upon consciousness.

The third compound, *anhalonine*, is one of the methylene-dioxy groups that has been evaluated. It has been evaluated at 100 mg., with no central effects whatsoever.

The fourth compound—the most toxic—is *lophopherine*, which is extremely toxic to cold-blooded animals, and was approached very cautiously by Heffter in his evaluations. At 20 mg., he had quite a radical vaso-dilation and an immediate headache. He pursued it religiously up to 50 mg.—at which there was quite a drop in heart rate and a compensatory increase in blood pressure, but no mescaline-like central effects whatsoever, no visual effects and no inter-pretative effects akin to mescaline.

Shulgin's conclusion, after three decades of interest in the chemistry of peyote, is that "the tetrahydroisoquinolines have to be more or less discarded as being major contributors" to this cactus' ability to affect mental states. He

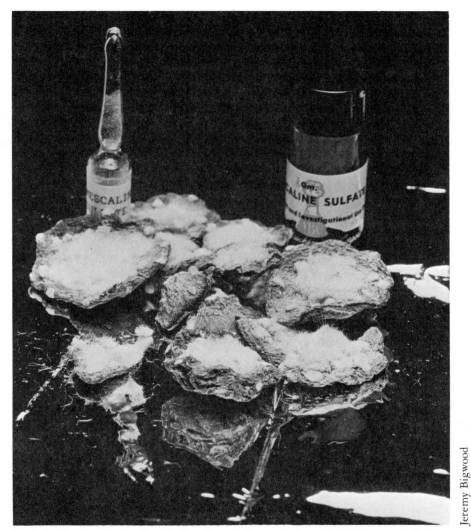

Jeremy Bigwood

Dried peyote buttons beside bottles of the major synthetic form of their psychoactive compound.

feels that these compounds may have secondary effects and may augment or interact with mescaline. "But for a first approximation, mescaline itself has to be considered as the principle component of the peyote that is active."

Escaline, Proscaline and Similar Synthetic Compounds
The mescaline molecule is the simplest of the β-phenethylamines. Hundreds, if not thousands, of similar compounds have been synthesized in

laboratories. These compounds bear a chemical structure that resembles ephedrine, which in the 1920s was "the primary reference standard" for stimulatory action in the central nervous system.

Gordon Alles, a pharmacologist associated with the Medical School of the University of California in Los Angeles and the initial sponsor of Edward Anderson's peyote studies, was very interested in this area of chemistry and eventually synthesized a number of psychoactive compounds that have chemical structures similar to that of mescaline. The best known of these are amphetamine and MDA. His discoveries inspired further investigations that led to the creation of quite a number of "one-ring" substituted phenyl-isopropylamines, which look much like mescaline on the molecular level but so far rarely have been found in the natural world. Many of these compounds will be discussed in Chapter Five.

Five compounds are identical to mescaline except for modification at one point on the molecule's ring, but these are expensive to make and so far have been experienced by only a few people.

Mescaline
($C_{11}H_{17}O_3N$, or β -3,4,5-trimethoxyphenethylamine)

Escaline   *Proscaline*

Escaline and proscaline are the best known of these analogues and differ from mescaline only in that the methyl group in the 4-position on the ring has been replaced by an ethyl or by a propyl group. Both compounds, in Shulgin's words, "appear to be qualitatively indistinguishable from mescaline in their action." There are two main differences: these "substituted" compounds cause less nausea than mescaline and are active in dosages of 40-80 mg., and thus exhibit about a five-fold increase in potency.

Also synthesized are 2-6-dichloral-TMPEA (trimethoxy- β -phen-ethylamine) and 2-chloral-TMPEA—these are the 2,6-dichloral and 2-chloral analogues of mescaline—and 4-thiomescaline, a compound in which a sulfur atom replaces oxygen in the 4-position. The last has been found to affect the central nervous system. In the *Journal of Psychedelic Drugs* for January-June

1979, Shulgin discusses escaline and proscaline, and makes this important note on the sulfurated variant:

> It is active in humans at 10-25 mg so it represents a 12-fold increase in potency over mescaline. Of all the compounds mentioned in this review, it comes most closely to being what should properly be called a psychotomimetic. It produces a very intense and disorganized psychotic state that has some aspects of visual distortion but primarily disrupts the mental integrity.

PHYSICAL EFFECTS

Taste and Nausea

Peyote has a bitter taste and causes many users to feel nauseous. Referring to ingestion, Indians have often said that peyote is "a hard road." San Pedro has a similar taste, but among those who have tried both cacti it is generally considered easier to swallow and keep down. Crystals of mescaline, while lacking the acrid taste, may also cause nausea in a substantial number of people. Discussing this aspect of the mescaline experience, Robert DeRopp has commented that use of peyote "is about as unpromising a passport to an artificial paradise as can be imagined."

For some people, the nausea is an insurmountable barrier. William James had perhaps the most extreme reaction on record: eating just one button, which wouldn't be enough to prompt mental activity, caused him to be "violently sick" for twenty-four hours.

Nausea and gagging occur sufficiently often in Native American Church practices that there is usually an official, aside from those already described, who is designated as the "shovel man." He is prepared with a tin can to deal with any such difficulties.

Many of the Huichols and North American peyotists claim that when one eats peyote, one is "tasting oneself": if the user is pure, this cactus is "sweet." Barbara Myerhoff, accompanying the Huichols during their 1965 and 1966 hunts, recorded that they urge new participants to "Chew it well. It is sweet, like tortillas." No one vomited, but no one savored it either:

> Huichols eating it look like anyone else with a mouthful of peyote: they grimace, sucking in their cheeks and moving their eyebrows up and down in a most characteristic manner—a reaction to the shockingly sour taste of the cactus.

The Indians generally fast before using peyote to diminish the potential for nausea; consumption of food and especially alcohol prior to peyote ingestion greatly increases the chances of vomiting. Sometimes the gag reflex is triggered purposely, as when they are trying a cure.

The Indians are interested in the mental and healing effects brought about by peyote, so they consider the initial problem of taste and nausea as inconsequential. Certainly, it is much less trying to the physical organism than other traditional methods used to achieve "visions" of the Great Spirit. Though peyote may be a shock to the stomach, its brief stress hardly compares with going out into the wilderness alone for a fortnight, carrying along just moccasins and a loin cloth, much less with some of the other ordeals endured to raise altered states of consciousness—one extreme example being that of swinging by ropes inserted around muscles in the chest.

It's interesting that some of those who wrote about their use of peyote during the 1950s and 1960s were able to reconcile themselves to peyote's gagging effect as basically compensatory. Beringer earlier had described this experience as one in which the user gets the hangover first, then the inebriation. More than a few people believe at some level that they may not have a profound or even enjoyable experience without having to pay for it.

A surprising effect noticed among many who have gagged after ingesting peyote is that this frequently results in their getting enormously "high." Even when it seemed that nothing could have been kept down, results can be profound. After nausea has conferred a certain seriousness on the experience, there is probably some psychological release felt at the point of vomiting that propels these people immediately into a psychedelicized state.

A myth that purports to explain the bitterness and nausea associated with the psychedelic cacti has gained some currency. Some people believe that the tufts and center of the peyote button contain strychnine; others have made the same assumption about the core of the San Pedro. Strychnine is absent in both cases.

The tufts in peyote are inert, and in at least one experiment a whole handful of this hairy material was ingested without producing any effect. The Huichols always eat these "eyebrows of the peyote." Some people prefer to remove this non-psychoactive section, but it is a personal preference, like not eating the inner "choke" of an artichoke. As to the San Pedro core, the Indians of the Andes slice up and then boil the entire cactus when they are preparing their psychoactive concoction.

One might well ask: "If there is nausea and vomiting, then doesn't it mean the plant must be toxic?" Masters and Houston answer in their *The Varieties of Psychedelic Experience* that "although toxic elements are present, the margin of safety is very great and serious poisoning is virtually unheard of."

Coursing through the Body

Following the consumption of mescaline or peyote, there's often a slight increase in pulse rate and blood pressure accompanied by sweating, salivation and possibly a small rise in body temperature. The most prominent visible alteration is dilation of the pupils. As with amphetamine and LSD, mescaline may later leave the user feeling ravenous. Like pot, it frequently also brings on a desire for sweets.

Peyote and mescaline are often thought to be spectacular mental drugs because they produce visual and other cerebral sensations. Curiously, little more than about 2 percent of ingested mescaline ever penetrates the blood-brain barrier. When mescaline was tagged with radioactive molecules of carbon, investigators were surprised to observe that nearly all of it went to the liver. From there it goes to the kidneys and is expelled within six to eight hours.

Because mescaline lodges for the most part in the liver, some concern has been expressed about its use by those with liver ailments. It is worth noting that during the 1950s and 1960s this drug was given to a number of alcoholic mental patients, many of whom had severely diseased livers, with little untoward effect.

Medical and Health Aspects

There is a long list of ailments that this psychedelic is said to be useful in treating. Indians have employed it for everything from dandruff to wounds to cancer, including TB, VD, diabetes, flu, cramps, pneumonia, rheumatism and toothache Even among Indians opposed to using it in religious rites, there's great respect for its medical efficacy.

Indians use peyote as much for the maintenance of good health as for religious worship. Frank Takes Gun, often referred to as the national president of the Native American Church, comments:

> At fourteen, I first used Father *Peyote*. This was on the Crow Reservation in Montana, and I was proud to know that my people had a medicine that was God-poweful. Listen to me, *peyote* does have many amazing powers. I have seen a blind boy regain his sight from taking it. Indians with ailments that hospital doctors couldn't cure have become healthy again after a *peyote* prayer meeting. Once a Crow boy was to have his infected leg cut off by reservation doctors. After a *peyote* ceremony, it grew well again.

Western notions of physiology and healing tempt us to dismiss such reports as nothing more than exuberant "witch doctor talk." However, it is a matter of record that these economically deprived people generally enjoy better-than-average health, and reliable observers have confirmed that when they do become sick and turn to peyote, the cactus seems to help them. Louise Spindler, an anthropologist who studied the Menomini tribe, was among the earliest to notice these effects, describing how women peyotists often kept a can of ground peyote for brewing tea, used in "an informal fashion for such things as childbirth, earaches, or for inspiration for beadwork patterns." Edward Anderson points out that in some Indian languages the word for peyote is the same as for medicine—*azee* (Navajo), *büsing* (Delaware), *puakit* (Comanche), *makan* (Omaha), *o-jay-bee-kee* (Shawnee), *walena* (Taos) and *naw-tai-no kee* (Kickapoo). R.E. Schultes has commented that peyote use for medicinal purposes is so well known that it was made into a verb by rural Mexicans: *empeyotizarse* means to self-medicate.

Dr. T.T. Peck of the San Jacinto Memorial Hospital in Baytown, Texas, made similar observations. He first became interested in LSD as a result of having seen the effects of peyote:

When I went into general practice as a country doctor in Texas, I was very impressed that some of our Latin American patients, despite their poverty and living conditions, were extremely healthy. One day, I asked one of my patients how he stayed so healthy, and he told me that he chewed peyote buttons ... then I became interested in these drugs that could promise physical as well as mental health.

In the late nineteenth century, American medical professionals became aware of peyote's health benefits after observing its effects among Indians. Once he became familiar with use of the cactus in treating illnesses, James Mooney recommended it to Dr. D.W. Prentiss and Dr. Francis P. Morgan, the latter a noted pharmacologist, and they decided to undertake tests with the peyote buttons Mooney supplied.

Their subjects were suffering from a variety of physical complaints—chronic bronchitis with asthmatic attacks; neurasthenia; nervous prostration; chronic phthisis with facial neuralgia and catarrh; persistent cough; and even "softening of the brain." A report by Prentiss and Morgan appeared in the August 22, 1896 *Medical Record*, proclaiming that the "effect of the drug was little less than marvelous" in one case; they sang the praises of peyote with almost equal gusto in others. They recommended it for use as an antispasmodic and for treatment of general "nervousness," insomnia and color-blindness. One example:

> Gentleman, aged fifty-five years. Chronic bronchitis with asthmatic attacks. Much distressed by an irritative cough which kept him from sleeping.... In a letter received from him recently he states that he has improved very much, being able to sleep all night without rising, which he has not been able to do for two years; and that, although he has no need of it upon some days, he carries a piece of a button in his pocket constantly, as its use relieves the tickling in his throat at once and gives better relief than any other remedy which he has ever tried.

Westerners tend to maintain a distinction between peyote as a vision-producer and peyote as a medicine. Among Indians, these qualities are regarded as being much the same: peyote is thought to put them in contact with the spirit world from which illness is derived. From their point of view, Western medicine is based on human intervention. Peyote visions, being a kind of divine intervention, are thus more powerful and provide a surer means by which to learn how to cure ailments.

One would think that by now questions about the medicinal efficacy of peyote and mescaline would be settled, but so far there haven't been good controlled studies of comprehensive scope. One constituent in peyote—peyocactin, which is also called hordonine—has been shown by James McCleary and his colleagues at California State University, Fullerton, to be an antibiotic active against a wide spectrum of bacteria, having an inhibitory action against at least eighteen strains of penicillin-resistant *Staphylococcus aureus.* This antibacterial characteristic may account in part for its healing effects when applied to wounds.

Another area that should be probed further is peyote's effect upon eyesight. The peyote literature includes many reports of restoration of vision, to which I might add my own report: having worn glasses since the age of three because of astigmatism and near-sightedness, I gave them up after taking a fair amount of peyote. In the absence of clinical data, all we have to go by is a large amount of individual testimony. Much of this is of a remarkable sort.

MENTAL EFFECTS
Similarities and Differences with LSD

LSD and mescaline cause dramatic changes in the web-spinning activities of spiders. Moreover, we can easily distinguish between the two substances by observing the webs constructed under the influence of one or the other psychedelic. The web is more regular or "perfect" under LSD and more abstract and irregular under mescaline. This difference is especially interesting because most "blind" studies of mental effects have shown that human volunteers are unable to differentiate between these two compounds.

In much of the writing about psychedelics, little effort has been made to clarify the differences between LSD and mescaline effects. In *The Varieties of Psychedelic Experience*, for example, Masters and Houston specify the agent ingested by their 206 subjects (of whom 89 received mescaline) but then seem to take it for granted that stages and characteristics of mescaline experience will be the same as those under LSD. They noted no great differences between the effects of LSD and mescaline in the creativity studies cited in Chapter One. Aldous Huxley, writing to Humphry Osmond in December of 1955 about his first experience with LSD (75 mcg.), emphasized the resemblances (and re-emphasized them later after more experiences with LSD):

> The psychological effects, in my case, were identical with those of mescaline, and I had the same kind of experience as I had on the previous occasion— transformation of the external world, and the understanding through a realization involving the whole man, that Love is the One .... I had no visions with my eyes shut—even less than I had on the first occasion with mescaline, when the moving geometries were highly organized and, at moments, very beautiful and significant (though at others, very trivial) .... Evidently, if you are not a congenital or habitual visualizer, you do not get internal visions under mescaline or LSD—only external transfiguration ....

Some people more experienced with both psychedelics have reported noteworthy differences in their responses to LSD and mescaline. They generally indicate that peyote and mescaline are "warmer" and "more earthy" than LSD, which is usually seen as being more "cerebral." The mescaline present in the cactus appears to increase considerably a feeling of fellowship

Die Wirkung von Substanzen auf den Netzbau der Spinne als biologischer Test (Peter Witt, Berlin, 1956)

Normal net of Zilla-x-notata Cl. Nets made by this spider after consuming drug-dosed flies appear opposite.

that is only sometimes prompted by LSD. Shulgin remarks that under mescaline "There is a benign empathy shown to both inanimate and living things, especially to small things." Allen Ginsberg and others have suggested that mescaline—more than other psychedelics—produces a state of mind very receptive to the complex of benevolent attitudes expressed in Wordsworth's nature poems.

There haven't yet been any studies comparing effects from mescaline with those from peyote. The Church of the Awakening used both fairly extensively and characterized mescaline effects as "identical with those we had obtained through the use of peyote itself" (in John Aiken's words).

There are many reports about the effects of peyote and mescaline coming from people who have used these substances in remarkably different ways and in a multitude of settings: from use in experimental laboratories to

Typical hashish-inspired net.

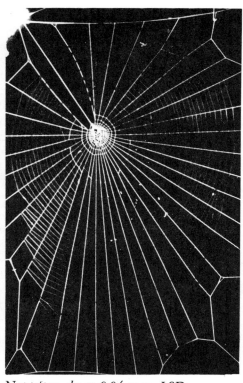

Net after about 0.04 mcg. LSD.

Net after a high caffeine dose.

Net after mescaline sulfate dose.

recreational use to use as part of a meditative regimen. These reports emphasize a variety of major effects, which will be illustrated under the following
categories: sacramental aspects, visual effects, auditory effects, dimensions
outside time and space, creative potential, psychological safety and psychotherapeutic potential. Several may occur within a single experience. In his
studies, Beringer found that he was unable to predict what would come up in
any particular mescaline session, even if he knew the experiencer well. Prem
Das, writing in *Art of the Huichol Indians*, agrees that the "spirits" in peyote
don't do "what one expects."

Dosage and Timing

Some prefatory comments about dosage and timing are in order. Generally speaking, three fairly large peyote buttons—each perhaps 1½" across—
are required to achieve any marked effect upon feelings, intellect and cognition.
Peyotists in the Native American Church often take thirty to forty over a
single night. (James Mooney recorded having heard of someone who took
ninety!)

The Huichols often use one to four buttons for lesser effects, inhibiting
"hunger, thirst, fatigue, and sexual desire" (according to Kal Muller, who
lived for two years among these Indians). During their annual pilgrimage,
peyote hunters consume many more, which are further potentiated by fasting
and sleeplessness to produce "visions" and "communication with deities."
Hoffer and Osmond assess an average peyote button as containing less than
25 mg. of mescaline.

Early studies of mescaline, detailed in Kluver's book, generally involved
doses of a fifth to a half of a gram. Shulgin puts the average dosage used in
experimental investigations at between "300 and 500 mg of the sulfate salt,
which is equivalent to 225-375 mg of the hydrochloride."

When mescaline or peyote is swallowed, mental changes usually begin
to occur within an hour; injection of mescaline brings them on more quickly.
Sometimes, however, the effects don't come on until the passing of another
hour, and sometimes not until after another two or three hours. Over this
interval, most of the physically distressing effects disappear, and the user
then is in good humor and "at languid ease" (as Weir Mitchell expressed the
transition).

Over the next two to four hours, the experience flows to a peak and
then descends over another four to six hours, if the mescaline was taken all at
once. The sedative, possibly jaw-tightening effects from lophophorine and
other alkaloids wear off fairly quickly. If peyote is taken over an entire night,
as is usual among many Indians, the state of being "high" is extended, of
course, as are some anesthetic effects (so that one can sit for twelve to fourteen
hours without feeling much pain).

Sacramental Aspects

Peyote and mescaline are "psychedelic," which for many users connotes
an experience that is "mystical," "sacred" or "blissful" (even if there are diffi-

culties along the way). The psychedelic state of mind can range from the philosophical to the personal and usually includes a lucid recognition to the effect that "I have seen so many things in myself that need changing." The mescaline experience almost always permits excellent recall of such perceptions, and Indians have said that peyote has brought about a better life for many of its users.

Louis Lewin went to the heart of this matter when he sorted through the many extraordinary aspects of the mescaline experience and declared the most important one to be "modifications of the spiritual life which are peculiar in that they are felt as gladness of soul." Huxley called it "without question the most extraordinary and significant experience this side of the Beatific Vision":

> Words like Grace and Transfiguration came to my mind, and this of course was what, among other things, they stood for .... The Beatific Vision, *Sat Chit Ananda*, Being-Awareness-Bliss—for the first time I understood, not on the verbal level, not by inchoate hints or at a distance, but precisely and completely what those prodigious syllables referred to.

Among Tahamaris, Huichols and Native American peyotists, the cactus is valued as a medium for revelations from deities or their representatives or from peyote itself. Most Huichol children are brought up in an environment of reverence for peyote; its centrality in their culture is illustrated by the fact that nursing mothers are especially encouraged to take peyote. About two-thirds of Huichol young men are peyotists, taking the cactus on many occasions during the year and making extensive preparations for their "sacred hunt." To fill in the details of how fully peyote use organizes Huichol culture, the Fine Arts Museums of San Francisco's book *Art of the Huichol Indians* observes that the cactus "is used for controlling the rain, for curing, for blessing the people, for locating the deer and planning the sacred deer hunts, in the election of Huichol governing officials, and in many other ways." Of all accounts of peyote's effects among North American Indians, the most sympathetic possibly comes from Humphry Osmond, who joined in the ceremonies of a peyote group in North Battlefield, Saskatoon, Canada (reprinted in his *Psychedelics*).

In the early 1950s, J.S. Slotkin was invited by Native American Church leaders to live among them in order to report on their peyote practices. He observed many peyotists who had "religious" experiences—intimations of God taking care of them and visions of the "Great Spirit." Jesus appeared before one woman and comforted her after the death of her son. Slotkin mentions a couple of instances involving Indians who were atheists until taking peyote. John Aiken cites a similar response.

Arnold Mandell, the founding chairman of the Psychiatry Department at the University of California at San Diego, noted that despite much emphasis on the "visuals" aroused by peyote, both Weir Mitchell and Havelock Ellis had metaphysical experiences under its influence. Ellis described a "detached yet acutely aware brain state" and characterized his experience in terms of the "majesty of its impersonal nature." Mitchell told the American Neurological Society in 1896 that peyote use revealed "a certain sense of the things about me as having a more positive existence than usual."

From people most sensitive to religious matters come still more impressive reports. John Blofeld, who was especially interested in Buddhism, had great doubts about Huxley's claim that mescaline could induce yogic experiences of a high order (see Ralph Metzner's *The Ecstatic Adventure*). After taking a quarter of a gram of mescaline, he began to contemplate the patterns that embellish sacred buildings, and "for the first time, I saw them as not arbitrary decorations but profoundly meaningful." His first mescaline experience wasn't painless: it started with a sense of "appalling mental torture." Eventually Blofeld made a "total surrender" and "ceased to cling ... to self, loved ones, sanity, madness, life or death." The experience was transforming:

> From hellish torment, I was plunged into ecstasy—an ecstasy infinitely exceeding anything describable or anything I had imagined from what the world's accomplished mystics have struggled to describe. Suddenly there dawned full awareness of three great truths which I had long accepted intellectually but never, until that moment, experienced as being fully self-evident.

These were: (1) an awareness of undifferentiated unity, (2) an awareness of unutterable bliss ("so intense as to make it seem likely that body and mind would be burnt up in a flash") and (3) an awareness "of all that is implied by the Buddhist doctrine of 'dharmas,' namely, that all things, whether objects of mental or of sensory perception, are alike devoid of own-being, mere transitory combinations of an infinite number of impulses." Blofeld comments that these "impulses" are analogous to electrical charges, and "This was as fully apparent as are the individual bricks to someone staring at an unplastered wall. I actually experienced the momentary rising of each impulse and the thrill of culmination with which it immediately ceased to be."

This kind of report is fairly typical among people coming to mescaline from a background of religious study. Houston Smith commented that when he took mescaline he felt as if some five layers of consciousness were perceptible ("I was to some degree aware of them all simultaneously"). He wrote that

> the emanation theory and elaborately delineated layers of Indian cosmology and psychology had hitherto been concepts and inferences. Now they were objects of direct, immediate perception ....
>
> It should not be taken from what I have written that the experience was pleasurable. The accurate words are significance and terror—or awe, in Rudolf Otto's understanding of a peculiar blend of fear and fascination.

Visual Effects

Heinrich Klüver said of the "mescal" experience that the visual effects were its primary aspect, and he attempted to describe them using a limited number of "form-constants." For instance, *grating, lattice, fretwork, filigree, honeycomb or chessboard designs* represented one form-constant. Closely related were *cobweb figures.* Klüver also noted *spirals,* and images "designated by terms such as *tunnel, funnel, alley, cone* or *vessel.*"

This schematization of images seems to be only a crude description of the visual experience apparent from most mescaline reports. One of Beringer's subjects, a physician, saw "fretwork" constantly but also felt himself become part of it. Hoffer and Osmond comment that one of their subjects had similar crystalline perceptions: "He saw a square screen or lattice before him. . . . At each node on the screen there was a nude girl dancing in time to the music."

Klüver classified other visual aspects of the mescaline experience, notably *increase of dimensionality* (often involving perception of a shift from two to three dimensions), *increase of vividness* and *variation in perception of size.* Zaehner presents an illustration of increased dimensionality: when he looked at pictures in books, the "things depicted seemed to be trying to escape from the material in which they were depicted." Illustrating the increase in vividness, Ellis said that as he ate a piece of biscuit

> it suddenly streamed out into blue flame. For an instant I held the biscuit close to my leg. Immediately my trousers caught alight, and then the whole of the right side of my body, from the foot to the shoulder, was enveloped in waving blue flame. It was a sight of wonderful beauty. But this was not all. As I placed the biscuit in my mouth it burst out again into the same colored fire and illuminated the interior of my mouth, casting a blue reflection on the roof. The light in the Blue Grotto at Capri, I am able to affirm, is not nearly as blue as seemed for a short space of time the interior of my mouth.

An example of changes in size occurred during Osmond's first experience with mescaline:

> At one moment I would be a giant in a tiny cupboard, and the next, a dwarf in a huge hall. It is difficult enough to explain what it feels like to have been Gulliver, or Alice in Wonderland, in the space of a few minutes, but it is nearly impossible to communicate an experience which amounts to having been uncertain whether one was in Brobdingnag or Lilliput.

Indians have been fairly reticent to outsiders about describing their peyote visions, perhaps regarding them as private. Many apparently consider the visual effects to be of minor importance, although Slotkin's *The Peyote Religion* (excerpted in Ebin's *The Drug Experience*) frequently mentions visions of Christ, the Great Spirit or a personal totem.

Kal Muller, in *Art of the Huichol Indians,* describes an impressive instance of "visuals" from a peyote pilgrimage undertaken by an Indian seeking to determine if he should become a shaman:

> The father of a Huichol friend of mine, a middle-aged shaman, told me that he had gone to Wirikuta as a young man and had eaten thirty-five peyote buttons at one sitting. Two unknown old men appeared at his side, just like the assistants of the *tsauririka.* One told him to look into the fire, where he saw a typewriter, writing by itself. The other told him to pull the sheets out of the typewriter and read what was on them. He did, even though he cannot read. The

sheets kept coming out of the typewriter all night, and he kept "reading" and chanting what he saw. The next day the other pilgrims told him that during the whole night he had performed as a *tsauririka*, singing in a complicated ritual, and that surely the gods wanted him to become a shaman.

The earliest reports among whites were by skilled literary men—Weir Mitchell and Havelock Ellis. Writing toward the end of the nineteenth century, both emphasized the visual qualities of peyote:

> *Mitchell:* The display which for an enchanted two hours followed was such as I find it hopeless to describe in language which shall convey to others the beauty and splendor of what I saw. Stars, delicate floating films of color, then an abrupt rush of countless points of white light swept across the field of view, as if the unseen millions of the Milky Way were to flow in a sparkling river before my eyes . . . zigzag lines of very bright colors . . . the wonderful loveliness of swelling clouds of more vivid colors gone before I could name them . . . . All the colors I have ever beheld are dull in comparison to these . . . .

> *Ellis:* At first there was merely a vague play of light and shade which suggested pictures, but never made them. Then the pictures became more definite, but too confused and crowded to be described, beyond saying that they were of the same character as the images of the kaleidoscope, symmetrical groupings of spiked objects. Then in the course of the evening, they became distinct, but still indescribable—mostly a vast field of golden jewels, studded with red and green stones, ever changing . . . . The visions never resembled familiar objects; they were extremely definite, but yet always novel; they were constantly approaching, and yet constantly eluding, the semblance of known things. I would see thick, glorious fields of jewels, solitary or clustered, sometimes brilliant and sparkling, sometimes with a dull rich glow. Then they would spring up into flower-like shapes beneath my gaze, and then seem to turn into gorgeous butterfly forms or endless folds of glistening, iridescent, fibrous wings of wonderful insects . . . .

Havelock Ellis gave a small amount of his peyote to the poet William Butler Yeats, who wrote back to Ellis about the impressive "visuals":

> I have never seen a succession of absolutely pictorial visions with such precision and such unaccountability. It seemed as if a series of dissolving views were carried swiftly before me, all going from right to left, none corresponding with any seen reality. For instance, I saw the most delightful dragons, puffing out their breath straight in front of them like rigid lines of steam, and balancing white balls at the end of their breath! When I tried to fix my mind on real things, I could generally call them up, but always with some inexplicable change. . . . in the evening I went out on the Embankment and was absolutely fascinated by an advertisement of "Bovrin," which went and came in letters of light on the other side of the river. I can not tell you the intense pleasure this moving light gave me and how dazzling it seemed to me.

Several investigators have since argued that the early emphasis on peyote's aesthetic appeal probably slowed scientific study. It may well be, as Lewin felt, that visuals are not the most important part of the experience.

Nonetheless, heightened color and luminescence are transformations in consciousness experienced by most users and must to some extent be acknowledged as hallmarks of this chemical.

Colors appearing most commonly in Indian experiences are said to be yellow, blue, green and red, inspired perhaps by the colors in fire and on the tepee or hogan walls. In the experiments carried out by Ellis and others, the color emphasis was on blue or violet, though Heinrich Klüver found no color to be excluded.

Writing about colors and visions seen under a psychedelic, Huxley addressed himself to the central questions. Once blinded, and thus especially appreciative, he reported that visual transformations can have resonance on other levels. He had expected to enter into "the kind of inner world described by Blake and A.E. [George William Russell]." That wasn't what happened:

> The change which actually took place in that world was in no sense revolutionary . . . at no time were there faces or forms of men or animals. I saw no enormous spaces, no magical growth and metamorphosis of buildings, nothing remotely like a drama or a parable.

But,

> I was not looking now at an unusual flower arrangement. I was seeing what Adam had seen on the morning of his creation—the miracle, moment by moment, of naked existence . . . .

> The books, for example, with which my study walls were lined. Like the flowers, they glowed, when I looked at them, with brighter colors, a profounder significance. Red books, like rubies; emerald books; books bound in white jade; books of agate; of aquamarine, of yellow topaz; lapis lazuli books whose color was so intense, so intrinsically meaningful, that they seemed to be on the point of leaving the shelves to thrust themselves more insistently on my attention . . . .

> A rose is a rose is a rose. But these chair legs were chair legs were St. Michael and all angels . . . . Confronted by a chair which looked like the Last Judgment—or, to be more accurate, by a Last Judgment which, after a long time and with considerable difficulty, I recognized as a chair—I found myself all at once on the brink of panic. This, I suddenly felt, was going too far. Too far, even though the going was into intenser beauty, deeper significance . . . .

Huxley brought to bear a great deal of erudition in art, philosophy, mysticism, history and psychology. There is probably no better discussion of color transformation and the psychedelics' ability to transport the user to what Huxley called "the Other World" than in the book he published in 1955 entitled *Heaven and Hell*.

Auditory Effects

As mentioned at the beginning of this chapter, Indian myths concerning the discovery of peyote generally involve *a voice*. A prominent auditory component also distinguishes peyote and mescaline from other psychedelics.

Don Juan, the Yaqui shaman-teacher in the books by Carlos Castaneda, described *Datura* and mushrooms as *powers* or *allies*, as opposed to peyote, which he described as a *teacher*. Indians have generally been quite clear in maintaining that peyote provides them with their songs. Peyotists often "hear" where they should look for this cactus. Some Indians even complain that they can't sleep near peyote because there was so much noise at night!

Peyote seems to bring on synesthesia, a mixing and reciprocal action among the five senses, so that the drumbeat maintained throughout the ceremony evokes pictures in the head as it heightens aural sensations (see Osmond's description of drumming and his reaction in *Psychedelics*).

Discrimination of tones under the influence of mescaline can become acute. To quote Lewin and a physician to whom he gave mescaline, music was sensed as "sweet and harmonious" and as coming "from infinity, the music of the spheres." When Slotkin first took peyote, he was greatly impressed with his altered auditory responses:

> It was about an hour before I began to notice any sensory effects. The drumming remained constant to me, but the singing wavered from high to low pitch in a way that no singer could ever do. Then the song seemed to come from all over the tipi, rather than just from the singer, and for a while it seemed to come from the top of the tipi. If I closed my eyes, I had no idea of where the music was coming from—even when the singer was the man next to me.

At a later meeting, Slotkin noted that under peyote's influence he could hear whispers from some distance away.

Memoirs of the American Museum of Natural History (Lumholtz, 1900)

Early Huichol representation of the face painted for "mother of corn" during peyote festivals.

Another face painting often seen in such ceremonies, this one for "grandfather of fire."

Dimensions Outside Time and Space

As with other psychedelics, "out-of-body" experiences occur in many peyote and mescaline trips. Users have often felt weightless and had a sense of "flying." More than a few have reported seeing their body become "luminescent" or "transparent" as they looked on from some distance away. One of Ellis' subjects felt a blue flame wafting from the back of his head, then found himself becoming transparent like a Chinese lantern.

Out-of-body experiences associated with the San Pedro cactus are discussed in Douglas Sharon's *Wizard of the Four Winds*—the story of Eduardo Palomino, a Peruvian sculptor, teacher, fisherman and shaman. Asked about the cactus' effects, Eduardo told Sharon that first there is

> a slight dizziness that one hardly notices. And then a great "vision," a clearing of all the faculties of the individual. It produces a light numbness in the body and afterward a tranquility. And then comes a detachment, a type of visual force in the individual inclusive of all the senses: seeing, hearing, smelling, touching, et cetera—all the senses, including the sixth sense, the telepathic sense of transmitting oneself across time and matter . . . . It develops the power of perception . . . in the sense that when one wants to see something far away . . . he can distinguish powers or problems or disturbances at great distance, so as to deal with them . . . . Then the individual, sometimes by himself, can visualize his past or . . . the present, or an immediate future.
>
> By means of the magical plants, and the chants and the search for the roots of the problem, the subconscious of the individual is opened up like a flower, and it releases these blockages. All by itself it tells things.

Sharon spent four years with Eduardo, eventually becoming his apprentice and helping in nine curing sessions. At first he had been skeptical about Eduardo's claim that he could see events and people at a great distance. Eduardo tried to explain:

> The flight is spiritual . . . . One invokes, and his spirit soars to those haunts. One asks for the lagoon, invokes, and then the spirit makes the trip. The journey of the spirit also causes one to visualize the lagoon in . . . an almost objective manner . . . . Spiritually one is there and one sees it up close.
>
> *Q: Does your being actually arrive there?*
>
> My material being, no. My spiritual being arrives, yes; and I perceive in an objective fashion, as if I were in the place.

As for changes in time perception, consider an extreme example, the experience of Christopher Mayhew, a Member of Parliament during the 1950s who offered to take mescaline under the supervision of Humphry Osmond and before BBC cameras—surely one of the best-documented trips ever.

Although many people under the influence of psychedelics have seen "trails"—the simultaneous perception of several discrete moments, like the arc of a lighted cigarette in a dark room—Mayhew experienced this phenomenon to an unusual degree. For the *London Observer* he described his experience as an "Excursion Out of Time":

What happened to me between 12:30 and 4 o'clock on Friday, December 2, 1955? After brooding about it for several months, I still think my first, astonishing conviction was right—that on many occasions that afternoon I existed *outside time.*

I don't mean this metaphorically, but literally. I mean that the essential part of me . . . had an existence, quite conscious of itself . . . in a timeless order of reality outside the world as we know it.

Mayhew's experience began with color hallucinations but soon led to a preoccupation with the very strange "behavior" of time. Time kept slipping out of sequence—he would see a cup at his lips before he actually removed it from the table—and he couldn't tell how far along he was in the experience. Even his watch did not help. Although his eyes registered various clock times, the hours were not in proper sequence, and he would see two-thirty after he had seen three o'clock. Finally, it was the arrival of a tea-tray that enabled him to judge that the duration of the drug would soon be coming to an end.

Time worked even more extravagant magic when it sent him into another dimension, where "I would be aware of a pervasive bright pure light, like a kind of invisible sunlit snow":

I would become unaware of my surroundings, and enjoy an existence conscious of myself, in a state of breathless wonderment and complete bliss, for a period of time which—for me—simply did not end at all. It did not last for minutes or hours, but apparently for years. .

For several days afterward, I remembered the afternoon of December 2 not as so many hours spent in my drawing-room interrupted by these strange "excursions," but as countless years of complete bliss interrupted by short spells in the drawing-room . . . .

On the first occasion when I "came back" in this way from an excursion I assumed that a vast period of time had elapsed and exclaimed, in astonishment, to the film team: "Are you still there?" Their patience in waiting seemed extraordinary; but in fact, of course, no time had elapsed, and they had not been waiting at all . . . .

These "time phenomena," contrary to everyday consciousness, seemed totally convincing—not hallucinations but another part of reality. Mayhew is definite on this:

The common-sense explanation is that since events in our drawing-room actually happened in a normal sequence (with plenty of witnesses, including the camera, to prove it), I just *couldn't* have experienced them in some other order, so I must have merely *thought* I did—I was deluded.

For anyone else than myself, this must be easy to believe; but for me, it is impossible. I am not—I repeat—saying that events *happened* in the wrong order, only that I *experienced* them in the wrong order. And on this point I cannot doubt my own judgment.

Creative Potential

Ellis thought that peyote would never appeal to most people because it was so predominantly an intellectual experience, promoting what he called a "detached but acute brain state." Lewin called it "purely intellectual" and noted many instances of "disorders of location." These observations are fascinating in themselves, but we should note that many users have been able to direct the peyote or mescaline experience into creative channels.

Arnold Mandell, speaking of the "unapologetic belief in symbols" among Huichols, suggests that peyote enables them to be restored to a state of naiveté—often a prerequisite for creativity. *Art of the Huichol Indians* amply illustrates how visions seen during peyote ceremonies find expression in tribal art forms. Alice Marriott and Carol Rachlin devote a chapter of their small book *Peyote* to Native American artists working with paint, metal and beads, especially Carol Sweezy of the Arapaho and Ernest Spybuck of the Shawnee:

> Most of the leading Indian easel artists and metal craftsmen of the twentieth century are or were (for some are dead now) peyotists. Monroe Tsatokee's "Fire Bird," reproduced again and again in books on Indian art, is probably the best-known modern Indian painting in existence.

The optimal condition for prompting creativity is to have a defined problem in mind that is stated in familiar terms—at least this was the assumption made at the Institute for Advanced Studies in Menlo Park, where qualifying volunteers were given mescaline. The results were that many of the subjects were able to solve artistic and technical problems after a single session.

The case of architect Eric Clough is illustrative: he needed a design for an arts and crafts shopping center in a resort-university community. In Metzner's *The Ecstatic Adventure*, Clough describes receiving the mescaline in the morning and then, blindfolded, traveling in his mind through jungle terrain and scenes from pre-Columbian civilizations. About an hour after a small lunch, Clough was asked to concentrate on his design problem:

> I looked at the paper I was to draw on. I was completely blank. I knew that I would work with a property 300′ square. I drew the property lines (at a scale of 1″ = 40′) and I looked at the outlines. I was blank.
> Suddenly I saw the finished project. I did some quick calculations . . . it would fit on the property and not only that . . . it would meet the cost and income requirements. It was contemporary architecture with the richness of a cultural heritage . . . it used history and experience but did not copy it.
> I began to draw . . . my senses could not keep up with my images . . . my hand was not fast enough . . . . I was impatient to record the picture (it had not faded one particle). I worked at a pace I would not have thought I was capable of.
> I completed four sheets of fairly comprehensive sketches. I was not tired

but I was satisfied that I had caught the essence of the image. I stopped working. I ate fruit . . . I drank coffee . . . it was a magnificent day.

While making drawings two weeks later, Clough found that his image of the shopping center remained sharp and that he was able to complete the drawings without referring to his original sketches. He also discovered he could view the project from different angles and examine minute construction details. His design was subsequently accepted, and since then he has been able to design other projects in the same way. Interviewed by *Progressive Architecture* about his use of mescaline, Clough suggested that "All architects ought to have this experience." He also confirmed that this faster, sharper and clearer procedure of "imaging" projects remained with him.

Psychological Safety

A 1971 report to the American Psychological Association by Dr. Robert L. Bergman, chief of the U.S. Public Health Service's mental health program on the Navajo Reservation, should be of interest to those concerned about the possibility of psychological damage from peyote and mescaline:

> For a period of four years, we have followed up every report of psychotic or other psychiatric episodes said to arise from Peyote use. There have been forty or fifty such reports. The vast majority have been hearsay that could never be traced to a particular case. Some have been based on a physician's belief that Navajo people use Peyote and if a particular person became disturbed it must be for this reason.

The study found "one relatively clearcut case of acute psychosis and four cases that are difficult to interpret." The clearcut case involved a Navajo who attended a peyote meeting after having had several drinks. "Ordinarily, no one is allowed to participate if he has been drinking, but the road man did not realize that this person had been." The Navajo became panicky and disoriented, then violent, but recovered within twenty-four hours and was reported to have remained well at a follow-up six months later. "It is noteworthy," Bergman adds, "that members of the church warn that the combination of alcohol and Peyote is very dangerous." Reactions in the other four cases were minor, and their relationship with peyote was doubtful.

There is only very rare evidence for serious psychological problems arising from use of peyote or mescaline. In John Aiken's analysis, mescaline experiences can be unpleasant but not harmful. Hoffer and Osmond cite three instances of prolonged reactions, which are about the only such citations in the literature.

Bergman's summary of how Native Americans minimize potential hazards can be generalized to other users. The crucial factors seem to be

> a positive expectation held by Peyotists, an emphasis on the real interpersonal world rather than the world within the individual, an emphasis on communion rather than withdrawal during the drug experience, an emphasis on adherence to the standards of society rather than on the freeing of impulses . . . .

The whole spirit of the religion seems best characterized as communion—with God and with other men. Meetings are experienced as a time of being close and growing closer to one another. Distortions of time sense are counteracted by the various events of the service which take place at precisely defined times of the night . . . .

Road men are trained to look after people who become excessively withdrawn. If a participant begins to stare into the fire fixedly and seems unaware of the others in the meeting, the road man will speak to him, and if necessary go to him to pray with him. In the process of praying with such a person, he may fan him with an eagle feather fan, splash drops of water on him and fan cedar incense over him. All of these processes are regarded as sacred and helpful, and it appears to me they provide stimulation in several sense modalities to draw one back to the interpersonal world. Another safeguard is the custom that no one is to leave the meeting. Considerable efforts are made if necessary to prevent someone who has been eating Peyote from going off into the night alone. This factor is probably important too, in the customary activities of the morning after the meeting. Everyone stays together and socializes until well after the time the drug effect is over.

Psychotherapeutic Potential

The direct experience of mental health professionals with peyote and mescaline was an early benefit from clinical investigations, significantly changing some treatment directions. In *Psychedelics*, E. Robert Sinnett recounts how taking 200 mg. of mescaline sulfate with three "psychiatric residents" enlarged his sensitivity:

> Although I had had much clinical experience working with schizophrenics as well as academic preparation in clinical psychology and two years of psychoanalytically oriented psychotherapy, new vistas and understandings were made available to me . . . . It seemed to me that the implications for doing rehabilitation and psychotherapy with psychotic patients are far-reaching . . . .
>
> I had not been able to intuitively understand the silly laughter of the hebephrenic or inappropriate affect until this time. Also, I was unaware of the social plight of the schizophrenic, who must receive feedback of his strangeness even from highly trained professional staff . . . . I look on the mescaline experience as having been a provocative, rich source of data for speculation—richer, I am embarrassed to say, than much of my formal scientific research and study.

Few studies have involved giving mescaline to mental patients, although Hoffer and Osmond discuss some from the 1950s in *The Hallucinogens* (pp. 38-39). Results indicated that larger than usual dosages were needed for schizophrenics, who generally responded with accentuation of their symptoms. In the early 1960s, Charles Savage and associates gave a single high-dose combination of LSD and mescaline to seventy-four chronic neurotics and reported that psychological tests before and six months after their sessions showed "marked improvement in twelve, some improvement in twenty-two, and slight improvement in twenty-six."

In my book *Psychedelic Baby Reaches Puberty,* a friend described how he benefited psychologically from his use of mescaline. His account indicates some of the psychological possibilities in mescaline visions:

> I sensed that something very strange was about to happen. We were sitting in Frank's apartment, doing nothing, when suddenly I found I had a strong urge to read. I picked up *Hamlet*—which was lying around—and started reading aloud the speech "To be or not to be." After I was well into it, Frank surprised me by saying to his roommate something like, "Doesn't he read that just like a radio announcer, just perfectly delivered?" Well, I've never been able to read anything perfectly in my life. "No, no, no," I said, even though I sensed that something somehow was up, because I had read it without stuttering or stumbling. In fact, after I thought about it, I decided that it was indeed a pretty good performance of "To be or not to be," perhaps better than any I had ever heard.
>
> During all this, by the way, my voice became lower, and since then it has remained lowered. It has become relaxed. I don't understand what happened as I read, but there is no doubt that my voice has changed. I still feel a slight catch in my throat, though, and, as I'll indicate shortly, I have an idea why.
>
> About this time I started getting dizzy. Frank had prepared a darkened room for me with a couch. He asked me to sit there quietly for a while . . . . After I had been in the dark for five or ten minutes, suddenly weird things began to happen. I started feeling that I was really crawling into the womb. Then other fantasies began. I would find myself making out—just all kinds of sexual passion. Then I discovered I was sucking my mother's nipple and biting the pillow and other odd sex things.
>
> I started feeling pains in my legs. I was in the fetal position, and I felt myself being pulled; it felt as though I was coming out for the first time from my mother's womb. This really shook me. But then it occurred to me that, by God, when I was born I was born feet first. I also felt for a while that I was strangling, and I remember being told that I was almost choked to death by the umbilical cord. This had something to do with my difficulty in speaking. . . .

After seeing many images relating to childhood, Frank told my friend that he thought he was simply enjoying the fantasies, and wanted him to concentrate on his soured relationship with his girlfriend. He said he would return in five or ten minutes, when he would want my friend to tell his life story. He then left, and my friend began to get terribly cold. When Frank returned, he

> asked me what I was doing and I told him to go away. 'I'm freezing," I said, "and I want to be left alone." I added that there wasn't any reason for him to pry into my life story. He immediately replied that if I didn't crawl down toward the other end and flatten out on the couch, he would force me to. I refused, and he then began yanking on my feet. This symbol of birth feet first was so vivid I almost laughed, but at the same time I simply did not want to leave my end of the counch. It was just too painful.
>
> Frank continued pulling, and gradually I began slipping out flat. And then all of a sudden I had another remarkable insight. It suddenly came to me that

it was up to me to save myself if I was going to be saved at all. At the moment that Frank was pulling on me, I suddenly became aware that it takes a lot of energy to survive in the world, and that up till then this was effort I had been unwilling to expend . . . .

But during the moment Frank was pulling me out flat on the couch, I knew without question that I needed to exert my will. I knew I had to do things myself. So I said, "All right, I won't be cold any more!" And I threw off the blankets, and it wasn't cold. I no longer felt cold.

All of a sudden I knew I could ignore my fears of my subconscious mind. The fears of my subconscious are real, but I knew I could ignore them. I could conquer the fears. All at once I felt as though I could remember anything and do anything. Problems suddenly seemed to disappear and I had a great feeling of relief.

I turned to Frank and told him that I'd solved everything and that I might as well go home. "Go home?" he asked. "Man, you're really under it." He insisted that I stay, and finally I agreed. But since all my problems seemed solved, since I no longer was preoccupied by the psychological aspects of the experience, I began paying attention to music and colors and had a very pleasant time.

FORMS AND PREPARATIONS

Peyote can be eaten fresh or in its dried state, or it can be made into a tea by boiling. It can be extracted from the dried or fresh state and made into a tar that can be taken in capsule form by boiling the ground or blended material and filtering away the roughage. A coffee filter or even a stocking can be used, with the liquid being evaporated afterward. Mescaline is soluable in chloroform; it is one of the few freebase compounds that isn't soluable in ether.

Shipments of the cactus to Indians are still made by truck from Laredo, though the cactus ranches selling to whites closed down long ago. However, San Pedro can be purchased from Mr. Pedro, Box 4611, Berkeley, CA 94704

Jeremy Bigwood

San Pedro cactus is prepared for ingestion by slicing and then boiling for six to eight hours. It is then evaporated into a powder or capsulable resin.

or from other advertisers in *High Times*. It is usually sliced up and boiled for six to eight hours. A portion 6 to 10″ long and 2 to 3″ in diameter constitutes a normal dose.

Many ingenious techniques have been used to make peyote and San Pedro more palatable—to facilitate absorption of the psychoactive molecules without triggering the gag reflex. In most Native American Church rituals, the peyotists simply put a dried button in the mouth until it is soft enough to be chewed and swallowed. That takes some time. They pass around milk and may smoke. When peyote is ingested in this fashion, its cactus' soapy, bitter taste is soon displaced substantially by a numbness.

The next most popular method seems to be grinding peyote up and swallowing it inside gelatin capsules. Probably the most efficient method is to take it as a suppository or douche, which would cause it to be absorbed better. In *been down so long it feels like up to me*, Richard Farina suggests mixing cream, ice and rum in a blender, dropping in sliced bits of peyote and quickly swallowing the whole thing: the theory being that the rum is for taste and for anesthetizing the stomach while the cream lines the stomach and passes the peyote bits quickly to the intestines.

With fresh peyote, a good procedure is to chew it with the front teeth, then toss it in small bits to the back of the mouth and swallow immediately. Most efforts to cover up taste don't really work.

Peyote will burn if it is dried and powdered, and it can be smoked with grass. Many adherents of Indian practices will not use it this way. This combination intensifies the effects of marijuana; it gives a lovely, light high that sharpens vision without sending one on a major trip.

Mescaline usually appears as a clear crystal in the form of a sulfate or hydrochloride. The crystals are up to ¼″ (1/3 cm.) long. Shulgin puts the usual dosage of the sulfate salt at 300-500 mg., which is equivalent to 225-375 mg. of the hydrochloride. He adds that this dose is often administered in two installments about an hour apart in order to minimize nausea.

In the 1960s and 1970s, much that was sold as mescaline wasn't mescaline. The size of a capsule can be a helpful indicator, since at least a third of a gram is needed if the compound is to manifest psychoactive effects. Pharm-Chem indicated at one point that the chances were only one in fifty that a capsule sold as mescaline was the genuine product. Nowadays, however, most of what passes as mescaline is authentic.

Blotter #4

Upper right: mescaline sulfate (also called mescaline hemi-sulfate dihydrate) crystals and a straight pin for size comparison. The crystals look like tiny, translucent glass rods, but upon closer examination they appear more like a pile of lumber (left). The photo at the bottom enlarges this "lumber pile" ten times.

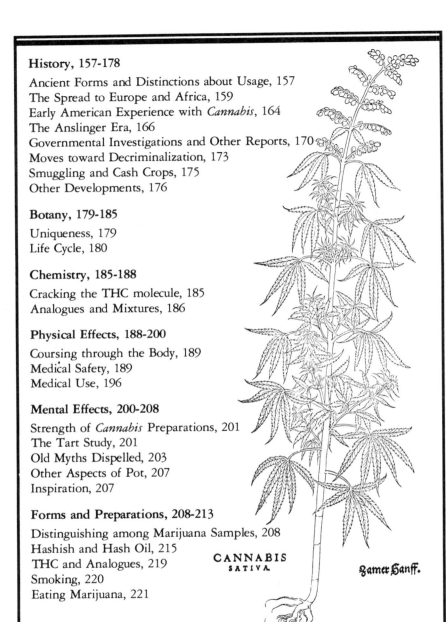

CANNABIS
SATIVA

Ʒamer Ƕanff.

Leonard Fuchs' woodcut of Cannabis sativa *in an early herbal from 1543. This plant is the main source of marijuana, a mixture of its leaves and flowers, and of hashish, made from the resin in its flowers. This plant is also grown for its strong fibers, which have been used in producing hemp rope, fabrics and fine papers.*

CHAPTER THREE

Marijuana and Hashish

> *... icon for the faithful, a windfall for the glib, a bonus for
> under-employed experts, a thrill for the naive, a whipping-boy for
> the ambitious, a tool for mystic explorers, a tantalizing mystery
> for scientists, a cash crop for peasants; hassles, joy, shouting,
> tranquility, apoplexy, fear, rebellion all wash over Western
> man in the presence of the little green weed.*

> —William Daniel Drake, Jr.

HISTORY

Ancient Forms and Distinctions about Usage

Origin of the marijuana plant is lost in pre-history, although it is likely native to central Asia, or possibly China. It is among humanity's earliest cultivated crops, going back to the beginning of agriculture. Now it may well be the most widely distributed cultivated plant. Earliest archaeological evidences date back some 10,000 years and show twisted strands of hemp being used in Taiwan in the making of patterns on clay pots. The ancient Chinese wove clothes, shoes and rope from the fibers of this plant, and produced the first paper from it.

Even today (late 1982), debate continues as to whether there is more than one species of the *Cannabis* plant. Most experts now agree that there are at least three species, with the most important differences among them appearing in the seeds, stalk, growth habits and, to a lesser extent, resin content.

The species probably appearing first in China is known scientifically as *Cannabis sativa* Linneaus, classified in 1753 by Linneaus, the father of modern botanical identification. Until quite recently *Cannabis sativa* was the main species spread throughout North America. This form is distinguished by its height, often up to fourteen to sixteen feet—sometimes over twenty feet. It produces strong fibers but generally not very much resin, which contains the psychoactive ingredient in marijuana. However, certain strains of the species, such as "Acapulco Gold" and "Homegrown Haze," exude a considerable amount of resin.

The earliest reference to mind-altering effects from *Cannabis* appears in the *Atharva-Veda* of the second millenium B.C., when it was already regarded as one of the five sacred plants of India. Ernest L. Abel in his *Marihuana: The First Twelve Thousand Years*, describes much of the early use of *Cannabis* in the daily life of China and India. Schultes and Hofmann in *Plants of the Gods* document its use in Tibet:

Cannabis sativa, *the most common and tallest species, was once grown mainly for fiber but now is the black market staple.*

Cannabis indica *is believed to be the most potent species. Cultivated for its inebriating qualities, it is short, bushy and very resinous.*

Cannabis ruderalis *is a rare Siberian species —short, without much mental effect, little known in the West, maturing within only two months.*

The Tibetans considered *Cannabis* sacred. A Mahayana Buddhist tradition maintains that during the six steps of asceticism leading to enlightenment, Buddha lived on one Hemp seed a day . . . . In Tantric Buddhism of the Himalayas of Tibet, *Cannabis* plays a very significant role in the meditative ritual used to facilitate deep meditation and heightened awareness. Both medicinal and recreational secular use of Hemp [are] likewise so common now in this region that the plant is taken for granted as an everyday necessity.

Cannabis indica Lamarck, classified by Lamarck in 1783, is a shorter plant that's more densely branched. Seldom over eight feet tall, it has short, brittle fibers and thus is not very useful for fiber but generally contains the greatest amount by weight of *Cannabis* resin. Until recently, it's cultivation has been mainly restricted to India, Persia and the Arab countries, where its leaves are often made into a milkshake and its resin is pressèd into hashish.

The third species of the marijuana plant, *Cannabis ruderalis* Janischewsky, was identified in 1924 in southern Siberia, but it also grows wild in other parts of Russia. Rarely over two feet tall, this species has little psychoactivity in its resin but matures much faster than the others (in about seven weeks).

The earliest record we have of *Cannabis ruderalis* comes from the tireless Greek traveler Herodotus, often considered the first Western historian. In 450 B.C., he described the funeral rites that took place when a king died among the Scythians, a nomadic tribe that roamed the steppes from Turkestan to Siberia. To purify themselves the Scythians set up small tepeelike structures covered by rugs, which they would enter to inhale the fumes of hemp seeds thrown onto red-hot stones. "It smolders and sends forth such billows of smoke that no Greek steambath could surpass it," comments Herodotus. "The Scythians howl with pleasure at these baths."

Historians considered this passage by Herodotus to be romantic embellishment until the late 1940s, when in the Altai mountains of Siberia Scythian tombs were found that had been covered with ice since about 400 B.C. Alongside these tombs were well-preserved corpses and little tents containing copper cauldrons filled with stones, ice and hemp seeds. Differences in *Cannabis* seeds enabled Janischewsky to distinguish *C. ruderalis* from the *sativa* and *indica* species, and when Soviet botanists examined the frozen seeds they were declared to be of the *ruderalis* species. *C. ruderalis* remains largely unfamiliar to botanists outside the U.S.S.R.

The Spread to Europe and Africa

Of the three species of *Cannabis*, the *sativa* type was the first to be spread widely around the globe, probably because of its having strong fibers and lots of edible seeds. The earliest known pharmacy book, published in China in the third millenium B.C. recommends hemp for everything from rheumatism to constipation—even absent-mindedness.

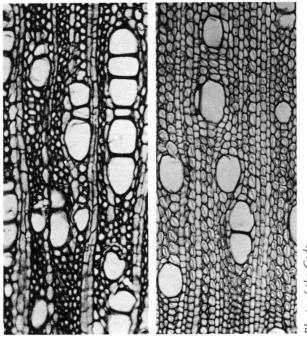

*Differences in the internal structure of wood
between* Cannabis sativa *(left) and* C. indica.
*These microscopic cross-sections illustrate how the
usually single conductive vessels in the former
species vary with the consistently grouped vessels
in the latter.*

There appears to have been little acquaintance with this herb in the
West until classical Greek times, when it was brought westward by various
barbarian tribes, mainly the Scythians. Democritus wrote that it was occasionally drunk with wine and myrrh to produce visionary states; Dioscorides and
Galen indicated that it was valued for its medicinal and therapeutic uses.
Galen also recorded that this herb was often passed around at banquets to
promote hilarity and joy.

Strangely, the ancient Greeks and Romans paid hardly any attention to
the fiber in this plant, although its use for ropes and sails had been introduced
from Gaul as early as the third century B.C. It was not until the first century
A.D. that Pliny the Elder outlined the grades and preparations of hemp fiber.

Scythians and other tribes introduced hemp into northern Europe as
well. An urn containing leaves and seeds of the *Cannabis* plant, unearthed
near Berlin, is believed to date from about 500 B.C. Although few records
remain from this time, it is evident that the hemp plant soon made its way to
England, Scotland and Ireland. Archeological remains show that hemp was

growing at Old Buckenham Mere in England by 400 A.D. From this point on, there was a tremendous spread of its cultivation in the British Isles. The plant was valued then for its fibers (made into cloth) and its seeds (which, as earlier in China, were used for food and oil).

Paracelsus, often regarded as the father of alchemy, first became acquainted with *Cannabis* products while in Basel, Switzerland, where the pharmaceutical firm of Sandoz now stands. It was also there that the botanist Leonhardt Fuchs sketched a charming, classic drawing of the *sativa* plant in 1543. By this time, the inebriating effects of *sativa*'s resin had been discovered by Europeans. Francois Rabelais, writing in the early sixteenth century devoted three small chapters of his *Third Book of Pantegruel* to this herb's botanical and psychoactive properties.

Meanwhile, the *indica* species of the plant spread gradually from the Far East to Egypt and Persia. Schultes and Hofmann cite a "questionable specimen of Hemp" in an Egyptian tomb dating as far back as three or four thousand years ago. Arab traders brought *Cannabis* to the Mozambique coast of Africa around the thirteenth century. From there, its use spread rapidly inland to virtually all African tribes. Archeological evidence of this transmission includes fourteenth-century waterpipes containing *Cannabis* residue.

European interest in the *indica* species of *Cannabis* began in the nineteenth century, as a result of the British colonization of India and Napoleon's conquest of Egypt (his doctors brought back many kilos of hashish in the 1790s). By the 1840s, monographs by Aubert-Roche, O'Shaughnessy and Moreau had spurred inquiry into how the drug would be useful in Western medicine.

W.B. O'Shaughnessy brought *Cannabis* into Western medical practice. He had been associated with the British East India Co. as a surgeon and was a professor of chemistry at the University of Calcutta. In 1839, he published a forty-page article describing the history of *Cannabis* products in the East, tests he had carried out on animals confirming the drug's safety and his successes with this agent as an analgesic in the treatment of rheumatism, severe convulsions and tetanus.

French psychologist Jean Joseph Moreau de Tours, observing the effects of *Cannabis* preparations in Egypt and other parts of the Near East, suggested that this drug might be used by doctors, enabling them to understand and to empathize with psychotic states experienced by asylum patients. His view predated the classification of any pharmaceuticals as "psychotomimetics."

Awareness of the effects of *Cannabus* spread beyond medical circles after Moreau gave a sample to Theophile Gautier, one of the leading French literary figures at the time. The after-dinner experiences at "Le Club des Haschischins" became notorious, and perhaps as a consequence accounts of the drug were somewhat exaggerated. Dr. Moreau, who usually administered the drug, noted that he became aware that the effects had begun when he

W. B. O'Shaughnessy, Professor of Chemistry and Natural Philosophy at the Medical College in Calcutta, introduced Cannabis *into Western medicine in 1839.*

found himself fencing with a bowl of fruit. Baudelaire claimed that "if you are smoking, by some sort of transposition or intellectual *quid pro quo*, you will feel yourself evaporating and will attribute to your pipe, in which you feel yourself crouching and packed together like tobacco, the strange power of *smoking yourself* . . . ."

A contemporary drawing of Theophile Gautier, founder of "Le Club des Haschischins."

J.J. Moreau (de Tours) theorized that Cannabis *could prompt a "model psychosis" for those who wanted to study aberrent mental states. He also supplied extracts from this plant in small cakes to members of "Le Club des Haschischins."*

Early American Experience with Cannabis

In the *Journal of Psychedelic Drugs* (vol. 11, p. 78), Dr. Jose Luis Diaz from the University of Mexico presents suggestive but uncertified evidence that marijuana may have been known to the Náhuas and other New World tribes before the arrival of the Spaniards. Whether or not *Cannabis* was growing in the Americas already, the Spanish seem to have taken their own to Chile in 1545 and then to Peru in 1554.

In 1606, the British took it to Canada to be cultivated for maritime purposes. In 1611 (at the time of the Jamestown Settlement), they brought it to Virginia; in 1632, the Pilgrims brought hemp to New England.

During the century and a half that preceded the American Revolution, *Cannabis* production for textiles throughout New England was subsidized. By 1762, Virginia farmers were penalized if they didn't grow it. It has been estimated that about half of the clothes worn at the time of the American Revolution were made of hemp.

Several of our Founding Fathers, including George Washington and Thomas Jefferson, cultivated *Cannabis*. In an entry in his diary, Washington expressed his desire to be present for the separation of male and female hemp plants. Some have argued that he may have been interested in the resin yield of the female plants, but it is more likely that he wanted to improve the fiber quality of the females (which decreases when they are pollinated). No hard evidence indicates that Washington or any of his contemporaries was interested in using *Cannabis* recreationally.

During the War of Independence, as Kentucky and Ohio were being opened up for settlement, vast tracts in both these states were set aside for hemp planting to provide the fiber with which to make clothes, rope, flags, altar cloths, food bags and fine paper.

By the middle of the nineteenth century, medical interest in *Cannabis indica* passed from Europe to North America. Soon such *Cannabis* preparations were available at the corner drugstore.

In 1857, Fitz Hugh Ludlow acquired a tincture of the *indica* species, stealing some to try it out. Afterward he paid six cents a dose for "Tilden's Extract." Then only sixteen, his imagination enflamed by *The Thousand and One Nights*, Ludlow called the preparation "the drug of the traveler" because it allowed him to journey mentally around the globe as well as into more mystical, often frightening regions. Encouraged by writings from Bayard Taylor, an American who had reported on his use of *Cannabis* products in the Near East, Ludlow set about recording his experiences. Ludlow's article in *Putnam's Monthly Magazine* (1856) and his anonymous *The Hasheesh Eater* (1857) were the first accounts of the psychoactivity of *Cannabis* published in North America. Although *Cannabis* extracts were readily available over the counter, few people at this time were ready to dabble in psychic experiments.

Fitz Hugh Ludlow wrote the first American contributions to Cannabis *literature. He is reported to have "turned on" many people, including Thoreau and Melville.*

With the end of the Civil War, the importance of hemp as a commercial crop declined. Emancipation of the slaves cut into the number of laborers harvesting hemp. More importantly, the invention of the cotton gin gave cotton a decided economic advantage over hemp and flax. The development of cheap wood pulp reduced the need for hemp as a source of paper, although it was still used in the manufacture of cigarette papers, money and Bibles.

Recreational use of hemp among Americans first showed up in about 1910 in New Orleans and in a few border towns as marijuana cigarettes were brought over by Mexican laborers. (They had already been used in central

South America and the Caribbean regions for half a century.) Marijuana caught on as a cheap substitute for alcohol among border guards and river travelers and within five years the practice was carried up the Mississippi River into the Ohio Valley. From there, it spread east into New York (especially Harlem). With the passage in 1920 of the Eighteenth Amendment, prohibiting sale of alcohol in this country, interest in *Cannabis* as a euphoriant rose.

The Anslinger Era

A year of considerable importance to this history is 1930, when Treasury Secretary Andrew W. Mellon appointed his niece's husband Commissioner of the newly created U.S. Narcotics Bureau. Harry J. Anslinger reigned as Commissioner for three decades. Anslinger was to the inhibition of *Cannabis* use what Andrew Comstock had at the turn of the century been to the inhibition of American sexual freedom. Although not particularly concerned about marijuana when he took office, he soon became obsessed with "the evils" of this weed, seeing a curse for humanity in the leaves and flowers of the *Cannabis* plant.

Fear about this largely unknown substance had already been stirred up, especially in the southwestern states, where it was used mainly by blacks and Mexicans. Prohibitions against nonmedical usage had been enacted in California (1915), Texas (1919), Louisiana (1924) and New York (1927). In the mid-1930s, Anslinger did his best to escalate the fear into hysteria. Drawing on his experience as a journalist with a stacatto, sensational style, he came out with "Marihuana, the Assassin of Youth," the first in a series of articles and books recounting the horrors committed under the weed's influence: murder, suicide, seduction of schoolchildren by "friendly strangers." (Several of his examples have since been refuted.)

Once Anslinger got going, he showed little interest as Commissioner in any news about the drug unless it could be worked into his atrocity file on "the Killer Drug," which he claimed was "a powerful narcotic in which lurks *Murder! Insanity! Death!*" The nation's papers loved it. By 1937, forty-six of the forty-eight states had banned marijuana.

Anslinger abandoned his earlier hopes for federal prohibition, because even he had come to doubt the constitutionality of such a law. Someone suggested that the U.S. might impose a "transfer tax" to be collected by the U.S. Treasury. Nonpayment of the tax would constitute a felony. In the ensuing congressional hearings, the Narcotics Bureau took a firm line; Anslinger even told legislators, "You smoke a joint and you're likely to kill your brother."

In all of the testimony, only one person raised any substantial objection to the Anslinger proposal. Dr. William Woodward, a legislative counsel for the American Medical Association, argued that *Cannabis* in medical preparations had not been abused and that the new provisions would cause hardship for doctors. He was quickly hooted down. House hearings concluded with no significant changes in the proposed bill, which then sailed through

Harry J. Anslinger (1893-1975) was the U.S. Narcotics Commissioner who engineered the federal—and later international—laws against marijuana that gave it the legal status of an addictive narcotic.

the Senate. In August 1937, FDR, who had come into office on a platform of repealing Prohibition, signed the Marihuana Tax Act. In addition to imposing the tax requirement, the law also declared *Cannabis* a narcotic. The new penalties for its use or distribution were five to twenty years for a first offense, ten to forty for a second.

The tax was to be assessed at $1 per ounce for those who registered and were considered legitimate users; for "illegitimate transfers," the tax was $100 per ounce. "At that time," comments Larry Sloman in his *Reefer Madness*, "cannabis was going for thirty-eight cents a pound on the licit market."

The year before, some twenty firms using hempseed oil in products such as soap, paint and linoleum had imported more than 30,000 tons of seeds, which became contraband under the new law because they could be used to grow plants. The only exception allowed was for sterilized seed for the birdseed industry, then producing four million pounds annually. Industry lobbyists maintained that birds deprived of *Cannabis* seeds would not sing.

The Narcotics Bureau hinted originally that special provisions would be made for medical usage but did not follow through. At the time, twenty-eight medicinal *Cannabis* preparations were for sale by companies such as Parke-Davis, Squibb and Lilly. Packages of marijuana cigarettes were even being sold as a cure for asthma. The new law put all of these products out of existence, and in 1941 the drug was dropped from the American *Pharmacopoeia*—after about a century of widespread use.

Much of Anslinger's efforts then went into eradicating this weed wherever it was growing. In 1937, more than 10,000 acres in the U.S. were under hemp cultivation. The plant was hardy and prone to escape into neighboring fields, making it all the more difficult for Anslinger to check the natural spread of hemp.

Anslinger had to give way after the Japanese took over Manila and the government became concerned about its supply of rope. In a crash program in 1943, 146,000 acres in the U.S. were seeded in half a dozen midwestern states. The Department of Agriculture produced a film about cultivation entitled *Hemp for Victory*. Despite great efforts to eradicate *Cannabis* traces later, patches remained in Indiana, Illinois, Wisconsin, Iowa, Kentucky and elsewhere. The strains, grown for rope, produced only small amounts of resin. Marijuana was not produced for its resin in any quantity in the U.S. until the 1960s.

In 1943, Anslinger turned his attention instead to a campaign against marijuana-smoking jazz musicians, and his instinct for the sensational got him all the funding from Congress that he ever requested. Anslinger may have used personal favors to gain congressional support: in 1978, Capitol Hill journalist Maxine Cheshire revealed that Senator Joseph McCarthy was addicted to morphine and regularly obtained it "through a druggist near the White House, authorized by Anslinger to fill the prescriptions."

After retiring from the Narcotics Bureau, the indefatigable Anslinger went on to head the American delegation to the U.N. concerned with drug use. By 1961, he managed in this capacity to get sixty nations to sign a "Uniform Drug Convention," which pledged to end *Cannabis* use within twenty-five years. Signing nations can, however, drop out by request. Shortly after, serious efforts to legalize marijuana usage got underway in the West.

MARIHUANA
THE ASSASSIN OF YOUTH

A TYPICAL FIELD OF MARIHUANA

THE LEAF

Compound, composed of five, seven, nine or eleven—always an odd number—of lobes or leaflets, the two outer ones very small compared with the others. Each lobe from two to six inches long, pointed about equally at both ends, with saw-like edges; and ridges, very pronounced on the lower side, running from the center diagonally to the edges. Of deep green color on the upper side and of a lighter green on the lower. It is the leaves and flowering tops that contain the dangerous drug. These are dried and used in cigarettes and may also produce their violent effects by being soaked in drinks.

THE FLOWERS

When mature, are irregular clusters of seeds light yellow-greenish in color.

Equipment Needed for Tests

Several glass slides
Two glass stirring rods
Porcelain SPOT plate
HCL in alcohol—4-oz. bottle
KOH in alcohol—4-oz. bottle
One small funnel
Two test tubes.
Approximate cost of above . . $1.50

Physiological Reaction

The effects of marihuana are most unpredictable.

Of the physiological reactions which may be apparent, we quote Dr. Herbert J. Kirchner, in charge of city prisons, city of Los Angeles, and a physician of wide experience in this field:

"The eye always presents a widely dilated, fixed, staring pupil, with the white of the eye severely bloodshot (orange-red). The breath has the characteristic odor, as elicited from burnt marihuana (burnt rope). There is no sensory disturbances of balance or gait, as elicited in acute alcoholic intoxication. The person under the influence may be hilarious, possibly hysterical, weeping or laughing, talks very rapidly, and in a loud tone."

In conclusion, it is important to recognize, that both the prolonged use of large doses by habitues, and the single large dose taken by a novice may cause criminal maniacal acts. Moreover, even small quantities can destroy the will power and the ability to connect and control thoughts and actions, thus releasing ALL vicious inhibitions.

THE PLANT

Attains a height, when mature in August, of from three to sixteen feet, the stalk a thickness of from one-half inch to two inches. Stalk has four ridges running lengthwise, and usually a well marked node by each branch, these appearing at intervals of from four to twenty inches. A leaf appears immediately under each branch. Green plant has a peculiar narcotic odor, is sticky to the touch, and covered with fine hair barely visible to the naked eye. Often hidden in fields of corn or sunflowers.

Test For Marihuana

Put substance in small funnel, plugged with cotton. Add 5cc (one thimble full) of petroleum ether (low boiling point) so that liquid filters through the substance.

Pour one-half of this extract into a small white porcelain dish and evaporate; add to the evaporated portion a few drops of one per cent solution potassium hydroxide (KOH) in alcohol. The residue should become purple in a minute or so and the color deepen on standing.

Add to the other half in the test tube about 1cc of solution of hydrochloric acid in alcohol, and shake. When settled the lower layer should be distinctly pink.

IT IS A CRIME for any person to plant, cultivate, possess, sell or give away Marihuana.

It is frequently used by criminals to bolster up their courage. Most dangerous of all is the person under the influence of marihuana at the wheel of an automobile. Their illusions as to time and space destroy their judgment as to speed and distance. When eighty miles an hour seem only twenty, they often leave a trail of fatal accidents in their wake. A user of marihuana is a degenerate.

STAMP IT OUT

Division of Narcotic Enforcement

PAUL E. MADDEN, *Chief*

STATE BUILDING

San Francisco   Los Angeles

An example of Anslinger's influence on anti-pot propaganda.

An example of the anti-marijuana literature produced during the 1940s.

Governmental Investigations and Other Reports

Tales about this mysterious herb from the East aroused the apprehensions of the English Parliament toward the end of the nineteenth century, which established a Commission in 1893 to look into the use of *Cannabis* in India. The resulting *Report of the Indian Hemp Drugs Commission* will probably stand as the most extensive, systematic examination of the subject ever, comprising testimony from just under 1,200 "doctors, coolies, yogis, fakirs, heads of lunatic asylums, bhang peasants, tax gatherers, smugglers, army officers, hemp dealers, ganja palace operators and the clergy" (Norman Taylor). The final report ran to seven volumes (3,281 pages); an additional secret volume was made for the military. Here are some conclusions:

> On the whole, if moderation and excess in the use of drugs are distinguished, which is a thing that the witnesses examined have, as just remarked, found it very hard to do, the weight of evidence is that the moderate use of hemp drugs is not injurious . . . .
>
> The question of the mental effects produced by hemp drugs has been examined by the Commission with great care. The popular impression that hemp drugs are a fruitful source of insanity is very strong, but nothing can be more remarkable than the complete break-down of the evidence on which it is based. Popular prejudice has over and over again caused cases of insanity to be ascribed to ganja which have had no connection whatever with it; and then statistics based on this premise are quoted as confirming or establishing the prejudice itself . . . .

> Absolute prohibition is, in the opinion of the Commission, entirely out of the question . . . .
>
> There is no evidence of any weight regarding mental and moral injuries from the moderate use of these drugs . . . .
>
> Large numbers of practitioners of long experience have seen no evidence of any connection between the moderate use of hemp drugs and disease . . . .
>
> Moderation does not lead to excess in hemp any more than it does in alcohol. Regular, moderate use of ganja or bhang produces the same effects as moderate and regular doses of whiskey. Excess is confined to the idle . . . .

Many other governmental examinations of *Cannabis* use have been undertaken since 1894. In *every* case, the conclusions have been similar to those reached by this nineteenth century commission: that the use of this drug in moderation is essentially innocuous; that existing penalties should not be increased; that its use does not lead to addiction, lunacy, violence or crime; and that virtually all reports causing public outrage have been either exaggerations or total fabrications.

Early in this century, much concern about use of marijuana was aroused in the Panama Canal area. The Army's investigative body came to the same conclusions as the 1894 Indian Hemp Commission: that *Cannabis* is comparatively innocuous, that it's not addictive, etc. Another commission established soon after in New Orleans produced the same findings. The most famous of all these investigative bodies, the LaGuardia Commission, reported in 1943 on the use of marijuana in New York City with the same results.

More recent findings that *Cannabis* is *not* harmful appear in the English *Wootton Report* of 1968, the Canadian *Le Dain Report* of 1970 and the much-publicized report of the U.S. President's Commission on Marijuana and Drug Abuse, the *Shafer Report* of 1972. Similar findings have come from South Africa, Australia and from a New York Academy of Sciences Conference on Chronic Cannabis Use in Manhattan in 1976. The latest such commission, a panel from the National Academy of Sciences, in 1982 urged removal of penalties for *Cannabis* use, after finding "no conclusive evidence that marijuana causes permanent, long-term health damage in humans, is addictive, leads to use of 'harder drugs,' affects the brain structure or causes birth defects."

In 1951, the U.N.'s *Bulletin of Narcotic Drugs* released results of a survey indicating that there were then approximately 200 million *Cannabis* users in the world. It also produced a bibliography of 1,100 titles that related to *Cannabis*, only some 350 dating from before the twentieth century. A more substantial bibliography was prepared in 1965 that included 1,860 titles. O.J. Kalant revised the list at the end of the decade; he cited 1,073 titles in English, 309 in French, 232 in German, 116 in Portuguese, 85 in Spanish, 38 in Italian and 111 in other languages. Ernest L. Abel toward the end of the 1970s produced a bibliography for NIMH of 3,045 titles. A U.N. report in 1982 increased the worldwide estimate of *Cannabis* users to more than 500 million.

The poet Allen Ginsberg, who first smoked pot in 1948, appeared at one of LeMar's earliest demonstrations to legalize marijuana—February 1965, outside the Women's House of Detention in Manhattan.

Moves toward Decriminalization

In 1961, Americans generally showed little interest in marijuana's mental effects, although the casual use of "tea" was widespread in jazz, beatnik and artistic circles. Later in the 1960s, fascination with LSD and "magic mushrooms" changed the image of *Cannabis*; many people started to regard it as a similar but considerably milder substance. Folk and rock musicians greatly encouraged this new image as they made oblique and enticing references in their lyrics to marijuana. Many of these songs made it to radio and were played nationwide. Writers such as John Rosevear, author of *Pot*, also spread the word.

In 1964, the Thelin brothers opened the first "headshop." Soon, every major city in the U.S. was bristling with headshops purveying books, records, posters and paraphernalia related to pot. Reprints of marijuana posters from the Anslinger era, such as one headlined "Reefer Madness," were snapped up for laughs, and many bought a new one showing the poet Allen Ginsberg with a sign that declared, "POT IS FUN."

By the mid-1960s, a flood of articles, books and records had dramatically changed the lurid image of "Marihuana, the Killer Drug," and experimentation with marijuana became commonplace among Americans of all classes. *Cannabis*, although still illegal, moved a long way toward being accepted socially and morally, attaining a status similar to that of whiskey during Prohibition.

At about this time, a group called LeMar was organized in Manhattan and at the University of Buffalo for the purpose of lobbying for marijuana's legalization. Before long, a similar group formed in England, going by the name SOMA. A *Marijuana Review* began making periodic appearances. Before the 1960s were over, the National Organization for the Reform of Marijuana Laws (NORML) was lobbying for marijuana law reform.

In 1970, Anslinger's "transfer tax" on marijuana was declared unconstitutional by the U.S. Supreme Court. In 1973, following the lead of such university cities as Ann Arbor, Eugene and Berkeley, Oregon became the first state to take steps toward legalization by minimizing the penalty for possession of small amounts. In 1975, the Supreme Court of Alaska ruled that the constitutional "right of privacy" protected marijuana possession for personal use in the home by adults. Alaska legalized possession of any amount of marijuana for private use, with a one-ounce limit for public possession. Personal cultivation was also legitimatized.

During our bicentennial year, California, Colorado, Ohio, South Dakota, Minnesota and Maine made possession of small quantities (generally an ounce) a misdemeanor to be settled with a small fine. Massachusetts and Texas, which had enforced some of the harshest anti-marijuana laws in the world, lowered their penalties drastically. Texas released just under 300 prisoners convicted under its previous marijuana laws. In New York, in spite of the unreasonably harsh "Rockefeller laws," only cases of excess have been tried and many of these have been reversed since.

In 1976, the board of governors of the California State Bar voted 11-2 against sanctions on personal cultivation of marijuana: "unless one hopes to promote marijuana traffic, it is irrational to punish people more for producing their own marijuana than for buying it."

Later that year, the outgoing Ford Administration eased the previous federal stand against decriminalization, encouraging discussion of this issue for the first time in a policy statement from the Strategy Council on Drug Abuse. Ford's chief advisor on drugs, Robert DuPont, stated that marijuana was less harmful than alcohol or tobacco and urged decriminalization of limited home production.

The media, once Anslinger's chief allies in whipping up anti-marijuana hysteria, adopted a calmer tone, as evidenced by the following excerpt from the *New York Times,* January 5, 1976:

Scientists Find Nothing Really Harmful About Pot

Several recent studies of chronic marijuana users, conducted independently in half a dozen countries, indicate that the drug has no apparent significant adverse effect on the human body or brain or on their functions.

The research essentially corroborates and expands on the results of an earlier study of marijuana use in Jamaica that found no signficant correlation between heavy use of the drug and impaired physical, intellectual, social and cultural activities.

The findings were reported Tuesday in research papers delivered at a New York Academy of Sciences Conference on Chronic Cannabis Use that attracted more than 100 researchers from ten countries.

Lenny Bruce used to say that pot would be legalized in America after two conditions were fulfilled: (1) when the sons and daughters of politicians got busted, and (2) when law students began smoking weed and then graduated to practice law. Both conditions were met during the 1970s. Among those busted were Kim Agnew, two Kennedys, a McGovern, a Colson, a Cahill, a Ford and two Carters. In November 1975, Marion Hugh Scott Concannon, the daughter of then Senate Republican leader Hugh Scott, was convicted of having sold an ounce of hashish to a narcotics agent and sentenced to two days of "socially useful" work each week for six months, a $100 fine and two years probation. Earlier, this same charge could have resulted in life imprisonment. After Jack Ford publicly admitted that he smoked pot, his father praised him for his honesty!

The Carter administration, taking office in 1977, indicated that the removal of heavy penalties for marijuana use was on its agenda, but a succession of drug-related embarrassments removed it before long. One of Carter's sons was thrown out of the Navy after "a marijuana incident." ("That's not a punishment," proclaimed a Yippie, "that's a reward!") The Secret Service quietly withdrew its watch on another Carter son and his wife whenever they visited a particular set of close friends and allegedly smoked pot. Then came a highly publicized incident involving Carter's chief expert on drugs,

Dr. Peter Bourne. Bourne prescribed Quaaludes for an associate and to protect her identity used a phony name for her. Bourne was forced to resign. No sooner had the dust settled than Hamilton Jordan, Carter's chief of staff, was charged with having snorted cocaine at a NORML party during the presidential campaign. This case dragged on and on. The Carter administration's early intention to decriminalize marijuana faded.

Efforts toward decriminalization and legalization continue. Millions of lives are still being affected by the lag in reform of marijuana laws. Figures from NORML indicate that over the last six years, half a million Americans annually have been arrested on marijuana-related charges. Some 90% of these cases involved possession of less than an ounce.

Smuggling and Cash Crops

In 1969, U.S. Customs officials confiscated 57,164 pounds of marijuana—somewhat under 30 tons. During 1975, six years later, the figure for confiscated pot had risen to 253.3 tons—and the next month alone brought in 86 tons, almost three times what was intercepted during all of 1969. In another six years, the announced 1981 confiscation amounted to 74,000 pounds of hashish and about 1,500 tons of marijuana.

Until the 1960s, nearly all of the strongly resinous marijuana smoked in the U.S. had been imported, generally in small batches. By the mid- and late-1960s, pilots—many trained in Vietnam—were flying loads from Central or South America in greatly increased numbers, enough to attract notice.

In 1974, Customs agents began using NORAD (North American Air Defense system) radar equipment. More than 150 planes a day crossed the Mexican border into the U.S. without radioing ahead and landing for inspection. For two months in 1975, the DEA (Drug Enforcement Administration) conducted "Operation Star Trek" to track planes that crossed into the southwest U.S., estimating the number of suspect aircraft at more than 250 a day. Very large amounts of capital were moving into the *Cannabis* market.

In the early 1970s, much of the powerful grass arriving on the East Coast of this country originated in Jamaica. During 1974, the DEA began "Operation Buccaneer"—its first overseas paramilitary effort, said to be "at the request of the Jamaican government." "American aircraft, helicopters, flamethrowers and herbicides," according to former *High Times* editor Pamela Lloyd, soon "scorched one-fifth of the island's surface." U.S. Customs and the Coast Guard made their first massive busts at sea, intercepting vessels headed for the southeast U.S. coast. A year later, vast stands of Mexican marijuana were sprayed with the deadly herbicide paraquat.

Marijuana from Jamaica and Mexico soon became a rarity in the U.S. Massive amounts arrived from Colombia—selling wholesale in New York for about $300 a pound and to users for $25-$35 per ounce, and sometimes more. This trade carried on surprisingly well; one Colombian official even expressed outrage in 1977 at "the DEA's attempt to convince us to destroy a crop with such great economic potential." Colombian marijuana dominated the import market during the late 1970s, although its potency began to decline, perhaps because the demand was too much. In this as in all areas of economic enterprise, quality tends to go down as the pressure for production increases.

Meanwhile, the potency of home-grown *Cannabis* products quickly increased. Word spread rapidly that some of the marijuana from Hawaii and California was superb. By 1977, many people were paying up to $250 an ounce for "Hawaiian," which was about as expensive as *Cannabis* ever got.

The $250 price tag on an ounce of a "weed" was an economic development with economic consequences. Clear instructions became available soon after for producing the potent "sinsemilla" (seedless female) version of marijuana. Regions of the country blessed with favorable growing conditions began experiencing a considerable economic revival.

Several agriculture officials in California, a particularly good growing region, stated in 1982 that the economic value of *Cannabis* exceeded that of ordinary crops—even all of them taken together. Nationally, revenue generated by *Cannabis* production was said to rank with the revenues of Exxon and General Motors. An assistant D.A. in Santa Cruz County, California, Ralph Boroff, put the new valuation squarely before the state's legislature when he declared, "I don't understand why everybody isn't growing at least five plants, because it is just so lucrative. You are looking at a thousand dollars a plant. It is something that is very easy to do."

If one plant alone can be worth $1,000, the grower becomes very interested in obtaining the best seeds available. So reasoned a few people who were selling single seeds for up to $5. (The seed business also fills a need brought about primarily by growing sinsemilla. Normally seeds would be available to start the next year's crop from the old crop.)

Other Developments

Marijuana's future as part of American life was further enhanced by the rediscovery of its medical potential. In 1974, Dr. Frederick Blanton from Fort Lauderdale reported on the successful treatment of glaucoma using Jamaican ganja. In 1976, government-grown pot from the University of Mississippi was prescribed for a glaucoma victim, and three years later, Florida, New Mexico, Hawaii, Indiana and Illinois legalized marijuana for medical research. Far from being the "killer drug," marijuana has been shown to be more effective than any other means in relieving the nausea associated with cancer chemotherapy.

Over the last decade, perhaps as much has been learned about *Cannabis* as was discovered over its entire previous history. The chemistry required equipment not available until just before this, and serious genetic

Catalog
of
S E E D S

Effective February 1981
ALL VARIETIES LISTED IN ORDER OF MATURATION

PURE VARIETIES

HYBRID VARIETIES
♀ *first* / ♀ *second*

Mature in October

$2.00 Afghani #1
$2.00 Afghani #2
$3.00 Afghani #2 Purple
$2.00 Skunk #1
$2.00 Skunk #2

Mature in November

$2.00 Nepali
$3.00 Malawi

$2.00 Nepali/Afghani
$2.00 Malawi/Nepali
$2.00 B. Early Haze/Afghani

All above can be grown outside most years in S.F. Bay Area

All below require a greenhouse in S.F. Bay Area

Mature in December

$2.00 South Indian #1
$1.00 South Indian #2
$5.00 South Indian #3
$5.00 Original Haze #1
$5.00 Original Haze #2
$5.00 Original Haze #3
$5.00 Original Haze #4
$5.00 Burning Bush

$1.00 Nepali/Haze
$1.00 Haze/Nepali
$1.00 Nepali-Haze/South Indian
$2.00 B. Early Haze/South Indian
$2.00 Haze/South Indian
$1.00 Thai-Haze/South Indian
$5.00 South African/Haze
$2.00 Burning Bush/Nepali
$2.00 Burning Bush/South Indian

Mature in January

$5.00 Extra Late (New Years) Haze

10% discount on $100.00; 25% discount on $1000.00 (except Skunk #1)
Special: 10 each of 25 kinds (250 for $500) while they last.

High Times

Prices from a contemporary marijuana seed grower. Once the seeds have been collected, an entrepreneur's entire business can fit easily into a shoebox.

work on hybridization is a recent development. This is changing the traditional image of pot greatly, with many strains now being as much as a dozen
times as strong as most pot known in the 1960s. A recent idea that is sure to
occur to many growers in the future is the making of *sinsemilla* hashish.

This chapter can only touch the surface of the profound change in
American attitudes toward marijuana and its impact on American life. The
myths promulgated by Anslinger have been almost entirely discredited
because of massive personal experimentation. By the 1980s, the domestic
pot industry had grown to at least $8 billion in volume annually, with total
daily U.S. consumption conservatively estimated at about thirty tons. There
are several interesting and important stories yet untold. One concerns the
efforts of Rastafarians to use it legally in their religion. Another concerns
renewed efforts by U.S., Florida and California officials to poison pot users
with the pesticide and plant killer known as paraquat. Yet another is the
Supreme Court's refusal in January 1982 to hear the appeal of a Georgia man
sentenced to forty years in prison for the sale of nine ounces of marijuana
(for $200); even at this late date, that sentence isn't considered "cruel and
unusual punishment."

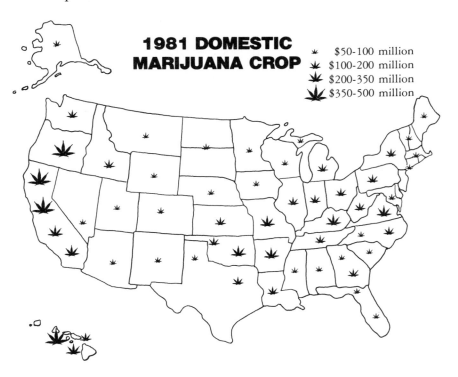

1981 DOMESTIC MARIJUANA CROP

$50-100 million
$100-200 million
$200-350 million
$350-500 million

NORML's estimation of the value and distribution of homegrown pot.

BOTANY

Uniqueness

Cannabis species are exceptional, unique from many viewpoints in biology, chemistry and pharmacology. They are among the oddest manifestations in the plant kingdom, something perhaps tossed off by the Creator as a wild afterthought on the seventh day.

Cannabis was originally classified as a member of the *nettle* family (Urticaceae) and then of the *mulberry* family (Moraceae). It is now considered most closely related to the *hop* plant and is thus a cousin to the *fig* tree! Classification is difficult because structurally it belongs in one place, while its sexual characteristics suggest it should be elsewhere. Over the last century or so, there has arisen a plethora of technical names for its variants: *kif, vulgaris, pedemontana, chinensis, erratica, foetens, lupulus, mexicana, macrosoerma, americana, gigantea, excelsa, compressa, sinensis,* etc., and there are those yet arguing for a single species. The law is beginning to accommodate to modern findings of three: *sativa, indica* and *ruderalis.* "In spite of its great age as one of man's principal narcotics and its utilization by millions of people

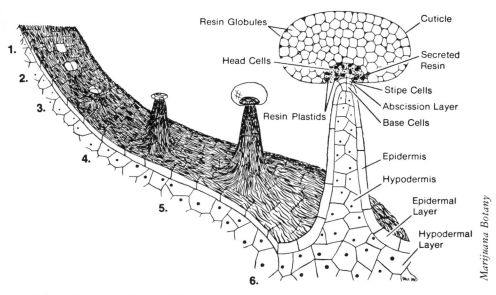

Robert Connell Clarke's illustration of the development of the resin-producing glandular plant hair with a stalk (the capitate-stalked trichome): (1) single cell stage; (2) trichome intially divides; (3) head and stipe cells differentiate; (4) epidermal stalk elongates as head cells finish dividing; (5) resin secretion begins as stalk continues elongating; and (6) stalk elongation ceases and resin secretion is highest.

Pam Elias

These drawings of Mexican Cannabis *illustrate typical differences between male (at left) and female plants.*

in many cultures," remark Richard Evans Schultes and Albert Hofmann, "and notwithstanding the great economic value of the plant for uses other than as an intoxicant, *Cannabis* is still characterized more by what we do not know botanically about it than what we know."

Life Cycle

These amazing plants tend to put off most pests—and thus don't rely on insects for pollination. Instead, *Cannabis* as a genus has gone its own way with individual plants being male or female but sometimes hermaphroditic. In the wild, *Cannabis* grows about half male, half female. Environmental conditions can change this ratio by as much as nine to one—the more light available, for instance, usually the more females. Generally speaking, adverse conditions result in more males. If conditions become extreme, the plant often becomes hermaphroditic with separate male and female branches, fertilizing itself for reproduction.

Its favorite conditions include light, dry, sandy, slightly alkaline soil. Still, it grows just about anywhere thistles or dandelions will sprout, except in clay or undrained soil. Distributed by hand, the seeds attain as much as a 60 to 80 percent germination rate. Because germination vigor is increased considerably with even slight care, seeds are often poked into the soil (½″ to ¾″ deep) with the pointed end up, rounded end down. *Cannabis* can also be reproduced by means of cuttings.

If it is to be transplanted, both the plant and the soil should be watered the night before. The new soil should be as similar as possible to the old. Transplanting should take place on a cloudy or drizzling day or in late afternoon, because bright and sunny conditions can provide a shock that may stunt further development.

When planted closely, *Cannabis* tends to develop fibrous qualities and to stretch taller. (*Cannabis* produces about four times as much useful fiber per acre as saplings.) To promote resin development, it is best to keep seedlings at least six feet apart. Nourished by humus or other sources of nitrates and by a fair amount of light and water, the yield can be close to eight or nine tons of resinous flowers and leaves per acre—about a kilogram per square meter—or enough for about fifteen million joints.

In the northern hemisphere, seeds are usually planted in April or May. Depending upon conditions—more than ten hours of light a day, for example, greatly hastens growth—maturation of the male plants takes ten to twelve weeks. For about the first month, the two sexes are indistinguishable; then the males tend to get taller and the females become bushy and squat. Eventually, the young female plant has at least twice the weight of the male.

The male reaches the day of flowering after about three months, toward the end of the summer when days get shorter. About two hours before sunrise, the developing flowers swell; about an hour later, the first flower opens, usually two-thirds of the way up and near the stem. Gradually the rest of the flowers open, spreading out toward the extremities. The final unopened flower at the top often completes this phase some eight to ten hours later, but flowering can take up to a week for some strains. This daily cycle of flowers opening is repeated up to two weeks.

At the first breeze the entire load of pollen drops—apparently the supreme moment for the male. It begins to lose its color and waxy texture soon after, then gradually wrinkles and dries over the next few days, from the base of the plant up. Contrary to a rumor circulated for years, leaves and flowers of the male plant are psychoactive, though they diminish in potency rapidly after pollination. They should be harvested before shedding their pollen, unless the pollen is needed for seed production.

In the wild, the female reaches its mature stage at the same time as the male. It prepares for conception by lowering its leaves and thrusting forth its pistils. If the female is pollinated, seeds begin to grow and ripen some ten days to four weeks later. Then the seeds of most types drop off and the plant itself dies. If the seeds are kept dry and under 75° F., they remain viable for years.

Sam Selgnij: *Blotter #4*

The stalk of Cannabis *can get quite thick, above shallow, matted roots.*

Under cultivation, pollination can be interrupted to prevent seed production; the female plant reacts by producing larger amounts of resin in the topmost flowering clusters. In certain areas of India, someone called the "ganja doctor" traditionally weeds out all the males when sexual characteristics are first noted in a crop—not because there's no psychoactive effect, but because removing the males will prevent pollination and greatly increase the females' resin production.

The stage of development at which pollination normally occurs is when the maximum amount of flowers appears. Resin accumulates quickly in the flowers, especially if the lower parts of the plant have been pruned or cut back. As time passes, the resin content diminishes once again. Researchers at the University of Mississippi pot farm have shown that resin content varies as well in terms of the time of day.

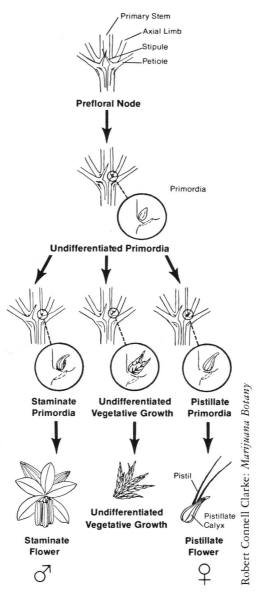

Primary Stem
Axial Limb
Stipule
Petiole

Prefloral Node

Primordia

Undifferentiated Primordia

Staminate Primordia

Undifferentiated Vegetative Growth

Pistillate Primordia

Undifferentiated Vegetative Growth

Pistil

Pistillate Calyx

Staminate Flower

♂

Pistillate Flower

♀

Robert Connell Clarke: *Marijuana Botany*

The first sign of sexual differences appear along the main stem, behind the leaf spur. The males can be identified by their curved claw shape, followed by the differentiation of round pointed flower buds having five radial segments. Females are recognized by the enlargement of a symmetrical tubular floral sheath that appears earlier. In some instances, especially among hybrids, small non-flowering limbs will form at the nodes that are often confused with male flowers.

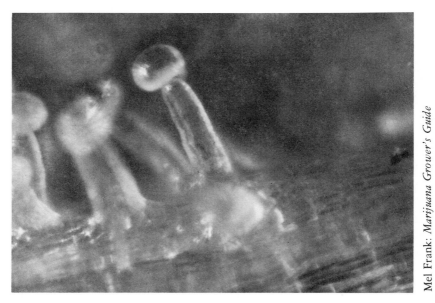

Micro-optical photographs of resin production. Above: surface tissue of marijuana, showing resin glands. Below: close-up of resin being exuded from resin gland.

Robert Connell Clarke:
Marijuana Botany

A male plant bagged for pollen collection.

The most potent crop is that made out of females that have not been allowed to seed when mature ("*sinsemilla*," from the Spanish for "without seeds"). Anyone interested in the cultivation of this connoisseur's grass should consult Jim Richardson's *Sinsemilla Marijuana Flowers,* Robert Connell Clarke's *Marijuana Botany* or Kayo's *The Sinsemilla Technique.* These books illustrate the great variety in appearances this single type takes, offering clear graphics to help farmers distinguish between the sexes. This crop is somewhat painstaking to grow, because all male plants have to be culled and the seedless buds should be picked by hand. It also results in less weight, because there are no seeds (which add substantial weight). Many think *sinsemilla* production is very much worth undertaking, and it is increasing over time. Domestic grass is becoming very potent as we see the improvements in selectively bred generations.

CHEMISTRY
Cracking the THC Molecule
For more than a century, numerous attempts to isolate and to synthesize the psychoactive components of marijuana resin were unsuccessful. Only in the last twenty years have researchers gained a chemical understanding of this complex and large family of molecules.

The first important discovery came in 1895, when three Cambridge chemists isolated the parent molecule of the group, cannabinol, and established the family's skeleton structure. One of the three Englishmen nearly lost his life in a lab fire while undertaking further experimentation. The other two did lose their lives—in separate lab explosions as they tried to probe deeper into the cannabinols. Unlike most of the compounds covered here, *Cannabis* is not an alkaloid and had to be extracted at that time with some highly flammable and explosive substances. Despite many subsequent efforts, cannabinol wasn't successfully isolated again until 1932.

By the beginning of the 1940s, Roger Adams and coworkers at the University of Illinois—commissioned by the LaGuardia Commission—were able to demonstrate a simpler method for synthesizing cannabinol and isolated the second important member of this family: cannabidiol. From their work, and that of A.R. Todd at about the same time, it became clear that these first two molecules are barely psychoactive and that the important components are produced by tetrahydrocannabinols (THCs).

Here are the structures of the three principal tetrahydrocannabinols and of the parent, which differ mainly in chemical bonding:

Δ^1-trans-
tetrahydrocannabinol

Δ^6-trans-
tetrahydrocannabinol

*Cannabinol, the
parent of this family*

*Cannabidiol (CBD), a
potentially active cannabinol*

Analogues and Mixtures

The molecules at the top seem to be the main constituents that affect the mind and are particularly interesting because, unlike other psychedelics, they don't contain nitrogen. More than sixty cannabinols—generally referred to as "cannabinoids" in scientific papers—are produced in a typical flower (which contains yet another four hundred identified compounds). As a researcher into these areas has noted, "cannabinol and all reduction products of its toluene ring can be considered to embody cannabis activity." To put this another way, the quality of marijuana is much determined by the mix concocted in each plant: variation in effect is akin to the differences in wine that are due to winds, soil, sun and seasons.

Hemp growing wild generally appears as a diploid plant (meaning that it has two sets of chromosomes per cell). During World War II, a government researcher named H.E. Warmke was looking for a way to improve the fiber of hemp and cut down on resin content. He discovered that Colchicine, a highly toxic alkaloid frequently used nowadays to alter a plant's chromosomes, brought about nontoxic, polyploid (meaning multiples of chromosomes per cell) hemp plants in second and later generations . . . which produced greater concentrations of THC in the resin. Unfortunately, the procedure is dangerous and generally kills the treated seeds. If you are interested, you can read the somewhat disputed details in W.D. Drake's *Connoisseur's Handbook of Marijuana* or in Robert Connell Clarke's *Marijuana Botany*.

Warmke showed that through some contriving the THC yield can be increased so as to give more psychic effects. Since then there have been a number of reports hinting that we're well on our way toward a Luther Burbank solution to the growing demand for more THCs in marijuana. In Canada, a government test station almost a decade ago produced *Cannabis* three times as strong as the average imported marijuana available on the streets, and the U.S. test station in Mississippi soon after reported a five-fold increase in strength. Domestic *Cannabis (sinsemilla)* from California has been analyzed at over 12 percent THC.

A stimulating and light grass is distinguished from grass that is heavy or puts one to sleep by the distribution and quality of cannabidiol and various THC components. The differences are reflected to a considerable extent in the color and smell of the leaf. Although few people have tried anything more psychoactive than the delta-1 and delta-6 THC molecules, chemists have now produced more than eighty cannabinols synthetically—including some that contain nitrogen, and acetylated ones that are very potent. More than 3,000 papers have been published on various THC analogues, the most prominent being "Nabilone" (from Eli Lilly) and "levantradol" (from Pfizer). These and many others exhibit no psychoactivity but have some of the medically beneficial effects of THC. These patentable compounds have been of special interest to chemical companies looking for something more reliable and with less problems for some patients than THC.

It may well be that as researchers continue to explore different molecular bondings and arrangements, they may find a way to remove some sleepy components or otherwise spice up the effects. Just as the cigarette called "Merit" is said to emphasize certain fractions of more than 2,000 available in tobacco, similar techniques of analytical fractometry may help bring about similar consequences as production of marijuana becomes more sophisticated.

A means of chemically altering and improving low quality marijuana is already available. "Isomerization" changes "lower-rotating" forms of cannabinols into those that are "higher-rotating." Simple processes use sulfuric acid and long, low-temperature boiling in alcohol, changing cannabidiol and THC-acid—which are prevalent in weak grass but are not psychoactive—into THCs. In pamphlets such as *Cannabis Alchemy* (Level Press/High Times) and *The Marijuana Consumer's and Dealer's Guide* (Chthon Press), this inexpensive technique is detailed.

With the "Isomerizer," the process is much easier. More than 200,000 Isomerizers are said to have been sold with the expectation that the device will increase potency of weak marijuana up to six times. After five or six years on the market, however, the isomerizing process hasn't really become popular. The main reasons appear to be because it's still too much trouble and most people don't enjoy the taste of the "Iso-hash" or oil which result since there is generally a lingering odor from bicarbonate of soda that is used to neutralize the sulfuric acid. Some complain that Iso-hash doesn't get them all that high. Robert Connell Clarke's *Marijuana Botany* provides a fuller discussion.

Iso-I   Iso-II

The Isomerizer boils grass in alcohol at low temperatures, which after addition of sulfuric acid (that is later neutralized) transforms cannabidiol and THC-acid into psychoactive THCs.

PHYSICAL EFFECTS

According to the fifth annual report prepared for Congress by the National Institute on Drug Abuse, appearing in February 1976, more than *half* of all Americans between eighteen and twenty-five had at least tried marijuana by 1975. Dr. Robert DuPont, then the government's top official on drug abuse, announced that alcohol and cigarettes were far more dangerous to health than marijuana, which, he said, lacks the lethal effects of either alcohol or tobacco. He added that young people are more likely to start with alcohol and tobacco, moving on to marijuana, than the other way around.

It has been well established that marijuana has almost no dangerous physical effects. Unlike most euphoriant drugs, it has few drawbacks: (1) there's no addiction, not even, as one writer has put it, "at the remotest cell," (2) while it may impair immediate memory, it doesn't obliterate recall later as alcohol can; (3) it produces some tolerance, but one can smoke it regularly and still get high; (4) it causes no alcohol-type hangover. (Some users may feel a bit slow the following morning, but this sense is mild compared with the after-effects of an alcohol binge.)

Coursing through the Body

The cannabinols are carried to most organs; a tiny amount then accumulates and resides for an extended period in the liver's fatty tissues, while the rest is soon excreted. Cannabinols appear only briefly in the brain, going mainly to the frontal and parietal regions, where it used to be thought that they stimulated increased alpha-wave production. (Now, it is thought there's no uniform significant change in brainwaves—see *Marihuana Reconsidered,* pp. 56-57.) Some increases occur in the pulse rate, as the heart compensates for a slight lowering in blood pressure. Marijuana dries both the mouth and the eyes. If you peel an onion right after smoking pot, you probably won't cry. Contrary to popular opinion, pupil size is not enlarged, so the two most noticeable physical consequences are: (1) dryness in the mouth and (2) redness in the eyes.

Medical Safety

Beginning in the late 1960s, a handful of doctors managed to produce a few isolated reports suggesting there might be adverse health effects from prolonged use of *Cannabis.* They revived the charge that it's an "assassin of youth." Such reports have been instantly and sensationally reported by much of the media.

All claims about health drawbacks associated with the use of pot—aside from the effects of its being smoked—have been either refuted by other investigators or compromised when their results couldn't be replicated. Some of these reports have been received by their authors' colleagues as irrelevant, highly suspect or worse. Since professional embarrassment has not deterred marijuana's critics, their alarming and widely-promulgated allegations should be confronted head-on.

What are these charges against marijuana? Deleterious health effects attributed to marijuana include:

disruption of basic
   cellular functions
hormonal imbalance (resulting
   in large breasts in males)
interference with the body's
   defenses against infection

impairment of sperm and
  egg production
chromosomal damage
birth defects
weakening of the heart
eye damage
THC concentrations in
  the brain and testes
brain damage
impotence and frigidity
cancer
addiction
and escalation to
  other drugs

It might be best to respond to such charges by citing the conclusions
from the most recent marijuana study, undertaken by the National Academy
of Sciences and sponsored by the National Institute of Health. The report
took over fifteen months to compile. Dr. Arnold Relman, chairman of the
study committee and editor of the *New England Journal of Medicine*, has
called it "the broadest, most comprehensive, least biased assessment" yet
made of marijuana's effects on human health.

It was issued February 26, 1982, well after the listed charges against
marijuana had been thoroughly aired. This report found "no conclusive
evidence that marijuana causes permanent, long-term health damage in
humans, is addictive, leads to use of 'harder' drugs, affects the brain structure
or causes birth defects." The study called attention to positive effects, noting
evidence that marijuana may be useful in easing the side effects of cancer
chemotherapy and in treating glaucoma, asthma and certain seizure conditions
such as epilepsy.

The panel did find short-term effects: on "immediate memory," "oral
communication" and "learning," and said that it sometimes "may trigger
temporary confusion and delirium." Noting that "about a quarter of the entire [U.S.] population has tried it at least once," Relman reported the study
group's recommendations: (1) more work to produce marijuana derivatives
with increased therapeutic action and less side effects, (2) a high-priority
national effort to find out more about this drug, and (3) the decriminalization
of penalties for personal marijuana use.

In 1975, a "first, intensive, multidisciplinary study of marijuana use and
users," entitled *Ganja In Jamaica*, was sponsored by the Center for Studies of
Narcotic and Drug Abuse, a division of the National Institute of Mental
Health. This study focused on people who had smoked marijuana in huge
quantities for between twelve and thirty years; conclusions drawn then were:

there is little correlation between use of *ganja* and crime, except insofar as the possession and cultivation of *ganja* are technically crimes. There were no indications of organic brain damage or chromosome damage among the subjects and no significant clinical (psychiatric, psychological or medical) differences between the smokers and controls.

The "single medical finding of interest," wrote Raymond Philip Shafer, Chairman of the U.S. National Commission on Marijuana and Drug Abuse, was "indication of functional hypoxia [oxygen deprivation] among heavy, long-term chronic smokers." This finding probably relates to ingestion of very large quantities via smoking (up to a pound of grass a week among Rastafarians, usually mixed with tobacco).

The preface to the report's 1976 edition gave even more reassuring information:

> . . . the relatively benign findings of the Jamaica project have generally been quite favorably received. Nevertheless, some have questioned the relevance of the psychological and neurological results and dismissed the findings as being pertinent only to Jamaica. In the year since the original publication of this research, the results of a number of rigorous multidimensional studies of cannabis use in other countries, undertaken by other scientific teams, have helped to lay these allegations to rest and have strongly bolstered the major findings of the Jamaica project and the cross-cultural applicability of these conclusions . . . .

> Under the auspices of the University of Florida, a medical anthropological study of urban, working-class, chronic cannabis smokers has been carried out in Costa Rica . . . . No evidence of pathology could be found after extensive medical examination. The results of psychological and brain function tests indicated that "chronic marihuana use is not associated with permanent or irreversible impairment in higher brain functions or intelligence." The Costa Rica project also included the examination of testosterone levels and immunology as related to cannabis use, areas of research not undertaken in the Jamaica study. No relationship between marihuana use and testosterone levels was found nor were there indications of impaired immunological response. Significantly, the study established that the use of cannabis did not impair the subject's ability to function well at home or at work and no evidence was found to support the hypothesis that heavy cannabis use precipitates an "amotivational syndrome." As in Jamaica, marihuana is utilized in Costa Rica to cope with the exigencies of daily life, not to withdraw from society. Another intensive study, clinical in orientation, was conducted by a multidisciplinary team at the University of Athens. The results of this research on Athenian workers confirms both the Costa Rican and Jamaican findings on all comparable variables.

> A major study of the behavior and biological concomitants of chronic marihuana use has been undertaken at McLean Hospital in Massachusetts. This team also found no evidence that chronic marihuana use impaired cognitive or neurological function nor that motivation to work for money was decreased even after heavy consumption. Another significant finding was that high

marihuana dosages did not suppress testosterone levels . . . . Finally, a longitudinal study of the grades of 1,380 UCLA undergraduates revealed no evidence
of brain damage or lack of motivation due to marihuana use. As the researchers
reported, "the dire consequences that were predicted have not materialized."

Such cross-cultural findings that marijuana presents no threat to
health should have ended concern about the alleged hazards. Since then,
additional investigations of marijuana users in Greece, Guatemala and Egypt
(the last, called "The Egyptian Study of Chronic Cannabis Consumption,"
was issued in 1980 by the Cairo-based National Center for Social and Chrim-
inology Research) have replicated the Jamaican findings. However, opponents
to marijuana continue to press their claims unsupported. Norman Zinberg in
1978 commented:

> It is important to remember that the Jamaica study is one of the finest pieces
> of research ever done. Subjects who had smoked very strong marijuana for
> between 12 and 30 years were studied physiologically, psychologically, socially
> and anthropologically. They were compared to a control group. They were
> studied in both hospital and natural settings. While at work they had devices
> strapped to their backs that could measure their lung input and output. This
> study found that there was no way to differentiate marijuana smokers from
> the control group. There was no evidence of greater lung pathology in the
> group that smoked marijuana than in the control group.

To illustrate the persistence of the critics, there were then alarming
charges of chromosome damage: these people jumped on the research
observation that THC, like many vitamins, is absorbed by fatty tissues in the
body and released slowly—unlike alcohol, which is metabolized quickly and
excreted within a few hours. Since the brain, ovaries and testicles are composed of much fat, they leapt immediately to the conclusion that THC *must*
accumulate steadily in these vital organs as a result of regular pot smoking.
(The original researcher objected strongly to any such interpretations of his
findings.)

After extensive study of the charge that excessive chromosome damage
is caused by marijuana, the National Academy of Sciences and relevant
researchers have concluded that it is not supported by the evidence and dismissed the charge. Concern about THC possibly lodging in the brain or repro-
ductive organs has lingered because finding conclusive evidence one way or
the other on such a matter is difficult. Recently, reassuring conclusions have
been reached on the basis of high-dose THC animal experimentation:
"Kinetics of Cannabinoid Distribution and Storage with Special Reference
to Brain and Testis," in the August-September 1981 *Journal of Clinical
Pharmacology*, reports on the "oil solubility" charge. This research was
sponsored largely by the National Council on Marijuana, an anti-drug organization.

It has long been known that the body seems capable of metabolizing
and disposing of "lipophilic" vitamins by trapping them in fatty acids in the
digestive system, somehow prohibiting their access to the gonadal and brain

systems, where they might exert toxic effects. Dr. Gabriel Nahas, associated with the College of Physicians and Surgeons at Columbia University and an anti-marijuana advocate for more than a score of years, argued that THC escaped this natural defense because it wasn't a vitamin. The study mentioned above tested this hypothesis.

Nahas and Dr. Colette Leger of the Hospital Fernand Widel in Paris injected rats intramuscularly on a regular basis with large doses of radioactively labeled THC. They then killed these animals to examine the testes and ovaries at various intervals after administration. Examinations determined that THC concentrations in testes and ovaries were extremely low, barely rising to a single *billionth* of a gram per gram of body tissue, and that these "concentrations" were almost entirely eliminated within twenty-four hours of a single dose. THC concentrations in the brain were found to be slightly higher but were eliminated faster. Most THC turned out to be trapped and neutralized in the digestive system—exactly the same pattern as with vitamins.

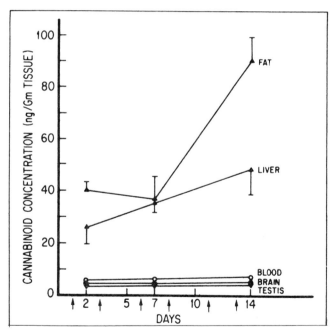

This graph shows the concentrations of THC in various parts of rats after injection of the human equivalent of 140 joints of marijuana, given regularly for fourteen days (equivalent to six months in a human). The associated report concluded, "These data illustrate the efficiency of the blood-brain barrier and the blood-testicular barrier in limiting the access and accumulation of this highly lipophilic substance into brain and testis."

Similar results appeared when the rats were regularly given massive dosages. Nahas and Leger concluded, "Concentrations of cannabinoids in brain and testis remained lower than in the blood and did not reflect any significant accumulation of the drug in those tissues."

In December 1976, *Psychology Today* published "The War Over Marijuana," a review by Dr. Norman Zinberg of the preceding seven years of marijuana research. At a conference in San Francisco in late 1978, Zinberg, associated with the earliest "scientific" investigation of marijuana and from the Harvard Medical School, described further developments regarding "Cannabis and Health" (a transcript of his remarks appears in the *Journal of Psychedelic Drugs,* January-June 1979):

> In that article I covered a number of salient theories—steppingstone to heroin, amotivational syndrome, brain damage, chromosome damage (i.e., birth defects), immune responses, psychosis, incitement to crime, general health hazard and sex impairment. None of this research proved that use of marijuana caused problems.
>
> I showed that the idea of marijuana use as a steppingstone to use of harder drugs like heroin has been disproved by any number of learned commissions, yet the idea persists. Incidentally, there is now a study which indicates that most heroin users do not even like marijuana. The notion of the amotivational syndrome, a term created by Dr. Louis J. West in 1972, shows up again and again although there have been a number of studies, including a very large one at UCLA (Dr. West's school), which show that users of marijuana maintain their motivation as well as or sometimes better than nonusers. The Jamaica study (*Ganja in Jamaica* by Lomitas and Rubin) which was funded by the President's Commission on Marihuana and Drug Abuse notes that in Jamaica marijuana is used as a motivator. It is of particular importance to remember that marijuana users in any study have performed better in school than nonusers. I think that has more to do with the personality characteristics of users, who are more likely to be more adventuresome than otherwise, but it is still an important finding.
>
> The only article on the subject, printed in the *Lancet*, claimed that marijuana use caused brain damage. It was a terrible piece of work which did not even indicate all the different drugs and conditions of the population studied. Since publication of that work, there have been a number of studies, particularly in the last few years, with soft tissue X-rays that indicate definitely that marijuana use does not cause brain damage, but the original Campbell study survives.
>
> The same problems occur for theories about chromosome damage, reduction in testosterone production and so on. These areas have been studied thoroughly. It has been found that numerous substances affect testosterone production, but as changes are within a reasonable range it is a matter of no concern. In fact, we don't even know what it means that testosterone levels go up and go down day by day or hour by hour.
>
> One of the most widely publicized studies was of the effect of marijuana use on immune bodies. This work turned out to be fallacious but that has not prevented its being cited again and again. At different times people have claimed

marijuana use causes aggression, anxiety and is responsible for serious mental illness. Now, after more than 15 years and over 51 million users, we know that these studies have not been significant.

At the moment the new bugaboo is whether marijuana smoking may cause some of the same respiratory problems as cigarette smoking. One article by Dr. Tashkin has appeared which found a high tar content in smoked marijuana. I think it cannot be good for anyone to inhale any hot substance into the lungs, hold it and then exhale it. The current contention about marijuana, however, is that a single marijuana cigarette is infinitely more dangerous than an entire pack of cigarettes. As yet a specific refutation of the Tashkin study has not appeared, but several studies of lung cancer patients at the National Cancer Institute have expressed considerable doubt about that work, and it does not square with the results of the Jamaican, Greek and Costa Rican studies of long-term chronic marijuana use.

(The Dr. Tashkin referred to above is Donald Tashkin of UCLA. After a recent NBC television documentary claimed that each marijuana joint was equivalent to seventeen tobacco cigarettes in its potential for lung damage, Dr. Eugene Schoenfeld contacted him as the source of this alarming news "and found that NBC had totally distored his research findings. He meant to say no such thing.")

In his *Marihuana Reconsidered,* Dr. Lester Grinspoon notes the "striking observation that there has never in its long history been reported an adequately documented case of lethal overdosage. Nor is there any evidence of cellular damage to any organ." These observations are worth emphasizing because toxicity studies show this drug to be among the safest known. It has been estimated that a lethal dose would require ingestion of approximately seven pounds of flowering tops within a twenty-four hour period. Experiments have demonstrated that about 40,000 times the amount of THC ordinarily smoked in a joint is needed to kill a mouse. This is about equivalent to drowning the animal in hash oil.

These remarks about the campaign of misinformation are not meant to say that there aren't some people who oversmoke marijuana and afterwards feel "sluggish," temporarily "wiped out," or suffer related deleterious effects from it. Virtually every drug known seems to cause undesirable effects in some people who, for reasons largely unknown, are particularly "sensitive" to them. However, it's clear that marijuana is a lot harder to "abuse" than alcohol, downers or many over-the-counter drugs. As Dr. Zinberg suggests, even damage to the lungs by massive, long-term pot smoking hasn't yet been confirmed.

To sum up this discussion, it seems appropriate to quote again the panel from the National Academy of Sciences investigating marijuana users in the 1980s: there is as yet "no conclusive evidence that marijuana causes permanent, long-term health damage in humans, is addictive, leads to use of 'harder drugs,' affects the brain structure or causes birth defects." For a fully detailed account of the scientific evidence on alleged health risks from smoking pot, see Dean Latimer's "7 Marijuana Medical Myths" in the March 1982 issue of *High Times*.

Medical Use

Throughout history, *Cannabis* has been appreciated as a healing herb. By the time of Christ it was used in India and China for the relief of pain, reduction of fever, surgery, stimulation of appetite and treatment of diarrhea, dysentery, bronchitis, migraine, insomnia and a variety of neurological diseases. Between 1840 and 1900, more than a hundred contributions were made to the Western medical literature that recommended *Cannabis* for one ailment or another.

In 1923, two French doctors grouped the diseases for which they considered it helpful:

1. Troubles of psychic origin: melancholia, delirium, hysteria, painful facial tics, chorea, delirium tremens, migraine headaches, neuralgia, sciatica, insomnia with delirium and nightmares, neurasthenia.

2. Certain genito-urinary troubles: gonorrhea, prostatitis, cystitis, dysmenorrhea.

3. Troubles of the respiratory system: in the form of cigarettes, vapour, and inhalations against chronic catarrh, emphysema, asthma, whooping cough.

4. Painful troubles of the stomach and intestine: cancer, ulcer, anorexy.

5. Certain skin diseases: eruptions, herpes, chronic itching.

6. Infectious diseases: tetanus, cholera, pest, erysipelas, eruptive fevers.

Although some of these recommended treatments are yet of a questionable value, we are beginning to hear new, more specific claims of its medical benefits. *Cannabis* is now said to be most effective in quelling glaucoma—not only does it dry up the eyes, but it diminishes intraocular pressure as well.

What this means in human terms was dramatized during the summer of 1976. Robert Randall, who taught speech part-time in a community college near Washington , D.C., fought for and won the right to be the first person in the U.S. to be "exempted from Federal drug laws in order to use marijuana as medicine." His story was told by Daniel St. Albin Greene in *The National Observer* in July 1976:

Bob Randall *does* smoke pot—for a reason. He has glaucoma. He's going blind. And marijuana is the only drug that seems able to save his remaining sight.

Randall says . . . he needs four to six joints a day to control his intraocular pressure, which, unchecked, can cause irreparable damage to the optic nerves. He wants the Government to let his ophthalmologist prescribe take-home marijuana so he can smoke when he needs to, without fear of being raided.

But Randall can't wait much longer. He's already functionally blind in his right eye, and his left eye is getting worse all the time.

Washington ophthalmologist Ben S. Fine says: "It is clear that Mr. Randall's condition can no longer be adequately controlled on conventional medications.

PREPARED AT THE

LABORATORY OF TILDEN & CO.,

NEW LEBANON, N. Y.,

AND

98 JOHN STREET, NEW YORK CITY.

1858.

CANNABIS INDICA.

Indian Hemp, Foreign.

The true Cannabis Indica is imported from India. It is cultivated largely in parts of Europe and Asia.

MEDICAL PROPERTIES.

Phrenic, anæsthetic, anti-spasmodic and hypnotic. Unlike opium, it does not constipate the bowels, lessen the appetite, create nausea, produce dryness of the tongue, check pulmonary secretions or produce headache. Used with success in hysteria, chorea, gout, neuralgia, acute and sub-acute rheumatism, tetanus, hydrophobia and the like.

PREPARATIONS.

Fluid Extract.....................................Dose, 5 to 10 Drops.
Solid Extract....................................   "   1 to 2 Grains.
Pills...Half and One Grain.

TINCTURE OF CANNABIS INDICA.

Fluid Extract................. ....Half Ounce.
Diluted Alcohol ....Twelve Ounces.
Dose—Half to one dram, and gradually increased in *tetanus* every half hour until the paroxysms cease or catalepsy is induced.

DRAUGHT OF CANNABIS INDICA.

Tincture of Cannabis Indica.................Half Dram.

Harper's Weekly (1858)

A mid-nineteenth century description of some medical uses for Cannabis.

This failure of medical treatment will result in Mr. Randall's blindness unless another medication is available or surgery is undertaken . . . . Surgical intervention for pressure control is not always successful, may aggravate the condition rather than stabilize it, and, in some cases, may damage remaining areas of active, healthy vision."

Randall tried every conventional IOP [Intra-Ocular Pressure] medication. Some worked for a time, then diminished in effectiveness. Meanwhile, his ophthalmologist was perplexed by the wide fluctuations in his IOP readings. Randall couldn't bring himself to clear up the mystery.

Bob Randall set the legal precedent for
contemporary medical use of marijuana.

"Since 1968," he explains, "I had noticed that marijuana smoking relieved the eye problems. But I thought this was just a side benefit of being relaxed. Whenever I would get the symptoms, I'd smoke a joint, and they would disappear within a half-hour. Whenever I'd run out or couldn't make a connection, I'd get intense symptoms again."

Last winter Randall underwent 10 days of testing at UCLA. His IOP was measured after doses of every conventional glaucoma medication and after he had smoked Government-grown marijuana.

In February [UCLA's Dr. Robert S.] Hepler said in an affidavit: ". . . . We found his IOP rose soon after awakening, remained above normal for the greater part of each day, and became particularly elevated in late evening . . . . Marijuana's pressure-lowering effect, in combination with prescription medications, usually brought his IOP levels toward the normal range . . . . It would seem that he has benefited from the use of marijuana in the past and could gain significant medical advantage from a program of regulated use in the future. Marijuana, in combination with conventional medications, provides him with control of intraocular pressure unobtainable utilizing other medications alone."

Randall's request leaves the Government nettlesome alternatives. Stick to the law at the risk of his going blind for want of a drug that millions use illegally. Or exempt him and, while perhaps saving his sight, risk setting a precedent that might evoke a torrent of similar applications by people suffering from other diseases . . . .

Meanwhile, Randall waits, wonders about the irony of it all, and reads as much as he can, while he can. Sometimes, he says, he can feel the pressure inside his eyes.

"The big problem," he adds, "is getting people to understand without becoming either a pathetic figure or a hero. I'm neither. I'm simply a human being placed in this odd situation because of a convoluted law."

Other recent reports indicate that THC "is far more effective than any other drug in relieving the vomiting and nausea that plague thousands of cancer patients undergoing chemical therapy."

About 75 percent of patients receiving chemotherapy for cancer suffer moderate to extreme nausea and vomiting, and about 90 percent find no relief in conventional anti-nausea drugs. According to findings reported in the *New England Journal of Medicine* for the first twenty-two experimental patients "Marijuana drug treatments resulted in at least a 50 percent reduction in vomiting and nausea after therapy." In five instances, the patients suffered no nausea at all. A controlled study based on work at the Sidney Farber Cancer Center showed that no decrease in nausea or vomiting occurred when placebo, or dummy, treatment was used. Moreover, terminal cancer patients given synthetic THC at the medical College of Virginia tended to become more relaxed, emotionally stable, less depressed and frustrated, and tended also to gain weight (whereas cancer patients become emaciated). Dr. Stephen E. Sallan, leader of a team researching THC at the Sidney Farber Center in Boston, summed up other differences noted:

Until THC was given to them, patients undergoing chemotherapy could only look forward to hours and even days of sickness and misery. THC changed all that.

It made it possible for patients to lead a normal life following treatment. It also relieved their dread of the chemotherapy that—before they took THC—had made them so sick and miserable.

The only side effect from THC is that a patient gets a "high" similar to the kind that comes from smoking marijuana.

A booklet titled *Using Marijuana in the Reduction of Nausea Associated with Chemotherapy* discusses the timing of grass use with specific anti-cancer drugs and even supplies recipes and instructions (for advanced cases) for preparing suppositories. Priced at $2.50, it is shipped within twenty-four hours from Murray Publishing Co., 2312 Third Ave., Seattle, WA 98121, (206) 682-3560. The author, Dr. Roger A. Roffman, has just published the fullest account of recent uses of *Marijuana as Medicine*, and would like to hear from those who want to share their experience. He can be contacted at Box 5651, University Station, Seattle, WA 98105, (206) 543-5968.

In some therapeutic applications, one might say the soothing effect comes about mentally. For instance, marijuana seems to change the perception of pain so that it becomes something off in a distance, rather uninteresting—"Just as the pain in a delicate ear would grow less and less," as a

Jeremy Bigwood

Roger Roffman, author of Marijuana as Medicine, *conducted the first research study on GI marijuana use in Vietnam and has been the administrator of the Washington State Research Program on the Medical Uses of Marijuana.*

physician in the late nineteenth century put it, "as a beaten drum was carried further and further out of the range of hearing." This effect is evident when marijuana is used during the contractions of childbirth, as is the tradition in many places, and when fretful babies are calmed by blowing pot smoke over them. Still, psychological anesthetic action is clearly only part of the story. (*Cannabis* preparations may also have anti-bacterial action. Check out both *Marijuana Medical Papers* and the report in Drake's *Cultivator's Handbook* on THC's ability to knock out *Staphylococcus* strains, including some that have become resistant to penicillin and other antibiotics.)

MENTAL EFFECTS

The *subtlety* of this drug is one of its important qualities. Of all the substances considered here, marijuana is the most subtle. Some question whether it is a psychedelic at all, and beginners frequently fail to notice much effect.

The *inability to experience the drug unprompted* was a major finding in the first scientific study of marijuana (by Weil, Zinberg and Nelson in Boston, 1968). On identical amounts of the substance, regular users discovered they got quite high, while non-users noticed no changes. Researchers wonder whether this difference results from having learned to appreciate

the effects or from physiological changes that occur after one or more experiences with the drug.

"You will hear people say that one never gets stoned the first time,"
wrote Bill Burroughs, Jr., describing what happened after he "dipped into a
Mason jar of homemade *majoun*" and also tried some "tasty little hashish
candies" when he first went to visit his father in Tangiers at age fourteen:

> ... but I was so far gone that I couldn't even remember the onset. Only visions
> of the entire course of human history, from the apeman all asteam on the hos-
> tile plains on through the blessed virgin and plunging into the abyss of tech-
> nology. After two million years, Ian nudged me gently and said that he'd like
> to go to sleep . . . .

Strength of Cannabis *Preparations*

In India, three different strengths of *Cannabis* are usually distinguished
—*bhang, ganja* and *charas*. These correspond to leaves, flowering tops and
leaves, and the best of the resin from flowers. Most marijuana smoked in
America belongs to the first, bottom grade; all the rest costs a great deal. The
bhang-type *Cannabis* here is about a tenth as strong as *charas*, which also is
known as hashish.

What happens at lower concentrations is interesting but shouldn't be
confused with more full-blown "psychedelic" effects provoked by "hash" or
"hash oil," which can be up to 40 percent THC. The effect of cooked pot
tends to be minimal up until consumption of about 2 grams (about 2 table-
spoons) of commercial varieties—containing, say, 2 percent THC. The
experience is then stronger and longer lasting (usually for four to eight
hours, compared to half an hour to one or two hours when smoking).

Because THC-acid and much of the delta-6-*trans* isomer are converted
by heat or combustion into the delta-1 form, the effects of smoking and eating
are quite different. (Absorption from the lungs is said to be about three
times more effective than when marijuana passes through the stomach.)

One unexplained characteristic—probably having to do with the
differences in cannabinols in a leaf—is that when people use different batches
of marijuana, they develop less tolerance than if they use the same grass
regularly.

Deterioration in the strength of THC over time results from exposure
to light (mainly), heat and air.

The Tart Study

Probably the most relevant study to date about what might be considered
"typical" pot experience was made by Dr. Charles Tart and reported in his
book *On Being Stoned*. Tart conducted his research by leaving questionnaires
at various locations near where he was working, requesting that they be filled
out anonymously and returned. His book is an evaluation of the first 150
completed questionnaires that passed his test for validity (a consistency on

14 key items among 220) and comprises, as he estimates, approximately 421 years of pot experience, representing some 37,000 joints.

Tart's study confirms that when the drug is relatively familiar to the user, reactions are not nearly as bizarre and disoriented as the classic literature on *Cannabis* inebriation suggests. He concludes that there are definite effects of the drug and works out a kind of "phenomenology of marijuana." His findings can be presented in a chart grouping *characteristic* versus *rare* experiences:

Characteristic Experiences

Patterns, meaning in
  ambiguous material
Visual imagery more vivid
Greater spatial separation
  between sound sources
Understand the words of
  songs better
Hear more subtle changes
  in sound
New qualities to taste
Enjoy eating and eat very much
More in the here-and-now
Time passes more slowly
Distance in walking changed
Sexual orgasm has new,
  pleasurable qualities
New qualities to touch
Movements exceptionally smooth
Get physically relaxed,
  don't want to move

Touch more exciting
Forget start of conversation
Insights into others
More subtle humor
Ordinary social games hard to play
Less noisy than when drunk
Often forget to finish some task
Easily sidetracked
Spontaneous insights into self
Harder to read
Appreciate more subtle humor
Accept contradictions more readily
Almost invariably feel good
  when stoned
Less need to feel in control
  of things
More childlike, open to experience,
  filled with wonder
Easy to go to sleep at bedtime

Rare Experiences

Flat quality to world
Colors get duller
Sounds blurry
Precognition
Visual world looks flat
Feel possessed by a hostile force
Sense *chakra* centers
Perform magical operations
Feel possessed by good force
Feel energy in spine
Vomit
Feel nauseated, dizzy

Do antisocial things
People seem dead, like robots
Less need for sex
Déjà vu
Prolonged blank periods
Almost invariably feel bad
  when stoned
Body parts move by themselves
Worry about losing control
Harm other people
Tremble in hands
Sleep poor, restless

Old Myths Dispelled

Dr. Tart's data should lay to rest one of the nastiest myths the Anslinger brigade fostered about marijuana, i.e., that it leads to sexual and other violence. "Loss of control to the point of antisocial actions" is reported to be *the rarest* of all marijuana effects recorded in the Tart study (p. 192). This is consistent with what's been found elsewhere in several NIMH (National Institute of Mental Health) studies. One of the most meticulous of these, *The Blumer Report*, determined that use of the plant's leaves *reduced* violence in juvenile delinquents in Oakland.

As to sexual effects, in her report on the intimate lives of marijuana users (*The Sexual Power of Marijuana*), Barbara Lewis asks, "Is sexual power a wild plant?" Her findings are prefaced with the following summary:

> Whatever scientific research does exist on marijuana and sex supports what I learned in my interviews. In a study of twenty-one men and eleven women who had used pot more than ten times and were asked why they continued to do so, 73% said they smoked to "increase sexual satisfaction" . . . . The study, "The Marijuana Problem: An Overview," was published in *The American Journal of Psychiatry* in 1968. It was coauthored by Dr. William H. McGlothlin, a research psychologist at the University of California in Los Angeles, and Dr. Louis Jolyon West, now chairman of the department of psychiatry at the same institution.

*These books, other than that by Barbara Lewis (which **was** an opinion-shaper), were never very popular and didn't influence many people. At least thirty such pulp volumes have appeared.*

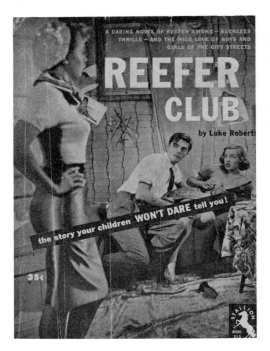

A DARING NOVEL OF REEFER SMOKE — RECKLESS
THRILLS — AND THE WILD LOVE OF BOYS AND
GIRLS OF THE CITY STREETS

REEFER CLUB

by Luke Roberts

the story your children WON'T DARE tell you!

35¢

VP 286 $1.50

PSYCHEDELIC SEX

ATILLA WAS A SEX CRAZED DEMI-GOD WHO SHOWED NO
MERCY TO HIS FEMALE SEX SLAVES . . . HE RAPED
AND PILLAGED THEIR BODIES TO SATISFY THE SEXUAL
CRAVINGS OF HIS HENCHMEN
by RALPH BENTON

ADULTS ONLY

Reefer Girl

The frank, biting story of a young girl of the slums,
and how she was caught in the toils of evil.

A NEW EXCITING NOVEL

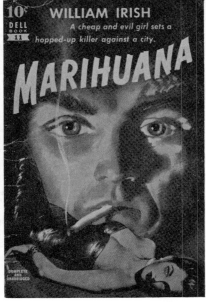

10¢

DELL BOOK

WILLIAM IRISH

A cheap and evil girl sets a
hopped-up killer against a city.

MARIHUANA

COMPLETE AND UNABRIDGED

DOPE DOLL

Sex And Suspe...
A Savage Set...
by
STEVE
HARRAGA...

Famous on two con...
for his masterful...
of breezy slaughte...
easy passion...

TWO GREAT BOOKS UNDER ONE COVER

Too Many Dames Can Ruin A Guy!

THE BIGAMY KISS

by
STEVE
HARRAGAN

GIANT

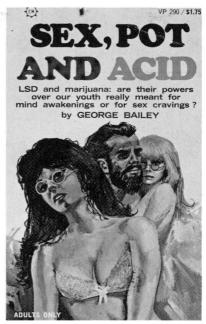

VP 290 / $1.75

SEX, POT AND ACID

LSD and marijuana: are their powers over our youth really meant for mind awakenings or for sex cravings?

by GEORGE BAILEY

ADULTS ONLY

FIRST TIME IN PAPERBACK—
THE $5.95 BESTSELLER—NOW 95¢

75980|95¢ ace

the Sexual Power of Marijuana

by BARBARA LEWIS

AN INTIMATE REPORT ON THE SEX LIVES
OF MARIJUANA USERS.

SHE TRADED HER
BODY FOR DRUGS—
AND KICKS!

Marijuana Girl

N. R. DeMexico

B328
35¢
K

NEVER WAS THERE
SO OUTSPOKEN A NOVEL
AS THIS...TELLING THE
PLAIN, UNCENSORED TRUTH
ABOUT TEEN-AGE
ADDICTS—AND THEIR
DESPERATE
SEARCH FOR
THRILLS!

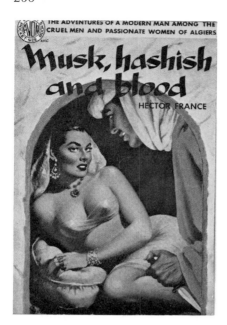

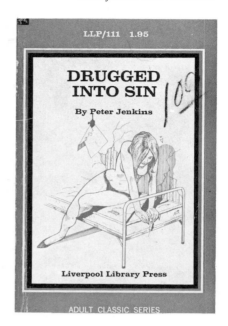

Dr. West was among the thirty-five psychiatrists, psychologists, physicians, sociologists, and pharmacological researchers with whom I talked. He had had contact with hundreds of marijuana smokers over the years. He expressed concern over some effects of the drug on some of its users. But he conceded that the continuing controversy over the question of whether pot is, technically, an "aphrodisiac" was irrelevant to most users.

"In real life and among real people," he said, "the fact is, the word is, the belief is, the expectation is, and the result is, that marijuana enhances sexual activity."

I also received considerable assistance from Dr. Erich Goode, assistant professor of sociology at the State University of New York in Stony Brook, Long Island, whose survey of 200 pot users was supported by the National Institute of Mental Health . . . . In 1967 he submitted a twelve-page questionnaire to 200 middle-class New York marijuana users. The questions dealt with every aspect of marijuana experience, including sexual response. The respondents' mean age was twenty-three.

A very substantial majority (68%) of these users reported that marijuana distinctly enhanced their sexuality. Even more interesting, 50% of the women and 39% of the men revealed that it actually excited their initial interest, sharpened their sexual desire—again, only when smoked with a desirable sexual partner. If smoked with someone deemed distasteful, they said, marijuana accentuates the feeling of distaste. Sex actually became repugnant. "It's not like alcohol, which often numbs a person to the unpleasant aspects of his partner," Dr. Goode commented.

Other Aspects of Pot

Some time ago someone showed me a hand-set booklet on

"the dangers of *not* smoking marijuana."

On a social level these dangers included such things as war, while on the personal level, it was claimed, *not* smoking made you forget you're a freak, made you think the President knows what he's doing, made you decide that nobody will love you unless you're someone other than yourself . . . .

Ken Kesey, who feels reluctant to recommend any other mental drugs because they have so often been impure, provides the ultimate pot commercial:

> But good old grass I can recommend. To be just without being mad . . . to be peaceful without being stupid, to be interested without being compulsive, to be happy without being hysterical . . . smoke grass.

Inspiration

The core of the matter is that most users of *Cannabis* find it inspiring in many ways. They claim not only that it can heighten sexual feelings but that it inspires religious feelings, increases creativity, helps them solve problems, helps to get them in touch with themselves and expands the scope of their minds. Rats given a diet of THC have been shown to be capable of learning how to run mazes faster than when they're left unstoned (see E.A. Carlini and C. Kramer, "Effects of *Cannabis Sativa* (Marihuana) on Maze Performance of the Rat," *Psychopharmacologica,* 1965, p. 175).

When people talk about marijuana adding a third dimension to pictures or new depths to colors or creating "synethesia" (when music can, say, become visual), they are discussing changes in normal external perception. Distortions in the sense of time and space are fascinating. The effects that come under headings of "insight" or "inspiration" are also common occurrences with marijuana use and these effects may prove beneficial to society at large. To drive this point home, read one more listing from the Tart materials, not *characteristic* or *rare* experiences this time but *common* experience:

Common Experience

Skip intermediate steps in problem solving

Insights into others

Thoughts more intuitive

Ideas more original

Converse intelligently even though things forgotten

Learn a lot about what makes people tick

Say more profound, appropriate things

Intuitive, empathic understanding of people

Sexual love a union of souls as well as bodies

Inhibitions lowered

Mind feels more efficient in problem solving

At one with the world

Events, actions become archetypal

Before leaving the topic of marijuana's mental effects, a word should be added about its ability to give access to long-buried memories, to facilitate rapport and to aid psychotherapeutic "transference." Let me cite the experience of Dr. Harry Hermon, who first became interested in this herb as a means to help his patients expedite their psychotherapy. A patient he had been treating without much success for some time came in one day, and the information Dr. Hermon had been seeking in vain to elicit for so long suddenly began to flow forth freely. Hermon was astonished. He asked what was different this time. His patient informed him that he had come in stoned.

"Stoned?" said Dr. Hermon. "What is this 'stoned'?"

And thus Dr. Hermon came to realize how effectively this weed could unblock a person's mind, an insight which launched him into an entirely new phase of his therapy and life.

Negative psychological effects occasionally yet appear among some users, mainly having to do with panicking, objections on the part of some people to seeing the past or present in a "new light," or overdoing marijuana smoking. A decade and a half ago, users generally considered smoking pot or hashish something to be prepared for and used it ritualistically. Since then the strength of much marijuana has increased and some people—mainly dealers and others with lots of time to kill—have perhaps overindulged. "Marijuana is a drug of low abuse potential," comments Dr. David E. Smith, who has treated all kinds of drug complications for more than a decade and a half at the Haight-Ashbury Free Medical Clinic. He and others treating people with drug problems point to the main symptom of pot "abuse" as a psychological compulsion to use it to the point of "loss of control" over other aspects of one's life, to where it seriously impairs one. "A little warms the heart," declares a Sacred Seeds package of high-potency skunk weed, "too much burns the soul."

FORMS AND PREPARATIONS
Distinguishing among Marijuana Samples

Marijuana appears as a mixture of leaves, twigs and possibly seeds, flowers and "buds" (clumps of leaves and flowers) of a *Cannabis* plant. The particular plant a batch of marijuana came from may have been an unseeded female, a female with seeds, a male or even hermaphroditic—an order which roughly indicates declining levels of THC content. It may have grown from *C. sativa* or *indica* seeds or have been a hybrid, reaching maturity or not in equitorial or temperate regions, or under lights of varying intensity and spectra, or hydroponically, with or without added nutrients, and close to other plants or apart from them. These factors, along with the time of year it was planted, whether it was transplanted, whether it was farmed with a knowledge of the effects of periods of light on it and the time of day it was picked, are some of the major variables affecting THC and CND levels in a marijuana sample.

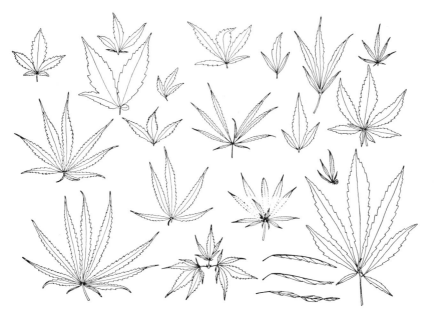

Robert Connell Clarke: *Marijuana Botany*

Cannabis *leaves appear in these and other shapes.*

Cannabis will grow almost anywhere given adequate drainage, but psychoactivity can vary by a factor of about twenty in various manifestations of the fresh, natural product. This is then affected by how it is harvested, dried and its age before use. This basic material can also be transformed into many grades of hashish, hash oil, isomerized forms or *Cannabis* butters for adding to or using with food. Marijuana has also been used in the making of beers, wines and liqueurs.

In some places, such as Amsterdam and in parts of the Near and Far East, fairly standardized types of *Cannabis* can be bought over the counter or enjoyed at "smoking clubs" without the complications that arise from its illegality here. Otherwise, the situation is more complicated and the novice or relatively inexperienced might appreciate a few pointers.

Jack Margolis and Richard Clorfene opened the section on "Buying Grass" in their *A Child's Garden of Grass* (1969) with some sensible advice:

> In buying grass, there are four things to remember: First, you don't want to get caught; second, you don't want to get bad grass; third, you don't want to overpay; and we can't remember the fourth.
>
> The first rule to remember in buying grass is "Know Your Connection." If you know and trust the person from whom you're buying the grass, you shouldn't have any difficulties. He won't be a cop or informer and, if the grass turns out to be a real burn (less than the correct quantity or bad quality), he'll probably make good.

The Hindu deity Shiva is frequently portrayed on advertisements for hashish and ganja shops, as in this Katmandu example behind kilos of hash "finger clusters."

The second rule to remember is, "Don't Trust Nobody." This applies even to people whom you know and trust. Undercover agents look and sound exactly like you do, and many informers are not actually agents; they're just people who have been put into the position of turning in other people because they themselves have been caught, and they've made a deal with the police.

Buying grass is usually relatively safe, because police usually bust people who sell it *to* them, rather than people who buy it *from* them . . . .

If you know your connection, there should be no problem, but if you don't then you should sample the grass first. Usually a seller will "puff" his wares— which means claiming that it's better than it is. Cases have held that puffing is legal, so if the grass turns out not to be as good as he said it was, you have no recourse in the courts. The smart thing is to bring some papers with you and sample it. (A seller of bad grass will usually say he is out of papers.)

In *The Marijuana Catalogue* (1978), Paul Dennis and Carolyn Barry described a test that applies for marijuana said to be "very good," "excellent," "bomber" or by other adjectives with implications of greatness:

> Sitting loose and relaxed, inhale the smoke slowly to your lungs' full capacity and hold it as long as you comfortably can . . . . Take six of these total lungfuls. If after ten minutes, fifteen at the most, you aren't feeling higher than the North Star on Christmas Eve, the grass in question is *not* superduper. If you feel fairly good, it's OK grass. If you feel just a little something, you think, you're going to have to burn your throat out to get high on it. After you try this test a few times, you'll learn your own reactions. You can become surprisingly sensitive to the various qualities of smoke *in the only infallible test*—your own subjective reaction.

If you are serious about testing the precise quality of a *Cannabis* sample, they also suggest that you

> don't take any more than two-thirds of a full joint—at least until you've made up your mind about its quality and the price you're willing to pay. Quite commonly a dealer will share an entire joint with you. Since the dealer may be doing a lot of smoking in the course of a day, he or she may actually not toke that much of the joint. So, without noticing it, you've ended up smoking most of the thing . . . .
>
> So the rule is, always sample some of the very bag you're buying; and if you don't know the dealer, watch that bag like the proverbial pea in the shell game. Also, even an honest dealer may offer a jay as soon as you come in— just to be friendly. Then later, when you try your stuff before buying, you realize you can't tell the purchased high from the gift one. If offered some smoke when you come in, say, "No, thanks. I'm OK." When the dealer hands you the bag you're considering buying, just say, "Mind if I try a little of this?" If the dealer claims the joint in his hand is the same stuff, just say you'd like to try the bag you're buying. Any honest dealer will say, "Sure." It's basic practice in reliable dealing.

A Two-Tier Market. Before the 1970s, most marijuana available in the U.S. had relatively low concentrations of THC by today's standards, and more intense *Cannabis* experiences were mainly propelled by various forms of hashish. Over the last decade, the marijuana market has split into two types of grass that are widely available—the result of genetic work on seeds, greater knowledge of how to cultivate resinous plants and particularly the growth of interest in *sinsemilla*. Now what is offered is poor to fair grass, and connoisseur grass and hash. Potency is divided in this way because of the economics of farming. Michael Starks in his *Marijuana Potency* enunciates the general principle after describing cultivation patterns and their results: "The consequences of these observations for the marijuana farmer are clear. You have two basic choices: high potency and low yield or lower potency and high yield."

Kayo cites a DEA study in his *The Sinsemilla Technique* on the THC content in various forms of marijuana. It reflects this division:

> THC levels in "normal" cannabis—that which grows wild or is imported from other countries—ranges from 0% to 2.5%. Domestic cannabis—that which is cultivated in the stressfilled environments of the United States—ranges from 2.8% to 7.6%.

Many people prefer strains without too much THC content. Others prefer to smoke small tokes of stronger *Cannabis* or to share half a joint with a friend (which in the better crops is sufficient for both). While the first tier is sold to the consumer in ounces or maybe quarter or half pounds, the second tier most often goes by the gram or possibly an ounce.

The ultimate test of a marijuana sample is smoking it. But much can also be learned by paying attention to some of the qualities evident in the leaves, twigs and whatever else is being presented:

Seeds. Their presence indicates that this isn't the most potentially resinous of plants, but rather a seeded female—which still can be very strong. There are various estimates indicating that about 40 to 50 percent of the "vital energy" in the female will go into seed production rather than resin production if fertilized. The weight one gets to smoke, of course, doesn't include the weight of seeds.

An examination of the seeds also enables one to determine something of the maturity of the plant when it was harvested. If they are round and dark, then they were probably harvested when resin and THC were roughly at their peak. If there are a lot of seeds that are smaller and yellower, then it was probably cut down early. Seeds from different locales can vary in size by a factor of two, with *C. sativa* varieties generally larger. *C. indica* seeds are distinguished from those of *C. sativa* by Michael Starks like this:

> *C. indica* tends to have small, almost spherical seeds . . . . *C. sativa* seeds are often highly compressed longitudinally so that when pressure is applied to the peripheral ridges, they easily fall apart, in contrast to those of *C. indica*. *C. sativa* seeds are the largest of the three species, often exceeding 5 mm in length.

Shake-to-Bud Ratio. If the marijuana is all loose leaves, or "shake," it can be male or female and of greatly varying THC and CBD content. The

Sam Selgnij: *Blotter #4*

Close-up of three Cannabis *seed varieties. The very small ones in the middle are from 9,000-ft. Himalayan wild Nepali hash plants.*

more flowers and leaf clusters, or buds, there are, the more likely that there are higher concentrations of THC. Many would consider *sinsemilla* shake stronger than much that is considered of commercial but not excellent quality. Young leaves can be fairly potent, as can male leaves. In his *Marijuana Potency*, Michael Starks discusses the complex nature of the cannabidiol (CBD) interaction with THC, gives values for specific varieties and writes that "it seems reasonable to assume that as CBD content approaches that of THC, the high will be diminished in intensity, but prolonged."

Leaf color can be predominantly brown, yellow, green, purple, black or various combinations of these and red streakings. Color becomes richer and more complex as the plant matures, but this is not much of a guide to the high that is experienced.

Resin itself, however, glints in the sun as tiny, brilliant points. Sometimes the resin becomes so thick that it actually crystalizes. The high doesn't actually accord with resin always, being a mix of the THC and CND interaction, but generally speaking this is so.

Smell. Many novelists and other writers have described the smell of marijuana as that of burning rope, perhaps getting off on the fact that it comes from the hemp plant. The actual smell is unlike any other herb, but is fairly pronounced and pervasive when marijuana is burned. As the plant matures the sharp, earthy smell of the leaves coming from chlorophyll diminishes as the more honey- and flower-like odors produced by resin and flowers increasingly predominate. Most users like the "taste" of all marijuana smoke,

The best marijuana "buds" appear as "colas," tightly packed flowering parts, as in this example called "candy cane cola." The name "cola" comes from the Spanish colas de zorro—*"foxtails."*

but prefer the more "resonate" smells produced at the end of the plant's life. The difference is much like that exhibited in bouquet of a wine as it ages and loses the astringent flavor produced by tannins.

Veteran smokers can easily tell if a sample of marijuana is bunk, ordinary or special by crushing a bud in one's fingers. When it breaks open, there should be a pungent smell. If its quite good, the fingers should also be somewhat sticky. Some strains have a strong pine, mint or skunk odor.

Ordinary imports of Mexican, Colombian and Jamaican generally have only small buds about 1-1½" long, which may constitute possibly a fifth to a tenth of the total. These are sufficient in most instances to get people quite high, as are just leaves alone. Fortunately, it takes only ten or fifteen minutes at most to know from direct experience whether the sample offered has effects predominantly up, strong, stony, psychedelic or whatever.

How should one check out a proferred "Thai" stick? These have been the only example so far of a special kind of *Cannabis* associated with exceptional packaging—small buds tied along a short skewer stick. (See back issues of *High Times* and *Cannabis* calendars for illustrative specimens.) Anyone interested in this question should roll fingers along a small part of the sample and see how sticky it is; smell it, checking out how "resonant" and complex the smells; and smoke a bit, giving it the ultimate test. Unroll about half an inch of the six inch skewer it is tied to and smoke that. If the results are not soon impressive, the sample is likely bogus.

Harvesting, Pressing and Aging. The best grass comes as "colas" or long "buds" which have been individually picked and often are hung upside down for at least three days to dry. They are hung upside down not to add THC to the leaves from other parts of the plant—as psychedelic myth long had held—because THC doesn't translocate. Hanging upside down gives the buds a tighter shape.

The bud is then manicured, or trimmed, of its loose leaves and sometimes vacuum-sealed in bottles or heat sealed into plastic containers. Kept cool, it will lose only about 5% of its content per year.

Most foreign shipments are compressed before shipment into "bricks" that weigh about a kilogram. Sometimes there are foreign objects inside, but this is rare. More important is that the crushing breaks up some of the protective shielding that keeps THC from turning into an inactive form through oxidation. The normal state to which grass is dried is not brittle, but as it ages it becomes more powdery and less powerful. This is why most people using quality grass, or often any kind, break open only a small amount at a time. Crumbled and exposed for any length of time to air, the THC in marijuana is sure to lose a significant amount of psychoactivity.

Hashish and Hash Oil

Grass is to hashish or *charas* as beer and wine are to hard liquor. As in the case of distilled spirits, some care is needed in the preparation of this strengthened *Cannabis* product.

Lawrence Cherniak: *The Great Books of Hashish*

A Himalayan hash press surrounded by hashish in various stages of completion. In the foreground are broken bits; in the middle left are "finger clusters" next to a plastic bag filled with chips warming in the sun; to the right of the press are well-pressed slabs in their plastic wrappings; and in the center are a dozen hand-pressed balls of Royal temple balls.

Traditionally, hash was collected by workers passing bareskinned through *Cannabis* fields, embracing the plants and then having the adhering resin scraped off their bodies. Nowadays, the practice generally is to clothe a worker in leather and then scrape the resin off the leather, or to simply rub the plant's buds with one's hands and then scrape the oily residue off one's hands. W.D. Drake's *The International Cultivator's Handbook* and Lawrence Cherniak's *The Great Books of Hashish* provide fairly full discussions of other methods of hash production, including one in which workers go into sealed beating or thrashing rooms clothed in loincloths and masks, seeking to extract the finest powder. Cherniak's book illustrates the processes and the products of Morocco, Lebanon, Afghanistan and the Himalayas in 168 superb color photographs.

Hashish was served at the Turkish Booth at the Centennial Exposition of 1876 in Chicago.

Blond Lebanese hash consists of a matrix including flower pistils, leaf and flower particle debris, non-resin-bearing cystolith hairs, conical trichomes and resin nodules. Above, this is shown magnified about 500 times by an electron scanning microscope. Below is water-pressed Afghani hash in which the resin nodules (magnified about 250 times) are largely undissolved.

The resin that has been collected gets pressed with animal fat, honey or a similar amalgam. Generally speaking, the quality of hash often corresponds to color—the darker it is, the more potent it usually turns out to be. But there are important exceptions. Good-quality Morrocan, for instance is frequently very potent, even though it looks rather white. Hashish deteriorates faster than marijuana because it is broken up finely when manufacturing begins. When it is well pressed, however, the interior will maintain its potency for about two or three years.

In the early 1970s, we first began to see fairly large amounts of "hash oil," a product distilled from marijuana leaves. Processes are detailed in Starks' *Marijuana Potency* from DEA papers. Here the rules of color are reversed: the darker the color, usually the less refined, the more harsh and the less potent the oil is.

The usual methods for smoking hash oil are: in a special glass pipe (an example can be found on page 331), on the end of a cigarette or rolled with tobacco or grass. Perhaps the most efficient way is to smear a drop or two on a cigarette paper and then roll that into a joint. Really fine quality hash oil is powerful enough that only a trace is needed. Dipping a container in hot water thins it, so that just a bit can be picked up by inserting a needle or paperclip and then smearing this on paper.

THC and Analogues

Delta-9 THC, because it has been around so long, is not patentable. For THC analogues, however, this is not the case. As a result, quite a few pharmaceutical houses have spent money trying to come up with something that would mimic THC's medical properties without THC's psychoactivity. Several candidates for this role were produced, with Lilly's "Nabilone" being considered for a while as the most promising. After a year of testing, however, dogs showed dramatic drops in blood pressure, and soon Lilly withdrew Nabilone from FDA consideration.

The U.S. government supplied marijuana until recently for a small amount of medical use. In August 1982, Surgeon General Julius Richmond announced that the government had decided to make THC pills available to cancer patients instead. Robert Randall and others concerned with medical use of marijuana attacked the decision. "I think it is unfortunate that the government decided to release what is known to be a medically inferior substance to marijuana and a substance which has a far higher potential for adverse side effects," Randall said. "In effect, the government is trying to flood the market with a phony synthetic and at the same time trying to retard research on the natural material." Roger Roffman's studies showed the natural substance to be more easily tolerated than the synthetic. Stephen Sallan of the Harvard Medical School said that smoking marijuana was more effective in reducing chemotherapy side-effects because it speeded up absorption of the active ingredient into the bloodstream.

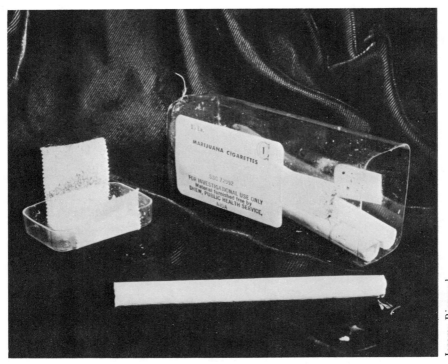

Jeremy Bigwood

Some of the joints produced by the U.S. government pot farm at the University of Mississippi for medical applications.

Smoking

The usual way to ingest marijuana is by smoking it. In this way THC acid is "decarboxylated" into THC and together with already-present THC passes into the lungs where it enters the bloodstream and is carried across the blood-brain barrier. This occurs quite rapidly, so that most veterans have some idea of the quality of a sample within a minute or two, although others might need to take longer.

Our present-day pipe appears to have been developed by the Indians of the Ohio Valley sometime around the second century B.C., if we are to believe the evidence of excavations of burial mounds. The notion of creating a joint—rolling a smoking mixture into a cigarette—seems to have developed originally among the Indians of Mexico prior to the time of Montezuma. By the time of *The Thousand and One Nights*, toward the end of the first millenium A.D., the hookah (or "hubbly bubbly") was well known.

Since then there have been some innovations in smoking: the bong, the carburetor, hash and opium pipes. *High Times* displays many refinements, including "The Tilt," which is said to heat marijuana only to the proper temperature for extraction of the THCs so that other oils are left in the residue. For those with sensitive throats, use of *hot water* in a bong reduces the amount of water-soluble, non-psychoactive components in *Cannabis* smoke and thus increase the amount of THC ingested per toke, while reducing the harshness on the lungs. "Passing the smoke through cold water tends to condense some of the desirable components," comments *High Times* in one of its advice columns, adding that since the majority of cannabinols (including THC) dissolve in alcohol, "the use of alcoholic beverages in a water pipe will give a less potent smoke." Many users prefer the taste when it is passed through cold water.

Eating Marijuana

In India and other areas with long marijuana experience, *Cannabis* is often made into something like a milkshake (*bhang*) or a kind of candy (most commonly known as *majoun*). These methods give effects, but experience has shown that if marijuana is to be ingested, its potency can be increased considerably by cooking it first in oil at low temperatures for about fifteen minutes.

Because cannabinols are not soluble in water, the general practice is to cook them in fat or butter (which when strained, produces the famous Indian product called *ghee*) or alcohol (in which they are soluble, although in this case all heating should be done at low temperatures and in the absence of an open flame since alcohol is highly combustible). A number of pamphlets on *Cannabis* cookery have been published, but many simply contain rewritten, familiar recipes to which grass has been added. Some, such as that by "Panama Rose," recommend that grass be boiled in water to make a tea—which is an effective way to lose most of the active principles if the grass itself is then simply thrown out like old coffee grounds. I recommend W.D. Drake, Jr.'s book *Marijuana Food* (Simon & Schuster) or Adam Gottlieb's booklet *Art & Science of Cannabis Cookery* (Level Press), which discuss culinary factors that should be taken into account with marijuana and provide all the basic recipes one might need.

Another point that should be remembered is that if the stomach is relatively empty, marijuana products are digested much faster. Thus, there are good grounds for *not* simply adding grass to a dish like spaghetti.

The basic recipe for marijuana butter paste given by Roger Roffman for his patients requires 1 to 1½ ounces cleaned marijuana, 1 quart of water and ¼ pound butter or margarine:

> In saucepan, combine marijuana, water, and butter or margarine. Simmer for approximately 45 minutes. Mixture will become green or mustard-colored as active ingredients of marijuana are dissolved in oil of butter or margarine. Refrigerate mixture to cool. If, after cooling, butter or margarine has congealed, reheat mixture just enough to return it to liquid form. Stretch cheesecloth over bowl and pour mixture through it to remove leaves and

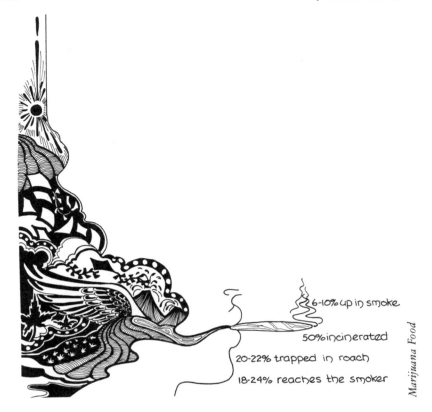

6-10% up in smoke

50% incinerated

20-22% trapped in roach

18-24% reaches the smoker

Marijuana Food

William Drake's view of the inefficiency of pot smoking. Unfortunately, eating is even less efficient because of incomplete absorption from the intestine. Using average marijuana containing 1 percent THC, smoking roughly one gram provides a minimal high, a condition also obtainable by eating about three grams. Michael Starks estimates that when pure, THC is roughly three times more potent when smoked than when eaten. "Smoking about 6 mg, or eating about 15 mg, of THC will feel like a minimal high to most people; whereas smoking 30 mg or eating 75 mg will tend to produce very intense effects, comparable to those from LSD."

other vegetable matter. Squeeze cloth *tightly* to prevent waste. Discard residue in cheesecloth. Refrigerate mixture again until butter or margarine congeals on top of liquid. (Active ingredients of marijuana are now dissolved in oil.) Carefully skim off congealed butter or margarine and discard liquid.

This paste can be used in any recipe instead of butter or margarine. The active ingredients aren't weakened by being cooked again. It can also be packed into capsules or shaped into suppositories.

Hasheesh Candy.—THE ARABIAN "GUNJE" OF ENCHANTMENT confectionized.—A most pleasurable and harmless stimulant.—Cures Nervousness, Weakness, Melancholy, &c. Inspires all classes with new life and energy. A complete mental and physical invigorator. Send for circular. Beware of imitations. 25 cents and $1 per box. Imported only by the

GUNJAH WALLAH CO., 476 Broadway, N. Y.

Two quick, efficient recipies: (1) To a brownie or corn bread mix weighing about 1½ pounds, add 1 cup of cleaned commercial grass that's been broken up by a blender and sautéed in butter or margarine for about fifteen minutes. Cut into nine or ten portions after baking as usual; take one or two at a time. (2) Melt half a cube (⅛ pound) butter in a pan and in this sauté a third to a half ounce of moderately potent grass for about five to ten minutes over low heat (not near any flames). Without allowing this to splatter, pour in eight ounces of vodka or rum rather swiftly and boil at a low temperature for another one to five minutes (depending upon how much alcohol you wish to evaporate). Strain the result, removing as much as possible of the juices into cups. Sweeten to taste with honey if desired; sufficient for two to four people.

A FRIEND WITH WEED IS A FRIEND INDEED!

This first known "mushroom stone," about a foot high and from the Guatemalan highlands, came to world attention when a German geographer published its picture in 1908. The meaning of this object by an unknown artist is uncertain, but it may speak for generations of mushroom worshipers. Some 300 similar sculptures have since been found. In 1952, a pencil sketch made of this one helped spark the rediscovery of Meoamerica's "sacred mushrooms."

CHAPTER FOUR
Psilocybian Mushrooms

"Will you help me learn the secrets of the divine mushroom?"

—R. Gordon Wasson

HISTORY

The fourth major category of psychedelics includes well over two dozen mushroom species at present. The number has risen recently and is expected to expand substantially in the near future as more mushroom species are analyzed.

Psilocybin and psilocin molecules are the primary psychedelic agents in the psychoactive mushrooms known so far, but four related molecules may in some way contribute to the mental effects. The term "psilocybian mushrooms" has been proposed to include all of the dozens of species containing psilocybin; it will be used in that sense here. Quite distinct isoxazolic molecules are present in the *Amanita muscaria* (Fly Agaric) and *Amanita pantherina* (Panther Caps) mushroom species, which are said by some people to create psychedelic states.

Although the histories of psilocybian and of *Amanita* mushrooms are entwined, the categories are quite different chemically, pharmacologically and in associated shamanic practices. The *Amanita* species will therefore be discussed in Chapter Nine of this book.

Of well over a half million plant species classified so far, about a fifth fall into the rather mysterious grouping of fungi. Many botanists consider these to be outside the usual concepts of "plant" or "animal." That some of these mushrooms are capable of causing impressive and often enlightening mental effects in humans is not, however, in doubt.

Fungi are distinguished from ordinary plants in two important ways. First, they lack—with a few exceptions—the green pigment chlorophyll that enables plants to make use of light in the production of organic substances. Second, they employ microscopic spores rather than seeds for reproduction. This chapter is concerned only with the rapidly growing, fleshy Basidiomycetes, the fungi popularly known as mushrooms or toadstools. The gilled "fruiting bodies" or carpophores of a mushroom are the sexual, "flowering" aspect; the larger part of the plant usually lives underground.

Scores of psilocybian mushrooms are of special interest nowadays, thanks mainly to the investigations of one couple: R. Gordon Wasson and Valentina Pavlovna Wasson. These two individuals were essential to the discovery that the largest natural production of psychedelics occurs in mushrooms. This revelation—quite as serendipitous as Hofmann's discovery of

LSD—came about in 1955. Their discovery (more accurately "rediscovery") is worth recounting because it greatly influenced subsequent developments.

From Antiquity until June 29, 1955

For millenia, psilocybian mushrooms were used by native Americans, living mainly in Central America but also as far south as Chile. These original mushroom users left few records, but they did establish a tradition of psychedelic mushroom use.

What we know of the Indian rites came from "gringos," and most of the relevant mushrooms go by botanical nomenclature that ends with the name of a non-native investigator. With only fragmentary evidence relating to earlier generations of mushroom worshippers, we must focus on fairly recent data.

The first important clues appear in sixteenth-century manuscripts written by Spaniards. The Friar Bernardino de Sahagún, who spent most of his adult life in Mexico, and Dr. Francisco Hernández, the personal physician to the King of Spain, both clearly described "mushrooms" used as psychoactive agents in tribal rites in post-Conquest Mexico. An educated Indian named Tezozómoc wrote in 1598 about the ingestion of "inebriating mushrooms" by celebrants at the coronation of Montezuma II.

In addition to these verbal accounts, drawings from Catholicized artists entitled *"Teonanácatl"*—meaning "wondrous," "awesome" or "divine" mushroom—also survive from the sixteenth century. One portrays a birdlike "devil" (a Spanish interpretation) dancing on top of a mushroom. Another depicts "the devil" encouraging an Indian to eat mushrooms.

A Náhuatl Indian dictionary prepared in 1571 distinguished a "mushroom of divine inebriation" from other "nanácatls," and another published in 1885 included the names for several inebriating mushrooms. In a translation of the latter, *Teonanácatl* is described as a "species of little mushrooms of bad taste, intoxicating, hallucinogenic."

Teonanácatl, *a sixteenth century drawing by a European from Sahagún's* Florentine Codex.

Teonanácatl, *a sixteenth century Indian drawing from the* Magliabechiano Codex.

Aside from these and other Spanish references, no effort seems to have been expended trying to identify *teonanácatl* until the twentieth century. A revival of interest, strangely enough, began as a scholar's squabble shortly after an authoritative misidentification in 1915.

After a search for *teonanácatl* in specimens of Mexican mushrooms, a prestigious American botanist, Dr. William E. Safford, concluded that there simply were none. He felt that the Spanish chroniclers must have confused them with dried peyote. In a talk entitled "Identification of teonanacatl of the Aztecs with the narcotic cactus *Lophophora williamsii* and an account of its ceremonial use in ancient and modern times," Safford—who was known for lengthy titles—declared that the dried mescal button resembled "a dried mushroom so remarkably that, at first glance, it will even deceive a mycologist"! He hypothesized that the Indians may have deliberately misled the Spanish in order to protect their use of peyote.

The few scholars who heard Safford or later read his handsomely-published report were mainly hearing about psychoactive mushrooms for the first time, only to be told that the mushrooms never existed. But there was one important dissenter—Dr. Plasius Paul (Blas Pablo) Reko, an Austrian physician who had engaged in extensive botanical collecting as a hobby while living in Mexico. Reko had become convinced that *teonanácatl* referred to mushrooms, not Safford's hypothesized peyote.

In 1919, Reko published a book entitled *El México Antiguo (The Old Mexico)* in which he proclaimed his belief that people were still using mushrooms in Mexico for "effectos narcóticos." He wrote in 1923 to Dr. J.N. Rose of the Smithsonian Institution:

> I see in your description of *Lophophora*, that Dr. Safford believes this plant to be the *teonanácatl* of Sahagún, which is surely wrong. It is actually, as Sahagún states, a fungus which grows on dung-heaps and which is still used under the same old name by the Indians of the Sierra Juárez in Oaxaca in their religious feasts.

Five years later, the journalist/novelist Victor A. Reko, a cousin of Blas Pablo Reko, wrote the first published objection to Safford's thesis. In an imaginative, popular book written in 1936—*Magische Gifte: Rausch- und Betaubungsmittel der Neuen Welt (Magical Poisons: Intoxicants and Narcotics of the New World)*—he declared that Safford's identification "must be contradicted":

> The nanacates are poisonous mushrooms which have nothing to do with peyote. It is known from olden times that their use induces intoxication, states of ecstasy and mental aberrations, but, notwithstanding the dangers attendant upon their use, people everywhere they grow have taken advantage of their intoxicating properties up to the present time.

Victor Reko gave the names *"Amanita mexicana"* and *"A. muscaria* variant *mexicana"* for the mushrooms described in his book. This embellishment of his cousin's views was significant in again attracting attention to a mushroom as *teonanácatl*.

Although Dr. Reko was considered by many to be "only an amateur," and indeed one given to fantastic ideas, he continued steadfastly to argue that there were Mexican tribes still using mushrooms for their shamanic ceremonies. In 1936, more than two decades after Safford "closed the case," Dr. Reko heard from Robert J. Weitlaner, an Austrian-born engineer who had given up that profession to study Indian ways. He told Reko that the Otomi Indians of Puebla (just northeast of Oaxaca) and of nearby regions were using mushrooms as inebriants and gave samples to Dr. Reko of what he said were the psychoactive mushrooms.

Dr. Reko, in turn, forwarded these samples to Dr. Carl Gustaf Santesson in Stockholm for chemical analysis and to the Farlow Herbarium at Harvard University for botanical examination. Reko's mailing arrived at Harvard in such rotted condition that the mushrooms were identified only as to genus (*Panaeolus*)—and perhaps incorrectly so.

The Harvard recipient was the young ethnobotanist Richard Evans Schultes, who had been a medical student until he happened upon Heinrich Klüver's first monography on "mescal visions." As Schultes later wrote to Klüver, reading that essay altered his life's course. Schultes changed his doctoral thesis to peyote use on the Kiowa reservation in Oklahoma and thereby began on a lifelong 'interest in mind-changing plants of the New World.

The appearance of Dr. Reko's mushrooms "out of the blue" encouraged Schultes to suggest that these—or something similar—may have been the mushrooms referred to in the Spanish chronicles as *teonanácatl*. Soon he and a Yale anthropology student, Weston La Barre, began summarizing the available evidence against Safford's arguments. In the *Harvard Botanical Museum Leaflets* of April and November 1937, Schultes disputed Safford's conclusion and uged that attention be redirected to identification of the mushrooms.

The next year Schultes began studies with Dr. Reko in northeastern Oaxaca among the Mazatec Indians. Soon the two heard reports about the existence of mushroom rites in and near the Oaxacan town of Huautla de Jiménez. They collected specimens of *Panaeolus sphinctrinus*, which was alleged to be the mushroom chiefly used in the rites. They also collected specimens of *Stropharia* (or *Psilocybe*) *cubensis*, a mushroom of lesser importance according to the native Mazatecs. These specimens remained in the herbarium at Harvard.

Soon after, Robert Weitlaner's daughter Irmgard and her husband, J.B. Johnson, along with others, attended a midnight mushroom ceremony—or *velada*—in which the shaman alone was said to have ingested *teonanácatl*. This ceremony was written up by Johnson for a Swedish journal, and soon forgotten.

All of these investigations ended with World War II. Dr. Reko went on to other pursuits, and Schultes was sent off to the Amazon to search out

Ethnopharmacological Search for Psychoactive Drugs

Plasius Paul (Blas Pablo) Reko, 1876-1953—a physician from Austria who conducted extensive botanical investigations in Mexico and held that mushrooms were still used by natives for creation of visionary states.

rubber sources. Santesson died shortly after completing his chemical analysis, and Johnson was killed in a minefield in North Africa.

We turn to the Wassons, whose contributions were prompted by an apparently minor incident in the fall of 1927.

R. Gordon Wasson is the American son of an Episcopalian minister who had written *Religion and Drink,* a book that examined biblical references to the drinking of alcohol by religious figures. He took the tact of a fundamentalist, which he was not, and implied that it would be quite unchristian to be critical of alcohol. The royalties of this book enabled the younger Wasson to study in Spain. He worked as an English teacher and then for a decade as a financial reporter for the *Herald-Tribune.* In 1926, he married a Muscovite pediatrician, Valentina Pavlovna.

A year later, the two were walking in the Catskill Mountains when Valentina Pavlovna dashed off the path to gather wild mushrooms. R. Gordon's initial reaction was one of disgust and fear that she might poison herself. He wouldn't even touch these "delicacies." Each of them was surprised to discover that the other had such intense, opposite feelings on the subject. The incident triggered a lifelong search of cultures manifesting either a great loathing of mushrooms or else a proclivity to treasure them. Soon they were dividing peoples into "mycophiles" ("mushroom lovers") and "mycophobes" ("mushroom fearers"). Their devotion to this eventually led them on a worldwide search for references and practices involving mushrooms—in museums, proverbs, myths, legends, folk tales, epics, history, poetry, novels, records made by explorers, and so on.

R. Gordon Wasson, who—while Vice President of the J.P. Morgan bank— was the first to reveal popularly the Indian use of "sacred mushrooms."

Valentina Pavlovna Wasson, who co-initiated ethnomycology, and was the first white woman to try psilocybian mushrooms.

    Twenty-five years later the poet Robert Graves and simultaneously an Italian printer of fine books, Giovanni Mardersteig of Verona, wrote to the Wassons about the search. They called attention to the Spanish chroniclers who had touched on *teonanácatl* and referred the Wassons to the "mushroom stones" then being discovered in quantity in the Guatemalan highlands, in El Salvador and in southeastern Mexico. Mardersteig even sent along a sketch that he made at the Rietberg Museum in Zurich. A few months later, Eunice V. Pike, a Protestant missionary to the Mazatecs, informed the Wassons that the local word for mushrooms meant "the dear little ones that leap forth." This correspondence led the Wassons to the leaflets by Schultes, written some fifteen years earlier.

    R. Gordon Wasson is not sure whether he or his wife was the first to put into words a hypothesis they came to agree on sometime in the 1940s— that as far back as 6,000 years ago, there were cultures that worshipped mushrooms. The discovery of the twenty or so mushroom stones seemed to be confirming evidence that the mushroom was the symbol of a religion, like the cross promulgated by Christians, the crescent moon by Moslems and

Two views of a "mushroom stone" in the Namuth collection of the pre-classic Mesoamerican period (1,000-500 B.C.). The figure emerging from the stipe is conjectured to be that of a young woman over a grinding stone or metate.

the Star of David by Jews. Although anthropologists and other experts referred to these artifacts as "mushroom stones," they seem to have thought of the term as merely descriptive, regarding these stone carvings as mainly phallic.

Schultes' papers, which pinpointed the town of Huautla de Jiménez in Oaxaca, gave the Wassons their most important clue about where to look for remaining mushroom cults. They contacted Schultes, who told them about Weitlaner, the Rekos and the mushroom *velada* witnessed by Weitlaner's daughter. He even arranged for a guide who had lived with the Indians of Oaxaca.

Thus began the Wassons' eight expeditions into the mountains of central Mexico. In their fifties, they undertook these trips in the spirit of pilgrimage.

Over three summer vacations, the Wassons searched the Oaxacan highlands for someone who could tell them about the sacred mushrooms. They spoke to all the herb venders they could find and collected many different species of mushrooms previously unknown to scientists. In retrospect, it may seem amazing how long it took to find the objects of their search. The problem was that while they did find psychedelic mushrooms (none of which were tried), they found no one who would perform the ceremony or talk about the use of mushrooms. There was no way to tell if they were psychoactive unless tried, and who were they to trust?

In the tiny village of Huautla de Jiménez, where he had traveled ahead of his wife, Wasson came upon the answer when he spoke briefly to Cayetano

Garcia Mendoza, a thirty-five-year-old official presiding at the town hall. The date was the 29th of June 1955. Feeling that he wouldn't have the chance to talk for very long, Wasson asked rather quickly, almost as if in an aside, "Will you help me learn the secrets of the divine mushroom?" Uttering the proper glottal stop at the beginning, Wasson used the term *'nti si tho* for the object of his search. The first syllable shows reverence and endearment, the second expresses "that which springs forth." To his utter surprise, the answer this time was: "Nothing could be easier."

Mendozá was as good as his word. Later that afternoon he took Wasson to his house where they gathered some of the mushrooms. By evening Mendoza had spoken to the famous *curandera* Maria Sabína, telling her without further explanation that she should serve Wasson, who then went with New York fashion photographer friend Allan Richardson to a mushroom ceremony.

Maria Sabína, right, the Mexican curandera *who revealed the experience of* teonanácatl *to R. Gordon Wasson. With her is her daughter, another* curandera, *who was present on that occasion.*

Richardson had promised his wife that if such an eventuality arose, he wouldn't try any mushrooms. At about 10:30 that evening, both he and Wasson were offered a dozen each of the large, acrid species known as *Psilocybe caerulescens* (or "Landslide" mushrooms). Over the next hour they consumed them.

"Allan and I were determined to resist any effects they might have," Wasson wrote later, "to observe better the events of the night." However, he soon began to notice harmonious colors and then geometric patterns that emerged in the dark. Then came "visions" of palaces and gardens. He later compared his experience to what the Greeks meant when they created the word *ekstasis*—a flight of the soul from the body. The experience continued until the very early morning. Wasson and Richardson thus became the first whites in recorded history to partake of the Mexican divine mushrooms. Wasson described this *velada*, or night ceremony, most fully in *The Wondrous Mushroom: Mycolatry in Mesoamerica.*

Three days after he ingested the sacred mushrooms, Wasson tried the experience a second time. A few days later, Valentina and their thirteen-year-old daughter Masha tried it. Six months later, back in New York, Wasson ingested dried specimens and found the effects even more fantastic.

The Wassons Mobilize Others

Meanwhile, the CIA had initiated a search for the so-called "stupid bush" and other botanicals that might derange the human mind. The CIA became especially interested in a shrub called *piule*, whose seeds, they were told, had long been used as inebriants in Mexican religious ceremonies. In early 1953, a scientist from "Project ARTICHOKE" went to Mexico in search of this plant. Before he left Mexico with bags of plant material, including ten pounds of *piule*, he heard wondrous stories about special mushrooms used in connection with religious festivals.

His collected samples went immediately to chemical labs. CIA scientists were excited by his findings and soon came upon the Spanish records relating to *teonanácatl*. Morse Allen, head of the ARTICHOKE program, was particularly fascinated by indications that mushrooms could be used "to produce confessions or to locate stolen objects or to predict the future." Putting high priority on finding the mushrooms, Allen even traveled to the best mushroom-growing area of Pennsylvania to secure potential growers if they should be found.

Shortly after Maria Sabina's 1955 *velada*, a botanist informant for the CIA in Mexico City sent along a description of R. Gordon Wasson's discovery. The report was brief, mainly indicating that the banker had envisioned "a multitude of architectural forms" after he had ingested the mushrooms. That was enough for the CIA to be interested in the Wassons.

The Wassons' next expedition took place during the summer of 1956, timed for the rainy season in Oaxaca so they could gather mushrooms. They were accompanied this time by the French mycologist Roger Heim, Director of the National Museum of Natural History in Paris and an acclaimed expert on tropical mushroom species. His role was to supervise the collecting of these fungi and to determine their taxonomy. Another Frenchman, a botanist colleague from the Sorbonne, also traveled to Oaxaca. Finally, to round out this interdisciplinary team, there was Dr. James Moore, ostensibly a chemist from the University of Delaware.

Moore was much more than a mere organic chemist at a university. He has recently been identified as an expert at synthesizing psychoactive and chemical weapons for the CIA on short notice; he was known as the CIA's "short-order cook." During the winter of 1955-56, he invited himself along when the Wassons indicated their intention to return to Mexico. As an enticement, he offered a $2,000 grant from one of the Agency's cover organizations, the Geschickter Foundation. The CIA man did not enjoy the journey or the mushroom ceremony:

> I had a terrible cold, we damned near starved to death, and I itched all over. There was all this chanting in the dialect. Then they passed the mushrooms around, and we chewed them up. I did feel the hallucinogenic effect, although "disoriented" would be a better word to describe my reaction.

After the collecting of specimens was completed, Moore returned to Delaware with a bag of the sacred mushrooms for analysis, hoping to isolate and then synthesize the active principle in large quantities for the CIA. Sidney Gottlieb wrote soon after that if Moore were successful, it was "quite possible" that the potentiating molecules "might remain an Agency secret" (not published in the scientific literature, unlike most academic discoveries).

While Moore worked on the problem of extraction and synthesis, Heim and his Parisian colleagues succeeded in the difficult task of cultivating the species from specimens and spore prints collected in Mexico. Heim wrote to Sandoz asking if its research team would assist in analyzing the mushrooms that had been grown. His colleagues had been unable to extract the active ingredients. Heim thought Sandoz, successful with LSD-25, might be in the best position to undertake such work. Albert Hofmann accepted Heim's offer with enthusiasm, having already read about the Wassons' discovery in a newspaper article.

Heim sent Sandoz 100 grams of dried *Psilocybe mexicana* that he had grown in cultures. The research team there first tested this on dogs, trying to establish what would be a reliable dose. The results were uncertain and almost depleted the mushroom supply. Hofmann ingested 2.4 grams himself to see if cultivation had ruined its psychoactivity.

While the dosage was moderate by Indian standards, the effects led Hofmann to conclude that humans provide a more sensitive testing of mind-affecting substances than animals. Using about a third of Hofmann's dose, his team members then made many tests of various fractionated extracts and soon isolated 4-OPO$_3$-DMT and 4-OH-DMT as psychoactive constituents.

Arthur Brack: *Sandoz 75 Jahre*

Psilocybe mexicana *mushrooms (pictured here as cultivated in the Sandoz labs) provided the material from which Albert Hofmann and his colleagues isolated psilocybin and psilocin. These mushrooms are rather small—up to 8 cm., about three inches, tall—and contain mainly psilocybin as their psychedelic agent.*

Hofmann, as it turned out, was probably the scientist best equipped to analyze the psychedelic agents, in that there is considerable chemical similarity between these substances and LSD (both contain the same kind of nucleus with a substitution at the fourth position in the indole ring). "Probably in no other laboratory in the world," wrote Hofmann later, "would there have been 4-hydroxy indole for comparison purposes." He and his colleagues found by extracting the alkaloids in the mushroom material and degrading them what the pschoactive principles looked like chemically; then they were able to use a route for synthesis somewhat like that for making LSD. Before long, they had published their methods for extraction and for synthesis in a Swiss chemical journal, where Hofmann gave the generic name for the two activating molecules as "psilocybin" and "psilocin" (derived from the *Psilocybe* genus to which *Ps. mexicana* belongs).

The rapid achievement of Hofmann's team was to end the CIA's dream of having its own clandestine reserve. Though Moore had the mushrooms first, he failed largely because he would not ingest the mushrooms back in the U.S. He had no way of telling whether his mushrooms were still active; even if he extracted the constituents in several solutions, he had no way of telling which solvent contained the active ingredients. There was no reason for him to test for indole tryptamines. Before long, Moore gave up his efforts and wrote Sandoz requesting a supply.

The first extensive accounts of the Wassons' discovery appeared in May 1957. They published a monumental two-volume work on their investigations, *Mushrooms, Russia and History*, and a shorter, more accessible report of seventeen pages in *Life* magazine. Only 512 copies of their *magnum opus* were issued (going for $125 then, and now selling at more than $2,000 a copy), but the *Life* article was seen by millions.

The third in a "Great Adventures" series, their article was titled "Seeking the Magic Mushrooms: a New York banker goes to Mexico's mountains to participate in the age-old ritual of Indians who chew strange growths for visions." The term "magic mushrooms" was invented by a *Life* editor; Wasson did not like it and still has reservations. John Marks characterized the tone of the presentation as giving these newly-revealed mushrooms "glowing but dignified respect." Coming soon after Huxley's writings about his ingestion of mescaline sulfate, the article caused quite a stir, introducing millions to the mysteries of psychedelics.

Among those most interested in the *Life* magazine article was Dr. Rolf Singer, a mycologist who carried its illustrations of the sacred mushrooms with him on a two-week trip to Mexico. He was accompanied by two Mexican graduate students in mycology, one being Dr. Gaston Guzmán, who was in the employ of Parke-Davis and who is at the time of this writing producing a monograph on the whole *Psilocybe* genus. This group followed the Wasson/Heim trail, eventually meeting up with R. Gordon Wasson in the remote mountains of Oaxaca. The Singer group was successful in its mushroom collecting. Upon returning to the U.S., Singer hurriedly published a paper and was thus able to establish scientific priority in the identification of mushrooms that the Heim team had been collecting for years. This haste divided the communities of mycologists and ethnobotanists, creating a rift that is deep even now, more than a quarter of a century later.

For all that, the Wassons were still the primary investigators of psilocybian mushrooms. They mobilized an impressive array of interested parties and resources for further study, involving institutions from the Bollingen Foundation to the Bank of Mexico. They recruited linguists, chemists, botanists and other specialists in Mexico, the U.S., Japan and the Urals—anywhere they found evidence of mushrooms being used as "entheogens."

By the time of Valentina Pavlovna's death from cancer at the end of 1958, most of the *teonanácatl* story had been uncovered. Commenting later on their search, Wasson said that even if they had been on the wrong track, theirs "must have been a singular false hypothesis to have produced the results that it has."

Sandoz Synthesizes Analogues and Distributes Psilocybin to Researchers

The patents on psilocybin and psilocin belonged to Sandoz Pharmaceuticals. After extraction, identification and synthesis of these naturally occurring molecules, Hofmann and his co-workers synthesized a series of analogues, or related compounds. These were essentially the same molecules except that: (1) the phosphoryl or hydroxy group at the top of the indole ring was moved around to other ring positions, and (2) different numbers of methyl groups (CH_3) and other carbon chains were added to the side chains and to the nitrogen on the indole ring to see how these changes would affect psychoactivity. These new compounds were tested on animals. The question of safety was significant in this case because these synthetic substances, unlike the mushrooms, were being tried for the first time.

Only two of these synthetic compounds were tested in controlled trials in humans, and they were eventually used in "psycholytic therapy" in several clinics in Europe. CY-19 (4-phosphoryloxy-*N, N*-diethyltryptamine) and CZ-74 (4-hydroxy-*N, N*-diethyltryptamine) are the diethyl analogues of psilocybin and psilocin; they produce experiences similar to their counterparts but are slightly less active by weight, and their effects last only about three and a half hours—compared with about twice that for psilocybin and three times that for LSD. They are considered particularly appropriate for psychotherapy using psychedelics as an adjunct, because they are less tiring, more manageable for the experiencer and therapist and easier to schedule.

Psilocybin, meanwhile, was sent to interested researchers at cost, becoming another psychedelic agent backed by a pharmaceutical house—after *Cannabis* tinctures, then mescaline, then harmaline and harmine, then LSD-25. Results from psilocybin studies began appearing in 1958, when the conclusions from six research projects were published. By 1962, Wasson was listing 362 items of relevant literature in a bibliography about psilocybin and the mushrooms containing this compound. The excitement in experimental psychiatry was intense. It was long before this psychedelic became available to any but a few in the small but expanding drug subculture.

On the 1962 expedition organized by R. Gordon Wasson to see Maria Sabína, Hofmann came along and brought a bottle of psilocybin pills. Sandoz was marketing them under the brand name "Indocybin"—"indo" for both

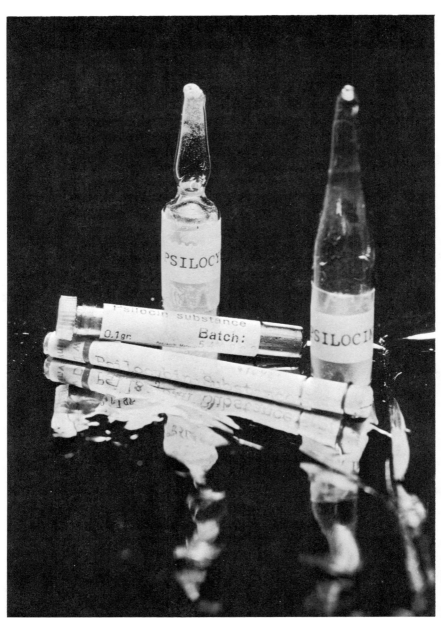

Ampules of early Sandoz psilocybin and psilocin.

Jeremy Bigwood

"Indian" and "indole" (the nucleus of their chemical structures) and "cybin" for the main molecular constituent, "psilocybin." ("Psilo" in Greek means "bald," "cybe" means "head.")

Hofmann gave his synthesized *teonanácatl* to the *curandera* who divulged the Indians' secret. "Of course," Wasson recalls of the encounter, "Albert Hofmann is so conservative he always gives too little a dose, and it didn't have any effect." Hofmann had a different interpretation: activation of "the pills, which must dissolve in the stomach before they can be absorbed, takes place only after 30 to 45 minutes, in contrast to the mushrooms which, when chewed, work faster because part of the drug is absorbed immediately by the mucosa in the mouth."

In order to settle her doubts about the pills, more were distributed, bringing the total for Maria Sabina, her daughter, and the shaman Don Aurelio up to 30 mg., a moderately high dose by current standards but not perhaps by the Indians'. At dawn, their Mazatec interpreter reported that Maria Sabina felt there was little difference between the pills and the mushrooms. She thanked Hofmann for the bottle of pills, "saying that she would now be able to serve people even when no mushrooms were available."

The Harvard Psilocybin Mushroom Project

Surprisingly little of the psilocybin experimentation involved human use. The best known investigations in this area were conducted by Dr. Timothy Leary and his associates at Harvard University—in the same building used by William James when he studied religious mysticism, "laughing gas" (N_2O), and the nature of altered consciousness.

Leary, who was Irish and Catholic in extraction and whose father was Eisenhower's dentist, had been rebellious and was expelled from West Point, but later he was well-received as a psychologist, speaker and author of two works, widely recognized among psychologists, a textbook and a psychological examination still employed for categorizing personality types. In 1960, while Leary was working as research director at the Kaiser Hospital in Oakland, he was offered a lectureship at Harvard for the fall.

In the summer of 1960, while on vacation in Cuernavaca near Mexico City, he ate seven small mushrooms beside the pool of his rented villa. Leary soon felt himself

> being swept over the edge of a sensory Niagra into a maelstrom of transcendental visions and hallucinations. The next five hours could be described in many extravagant metaphors, but it was above all and without question the deepest religious experience of my life.

Leary vowed "to dedicate the rest of my life as a psychologist to the systematic exploration of this new instrument." That fall he returned to Harvard and interested many graduate students and others in researching psilocybin.

INTERPERSONAL CHECK LIST
ILLUSTRATING THE CLASSIFICATION OF INTERPERSONAL BEHAVIORS
INTO 16 VARIABLE CATEGORIES

From Multilevel Measurement of Interpersonal Behavior, *Dr.*
Timothy Leary's first book (1957), which has been followed by more
than two dozen others.

Aldous Huxley was in Cambridge at the time, as a visiting lecturer at
M.I.T.; he was brought in as an advisor. On the day John Kennedy was elected
to the Presidency, Huxley and Humphry Osmond visited Leary. Afterwards,
they both agreed that Harvard would be a perfect place to conduct a study of
psilocybin, but they felt that Leary "might be a bit too square," in Osmond's
words. This evaluation has since caused Osmond to wonder considerably
about his and others' efforts to generalize personality assessment.

By late 1960, Leary had contacted Sandoz for psilocybin to be used for
"creativity studies" and had established an eight-member board to oversee
the Harvard Psilocybin Research Project. The board included Huxley,
psychiatrist John Spiegel (who went on to become president of the American
Psychiatric Association), David McClelland (Leary's superior), Frank Barron
(an associate who has since written much about creativity), Ralph Metzner
(later a close Leary colleague), Leary, and two graduate students who had
already started a project with mescaline.

During the winter term of 1961, another Harvard faculty member, Richard Alpert, became an important companion. Leary and Alpert were co-lecturers in a course on "game theory" called Existential Transactional Behavior Change. Alpert was asked by the chairman of the social relations department (McClelland) to keep an eye on Leary and this "mushroom project."

During early March 1961, however, Alpert himself took synthesized psilocybin—which Leary and others made a point of referring to as "the mushrooms" or "the mushroom pills." Within a few hours, he had an experience that was to turn his life around. He began by closing his eyes and relaxing. Here's a description of that first trip beginning his transformation that appeared in a New Age magazine of the mid-1970s:

> ... in the living room of Leary's house in suburban Boston, Alpert saw a figure in academic robes standing a few feet away and recognized himself in his role as Harvard professor. The figure kept changing to other aspects of his identity —musician, pilot, lover, bon vivant—that had somehow dissociated themselves from his body. And then to his horror he watched his body itself disappear as he looked down on it—first his forelegs, then all his limbs, then his torso—and he knew for the first time that there was "a place where 'I' existed independent of social and physical identity ... beyond Life and Death." About five in the morning he walked the few blocks to his parent's house in a driving snowstorm and began shoveling the driveway, laughing aloud with joy ....

Three psilocybin projects were set up in line with Leary and Alpert's specialty, the psychology of "game-playing." In early 1961, after initial psilocybin investigations, the Leary group began working in nearby Concord with convicts in the Massachusetts Correctional Institution, a maximum-security prison for young offenders. It was hoped that psilocybin could help prisoners "see through" the self-defeating "cops-and-robbers game" and become less destructive citizens. Leary got along well with the Irish warden, and soon six prisoners volunteered for the study.

The six volunteers grew in number to thirty-five over the next two years. Each underwent two psilocybin experiences during six weeks of bi-weekly meetings. Although the subjects were not very well educated, they were able to detach themselves from their everyday roles and "confront themselves," recognizing constructive alternatives to their formerly violent and self-destructive behavior patterns. The question was what would happen to these prisoners upon release. Would the insights gained from two fairly heavy doses of psilocybin help them to lead useful and rewarding lives? Or would they soon be headed back to prison? Dr. Stanley Krippner, who also was given psilocybin at Harvard and who has since worked in the fields of "dream studies" and parapsychology, summed up the results:

> Records at Concord State Prison suggested that 64 percent of the 32 subjects would return to prison within six months after parole. However, after six months, 25 percent of those on parole had returned, six for technical parole

violations and two for new offenses. These results are all the more dramatic when the correctional literature is surveyed; few short-term projects with prisoners have been effective to even a minor degree. In addition, the personality test scores indicated a measurable positive change when pre-psilocybin and post-psilocybin results were compared.

Although this psilocybin experiment included a lot of "tender, loving care" and no control subjects, it established a sound basis for hope. The results warrant at least one controlled study.

In a second area of experimentation, Leary and his associates gave the "mushroom pills" to about 400 graduate students, psychologists, religious figures, mathematicians, chemists, writers, artists, musicians and other creative individuals to study their reactions. Extensive records were kept but to date only a few of these accounts have been published.

One recording of a Huxley trip mentions only that he was given 10 mg. of psilocybin and that he "sat in contemplative calm throughout; occasionally produced relevant epigrams; reported the experience as an edifying philosophic experience." Alan Watts' description of the psilocybin experience as "profoundly healing and illuminating" for him appears as chapter nine in Ralph Metzner's *The Ecstatic Adventure*; Stanley Krippner's account is in Bernard Aaronson and Humphry Osmond's *Psychedelics*. In *Creativity and Psychological Health*, Frank Barron devotes a chapter to excerpts from the records made by artists and musicians given psilocybin.

The December 1963 issue of the *Journal of Nervous and Mental Diseases* summarized the findings on the first 129 men and 48 women tested: 70 percent considered the experience either pleasant or ecstatic, 88 percent felt they had learned something from it or had some important insights, 62 percent believed the experience to have changed their life for the better, and 90 percent expressed a desire to try the drug again.

Out of this work developed a third area of inquiry: the resemblance of mystical experience induced by psilocybin to mystical states brought about by spontaneous rapture or by religious practice. This eventually became a "double-blind" study, described by Leary as a "tested, controlled, scientifically up-to-date kosher experiment on the production of the objectively defined, bona-fide mystic experience as described by Christian visionaries and to be brought about by our ministrations." It was conducted by Walter Pahnke as part of his Ph.D. dissertation for the Harvard Divinity School.

His thesis focused on nine traits listed by Dr. W.T. Stace, Professor Emeritus at Princeton. These characteristics, Stace felt, were the fundamentals of mystical experience—"universal and not restricted to any particular religion or culture".

In a Boston University chapel on Good Friday 1962, twenty Christian theology students took part in Pahnke's experiment after having been exhaustively tested and screened. Ten were given 30 mg. of psilocybin. The others (as nearly as possible, a similar group) received 200 mg. of nicotinic

THE EFFECTS OF CONSCIOUSNESS-EXPANDING DRUGS ON PRISONER REHABILITATION

Second Annual Report; Psilocybin Rehabilitation Project:

All the professional work on this project was volunteer. The expenses for clerical assistance and salaries for ex-inmate workers were covered by generous donations from The Uris Brothers Foundation, New York, and the Parapsychology Foundation, Eileen Garrett, President.

Applications to three offices of the U.S. Public Health Service requesting support for continuing this project were refused.

Exactly two years ago the Harvard Psilocybin Project initiated a research program at Massachusetts Correctional Institution, Concord, designed to test the effects of consciousness-expanding drugs on prisoner rehabilitation.

The project was designed as a pilot study—necessarily exploratory—since little was known about the long-range application of the substances.

During the fall and the winter of 1960, much of my time and energy was going into the study of the effects of the psychedelic mushrooms. I was also carrying on an active program of lecturing, teaching, and field work in clinical psychology in the Harvard Graduate School. I had been brought to Harvard in 1959 in order to introduce existential-transactional methods for behavior change. After fifteen years of practicing psychotherapy and about ten years of doing research on psychotherapy, I had come to the conclusion that there was very little that one person called a doctor could do for another person called a patient by talking to him across a desk, or listening to him as he lay on a couch. I developed a lot of theories and a lot of methods on how behavior change could be brought about more effectively than the standard clinical interview method.

There are two main points to the theories I developed; first (transactional) I was convinced that the doctor had to suspend his role and status as a doctor, had to join the other person actively and collaboratively in figuring out the solution to his problem. As much as possible, the doctor had to turn over the responsibility to the man who knew most about the problem at hand, namely, the patient. I developed many techniques for getting patients to help each other.

The second point in my theory (existential) was that the doctor has to leave the safety of his consulting room and get out there in the field where the so-called patient is having his unique problems, and where he is going to solve his problems. I saw the role of the doctor as that of a coach in a game in which the patient was the star player. The coach can help, can point out mistakes, can share his wisdom, but in the last analysis, the guy who does

---

The opening page of the best presentation on the Harvard Psilocybin Research Project's two-year study with convicts—published in 1968 in Timothy Leary's High Priest *(Chapters 9 and 10) and in the* Psychedelic Review #10.

acid and a small amount of benzedrine to stimulate the initial physical sensations of a psychedelic. Neither the subjects nor their guides knew at first which drugs had been given to whom.

The experiment soon came to be known as "The Miracle of Marsh Chapel." In the following six months, extensive data were collected. These included tape recordings, group discussions, follow-up interviews and a 147-item questionnaire used to quantify these characteristics of mystical phenomena:

1) An experience of unity
2) An experience of timelessness and spacelessness,
3) A sense of having encountered ultimate reality
4) A feeling of blessedness and peace,
5) A sense of the holy and the divine
6) An experience of paradoxicality
7) A sense of ineffability
8) Transiency, and
9) Persisting positive changes in attitude and/or behavior

The reaction level in each of Dr. Stace's nine categories was found to be significantly higher for the psilocybin group than for the controls. Nine out of the ten who ingested psilocybin reported having religious experiences that they considered authentic, while only one from the control group claimed to have had even minimal spiritual cognition. More important in terms of genuine mystical experience, there was a lasting effect upon behavior and attitudes. Pahnke summarized these results:

> After an admittedly short follow-up period of only six months, life-enhancing and life-enriching effects, similar to some of those claimed by mystics, were shown by the higher scores of the experimental subjects when compared to the controls. In addition, after four hours of follow-up interviews with each subject, the experimenter was left with the impression that the experience had made a profound impact (especially in terms of religious feeling and thinking) on the lives of eight out of ten of the subjects who had been given psilocybin . . . . The direction of change was toward more integrated, self-actualized attitudes and behavior in life.

Subsequent requests by Pahnke for psilocybin and government approval to repeat his study were denied.

Use of Psilocybian Mushrooms Increases

Expensive and complicated to make, synthetic psilocybin was available to only a small number of those in the "drug subculture" and some with academic connections during the 1960s. As for the organic product, it was widely believed then that sacred mushrooms grew only in Mexico. Most who experienced them traveled to Huautla de Jiménez. *The Turn-On Book* and *The Psychedelic Guide to the Preparation of the Eucharist* described methods for growing *Psilocybe cubensis* on agar or grains, but these techniques were not very effective, did not produce many mushrooms, and went largely untried.

Additional species of mushrooms containing psilocybin and psilocin were discovered, and biosynthetic studies utilizing *Psilocybe cubensis* were initiated in many university laboratories. Still, only a few people having access to the mycological literature knew that *Psilocybe semilanceata*, which Heim and Hofmann had analyzed as being quite potent, grew extensively along the coast of the Pacific Northwest. Mycologists as a group were uninterested in publicizing psychoactivity. The main clues appeared in French, in Heim and Wasson's *Les Champignons Hallucinogenes du Mexique* (1959) and *Nouvelles Investigations sur les Champignons Hallucinogenes* (1967).

After the climax of anti-LSD propaganda in the late 1960s, interest in organic or "natural" psychedelics greatly increased. The appeal was fueled by Leary's *High Priest*, which devoted attention to mushrooms and psilocybin, and by the books of Carlos Castaneda. The first of these, *The Teachings of Don Juan: A Yacqui Way of Knowledge*, caught the popular imagination as many readers became fascinated with Don Juan's "smoking mixture" (allegedly a combination of mushrooms, *Datura* and other substances sealed in a gourd for more than a year).

In order to meet the new demand for "magic mushrooms," many dealers simply renamed their LSD, PCP or other compounds, some even claiming that their "psilocybin" had been cut with "organic rose hips," apparently to make it sound even more "natural." By the early 1970s, unscrupulous dealers were adulterating *Agaricus bisporus*—the common, edible, commercial mushroom, which is now called *A. brunnescens*—with LSD or PCP or both. This practice continued for several years. PharmChem, after analyzing hundreds of suspect mushroom samples, reported that it had found only *two* genuine specimens over a three year period. Bruce Radcliff of PharmChem dubbed the others *Pseudopsilocybe hofmannii.*

A new era in hunting mushrooms opened after publication of Leonard Enos' *A Key to the American Psilocybin Mushroom* (1970). This small book described fifteen species in sixty pages, providing a water-color picture of each. Enos had had personal experience with only two of the species that he treated, and thus his renderings of the mushrooms' appearances were inaccurate and sometimes fanciful. (In two cases, species known by two Latin binomials were drawn to look like different kinds of mushrooms.) He also provided a section on cultivation, which was overcomplicated and which no one seems to have used. Nonetheless, Enos' book stimulated much American fieldwork that resulted in several reliable guides by the end of the decade.

Starting in 1974, a group of a dozen people in the San Francisco Bay Area began experimenting with various techniques for growing psilocybian mushrooms, hoping to find a simple procedure for cultivation that would work for the users themselves. They had already grown several *Banisteriopsis* species and the San Pedro cactus in a search for a natural psychedelic that offered a high yield and could be grown indoors. They concluded that mushrooms presented the best opportunity.

In 1976, writing under the names O.T. Oss and O.N. Oeric, this group published the results of their mushroom experimentation in *Psilocybin: Magic Mushroom Grower's Guide.* This book described in clear English accompanied by photographs a fairly simple and effective technique for home cultivation of the potent *Stropharia (Psilocybe) cubensis* species that required no controlled materials. Simultaneously, spore prints became available through counterculture magazines, notably *High Times.*

The important differences in the Oss and Oeric method had to do with instructions for maintaining sterile conditions and with "casing." In 1971 J.P. San Antonio published a new laboratory procedure for producing *Agaricus brunnescens* in small amounts for scientific study: he showed that covering the mycelium, or vegetative stage, of this common mushroom with about half an inch of slightly alkaline soil could greatly increase the yield by causing it to "fruit" repeatedly (in "flushes" appearing periodically). Although it is unclear who deserves the credit for this breakthrough, the San Antonio technique was modified so that it worked with *Stropharia cubensis* grown on rye and other grains.

Oss and Oeric hoped that users cultivating these mushrooms in their homes would be independent of the illicit market, which at the time was producing and selling many spurious products. Further, they hoped that this

Jeremy Bigwood: *Psilocybin: Magic Mushroom Grower's Guide*

Jars of Stropharia cubensis *yielding up to a crop per week for about two months under optimum conditions (approximately 200 grams of mushrooms, about 20 grams dry weight).*

technique would become a permanent part of the subculture, immune from surveillance and anti-drug crusades. To a certain extent, these ends have been met. However, the authors did not realize that there would be as many large growers as have emerged.

Their technique was still so complicated that only a small percentage of users have even tried it. A large pressure-cooker is needed, and many

Photographs illustrating the main steps involved in psilocybian mushroom cultivation: (1) equipment needed for scalpel isolation of sterile flesh of Stropharia cubensis; *(2) step-by-step growth from spores to mushrooms; (3) inoculations of Mason jars filled with rye and water from stock culture; (4) mycelial growth after five, ten and fifteen days; (5) casing and spraying Mason jars; (6) fresh mushrooms and dried mushrooms ready for freezing.*

Jeremy Bigwood: *Teonanácatl*

couldn't get the hang of the spore-growing and sterilization requirements
for inoculation of the rye jars. Since a capital investment of only about $200
enables one to produce large volumes, some people have taken on the procedure as a full-time job, producing thousands of jars of these mushrooms.
This cottage industry has disappointed some in the Oss and Oeric group,
because it again has resulted in a kind of centralized capitalism.

In the half-decade since publication of the Oss and Oeric book, several
others have issued procedures for psilocybian cultivation. Many mushroom-
growing kits have been presented to the public. There have even been "dung
dealers" offering high-priced compost for sale.

Over this period, many interested parties have become knowledgeable
about mushroom growing, with a few people doing much additional experimentation. Among other current developments, we are seeing a fair amount
of cultivation of other psilocybian species such as of *Psilocybe cyanescens*
(which is large and full of psilocybin, but so far has been a poor "fruiter").
Also, procedures are becoming steadily simpler with time and practice.

BOTANY

Mushrooms containing psilocybin and/or psilocin belong to a broad
botanical order, the Agaricales (gill-bearing fungi), and are found mainly in
the *Psilocybe, Stropharia,* and *Panaeolus* genera. Well over two dozen
species of psilocybian mushrooms are now known, each exhibiting distinct
ranges in size, shape, habitat and potency. Potency goes from virtually
nothing to approximately 15 mg./gm. of the dry weight. The average is
perhaps 3.0 mg./dry gm., amounting to about 0.03 percent of the fresh
mushrooms. Mushrooms are generally 90 percent water.

The species that are presently considered most important will be discussed in terms of their unique qualities. First, some comments relevant to
them all.

Field Identification, Bluing Reaction,
Spore Prints and Preparation

When the Wassons asked their Indian guide about the source of mushrooms, he replied, "The little mushroom comes of itself, no one knows
whence, like the wind that comes we know not whence nor why." Actually,
psilocybian mushrooms begin as microscopic spores that grow on the tip of
cells near the mushrooms gills, called basidia. After maturing, they are
dispersed by the wind.

Out of perhaps a million such spores, only a few grow after reaching an
appropriate habitat. They develop threadlike into hyphae, thin cells that
mass together and spread underground to become the mycelium, which
corresponds to the leaves and roots of a green plant. When this structure
"fruits," the sexual part of the organism appears above ground as a mushroom.

As the mushroom expands through the absorption of water by osmotic
action, a protective veil develops under the gills. Eventually the cap breaks

the veil through an evaporation process caused by the sun, and the veil and stem are covered with spores, usually a dark purple-brown. Millions of spores rain down and then are carried by the rain and wind to where they will germinate and again produce mycelia, thus completing another cycle.

Anyone interested in collecting or growing psilocybian mushrooms should, of course, acquire a field guide by a competent author, such as Paul Stamets' *Psilocybe Mushrooms & Their Allies.* Additional valuable illustrations, photographs and descriptions can be found in Ott and Bigwood's contribution to *Teonanácatl,* Gary Menser's *Hallucinogenic and Poisonous Mushroom Field Guide,* and Richard and Karen Haard's *Poisonous & Hallucinogenic Mushrooms.*

When collecting, it's a good idea to grasp and twist only the stem (not the cap). All species should be separated in wax paper or paper bags (not baggies—mushrooms must breathe or they rapidly spoil), and care should be taken to see that they aren't crushed.

Notes made about the mushrooms' habitat often give valuable clues to identification of psilocybian mushrooms, as does a "spore print." This can be made by placing one specimen's cap on a sheet of white paper and, if possible, another on black paper. These mushroom caps should then be covered by a glass and left alone for several hours, until it becomes clear whether or not they are dark purple-brown. The remainder of the collection should be refrigerated (but not frozen) as soon as possible, because mushrooms deteriorate fairly rapidly in heat. They can be preserved in the vegetable bin of a refrigerator well over a week.

Some psilocybian mushrooms reveal a striking blue color characteristic in fresh specimens; this can aid in identification along with other traits, such as spore color and size, appearance of the gills, etc. When these mushrooms are scratched or bruised by handling, they stain blue or, if the surface color is yellowish, greenish blue. Some of these mushrooms exhibit this stain naturally, perhaps because of the heat of the sun or the pressure of raindrops.

There has been much mention of this test in the psychedelic literature, but it is by no means reliable. Some mushrooms "blue" only after the first "flush" of the fruiting bodies (growth of the fruiting bodies recurs, usually at one-week intervals). Some authors have concluded that this "bluing" occurs only in mushrooms containing both psilocin and psilocybin.

Bigwood and Michael Beug, after analyzing many collections of fifteen psilocybian species, concluded that bluing *per se* does not indicate the presence of psilocin. A few species containing only psilocybin exhibited a slight bluing reaction on the stems but would not blue when handled. The species containing both the 4-phosophorylated psilocybin and the 4-hydroxylated psilocin analogues, however, bruised a darker blue and often showed this characteristic even when untouched. It is unclear which tryptamine in the psilocybian mushrooms is responsible for the bluing, but pure psilocybin or psilocin when placed in pure water and left at room temperature discolors the water to a bluish-brown.

Harvested psilocybian mushrooms can be eaten fresh, or they can be dried, sealed and stored. The best procedure is to dry the mushrooms in a freeze-drier without heat. For most users, this is impossible, so a lamp or oven can do, as long as there is ventilation and the temperature does not exceed 90° F. in a dry atmosphere. (If you use an oven, leave the door cracked open.) A space heater can also be used. Whatever the means, the drying takes at least twenty to twenty-four hours and leaves the mushrooms in a brittle state.

The mushrooms should then be weighed, placed in a sealable container and frozen. No mushrooms should be frozen fresh, because they will disintegrate when thawed.

To produce a homogenous mixture from which known doses can be accurately weighed, grind the mushrooms in a blender or coffee mill. The resulting powder should be stored frozen at the lowest temperature possible in an airtight container filled to the top. The result doesn't look like mushrooms and probably cannot be identified by species even by a mycologist. It is quite easy to measure out doses for ingestion.

Freezing is most critical for those mushrooms known to contain psilocin, such as *Psilocybe cyanescens* or *Stropharia cubensis*, because they have a short shelf life at room temperature. For ingestion, such powders can be capped, blended into a "smoothie," or drunk with chocolate. A chocolate drink prepared with honey, spices and water (there was no milk in pre-Conquest America aside from corn whey) has long been associated with mushroom rituals and is quite pleasant served before a *velada*.

Stropharia (Psilocybe) cubensis *(San Isidro)*

This mushroom was originally collected in Cuba in 1904. It is the easiest of all mushrooms to grow—even easier than the commercial ones. Currently, it is probably the best psilocybian mushroom for most users and is certainly the most readily available. Its psychoactivity varies, however, and degenerates over time, especially when there is delay in moving the product from the grower to user. Some dealers have been known to open up bags of these mushrooms so they will gain more weight from ambient humidity, which breaks down the psilocybin and psilocin even further.

This species was collected by Schultes during his 1939 trip to Oaxaca and deposited at the Farlow Herbarium at Harvard University. After the Second World War, the mycologist Rolf Singer worked there identifying mushrooms; in an attempt to reorganize the taxonomy of the genus *Stropharia,* he came upon Schultes' specimens. In 1951, he placed *Stropharia cubensis* Earle in the *Psilocybe* genus, basing this identification on microscopic characteristics, particularly of the spore. He neglected to tell Schultes and didn't follow this work up, but the mushroom is now often referred to as *Psilocybe cubensis* (Earle) Singer.

Jeremy Bigwood

Stropharia (Psilocybe) cubensis, *the most popular psilocybian mushroom,
contains up to 14 mg./gm. of psilocybin dry weight. The potency of this
mushroom varies greatly, however, and deteriorates fairly rapidly over time.*

Some mycologists have disputed Singer's identification, arguing that the macroscopic features place this mushroom in the genus *Stropharia*. At the time of this writing, both designations are found in the literature—*Stropharia* in ethnopharmacological and some European mycological sources, *Psilocybe* mainly in the American, Mexican and botanical sources.

This mushroom is tropical and subtropical and appears in cowfields during rainy seasons or other times of high humidity. In the U.S., it is distributed mainly along the southeastern seaboard, but it can be found inland as far north as Tennessee.

It grows naturally in connection with cattle—particularly hot-weather-loving Brahmas—and especially in dung a few days old. It may be because of this that the Indians consider it inferior, only using it as a last resort. More likely, it has lower status because it wasn't indigenous to Mexico—it arrived with Spanish importation of Brahma cattle from the Philippine Islands—and thus doesn't have ancient associations in their shamanistic rites. In Mexico, the Mazatecs call this species "di-shi-tho-le-rra-ja" (sacred mushroom of cow dung), but its other names are Spanish (such as "San Isidro Labrador," St. Isidore the Plowman). The anthropologist Peter Furst has promoted the notion that it may have grown in deer dung, but attempts to grow it in that medium haven't succeeded. In cultivating it, dung isn't essential; it fruits very potently on rye and other grains. Rye-cultured specimens appear less robust than those in the field or those grown on compost, but in terms of psychoactivity they are about a third stronger on the average.

In the fields, this mushroom tends to come up singly or in small groups. Growth is rapid. In pastures, it often grows from the size of a pinhead to a full mushroom in little more than a day. It becomes rather large, generally attaining a height of 15-30 cm. (6-12"). It often appears whitish overall, sometimes with a steaking of "comic strip blue." The mushroom often blues without any apparent bruising, perhaps because of intense heat. When it opens, the cap usually gets lighter on the outside while the center gets darker—but not necessarily so. It can be light brown or light reddish-gold, and often the prominent annulus, or collar, is covered with spores.

Early studies made of this species estimated the concentrations of psilocybin at about 0.2 percent (2.0 mg./gm.) of the dry weight, along with a fairly high amount of psilocin. But the analytical tools then in use necessitated heating and are now considered obsolete. Current state-of-the-art equipment —such as High-Performance Liquid Chromotography (HPLC)—shows that much of the "psilocin" observed was actually psilocybin that had been transformed into psilocin by the analytical process.

Recently, Bigwood and Beug detected psilocybin in concentrations as large as 13.3 mg./gm. (1.3 percent) and psilocin in concentrations of 1.0 mg./gm. in a batch of dried *Stropharia cubensis* mushrooms. In the same strain, however, they also found psilocybin as low as 3.2 mg./gm. and psilocin at 1.8 mg./gm.

Moreover, they discovered that the same strain in the same container produced greatly varying amounts of psychoactive constituents in different "flushes" appearing about a week apart. For example, they recorded the following psilocybin content—in mg./gm. dry weight—for one sequence of five flushes: 8.3, 6.5, 13.3, 4.8 and 6.8. The potency of the third flush was twice that of the second and nearly three times that of the fourth.

The third flush did not show the highest psychoactive concentrations in other instances. The *only* consistency found was that in the first flush psilocin—and the psilocybin and psilocin analogues—were either barely present or entirely absent. Their strength then increased in subsequent flushes.

Bigwood and Beug's conclusion in 1982 was this:

> We found that the level of psilocybin and psilocin varies by a factor of four among various cultures of *Psilocybe cubensis* grown under rigidly controlled conditions, while specimens from outside sources ["street" samples] varied ten-fold. It is clear that entheogenic and recreational users of this species have no way to predict the amount of psilocybin and psilocin they are ingesting with a given dry weight of the mushroom. Thus, variations in the subjective experience come not only from effects of "set" and "setting," but also in very real measure from dosage differences.

Psilocybe semilanceata *(Liberty Caps)*

This is now the second most important psilocybian mushroom world-wide. Its popular name comes from its looking like caps worn during the French Revolution. Found in the northern temperate zone, it grows inland up to a thousand miles from the ocean—a rule covering its known habitat to date. It fruits in tall grasses and on cow fields mainly in the fall, only occasionally in the spring. (Unlike *Ps. cubensis*, it does not grow on dung itself.) This species is fairly small, about 10 cm. (4″) tall at most.

Reports of the psychoactivity of Liberty Caps predate the Wassons' journeys to Mexico. In C. McIlvaine's *One Thousand American Fungi* (1900), this species is described as a mushroom with strange effects that don't last long and are not toxic. The psychoactive ingredient, according to this classic text, can be removed by boiling the mushroom in water and then throwing away the water. In 1910, a professor at Yale and his wife took it a few times and had marvelous experiences and hilarity for a short while. At about this same time, reports circulated of its use in Norway, Maine by the artist community there.

Psilocybin was first detected in *Ps. semilanceata* by Heim and Hofmann in the early 1960s, but it was not used in Europe until at least a dozen years later. In the Pacific Northwest, use apparently began as early as 1965. The Royal Canadian Mounted Police confiscated some on the Vancouver campus of UBC at that time. Experimentation with this mushroom was only sporadic, however, until publication of Enos' 1970 book because very few people were

Psilocybe semilanceata *(Liberty Caps), a favorite in coastal temperate zones, are potent in psilocybin—averaging around 11 mg./gm. dry weight—which is stable.*

Teonanácatl

Psilocybe pelliculosa, *another psilocybian species that many people*
confuse with Liberty Caps, contains psilocybin and the same analogues
but has only half the potency of Liberty Caps. This one can be easily
distinguished by habitat. Rather than in cow fields, it grows on sawdust
or wood chip piles in forested areas where lumberjacks have been
working. It doesn't display the indrawn edge to its cap that is evident
in Liberty Caps, and often its stem and cap edge darken with age.

aware of the existence of psychedelic mushrooms in that area. Nowadays,
thousands of people in the northwestern U.S., Scandinavia (especially Norway), the British Isles and most of western Europe collect this mushroom.
    Ps. semilanceata is quite potent by weight, containing as much as 12.8
mg. psilocybin/gm. and averaging around 11 mg./gm. in dried specimens.

Unlike *Ps. cubensis,* which is highly variable in strength, this one is much more uniform with psychoactivity differing in samples by not much more than a factor of two. Three or four of these tiny mushrooms are often enough to energize the body and affect color perception and visual acuity. About twenty to thirty mushrooms constitute a strong dose, although some people have been known to take up to 100 at a time. It is recommended that users take no more than 2 or 3 dried grams the first few times.

Some people have observed that mushrooms containing both psilocybin and psilocin tend to lose their psychoactivity fairly rapidly, whereas those lacking psilocin tend to have a long shelf life. Liberty Caps have no psilocin, but they do contain psilocybin analogues. Specimens collected and analyzed in 1976 were reanalyzed after four years on a shelf without refrigeration. They were found to be almost as potent.

Most Liberty Caps do not blue, but some do so heavily. At this point, we don't know whether the latter are another species. Some mushrooms recently collected are quite similar in appearance to *Ps. semilanceata* and inhabit the same cow fields. These may be variants or other new species; of those that look like Liberty Caps and grow on pastures, none is poisonous. (A recently discovered psilocybian mushroom that is similar is known as *Ps. linaformens* and is common in Europe and Oregon, where it too is often called a "Liberty Cap.")

Panaeolus subbalteatus (benanosis)

This is the most prevalent of these psilocybian mushrooms, growing throughout the U.S. and found in various climates in many parts of the world. It grows singly or in clusters to a height of about 8 cm. (just over 3"), most commonly on composted dung, in both spring and fall. The tan cap develops a striking cinnamon-brown band around the bottom and flattens as it ages, with the central portion fading over time to a pale, warm buff color. Eventually it resembles a large floppy hat draped over a fairly thick, whitish stem that sometimes blues at its bottom. The spore print has a blackish-purple color.

Andy Weil claims that *Panaeolus subbalteatus* doesn't produce as good a psychedelic trip as most other psilocybian mushrooms and that it can bring on a side effect of stomach aches. These assertions have not been confirmed by most other users and many people like it—especially in the spring, when few Liberty Caps are available. It springs up on compost, straw and manure piles and often can be seen clustered in one- or two-foot rings along roads, on lawns and in open areas. It can be cultivated but only on compost, and spores from it can be bought from *High Times'* advertisers through the mail.

Panaeolus subbalteatus has a long shelf life and contains no psilocin; the psychoactivity comes only from psilocybin and its analogues. The amounts are low to moderate for psilocybin, varying from a little over 1.5 mg./gm. up to 6.0 mg./gm. dry weight.

Michael B. Smith: *Hallucinogenic and Poisonous Mushroom Field Guide*

Panaeolus subbalteatus, *a species seen commonly throughout North America and many parts of the world, contains low to moderate amounts of psilocybin. It is among the few psilocybian mushrooms that fruit in the spring.*

Psilocybe cyanescens *(Wavy Caps, Blue Halos)*

This species is the most potent psilocybian mushroom known. Although not as big as *Ps. cubensis*, it is probably the second largest growing in the U.S., generally reaching 6-8 cm. in height (about 3"). This mushroom, like *Ps. pelliculosa* and the few others that follow, don't grow on dung but rather on hardwoods and wood chips.

Ps. cyanescens likes to inhabit landscaped yards containing ground bark and often dwells under Douglas fir or cedar and in mulched rhodeodendron beds. The large cap, which starts out chestnut brown and becomes more caramel-colored with age, is wavy, so they've been called Wavy Caps. Because of the blue line around the edge of the cap, they are also known as Blue Halos. Generally this species grows in clusters, although sometimes it comes up singly. When it fruits, it is prolific. It is not unusual to hear of mushroom hunters gathering six to seven ounces dry weight at a time.

This mushroom contains psilocybin, psilocin and at least four analogues. It blues markedly when bruised and is less stable than Liberty Caps. It isn't

Teonanácatl

Psilocybe cyanescens, *a large species with an undulating caramel-colored cap, is the most potent psilocybian mushroom detected anywhere. It fruits prolifically from fall through winter in the Pacific Northwest.*

cultivated very easily, but is potent. In Bigwood and Beug samples, "Psilocybin levels were found to range up to 16.8 mg./gm. dry weight, with the total psilocin plus psilocybin levels reaching 19.6 mg./gm. dry weight—nearly 2% of the dry weight." Being large and the most potent psilocybian species, it is quite popular and one of the most sought after mushrooms in the Pacific Northwest.

Psilocybe baeocystis

This is another strongly-bluing Pacific Northwest species. It can be found growing on ground bark, wood chips, peat moss and occasionally lawns and is common on campuses. This popular mushroom appears from fall through midsummer; as many as fifty are often clumped together. Generally it contains rather low levels of psilocybin and psilocin. Its potency, however, is highly variable.

Teonanácatl

Psilocybe baeocystis *inhabits areas with bark and wood chips and is prevalent throughout the Pacific Northwest. Its psychoactivity is usually weak but in some instances rivals that of the strongest psilocybian mushrooms.*

Bigwood and Beug assess it as averaging about 2.8 psilocybin/gm. and 1.4 mg. psilocin/gm. dry weight. But one collection they examined was found to contain 8.5 mg. psilocybin/gm. and 5.9 mg. psilocin/gm.—rivaling concentrations in the strongest psilocybian species. This variability makes it riskier to use than most others. "One could eat a lot of weak ones to get an experience," comments Jeremy Bigwood, "and then go to another patch and get maybe 200 mg. of psilocybin plus." Extra caution in dosage is strongly recommended.

The edge of the cap of this species generally undulates, resembling a bottle cap or lawn umbrella, and the stem is often characterized by twisting bends. An important identifying characteristic is a brown spot that appears in the center of the cap after it is dried. *Psilocybe baeocystis* is bound to become more familiar because of increasingly widespread use of its host materials in industrial parks, around homes, etc.

Another psilocybian mushroom that also blues and has characteristics similar to *Ps. baeocystis* and *Ps. cyanescens* is *Ps. cyanafiberlosa*. It was originally collected between patches of the first two. This one has somewhat wavy caps like *Ps. cyanescens*, although they don't open up nearly so much, and the same chemical components as the others. It's normally weaker than *Ps. baeocystis*, often containing about 1.3 mg. of both psilocybin and psilocin/gm. dry weight.

Psilocybe stuntzii

This is another psilocybian mushroom that readily springs up on commercially prepared wood chips. It is a fairly small, stout mushroom, which in many people's opinion should be included in the *Stropharia* genus since it has a prominent annulus. It can be found on grasses, bark mulch and mulched lawns in the fall and summer; under the grasses there is always a

Teonanácatl

Psilocybe stuntzii *is a recent Pacific Northwest psychedelic find. Short, stout and a wood chip parasite, it is about the weakest of the known psilocybian mushrooms of North America.*

Paul Stamets: *Psilocybe Mushrooms & Their Allies*

Psilocybe stuntzii *growing beside* Galerina autumnalis. *These two mushroom species, the first psychedelic and the second poisonous, often grow so closely that they appear to be clustered. The most reliable differentiating factor is spore color—the* Galerina's *being rust-brown, the* Psilocybe's *being gray to lilac.* Ps. stuntzii *also has a prominent annulus, while* Galerina autumnalis *does not.*

layer of wood bits. The cap is sticky and has stripes on the edges that become flat, scalloped edges when the mushroom is mature. This is very likely the weakest psilocybian mushroom in the Pacific Northwest. The Bigwood and Beug studies show that its potency ranges from nothing to a high of 3.6 mg. psilocybin/gm. dry weight.

IMPORTANT NOTE: this species can easily be confused by the novice with the deadly species *Galerina autumnalis*, with which it sometimes clusters. The most potent psilocybian mushrooms grow on wood chips, and so anyone hunting for them should know how to identify the poisonous *Galerina*.

The two species in question can definitely be separated from one another by spore color: that of the *Galerina* species is rust-brown in contrast to that of the *Psilocybe* species, which is gray to lilac. Furthermore, their coloration is different, their "collars" look quite different, and the *Galerina* species presents lines radiating from the center of the cap. Only the psilocybian mushroom turns blue upon bruising. If there is any doubt as to identification, a mushroom that does not blue should be discarded as *Galerina*. (The toxic ingredient in *Galerina autumnalis* also appears in the common edible mushroom but in very small amounts.)

In December 1981 on Whidby Island in Washington State, some teenagers searching for psilocybian mushrooms made a mistake in identification. Two young men and a woman who ingested the mushrooms got sick the next day but were afraid to report their illness for fear of arrest by the authorities. They apparently waited yet another day before the symptoms got extremely bad, and then all three went to a hospital. The two young men survived, but the young woman died on Christmas Day.

Another fatality attributed to the search for psilocybian mushrooms occurred in 1960, when two adults and four children ate a large number of what they assumed were *Psilocybe baeocystis*. A six-year-old boy in this group died. Some of the mushrooms from this patch, photographed for an article, were clearly not *Ps. baeocystis* but *Ps. cyanescens*. Because these two species sometimes grow together with *Galerina autumnalis*, it's not unlikely that the six people ingested all three. Their symptoms were similar to those of the woman on Whidby Island.

This short description of the main North American species illustrates how varied psilocybian mushrooms are. People intending to gather or cultivate them should consult experts, particularly when identification of any mushroom is in question. Even clear photographs may be only somewhat helpful. It should be kept in mind that mushrooms change appearance as they age and often have different coloration in different regions.

CHEMISTRY

The psychoactive compounds in psilocybian mushrooms are psilocybin, psilocin and their *N*-de and *N*-di-demethylated analogues. Workers at Sandoz Pharmaceuticals and elsewhere have synthesized many related compounds. But only two have been tested in humans (these were lab-coded "CZ-74" and "CY-19").

All such compounds contain the white, crystalline "ring" structure of an "indole"—which chemists abbreviate as C_8H_7N and draw in this fashion:

indole

They also contain "ethylamine" side chains of various lengths. Taken together, the indole and side chain constitute "tryptamines." Nearly all psychedelic tryptamines exhibit a rare substitution at the position marked by an asterisk in the drawing above.

The psilocybin and psilocin molecular grouping bears a close resemblance to chemicals appearing in the brain. One of the psilocybian analogues is, in fact, one of the closest known compounds to the neurotransmitter serotonin, differing only with respect to the rare substitution just mentioned: it is 4- rather than 5-hydroxytryptamine. Psilocin, interestingly, is the nearest relative to bufotenine, once thought a psychoactive compound,

alkaline phosphatase

4-OPO₃-DMT (Psilocybin) → 4-OH-DMT (Psilocin)

4-OPO3-DMT (Psilocybin)
(4-phosphoryloxy-N, N—
dimethyltryptamine)

4-OH-DMT (Psilocin)
(4-hydroxy-N, N-
dimethyltryptamine)

5-OH-T, also called 5HT
(Serotonin)

5-OH-DMT (Bufotenine)

4-OPO3-DET (CY-19)
(4-phosphoryloxy-N, N-
diethyltryptamine)

4-OH-DET (CZ-74)
(4-hydroxy-N, N-
diethyltryptamine)

Psilocybin (at top left) is the main psychoactive compound in psilocybian mushrooms. Most of it is transformed upon ingestion by the enzyme alkaline phosphatase into psilocybin (top right), the second important psychedelic in these mushrooms.

Close cousins to psilocin are bufotenine (middle right), a substance in plants and animals that was once thought psychoactive, and the human neurotransmitter serotonin (middle left).

Two synthetics in this clustering that have been tested in people with good results are CY-19 and CZ-74, represented in the bottom drawings.

Other related compounds present in some psilocybian mushrooms are 4-OPO3-NMT (baeocystin) and 4-OPO3-T—both analogues of psilocybin—and 4-OH-NMT (norbaeocystin) and 4-OH-T—both analogues of psilocin.

which was first discovered in the skin secretions of toads (*Bufo vulgaris*, for which it was named) and later in plants, notably the tree known as *Anadananthera peregrina* from which *cohoba* snuff (see Chapter 6) is made.

Psilocybin and Psilocin

The major psychedelic agent in psilocybian mushrooms is psilocybin—the first indole derivative discovered to contain phosphorus. When ingested, the phosphorus radical is immediately "dephosphorylated" by an intestinal enzyme, alkaline phosphatase, into psilocin and phosphoric acid. Animal experiments suggest that psilocybin and psilocin appear at similar chemical concentrations at about the same time in various organs. Thus, the phosphorus radical is generally considered "dead weight" in terms of psychoactivity.

An important difference between psilocybin and psilocin is their relative stability—psilocin is easily oxidized, deteriorating soon afterwards. Hence Sandoz chose to develop psilocybin, which doesn't require freezing to retain potency, rather than the easier-to-synthesize psilocin. Unfortunately, mushrooms containing just psilocybin and its analogues—*Ps. semilanceata, Ps. pelliculosa* and *Ps. mexicana*—are all tiny. By weight, psilocin is about 1.4 times as strong as psilocybin—a ratio corresponding to their molecular weights. (Compared by weight, LSD is about 200 times as powerful as psilocybin.)

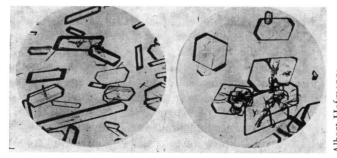

Psilocybin (left) and psilocin crystals viewed through a microscope.

Albert Hofmann:
contributing to
*Discoveries in
Biological Psychiatry*

Related Psychoactive Derivatives

Many users feel that psilocybin and psilocin in synthetic form produce a more lucid mental state than the mushrooms; they also seem to provide more physical energy. Mushrooms generally have longer effects and are more sedating.

These differences are probably caused by the presence of the psilocybin and psilocin analogues, which appear in small amounts but may act as sedatives. These analogues have so far been tested only on animals.

PHYSICAL EFFECTS

The amount of time required to produce somatic sensations from psilocybin, psilocin or psilocybian mushrooms varies with the mode of ingestion. If a high dose of mushrooms is chewed well and kept for some time in the mouth, effects may be perceived within seven to eight minutes. Psilocybin or psilocin placed under the tongue—or moderate amounts of the mushrooms retained for a while in the mouth—produces initial sensations within about fifteen to twenty minutes. If the mushrooms are immediately swallowed, however, only about half of the potentiating chemicals are absorbed by the stomach wall, and it then takes thirty to forty-five minutes (sometimes a full hour) before they cross the blood-brain barrier to prompt psychoactivity. When psilocybin and psilocin are injected intramuscularly, the effects are felt within five to six minutes.

Generally, the first signs that the effects are starting are involuntary yawning (usually without sleepiness) and a non-specific sense of restlessness or malaise. Some people experience nausea with mushrooms, most often after they use the bitter *Ps. caerulescens, Ps. Aztecorum* or similar acrid species. A few users feel a chill as the effects come on, weakness in the legs or slight stomach discomfort. Others feel drowsy and may want to curl up and go to sleep.

In most instances, yawning and a slight sensation of physical disorientation or giddiness are the characteristic experiences during the short take-off stage, which usually lasts half an hour and is followed by feelings of lightness and physical harmony. A few users find that bodily discomfort persists much longer.

High-dose studies of rats suggest that psilocin taken orally is distributed throughout the body. Concentrations in tissues appear highest about half an hour after ingestion, decreasing rapidly over the next three to four hours. The adrenal glands of the test animals show the highest concentrations after the first hour; until then, the kidneys have more. The small intestine, skin, bone marrow, lungs, stomach and salivary glands also have significant concentrations—greater, in fact, than those in the brain.

As with LSD, psilocybin and psilocin prompt few obvious physiological reactions in most people: mainly, dilated pupils and, in some users, a sensation of "dry mouth." A few studies have noted a slight rise in blood pressure, heart rate and temperature, but these reactions appear to result from apprehensions about the experience or from environmental factors.

Psilocin's primary physiologic effect upon the brain seems to be inhibition of the neurotransmitter serotonin, an effect resembling that brought about by LSD. This finding, together with a notable cross-tolerance exhibited between psilocin and LSD, suggests that both compounds act upon similar mechanisms—or possibly, as Hofmann puts it, on "mechanisms acting through a common final pathway."

Substantial tolerance can be built up by repeated doses taken in close sequence. In 1961, Dr. Leo Hollister gave psilocybin to a subject on a daily basis for twenty-one days, starting with 1.5 mg. and increasing it to 27 mg. On the twenty-second day, the subject showed hardly any reaction to 15 mg. After a rest of several weeks, however, the same dose produced the normal degree of psychoactivity.

In less extreme instances, psilocin tolerance tends to be less pronounced than is the case with LSD. Furthermore, cross-tolerance between these two compounds, when ingested alternately, is not as complete as tolerance developed after repeated ingestion of just one alone.

In the high-dose study of rats, all but 6 percent of the psilocybin was excreted within twenty-four hours. In humans, only 80 to 85 percent of psilocybin and its metabolites is excreted within eight hours, in the urine (about 65 percent), bile and feces (15 to 20 percent). Some 15 to 20 percent lingers on, stored in fatty tissues; significant quantities appear in urine up to a week later. A full 25 percent of the originally administered dose enters urine as psilocin.

Psilocybin, psilocin and psilocybian mushrooms show low toxicity. Doses up to 200 mg. of psilocybin/kg. of body weight have been given to mice intravenously without lethal effects. When dosage was increased to 250 mg./kg. of body weight, a few of the mice died. In terms of average human weight, this corresponds to about 17 or 18 gm. of psilocybin—more than 2,000 times the dosage recommended by Sandoz when it originally marketed this drug.

Extrapolation from animal studies to human use gives only a rough estimate of toxicity. It does seem safe to say that one would have to consume well over a kilogram of the most potent fresh *Stropharia cubensis* mushrooms—which vomiting would prevent—even to approach the lethal range. Jonathan Ott, an organizer of mushroom conferences and author of *Hallucinogenic Plants of North America*, said, "I know of no case where an adult has been made seriously ill by psilocybian mushrooms. Tens of thousands of intentional inebriations occur each year with psilocybian mushrooms in the Pacific Northwest alone, yet no conspicuous medical problems have emerged."

MENTAL EFFECTS

Psilocybian mushrooms, psilocybin and psilocin can produce profound, awesome effects upon the mind. In research reported over the first two decades of study, subjects given psilocybin and other drugs in blind experiments were generally unable to distinguish this substance from LSD or mescaline of comparable dosage until several hours had passed. Recognizing psilocybin at that point was possible because of the shorter duration of its psychedelic effects.

In terms of timing, psilocybian experience is characterized by the user's going "up" rapidly, nearly always achieving an enlargement in the scope of perception that persists for about two hours. Then a gradual decline is experienced over the next three to four hours, resulting in the restoration of ordinary consciousness. The quality of thoughts and feelings evoked during these two phases varies greatly, according to the user's mental set, surroundings and the dosage ingested.

Leo Hollister's Observations

In 1961, Leo Hollister and his associates at the Palo Alto Veterans Hospital reported on blind experiments in which they gave psilocybin orally and by injection to a group of "psychologically sophisticated volunteers (graduate students, etc.)." They found that the threshold oral dose was about 60 mcg./kg. of body weight—about 4 gm. for an average-sized person—"from which minimal but definite changes were produced." (An appropriate measure for drugs like amphetamines or barbiturates is perhaps body weight; in contrast, drugs stimulating the central nervous system, such as psilocybin and other psychedelics, probably vary in effect more directly in terms of brain weight.)

In their observation of psilocybin experiences, Hollister and his associates paid almost no attention to such factors as the mental set of individual subjects (despite their background in psychology) or setting, except to say that "the visual beauty of the colored images, especially when augmented by the stroboscopic light during the electroencephalogram, seemed to be a mystical experience to some." The account of mental effects, unfortunately, consists of about 130 words, collected below (from *Chemical Psychoses*, 1968):

Some alterations in mood, either euphoria or dysphoria
Concentration and attention are disturbed
Psychological functioning is impaired
Blurred vision, brighter colors, longer afterimages, sharp definition of objects, visual patterns (eyes closed)
Increased acuity of hearing
Dreamy state, loss of attention and concentration, slow thinking, feelings of unreality, depersonalization
Incoordination, difficult and tremulous speech
Colored patterns and shapes, generally pleasing, sometimes frightening, most often with eyes closed, occasionally superimposed upon objects in field of vision
Undulation or wavelike motion of viewed surfaces
Euphoria, general stimulation, ruminative state
Slowed passage of time
Transient sexual feelings and synesthesias
A few auditory hallucinations
Changes in the body image, the extremities appearing larger than normal
An unusual ability to perceive the feelings and motivations of people in the environment
Reports of great empathy

R. Gordon Wasson's Observations

When Abram Hoffer and Humphry Osmond took up the matter of mental effects in their book *The Hallucinogens*, they remarked that "the major difference between the mushroom effect and pure psilocybin seems to be the dryness of the scientific accounts and the richness of the accounts of self-experimentation." Probably no finer example of "richness" exists than in the descriptions of R. Gordon Wasson.

In *The Wondrous Mushroom*, Wasson wrote about four psilocybian experiences, highlighting the contributions of mental set and setting. All four experiences involved the same mushroom—*Psilocybe caerulescens*—taken in roughly the same dosage.

(Trip 1) As to mental set, his expectations had been building for some years. While his father was interested in *Religion and Drink*, Wasson became steadily more interested in religion and mushrooms, studying their significance in various cultures for a quarter of a century before he acquired a sample of *teonanácatl*. Another two years passed before he actually tasted it, as he waited to find someone who could perform the mushroom ceremony.

On the verge of a much anticipated but unfamiliar experience, Wasson derived an important sense of reassurance from his setting. He was in the company of Indians who were experienced users and who were taking the drug with him. The *velada* was conducted by a *sabia*—a wise-woman, "one-who-knows." Wasson had a close friend along for a companion.

The ceremony consisted of chanting that continued all night long, except for brief intermissions every forty minutes or so. The *sabia* Maria Sabina danced for two hours in the dark. The ritual aspect, in the context of feeling both adventurous and safe, seems to have influenced the quality (or tone) of Wasson's experience.

Early on, he saw architectural visions like the biblical descriptions of the heavenly city:

> The visions came in endless succession, each growing out of the preceding one. We had the sensation that the walls of our humble house had vanished, that our untrammeled souls were floating in the empyrean, stroked by divine breezes, possessed of a divine mobility that would transport us anywhere on the wings of a thought.

(Trip 2) That first experience was impressive—even "gala." Wasson and his associate Allan Richardson had many questions to clarify. Three days later, they asked if Maria Sabina would perform a second *velada*. This time Richardson didn't ingest any mushrooms because he intended to take photographs. Wasson accepted five pairs of the "landslide" (*derrumbe*) mushrooms, rather than the six pairs he had previously taken. He says the effects were just as strong. (He felt nauseous the first time and twice had to leave the room; on this occasion, he didn't have that problem.) The setting was the same, but his mental set was quite different. Here is how Wasson described it:

(It was raining in torrents all that night, so there was no moon.) But the Señora's behavior differed much from what we had seen the first time. Everything was reduced in scale. There was no dancing and virtually no percussive utterances. Only three or four other Indians were with us, and the Señora brought with her, not her daughter, but her son Aurelio, a youth in his late teens who seemed to us in some way ill or defective. He was now the object of her attention, not I. All night long her singing and her words were directed to this poor boy. Her performance was the dramatic expression of a mother's love for her child, an anguished thronody to mother love, and interpreted in this way it was profoundly moving. The tenderness in her voice as she sang and spoke, and in her gestures as she leaned over Aurelio to caress him, moved us profoundly.

(Trip 3) Three days later, Wasson's wife Valentina Pavlovna ingested five pairs and their thirteen-year-old daughter Masha took four pairs of the same mushrooms. They swallowed them during the afternoon in sleeping bags in a closed room. This was the first occasion, Wasson remarked,

> on which white people were eating the mushrooms experimentally, without the setting of a native ceremony. They too saw visions, for hours on end, all pleasant, mostly of a nostalgic kind. VPW at one point thought she was looking down into the mouth of a vase, and there she saw and heard a stately dance, a minuet, as though in a regal court of the seventeenth century. The dancers were in miniature and the music was oh! so remote, but also so clearly heard. VPW smoked a cigarette; she exclaimed that never before had a cigarette smelled so good. It was beyond earthly experience. She drank water, and it was superior to Mumm's champagne—incomparably superior . . . .

(Trip 4) Six weeks later, Wasson tried the mushrooms again in New York. Although dried, they apparently retained much of their potency, for he wondered subjectively "if indeed their power had not increased." Secure in his home and confident now about the mushrooms, Wasson found the setting was actually enhanced by a terrific storm ("Hurricane Connie"):

> As I stood at the window and watched the gale tossing the trees and the water of the East River, with the rain driven in squalls before the wind, the whole scene was further quickened to life by the abnormal intensity of the colors that I saw. I had always thought that El Greco's apocalyptic skies over Toledo were a figment of the painter's imagination. But on this night I saw El Greco's skies, nothing dimmed, whirling over New York.

Four experiences, catalyzed by the same mushroom, yielded four considerably different results. Two years later, Wasson amalgamated these into his generalized description of the effects of psilocybian consumption:

> The mushrooms take effect differently with different persons. For example, some seem to experience only a divine euphoria, which may translate itself into uncontrollable laughter. In my own case I experienced hallucinations. What I was seeing was more clearly seen than anything I had seen before. At last I was seeing with the eye of the soul, not through the coarse lenses of my natural eyes. Moreover, what I was seeing was impregnated with weighty

Jeremy Bigwood

Psilocybe caerulescens—*large and bitter tasting—was the sacred mushroom tried by R. Gordon Wasson. The mushrooms pictured here were found on a roadside near Rio Hando in Oaxaca, Mexico.*

meaning: I was awe-struck. My visions, which never repeated themselves, were of nothing seen in this world: no motor cars, no cities with skyscrapers, no jet engines. All my visions possessed a pristine quality: when I saw choir stalls in a Renaissance cathedral, they were not black with age and incense, but as though they had just come, fresh carved, from the hand of the Master. The palaces, gardens, seascapes, and mountains that I saw had that aspect of newness, of fresh beauty, that occasionally comes to all of us in a flash. I saw few persons, and then usually at a great distance, but once I saw a human figure near at hand, a woman larger than normal, staring out over a twilight sea from her cabin on the shore. It is a curious sensation: with the speed of thought you are translated wherever you desire to be, and you are there, a disembodied eye, poised in space, seeing, not seen, invisible, incorporeal.

Dosage Considerations

Along with mental set and setting, dosage is a major consideration in the quality of a psilocybian experience.

Albert Hofmann's view has been that the "medium oral dose" for psilocybin is 4-8 mg., which "elicits the same symptoms as the consumption of about 2 g of dried *Psilocybe mexicana* fungus." When Sandoz first distributed psilocybin, the pills contained 2 gm. each; it recommended four to five of these in conjunction with "psycholytic" psychotherapy.

After the "mushroom pills" arrived at Harvard, Leary's group quickly discovered that larger amounts produced more impressive results. Leary and another person took 20 mg., and a third person consumed 22 mg. In the first session of the Concord prison project, Leary took 14 mg., while the three volunteer convicts took 20 mg. each. By the time Michael Hollingshead arrived with his bottle of LSD, the Harvard group was using as many as three 20-mg. pills for each trip. Hollingshead therefore took three: "There was a certain amount of intensification of colors, but nothing compared to LSD. So then I took 100. And then, though it was a shorter time, it was very impressive."

On the subject of appropriate dosage, there is clearly some distance between Hollingshead and Hofmann.

Regarding native use of psilocybian mushrooms, R. Gordon Wasson reports that usually each adult Indian is given four, five, six or thirteen pairs. Thirteen pairs is common because thirteen is considered a lucky number. With the wide variations in both mushroom size and potency, such rough guidelines undoubtedly result in enormous differences in the amounts of psilocybin and psilocin consumed.

Questions as to the proper dose for a first trip are difficult to answer, and no answer will be attempted here. With individual variations in mental set and setting taken into account, any general recommendation is bound to be too high or too low in a significant number of cases. It is up to the initiate to decide whether he or she should seek a more than recreational experience the first time out.

For experienced users, Rolf von Eckartsberg illustrates a point about regulating the quality of the experience through dosage in "To Be Able to Say: Thou, Really to Love" (reprinted in *The Ecstatic Adventure*). Von Eckartsberg and his wife had taken three low-dose psilocybin pills. Soon he became aware that while she "was floating through space, giggling, squirming, fluttering like a butterfly," he felt incapable of any emotional reactions. "I found myself standing apart," he reported, "removed by worlds, only half real, half empty and half dead." He pulled himself out of this "peculiar lack of emotional underpinning" by taking "two more pills, one after the other, at about forty-minute intervals."

This additional propulsion soon resulted in "a wonderful openness, I am held in the grasp of a comprehensive clarity, lucidity, like very clear, warm, transparent glass." By the end of his report, von Eckartsberg declared "For the first time I feel like a complete human being, centered in myself, yet an open platform, nothing to hide, completely reconciled and in harmony, a true partner, a steady pole . . . ."

Dosages increased beyond a certain threshold can significantly alter psilocybian experiences, which range from heightened sensitivity to color and sound through feelings of "mental stillness" and acuity to enhanced rapport with others and mystical states. Amounts of psilocybin above 8 or 10 mg. can produce the same gamut of experience available with LSD. In psychotherapy, doses of 10 mg. psilocybin and over have been used to good effect in penetrating the defenses of compulsive-obsessive patients, in aiding "transference" and in reviving childhood memories for the purpose of dealing with early traumas.

If mental set and setting are sacramental, the results can be mystical, as with Wasson's first mushroom experience. However, circumstances need not be exceptional to evoke impressive responses, as Timothy Leary first learned after eating seven small mushrooms beside a pool: "the discovery that the human brain possesses an infinity of potentialities and can operate at unexpected space-time dimensions left me feeling exhilarated, awed, and quite convinced that I had awakened from a long ontological sleep." When Leary met Richard Alpert at the airport in Mexico City shortly after, he greeted him, saying he had just been through six hours that taught him more than all his years studying psychology. "That was impressive to a fellow psychologist," Alpert says.

Walter Houston Clark gives another example of how psilocybin can profoundly influence behavior, speaking about the Corncord prison project:

> The convicts Leary had were some of the toughest convicts in the Massachusetts prisons in 1961 and 1962. They were armed robbers. They ruled the other convicts when the guards were out of sight. They had no compunctions about breaking somebody's arm, if that was necessary to enforce their ideas. They volunteered for this and thought they were going to get control of the experiment.

Instead, these tough convicts all had profound religious experiences. One of the toughest of them told me about when he took psilocybin. He had a vision of Christ and he helped Christ carry his cross towards Calvary. Then he said that after the vision stopped, "I looked out of the window and all my life came before my eyes, and I said, 'What a waste!' " Well, that was the turning point in this person's experiences. He and other tough guys started an organization within the walls to continue with their own rehabilitation and the rehabilitation of others.

Gentleness

LSD and mecaline are generally thought to have more impact than psilocybin because of their longer duration; they are also perceived by many people as more coercive than psilocybin. The psilocybin experience seems to be warmer, not as forceful and less isolating. It tends to build connections between people, who are generally much more in communication than when they use LSD.

Although rare, some "hellish" experiences have resulted from psilocybin and mushroom use, mainly in the early studies, when these drugs were administered in inappropriate hospital settings by doctors unacquainted with their effects. A vivid account of one such trip appears in Ebin's *The Drug Experience*—a first-class example of how not to conduct such investigations.

Albert Hofmann provides two examples. The first occurred after swallowing thirty-two dried specimens of *Psilocybe mexicana* to see if Heim's cultivation from Mexican sources produced mushrooms that were still psychoactive; the second appears as "an experiment with psilocybin" in the spring of 1962 in his autobiography (pp. 162-168). Hofmann seems to be one of those people "exquisitely sensitive" to psychedelic effects; as with his first self-ingestion of LSD, these trips came on overwhelmingly. The first experiment involved a medium dose by native standards (2.4 gm.):

Thirty minutes after taking the mushrooms the exterior world began to undergo a strange transformation. Everything assumed a Mexican character. As I was perfectly well aware that my knowledge of the Mexican origin of the mushrooms would lead me to imagine only Mexican scenery, I tried deliberately to look at my environment as I knew it normally. But all voluntary efforts to look at things in their customary forms and colors proved ineffective. Whether my eyes were closed or open I saw only Mexican motifs and colors. When the doctor supervising the experiment bent over to check my blood pressure, he was transformed into an Aztec priest and I would not have been astonished if he had drawn an obsidian knife. In spite of the seriousness of the situation it amused me to see how the Germanic face of my colleague had acquired a purely Indian expression. At the peak of the intoxication, about 1½ hours after ingestion of the mushrooms, the rush of interior pictures, mostly abstract motifs rapidly changing in shape and color, reached such an alarming degree that I feared that I would be torn into this whirlpool of form and color and dissolve. After about six hours the dream came to an end. Subjectively, I had no idea how long this condition had lasted. I felt my return to everyday reality to be a happy return from a strange, fantastic but quite really experienced world into an old and familiar home.

In Hofmann's 1962 psilocybin experiment, undertaken with the novelist Ernst Junger, the pharmacologist Heribert Konzett and the Islamic scholar Rudolf Gelpke, each took 20 mg. of psilocybin. Hofmann summarized the experience as having "carried all four of us off, not into luminous heights, rather into deeper regions" and concluded: "It seems that the psilocybin inebriation is more darkly colored in the majority of cases than the inebriation produced by LSD."

At Harvard, in contrast, there were no bad trips on psilocybin. Michael Kahn, a psychologist who observed both the Harvard and Millbrook psilocybin scenes, gives an account of how the advent of LSD changed the setting, resulting in greater emphasis on solitary experience.

There were no "bad trips" in those days. We didn't know what a "bad trip" was. Hundreds of psilocybin trips—I never saw one. I didn't even have a word "bad trip" in my vocabulary. Those were benign, life-changing, growth experiences, because Tim's presence was so involving . . . . We were on a love trip; Timothy had us on a love trip and it was fantastic.

We just formed this incredible community. We saw each other every day, and we hung around together, and we planned sessions together, and we played together, and we exchanged lovers, and it was just fantastic . . . .

Then Michael came and introduced the LSD and some stuff happened that I really didn't like—I guess I should say I really didn't understand. Not so much to Timothy as the rest of us. LSD is a very different drug, and we began going on solo trips which we hadn't been doing so much. People would take these wild doses of LSD and disappear, and you wouldn't see them again for two days—including myself. You know, you get together with the gang expecting one of those love sessions, and somebody would give you 400 kosher mcg. of that stuff and you'd never see anybody again till two days later, and you'd all look around and there you'd been out in the Tibetan mountains.

It was fun, and it was exciting, and it was scary. And the bad trips began—and the scary things. But then what happened that really disturbed me a lot was that we got quite cliquey—which had never happened before.

You see, things like this would happen: we would finish the psilocybin session and we would go out to the Dunkin' Donuts or the Star Market to get breakfast. And you never saw such a beautiful bunch of people in your life as that as we were walking into those places. Everybody else who was waiting in line for the "Dunkin' Donuts" were our brothers and sisters. We would quick over to the end of the line, somebody would come in and we would keep going to the end of the line and we would strike up conversations with these people. We would have this far-out thing going with the Dunkin' Donuts on Sunday morning, you know.

LSD changed all that. We got snotty, we got put-downy, we got "in" and "out." We got looking at the people who hadn't had "the experience" as though they were inferior to us. We would go to parties and there would be "drug people" and "non-drug people," and we would be in little groups, and we would tell "in-jokes," and we would be groupy, and we'd put down people who tried to get in with us.

Auditory Effects

LSD and mescaline have a reputation for being spectacular hallucinatory drugs. In moderate to high doses, psilocybin and psilocybian mushrooms produce striking visual effects in most users who close their eyes even among people who are ordinarily not much as "visualizers." In contrast to most other psychedelics, psilocybian mushrooms have also impressed many users with auditory effects. Oss and Oeric describe the response when the experience is upbeat:

> The state of mind induced by a full dose of mushrooms is one of euphoria and calm lucidity, with no loss of coherence or clarity of thought. The hallucinations seen with the eyes closed are colorful, hard-edged, and highly articulated, and may range from abstract geometrical forms to visions of fantastic landscapes and architectural vistas. These hallucinations are most intense when the mushroom is taken in the setting preferred by the Mazatecans: inside at night in complete darkness. On the other hand, if one is in a natural setting and directs the focus of the senses outward to the environment, one discovers that one's senses seem keyed to their highest pitch of receptivity, and finds oneself hearing, smelling and seeing things with a clarity and sensitivity seldom, if ever, experienced before.

One of the most interesting papers published on mushrooms is Henry Munn's in *Hallucinogens and Shamanism.* Married to a niece of the shamans he writes about, Munn reports that the Indians hear the mushrooms say things and theorizes that psilocybin affects some verbalization and speech centers of the brain. Auditory hallucinations induced by these mushrooms occur both externally and internally (with "hearing," as we normally think of it, and with "inner voices"). Munn emphasizes the "ecstatic language" given voice through the shamans:

> The phenomenon most distinctive of the mushroom's effect is the inspired capacity to speak. Those who eat them are men of language, illuminated with the spirit, who call themselves the ones who speak, those who say. The shaman, chanting in a melodic singsong, saying *says* at the end of each phrase of saying, is in communication with the origin of creation, the sources of the voice, and the fountains of the word.

Jean Basset Johnson, among the first whites to observe a mushroom ceremony, also observed that inspired speech during a curing session attributed to the mushroom, not the shaman. Oaxacan Indians today claim that God gave them these sacred mushrooms because they could not read and it was necessary for him to speak to them directly.

The Great Oracle

The earliest report of mushroom ingestion comes from Tezozómoc, who commented on the celebrants at the coronation of Montezuma II seeing visions and hearing voices: "therefore they took these hallucinations as divine notices, revelations of the future, and augury of things to come." Indian users have traditionally employed the visualization and vocalization in psilocybian experiences for purposes of divination, prophecy, healing and worship.

Wasson describes these practices more specifically:

> Perhaps there is illness in the family and the mushroom is consulted to learn whether the patient will live or die. If the verdict is for death, the family does not wait but immediately prepares for the funeral, and the sick person loses the will to live and shortly afterward gives up the ghost. If the verdict is for life, the mushroom will tell what must be done if the patient is to recover. Or, again, if a donkey has been lost or if some money has been stolen, the mushroom is consulted and gives the answers. Among these unlettered folk, speaking languages that are not written, there is often no news of an absent member of the family, perhaps one who has gone as a "wetback" to the United States. Here the mushroom, as a postal service, brings tidings of the absent one, whether he is alive and well, or sick or in jail, or prosperous or poor, or whether he is married and has children.

Wasson had special reason to be interested: during the first ceremony, Maria Sabina asked him what question he wanted answered. After fumbling about, he asked about his son in Cambridge. She had never heard of the place. Later that evening, she reported that his son wasn't in Cambridge but at home. He was in emotional turmoil over a girlfriend and was about to join the Army. Although Wasson knew nothing of this at the time, all turned out later to be true.

Stan Krippner, one of the subjects of the Harvard Psilocybin Project, gives another example:

> . . . I found myself gazing at a statue of Lincoln. The statue was entirely black, and the head was bowed. There was a gun at the base of the statue and some-one murmured, "He was shot. The President was shot." A whisp of smoke rose into the air.
>
> Lincoln's features slowly faded away, and those of Kennedy took their place. The setting was still Washington, D.C. The gun was still at the base of the statue. A wisp of smoke seeped from the barrel and curled into the air. The voice repeated, "He was shot. The President was shot." My eyes opened; they were filled with tears . . . .

Of this, he wrote later:

> In 1962, when I had my first psilocybin experience, I gave this visualization of Kennedy relatively little thought, as so many other impressions came my way. However, it was the only one of my visualizations that brought tears to my eyes, so I described it fully in the report I sent to Harvard. Nineteen months later, on November 23, 1963, the visualization came back to me as I mourned Kennedy's assassination.

Hofmann has been quoted about the Mexican tone coloring his first mushroom experience—when the Germanic doctor hovering over him appeared as an Aztec priest. In Hofmann's 1962 "psilocybin experiments," Mrs. Li Gelpke, an artist, also participated. Here she describes a drawing she made at that time:

> Nothing on this page is consciously fashioned. While I worked on it, the memory (of the experience under psilocybin) was again reality, and led me at every stroke. For that reason the picture is as many-layered as this memory, and the figure at the lower right is really the captive of its dream .... When books about Mexican art came into my hands three weeks later, I again found the motifs of my visions there with a sudden start.

Similar phenomena have been noted by Wasson, who has conjectured that ancient Mexican art may have been influenced by visionary images appearing during mushroom sessions.

Andrew Weil's Observations

In *The Marriage of the Sun and Moon*, Andy Weil declares that he's a "mycophile" and describes three trips he took using the San Isidro mushroom (*Stropharia cubensis*). These three experiences with the same mushroom stimulated greatly varying responses. They may serve as a conclusion for this discussion, because they emphasize again the significant influence of mental set and setting.

(Trip 1) In 1972, Weil arrived in Huautla de Jiménez, where he had the good fortune to be taken into the house of a *curandera* living in a nearby village. As a healer, she used modern medicines and also mushrooms, which she regarded as the *gran remedio* that cures all ills. She had already collected a bunch of San Isidro mushrooms that were obviously meant for Weil, as she said. Weil had only a twenty-four hour permit to stay in the area.

He noticed larvae and insects among the mushrooms. The *curandera*, however, passed the mushrooms through the smoke from a dried chile pod placed on glowing charcoal, and instantly the insects crawled out of the mushrooms and died on a newspaper placed below. Weil ate two of the largest mushrooms (three-inch caps), and as the *curandera* prayed, he ate twenty smaller ones.

Protected by the sacred ministrations of the *curandera*, he was soon feeling "extraordinarily content and well" and experienced sensations of lightness. He felt "fresh, alert, healthy and cleansed." The healer communicated "much of her own vitality, optimism and goodness of spirit, leaving me elated and more confident in my own abilities and powers."

Going outside later, he recalled Wasson's suggestion that the word "bemushroomed" would be a good term for this state. He observed a full eclipse of the moon and later went to sleep. "In the morning, I awoke refreshed, feeling better than I had in a long time, and went off for a day in Huautla of shopping and negotiating with the military authorities ...."

(Trip 2) When Weil returned, the healer told him that some mushrooms were left over and that he might as well finish them that night. "I
really did not want to," writes Weil, "since I had just had a perfect mushroom
experience, but instead of telling her that, I agreed." They repeated the
service with incense and prayers beneath a picture of the patron saint Isidro,
who was being showered with "psychedelic rays . . . from some other dimension." This time, the experience took a different direction:

> A heavy bank of fog and clouds closed in, the temperature dropped, and
> suddenly nearly everyone in the house was sick. There was much crying and
> coughing from the bedroom, and I began feeling unwell, too. A great sense of
> depression and isolation came over me. I could not get to sleep. The mush-
> rooms seemed to be working against me, not with me, and I felt far away from
> where I was supposed to be.

Toward dawn, Weil was still awake and concluding that mushrooms,
like other psychedelics, "must be used in a proper context." He comments
on this lesson:

> To take them just because they are available, when the time is not right, is a
> mistake. The negative experience of this second night did not in any way de-
> tract from the goodness of the first night. If anything, it made me more aware
> of the value of that experience and more eager to retain it and use it in my life.
> I hoped that I would be able to be bemushroomed again, but I resolved to be
> patient until the right moment came.

(Trip 3) A short while later, outside Cali in Colombia, Weil ate *Stropharia cubensis* again. The mushroom seemed to be growing all over the
place, although its use was not traditional there. Whites and others "have
recently introduced Colombian Indians to the drug, the reverse of the usual
order of things." The setting this time was "an idyllically beautiful field with
clumps of woods, a clear river and enormous, gray, humpbacked Brahma
cows lying peacefully in the bright green grass." The resulting trip led him
to inquire further into setting:

> We sat in the grass, about ten of us, and let the mushrooms transport us to a
> realm of calm good feeling in which we drank in the beauty of the setting.
> There were color visions, as I had experienced before with San Isidro in Mex-
> ico. In Mexico I had eaten the mushrooms late at night, in darkness and
> secrecy, in the very shadow of menacing police authority. Now it was broad
> daylight, in open country, with no one around but friendly fellow travelers. In
> Mexico I had felt like an early Christian pursuing the sacrament in a catacomb,
> wary of the approach of Roman legions; here everything was aboveground
> and open. The Indians of the Sierra Mazateca say the mushroom should not
> be eaten in daytime, that they must be eaten at night. Yet here we were in full
> daylight having a wonderful time. In general, I prefer to take psychedelic sub-
> stances in the daytime, when their stimulating energies are more in harmony
> with the rhythms of my body. I feel that way about mushrooms, too. Is it
> possible, I wondered, that the Indian habit of eating mushrooms at night is

not so traditional as it seems but dates back only to the arrival of the Spanish and persecutions of native rites by the church?

Weil has since experimented with other psilocybian mushrooms; he feel that "the most interesting properties of mushrooms may not come to our attention if people use them casually and without thought."

FORMS AND PREPARATIONS

Illustrations of the psilocybian mushrooms in this book have so far been in the fresh state. When offered for sale, however, they generally have been already dried. Here is an example of *Stropharia (Pilocybe) cubensis* as it is ordinarily presented:

Jeremy Bigwood

Psilocybe cubensis *mushrooms, dried and bagged for future use.*

Dosage regarding mushrooms is complex—enough so that the reader is directed to the botany section of this chapter where rough guidelines are given for the most popular half dozen psychedelic species. Near the beginning of that section are also instructions for preparing uniform, stable doses—something that so far has not shown up much in the psychedelic subculture.

A Modern Herbal (Grieve)

Nutmeg, a psychoactive spice, is the dried seed within the fruit of an East Indian tree, Myristica fragrans.

CHAPTER FIVE

Nutmeg and MDA

3-4-Methylenedioxy-amphetamine . . . enhances intellectual and emotional thinking, together with an increase in the level of fluency and attention, at dose levels less than those required for the appearance of imagery and perceptual distortion.

—Roger Brimblecombe and Roger Pinder

HISTORY

Introduction to the MDA "Cluster"

Previous chapters describe the four groups of psychedelic substances that have had the greatest influence on humans to date (for speculations regarding the history and possible influence of Fly Agaric, see Chapter Nine). Of the five remaining groups of substances generally regarded as psychedelic, the one attracting the most interest in the U.S. currently appears to be the MDA cluster.

MDA-like compounds almost always come from the volatile oils found in a small number of plants: nutmeg, mace, saffron, calamus, crocus, parsley, dill and sassafras. More than a thousand synthesized compounds fall into this group. Only a few have been tried by humans.

MDA-like compounds—such as the TMAs, DOB, DOET, DOM, MMDA, PBR, TMPEA, DMPEA, DMA, PMA and MEDA—have molecular structures that resemble mescaline, dopamine and amphetamine. Moreover, the effects are often experienced as being like an interplay between mescaline and amphetamine—one or the other tendency predominating according to the structure of the particular compound. Thus this cluster often has been referred to as "psychedelic amphetamines." (A chemist would probably designate them as "alpha-methyl phenethylamines," "indolealkylamines" or "one-ring substituted amphetamines.")

An important feature common to members of the MDA cluster is that substitutions on the molecular ring can be made fairly readily; the process is expensive and requires sophisticated chemistry. Still, the chemistry is much simpler than for the four psychedelic groups already discussed, which is one reason why a tremendous number of these MDA-like substances have been synthesized. Many people feel that the number and variety of MDA analogues will enable researchers to make systematic comparisons of mental characteristics and chemical structures, thus providing an important key for understanding more about the nature of the human mind.

A Modern Herbal

Sassafras is a botanical source used in synthesizing MDA-like compounds.

The superiority of the synthetics over the natural MDA-like sources is pronounced. "Aminization" (chemical conversion to amine form) of plant oils heightens and clarifies mental effects and all but eliminates physical side effects often accompanying use of the botanicals. Users of the synthetics generally report increased relaxation, empathy and mental fluency, and many prefer this experience for being without the "distractions" of the psychedelic visuals that are characteristic of LSD and mescaline.

One can think of mescaline and LSD as one pole in the psychedelic field—evoking ego-death and rebirth, visions and much else that can appear with jolting unexpectedness. Most of the tested MDA-like compounds are gathered around the opposite pole—where shocks are rare and the emphasis is on ideas and enchanced rapport with people.

The MDA cluster is presented here as the first of five psychedelic clusters that are more exotic—at least in the sense of being used by fewer people than LSD, mescaline, marijuana and psilocybian mushrooms. It should be emphasized that now we begin to depart from consensus on what's truly "psychedelic." Effects from members of the MDA-cluster can easily be likened, and thereby denigrated in the minds of many, to those of cocaine or amphetamine. Although the MDA-like compounds are increasingly popular, their subdued effects couple them with the subtlety of marijuana for some.

Nutmeg and Mace

Nutmeg, which in the U.S. is mainly used as a garnish during Christmas festivities, is the dried kernel of *Myristica fragrans*, a tree native to the Spice Islands, near New Guinea. Now cultivated in many places, the tree grows to about fifty feet high and bears seeds for up to sixty years. Its fruit looks much like a peach and contains a brownish-purple, shiny kernel encased within a bright orange-red or red covering. The covering, or aril, is used for production of mace; the seed, dried in the sun for about two months and turned over each day, becomes nutmeg. Both the kernel and its covering contain psychoactive components within their oils.

Most of the natural substances that contain compounds similar to MDA have a history of use for their medicinal properties and their psychoactivity. The *Ayurveda* of ancient India refers to nutmeg and mace as *made shaunda*, generally translated as "narcotic fruit." An 1883 *Materia Medica* from Bombay records that "the Hindus of West India take Myristica as an intoxicant." Nutmeg has been used for centuries as a snuff in rural eastern Indonesia; in India, the same practice appears, but often the ground seed is first mixed with betel and other kinds of snuff. Restrictions on hashish in Egypt have brought about periods when nutmeg was used as a substitute.

Nutmeg appears in the Hindu Pharmacopoeia as a treatment for fever, asthma and heart disease. Since the seventh century A.D., Arab physicians have used it for digestive disorders, kidney disease and lymphatic ailments. Yemeni men are said to consume nutmeg to increase and maintain their sexual vigor.

Nutmeg and mace weren't known to the Greeks or Romans. They were not introduced to the West until 1512, when the Portuguese reached the Banda, or Nutmeg, Islands. The earliest record of nutmeg's mental effects comes from 1576, in the description of a "pregnant English lady who, having eaten ten or twelve nutmegs, became deliriously inebriated" (she was lucky not to have died).

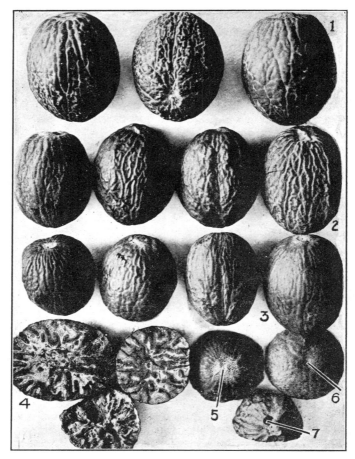

Myristica *(nutmeg); 1, Penang nutmegs. 2, Round
West India nutmegs. 3, Banda nutmegs. 4, Longitudinal,
cross and a broken surface of the seed. 5, Upper part
of the seed. 6, Base of the seed. 7, Wormy seed.*

The photos on these pages come from the *Squibb Handbook* of 1896;
Squibb's captions have been retained and illustrate variations appearing in
the *Myristica fragrans* species.

In the seventeenth century, nutmeg became an important article in the
spice trade, which the Dutch monopolized for a long while with their naval
superiority. "So precious were nutmegs," writes the botanist William Emboden in *Narcotic Plants,*

> that carved wooden replicas were sold to the ignorant via a black market.
> Slaves on the ships bringing nutmeg to Europe were castigated for consuming
> part of the cargo. They knew that a few of the large kernels of nutmeg seed

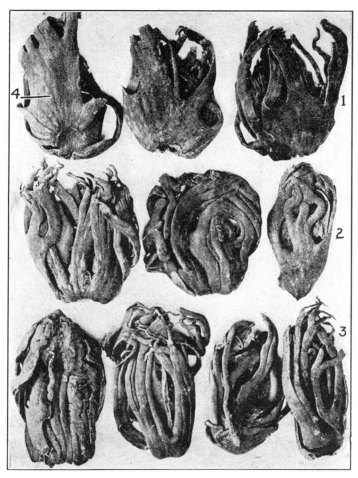

Macis: *1, Banda mace. 2, Siam mace. 3, West Indian mace. 4, Broad bands of Banda mace.*

would relieve their weariness and bring euphoric sensations of an other-worldly nature accompanied by pleasant visions. Nausea and dizziness followed as the price for this respite from reality. The more practical mind of the European saw this seed as potential medicine and did not hesitate to administer it in the event of severe illness. On that day in February 1685 when the feeble King Charles II was felled by a clot or haemorrhage, one of the numerous unsuccessful attempts to revive him included a decoction of nutmeg. His death a few days later did nothing to detract from the reputation of nutmeg as a useful drug. Nutmegs encased in silver were worn at night as an inducement to sleep, aphrodisiacal properties were ascribed to them, and they became a standard element in love potions. In London the rumour spread that a few of these nuts would act as an abortifacient.

Use of this commonly available substance as an inebrient has continued into this century. "Confirmed reports of its use by students, prisoners, sailors, alcoholics, marijuana-smokers and others deprived of their preferred drugs," write Schultes and Hofmann in *The Botany and Chemistry of Hallucinogens,* "are many and clear. Especially frequent is the taking of nutmeg in prisons, notwithstanding the usual denials of prison officials."

Calamus, or "Sweet Flag"

Another source of oils from which MDA-like compounds have been synthesized is a marsh plant growing in temperate zones of Asia, Europe and North America that's known botanically as *Acorus calamus* and popularly as sweet flag, sweet sedge, rat root, flag root, sweet myrtle, beewort or sweet calomel. This is an iris-like perennial growing five to six feet high that often borders streams and ponds where cat-tails are found. Its leaves have unusual crimped edges, and a horizontal creeping root may extend up to five feet long. The oils in this rhizome contain two psychoactive substances, asarone and β-asarone, which are the natural precursors to TMA-2, a compound that has ten times the potency of mescaline. (Asarone also appears in *Caucus carota,* a wild carrot from Central Asia.)

For at least 2,000 years, *Acorus calamus* has been used in India and China as a medicine. In Ayurvedic practice, the plant is called *racha* and recommended as a remedy for bronchitis, asthma and fevers. In China, where it's known as *shih-ch'ang pu,* it is used to relieve constipation and swelling. According to *Exodus* 30: 22-25, this was one of the constituents of a "holy annointing oil" that the Lord commanded Moses to make and rub on his body when he approached the Tabernacle.

This root was known to many early American settlers and to Walt Whitman, who wrote forty-five poems under the title "Calamus" in *Leaves of Grass.* (Invoking calamus in the thirteenth poem, Whitman realizes that he "must change the strain—these are not to be/ pensive leaves, but leaves of joy . . . .")

In the British Isles during the Depression of the 1930s, calamus was often chewed by people unable to buy tobacco. The root tastes much like ginger and, in small quantities of up to two inches, is stimulating and euphoric.

Calamus has also been used by many North American Indian tribes for the relief of fatigue. In larger quantities, the root causes one to "walk a foot above the ground." Even more of the root has been used and is still used in conjunction with puberty initiatory rites. In *The Hallucinogens,* Hoffer and Osmond recount the experiences of "an informant well acquainted with the habits of northern Canadian Indians." He used rat root collected in northern Alberta by the Cree:

> He reported that nearly all the Indians over age 40 used rat root regularly but the younger Indians were unfamiliar with it and its use was discouraged by physicians who practiced there. Rat root users seemed to be healthier, and

were not subject to alcoholism. The Indians used rat root (a) as an antifatigue medicine (they chewed about 1 inch of the dried root which had a diameter equal to a pencil); (b) as an analgesic for relieving toothache, headache, etc; (c) for relief of asthma; (d) for oral hygiene, and (e) to relieve hangover.

Our informant had over the years tested these medicinal qualities and generally confirmed them. It was particularly effective for alleviating fatigue. On one occasion, he walked 12 miles in the northern woods to fight a forest fire. He was out of condition and was exhausted at the end of the march. He chewed and swallowed 2 inches of rat root. Within 10 minutes the fatigue vanished and on the return march he seemed to be walking 1 foot above the ground and felt wonderful. The effect was very unlike amphetamine. On his return home he was very exhausted but after a night's sleep was normal.

The informant and his wife, a trained psychiatric nurse, were both sophisticated subjects with hallucinogens. They had taken LSD several times in well-controlled experiments at one of our research laboratories. They had both taken 10 inches of rat root 5 times and both agreed it produced an experience very similar to LSD.

Alles Discovers MDA's Psychoactivity

MDA, the archetype and simplest member of this cluster, was first synthesized in 1910 by G. Mannish and W. Jacobson, who described the process in a German journal. It wasn't until 1939 that animal tests were performed, when·the team of Gunn, Gurd and Sachs became interested in the substance while conducting adrenaline studies. Two years later, another team—Loman, Myerson and Myerson—thought this compound might alleviate Parkinsonism but discarded the idea when the drug produced muscular rigidity in the single patient tested. At about this time, MDA was rejected as a possible weight reduction agent by the Smith, Klein & French Co. because pronounced though not hallucinogenic effects interfered after a few days with the patients' ordinary routines.

Gordon Alles, the UCLA researcher who discovered amphetamine in 1927, was interested in MDA (3,4-methylenedioxyphenylisopropylamine) and its cousin 3,4-methylenedioxyphenylethylamine because of the structural closeness of these two molecules to ephedrine, the standard drug for testing central nervous system stimulation during the 1930s and 1940s. He decided that he would conduct what he called a "double-conscious" test of these substances—meaning that he would synthesize, measure and take them himself in order to compare their effects with what he knew about how ephedrine affected him. "I was quite well calibrated," he remarked later, "with 50 mg. doses of ephedrine and with similar doses of amphetamine."

After tests with dogs, which indicated that these two compounds were one third to one half as active in their peripheral effects as mescaline and amphetamine, Alles swallowed 36 mg. of MDA. During the following two hours, he noticed neither physical nor mental sensations. He then took an additional 90 mg.

Within a few minutes, he "realized that a notable subjective response was going to result." The muscles of his neck became markedly tensed, and he was closing his jaws tightly and grinding his back teeth. His gums became white and contracted. He perspired quite a bit but noted a slowed respiration rate. His pupils were "markedly dilated . . . . I had never seen dilation of the pupils in animals or man to such an extent."

About forty-five minutes after the second dose, smoke rings filled the air, moving in slow motion about him. In a closed room on the sixth floor of a university building, there "was no possible source of smoke rings." Yet,

> an abundance of curling smoke rings was readily observed in the environment whenever a relaxed approach in observation was used. Visually, these had complete reality; and it seemed quite unnecessary to test their properties because it was surely known and fully appreciated that the source of the visual phenomena could not be external to the body. When I concentrated my attention on the details of the curling gray forms by trying to note how they would be affected by passing a finger through their apparent field, they melted away. Then when I relaxed again, the smoke rings were there.

Talking about these smoke rings later, Alles commented, "I was as certain they were really there as I am now sure that my head is on top of my body." Further into the experience, he also noticed that

> Vision at a considerable distance was remarkable in clarity of detail. I had never looked out of the window a great deal before but I found that at a distance of three and four blocks away, I could make out very minute details of things.

Later, Alles said he was sure that the details were correct and that he wasn't able to make them out during normal consciousness "to anywhere near as great an extent." These visual effects only introduced what lay ahead. Looking at his "almost entirely black eyes," he had been fearful momentarily but thereafter had "a general feeling of well being," accompanied by a switch in his perception of the location of his consciousness:

> When I was very relaxed, my thinking became introspectively speculative. Awareness of the body and of its functionings became subject to a detached spatial consideration, and the reality of the place of detached observation for a time semed clearly transposed out of the body and to a place above and to the right rearward. I was compelled to turn my head several times and look into that upper corner of the room in wonder at what part of me could be up there and observing the subjective situation and behavior as if from that point. I observed this phenomenon from where I was seated.

There was also "remarkably clear and apparent" differentiation in the perception of sounds:

> Seeing the smoke rings that weren't there gave me the impression that perhaps I was also hearing things that weren't there. When I heard footsteps, I looked out into the corridor and found no one there. I repeated this a number of times. Somehow I felt this was not a hallucinatory phenomenon, and that I was hearing actual walking. Then I finally realized that I was hearing footsteps

not primarily in either my right or left ear, and that the sound must be coming through the window. (I was on the sixth floor of the Medical Office Building at that time). I looked out and saw people walking along the sidewalk. That was not sufficient correlation, so I sat down until I heard definite footsteps. Then I looked out and saw that a person was passing. After doing this three or four times I realized that there was a one-to-one correspondence between my hearing footsteps and the passing of a person on the street below.

Alles later added that until then he "had never even read an account of hallucinatory experiences" and that "if I had not persisted in looking for the source of the footsteps, I would have remained under the impression that I was having auditory hallucinations."

Another aspect of this experience was tactile:

I found that now, too, I had a qualitatively different sensation in my finger-tips. Then as I tried stronger stimulation of the finger ends, I experienced a peculiar phenomenon that I had never noted before; nor have I noted it since, under any conditions. If you watch as you touch a tabletop with your finger, you will notice that the time when you hit it, as determined visually, and the time when you feel it are in essential coincidence. However, under this drug, I found that I first hit the table, and then felt it; the feeling was a very definitely delayed phenomenon. I experimented with this for a half hour or more . . . .

Synthesis and Testing of Related Compounds

It was through Alles' work that MDA and its many relatives eventually came to public awareness. He took MDA several times, determining that minimal effects began with a dose of about 80 mg. Asked later about taking a higher dose again, his comment was: "I would not at all hesitate to do so for experimental purposes, if people could tell me just what they wanted to observe at the particular time. Just a simple repetition of the hallucinatory experience, I think, adds nothing to our knowledge."

In 1957, Alles attended a conference in Princeton, New Jersey, that was sponsored by the Josiah Macy, Jr., Foundation, and there he described his MDA experience. In 1959, the proceedings of the conference were published in *Neuropharmacology: Transactions of the 4th Conference* (edited by Harold Abramson). Five or six years later, MDA began showing up in the counterculture, and in 1970 it was "scheduled" as part of the Comprehensive Drug Abuse legislation.

The U.S. Army experimented at its Edgewood Arsenal in Maryland with quite a number of psychoactive substances in the 1950s. Although their results remain mostly undisclosed, Army scientists were using MDA (coded EA-1299) and some MDA-like compounds. Synthesis of MDMA, active in doses of the 75-100 mg. range and shorter and milder in its effects than MDA, was not reported in the scientific literature until 1960. It has since been established that MDMA was one of the "Experimental Agents" tested at Edgewood Chemical Warfare Service, where it was labeled EA-1475.

Gordon Alles discovered the psychedelic effects of MDA.

The next important MDA-like compounds to come along were the TMAs (there are six). TMA-2, the most interesting, was first synthesized in 1933, but its psychoactive effects weren't recognized until 1962, when the chemist Alexander Shulgin aminized it from asarone derived from the oils present in calamus. That same year Shulgin aminized myristicin, present in the aromatic oils of mace and nutmeg, and came up with MMDA. After more than 75 mg. have been ingested, this compound produces MDA-like effects that usually last under five hours, differing from MDA's effects in that there is often dream-like imagery when the eyes are closed.

In 1964, Shulgin synthesized DOM (2,5-dimethoxy-4-methyl-amphetamine) and determined that with a dose of 3 mg. the effects lasted eighteen hours or more; with a dose above 5 mg., the results are highly hallucinogenic and could persist up to three days. Two years after his report, a "new drug" with long-lasting effects was introduced to the counterculture under the name STP. Although it wasn't clear for some time, DOM and STP turned out to be the same. Apparently STP was synthesized independently by underground chemists experimenting with MDA derivatives.

STP was said to be an acronym for "Serenity, Tranquility and Peace," although for many it proved to be a foundation-shaking experience. Among the first to try STP was Richard Alpert, who took it in an apartment building on 57th Street in Manhattan and promptly tried to walk out the window. He was so scared by his response that he said the drug should not be released under any circumstances, that it was too intense. Later, considering that

New York City "was not perhaps the optimum" in experimental environments, he tried it again near Taos, New Mexico after fasting for five days. Alpert wanted to give STP "a fair shake." He has since described this experience as "an extraordinary, extraordinary trip. I was *really* impressed. I still thought it was maybe too strong an agent for most people—it might have been too fierce for their use. But it was certainly a profound psychedelic experience . . . ."

Despite such cautionary advice from the people who first tested it, in January 1967 some 5,000 tablets in 10 mg. dosage—more than three times Shulgin's recommendation for DOM—were distributed for free at the first "Human Be-in," in San Francisco's Golden Gate Park. Jeremy Bigwood recalls that

> by nightfall there were several thousand tripping hippies, along with a scattering of panic reactions to the intensely psychedelic STP experience. After a sleepless night there were still a couple of thousand tripping hippies—many of whom were no longer enjoying the voyage. Hundreds of people experienced hallucinatory episodes lasting three days, many ending up in the emergency rooms of various Bay Area hospitals wondering if they would ever come down.

STP continued to be available in some locales for another two years, even though the producers later agreed that their tablets presented much too strong a dosage. Questions were also almost immediately raised about the purity and actual content of these pills. Hospitals treating overwhelmed users reported that Thorazine (chlorpromazine) seemed to intensify and prolong STP's effects. Studies carried out the next year showed that Thorazine had a slight dampening influence on the DOM experience. Thus, some people felt that the STP pills must have contained other substances, which somehow were activated by Thorazine.

Another sticky situation arose in the early 1970s when it became clear that there is one physically dangerous member of this cluster: PMA (4-methoxyamphetamine). This compound, distributed mainly between 1972 and 1973, was often passed off as MDA. An effective dose of PMA can cause a dangerous rise in blood pressure. Use of this substance resulted in several deaths—although for some time it wasn't clear which drug had been ingested. Some people felt that MDA was involved, but it seems now that PMA was responsible. PMA is a dangerous MDA-like compound that appears to have been totally withdrawn from circulation.

Bigwood, writing in *Head* magazine (December 1977), pointed out that the alphabet-soup designations of the MDA cluster are a significant source of confusion. With so many compounds in this cluster, initials for a specific substance may be correctly passed from manufacturer to distributor, but are often jumbled after the compound has passed through several hands. The delay in identifying PMA as dangerous demonstrates the seriousness of this problem.

In 1974, Shulgin synthesized DOB, which is very much like DOM except that it's milder and much more manageable. Then followed his synthesis of DOET, another drug possessing moderated STP-like effects. These compounds have been tried out by a few people but are generally not as available as MDA.

In the 1980s, several related compounds have been distributed. They appear to have been used so far without problems.

CHEMISTRY

The oils from nutmeg, dill, parsley seed, calamus, crocus, saffron, vanilla beans, sassafras and other plants contain generous amounts of the precursors to the semi-synthetic MDA-like compounds. Recently dried nutmeg is about 15 percent extractable oil.

Most users feel mental effects from ground nutmeg with a 20 gm. dose, which has been assayed at 210 mg. myristicin (potential MMDA), 70 mg. elemicin (potential TMA), 39 mg. safrole (potential MDA), plus smaller amounts of other aromatic ethers and a number of terpene hydrocarbons (biological irritants).

Conversion of the non-amine oils in the presence of ammonia into the amine forms (TMA, MDA, etc.) has been demonstrated in the laboratory, giving rise to speculation that a similar process occurs in the body to create mental effects. "Although the addition of ammonia has been shown to occur *in vitro* with tissue homogenates," Shulgin has commented, "there is at present no evidence that any of these centrally active bases can be formed *in vivo.*"

The chemistry of related synthetics is extensive, because atoms and radicals on the ring and side chain are susceptible to replacement with relatively little laboratory manipulation. The best review of the effects of the synthetics known to have psychoactivity appears in Vol. 11 (*Stimulants*) of the *Handbook of Psychopharmacology* (Plenum Press, 1978), in which Shulgin discusses the chemistry and corresponding effects of forty-nine MDA-like compounds, dividing them into the following categories: eleven that are *methoxylated phenylisopropylamines*, with varying positions for and varying numbers of methoxyl groups; eleven that are *methylenedioxy phenylisopropylamines*, with or without methoxyl groups in addition; five that are *phenylisopropylamines with alkoxy substituents* in addition to, or instead of, methoxyl groups; twelve that are *phenylisopropylamines with alkyl groups on the aromatic ring*, with or without methoxyl groups in addition; and ten that are *phenylisopropylamines with a halo group or a sulfur on the aromatic ring*, with methoxyl groups in addition.

Most readers will find two other summaries more accessible: Shulgin's article on "The Phenethylamines Related to Mescaline" in the January-June 1979 issue of the *Journal of Psychedelic Drugs* and a more generalized treatment in Vol. III, Chapter Sixty of *Burger's Medicinal Chemistry* (4th ed., John Wiley & Sons, 1981).

60.22

Structure No.	Substitution Position of R					Name	Potency Relative to Mescaline	Ref.
	2	3	4	5	6			
60.22a	H	OCH₃	OCH₃	OCH₃	H	TMA	2	83, 84
60.22b	OCH₃	H	OCH₃	OCH₃	H	TMA-2	20	85
60.22c	OCH₃	OCH₃	OCH₃	H	H	TMA-3	<2	85
60.22d	OCH₃	OCH₃	H	OCH₃	H	TMA-4	4	75
60.22e	OCH₃	OCH₃	H	H	OCH₃	TMA-5	10	75
60.22f	OCH₃	H	OCH₃	H	OCH₃	TMA-6	10	75
60.22g	H	H	OCH₃	H	H	PMA	6	75
60.22h	OCH₃	H	OCH₃	H	H	2,4-DMA	6	78
60.22i	OCH₃	H	H	OCH₃	H	2,5-DMA	6	78
60.22j	H	OCH₃	OCH₃	H	H	3,4-DMA	~1	86
60.22k	OCH₃	OCH₃	OCH₃	OCH₃	H	—	6	75
60.22l	H	OCH₃	OCH₂φ	OCH₃	H	—	2	78
60.22m	OCH₃	H	OEt	OCH₃	H	MEM	20	78
60.22o	H	O—CH₂—O		H	H	MDA	3	87–89
60.22p	H	OCH₃	O—CH₂—O		H	MMDA	3	90, 91
60.22q	OCH₃	H	O—CH₂—O		H	MMDA-2	10	85
60.22r	OCH₃	O—CH₂O		H	OCH₃	MMDA-3a	10	85
60.22s	O—CH₂—O		OCH₃	H	H	MMDA-3b	3	85
60.22t	O—CH₂—O		H	H	OCH₃	MMDA-5	10	78
60.22u	OCH₃	O—CH₂—O		OCH₃	H	DMMDA	12	92
60.22v	OCH₃	OCH₃	O—CH₂—O		H	DMMDA-2	5	92
60.22w	OCH₃	H	SCH₃	OCH₃	H	p-DOT (Aleph-1)	40	93
60.22x	OCH₃	H	SEt	OCH₃	H	Aleph-2	80	78
60.22y	OCH₃	H	SPr(i)	OCH₃	H	Aleph-4	40	94
60.22z	OCH₃	H	SPr(n)	OCH₃	H	Aleph-7	60	94
60.22aa	OCH₃	H	CH₃	OCH₃	H	DOM (STP)	80	78, 95
60.22bb	OCH₃	H	Et	OCH₃	H	DOET	100	78, 96
60.22cc	OCH₃	H	Pr(n)	OCH₃	H	DOPR	80	14
60.22dd	OCH₃	H	Bu(n)	OCH₃	H	DOBU	40	14
60.22ee	OCH₃	H	Am(n.)	OCH₃	H	DOAM	10	14
60.22ff	OCH₃	H	Br	OCH₃	H	DOB	400	97
60.22gg	OCH₃	H	I	OCH₃	H	DOI	400	78

Characteristics of some psychoactive phenylisopropylamines as listed in Burger's Medicinal Chemistry. *Substitution of various molecules and molecular groups at various positions in the skeleton nucleus has been extensively tested and results in wide variations in potency (DOB is the strongest, exhibiting some 400 times the strength of mescaline). Those in the middle are the most popular in this series, but the recently-synthesized Aleph compounds, which contain sulfur and emphasize introspection, have also been well received.*

Ann Shulgin

Alexander Shulgin discovered the psychedelic effects of TMA-2, DOM, MMDA, DOB and other phenylisopropylamines.

Shulgin's interest in the relationship between structure and activity is also held by Roger Brimblecombe (of the research laboratories of Smith, Kline & French) and his colleague Roger Pinder (Australian Drug Information Services). As early as the mid-1970s, Brinblecombe and Pinder saw that substituted phenylethylamines would eventually reduce the status of mescaline, once the most potent psychedelic known but pre-eminent only because of its early isolation and identification. In their *Hallucinogenic Agents* (1975) they wrote that mescaline "can now be regarded as a naturally occurring example with relatively low potential of a much wider group of hallucinogens."

The writings of Shulgin, the Brimblecombe-Pinder team and many others are filled with speculations about how an alpha-methyl group adds to potency, how a tryptamine ring and amphetamine tail perhaps allows passage through the blood-brain barrier, how various chemical alterations keep monoamine oxidase from cutting the molecule's tail, thus increasing activity and duration. There's material here for fascinating rumination—what with the extreme variations in strength, in timing and in the experiential tendencies manifested by each compound.

One complication not often mentioned is that many of these compounds appear as optical isomers and in different forms as freebases or salts. The MDA molecule, for instance, presents itself in two mirror images that rotate plane-polarized light in opposite directions. Although they rotate light to the same degree, they have different strengths. The doses required to produce the same effect upon the central nervous system from the levorotary isomer, the dextrorotary isomer and the racemate (an optically neutral mixture of the two isomers) are estimated by Shulgin at 70, 225 and 125 mg. respectively. Of these three forms, the levo-isomer has the greatest effect in humans. The same is true of DOET, where the levo-isomer is roughly twice as strong as its mirror image.

In the discussion of mental effects below, most attention will be given to MDA and MMDA. Here are sketches of these two:

MDA	*MMDA*
(3,4-methylene-	*(3-methoxy-4,5-methylene-*
dioxyamphetamine)	*dioxyamphetamine)*

PHYSICAL EFFECTS

Nutmeg

In a *High Times* debate concerning synthetic versus organic psychedelics, Bruce Eisner argued that for most users synthetic mescaline sulfate is preferable to peyote and LSD is preferable to morning glories or ergot, because the "plant forms contain many other alkaloids besides the psychoactive ones, some of which make a person sick, and in the case of ergot, can lead to death." The same argument applies to the differences between nutmeg and MDA.

A number of accounts of nutmeg inebriation appear in *The Ethnopharmacologic Search for Psychoactive Drugs*, and particularly full discussions are given by an ex-convict in Hoffer and Osmond's *The Hallucinogens* and by another ex-convict in *Medical Botany* by Walter Lewis and Memory P.F. Elvin-Lewis. Nearly all such records agree that inebriation with nutmeg is accompanied by unpleasant somatic side-effects. The Church of the Tree of Life's *First Book of Sacraments* summarizes the physical effects:

> The usual prison dose is a matchbook of ground nutmeg—about 20 grams. This amount can cause some very severe psychological and physiological effects. These effects may vary somewhat with the individual, the dose and the potency of the material. Some people enjoy it, but most see it as a rather grueling experience. Many find it difficult to swallow the required dose. Some suffer nausea during the first 45 minutes. After that silly feelings and giggling often occur. This is soon followed by dryness of the mouth and throat, flushing

of the skin and reddening eyes. Occasionally a person will feel agitated and hyperactive, but more often he will feel heavy, intoxicated and unable to do anything but lie down. Motor functions may be confounded and speech incoherent. He may become overly conscious of his heart beat and become concerned about the seeming gaps between beats. Later he may enter a stuporous euphoric state in which he experiences profound peace of mind and dreamy visions. If he is able to move about he will usually feel like everything is in slow motion . . . .

A person under the spell of nutmeg is likely to find himself unable actually to sleep, but also incapable of being really awake. Sleepless stupor is the most apt description of nutmeg narcosis. This condition may last for 12 hours followed by 24 hours of drowsiness during which he may sleep a lot.

The after-effects are usually quite unpleasant: aching of the bones and muscles, soreness and aching of the eyes, running nose, tiredness, depression and possible headaches. One of the best things that can be said about nutmeg intoxication is that it is too unpleasant to be addicting . . . .

The MDA-like and STP-like Subclusters

MDA, MMDA and the other semi-synthetics are prepared by aminization of various natural oils, which seems to eliminate nearly all the unpleasant physical effects of the experience for most people.

Almost all users exhibit dilated pupils. Perhaps 10 percent of users feel transitory nausea, jaw-tightening, sweating or jitteriness, and most register some rise in blood pressure. Claudio Naranjo suggests that "Since individual incompatibility is consistent and bound to dose level," it is possible to identify those susceptible to physical problems

> through progressively increased test doses (i.e., 10 mg., 20 mg., 40 mg., 100 mg.). This should be done without exception throughout the time preceding any first therapeutic MDA session. Typical toxic symptoms are skin reactions, profuse sweating, and confusion; I have observed these in about 10 per cent of the subjects at dosages of 150-200 mg.

"Another outstanding quality about this drug complex," says Jeremy Bigwood,

> in contrast to everything else psychedelic is its "rush" effect. Things with 3,4-dioxy groups, like MDA, all have that rush—whether or not they are substituted in other positions. That rush seems to be a unique handle to that series. None of the others have that feeling—which is why some people have compared it to cocaine. Injected, it's very similar to cocaine or amphetamine. Even orally, it's similar.

These compounds seem to produce some of the paradoxical reactions often observed with amphetamine and thus should be handled with caution. A short pamphlet from Stash, a psychedelic information service, warns against use of MDA by "Persons with heart disease, severe high blood pressure, hyperthyroidism or diabetes mellitus." MDA was described by Alles as being a third as potent as amphetamine in vaso-constrictive effects. The

Spring Grove researchers of Turek, Soskin and Kurland studied ten subjects given 70 mg. of the levo-isomer orally and observed a drop in blood pressure "followed by a rise during the second and third hours after administration, returning to the pre-drug pressure at the fifth hour." MDA also induces sleeplessness in some people, although not as often or severely as equivalent amounts of amphetamine.

Many users feel tired and sluggish the following day, which led Weil to suggest that one should be in good physical shape with adequate energy reserves before trying such compounds. "For unknown reasons," he adds, "MDA seems to be especially hard on women and will activate any latent infections or problems on the female genito-urinary tract. Women should take lower doses than men (less than 100 milligrams), and should avoid the drug altogether if their pelvic organs are ailing." Stash comments that so far there haven't been any studies of possible birth defects and counsels that "it is wise for a woman to avoid *all* drug use if she suspects she is pregnant."

Most of the MDA-like compounds are fairly short-acting, but a few have long duration and thus form a significant subcluster, comprising DOET, DOB and the more volatile DOM, a compound that produces considerably different effects at different dosages. Brimblecombe and Pinder describe DOM/STP's physical symptomology:

> The highly active, 2,5-dimethoxy-4-methylamphetamine (DOM, STP) was first identified in an illicit sample of drugs, and was claimed by its users to produce effects lasting greater than 72 hours with potentiation by the usual hallucinogen antagonists like chlorpromazine. Subsequent scientific evaluations (Snyder, Faillace, and Hollister, 1967; Hollister, MacNicol, and Gillespie, 1969) showed these claims to be false, the effects of DOM lasting less than 24 hours and being attenuated by chlorpromazine. The drug is a potent hallucinogen, however, doses of 3-5 mg. producing mental changes with marked hallucinations 1 hour after oral administration, peaking after 3-5 hours, and lasting for 7-8 hours. Only mild euphoria was noted the next day and in only a small proportion of subjects. The typical hallucinogenic triad of symptomatology was evident: physiological effects like nausea, sweating, paraesthesia, tremors, and increased systolic blood-pressure; sensory changes such as blurred vision, multiple imagery, vibration of objects, distorted shapes, visual hallucinations, enhancement of detail, slowed passage of time, and increased contrasts; and psychic phenomena like loss of thought control, elation, difficulty in expression of self, floods of thought, blankness of mind, and ease of distraction.

It should be noted that doses above 5 mg. (as seen at the 1967 "Human Be-in") produce effects of greater intensity and duration.

MENTAL EFFECTS

Nutmeg

Although it's a psychedelic of last resort, plenty of people have tried nutmeg. Malcolm X recalled from his prison experience that it "had the kick of three or four reefers"; other reports range from great exultation to delirium.

The third syndrome is quite typical, as in this anonymous nutmeg account from *Drugs From A to Z*:

> . . . it's a kind of drunkenness, I suppose, in a way you would call it a hallucinatory experience, but mostly it's just being wacked out of your head, sort of. It's really not a specially pleasant high. There are certainly wild distortions of perception and the brain functions, sort of in spurts and spasms. . . .
>
> And you will get sick as well as high, more or less simultaneously. And you will not feel right the next day either. It is not exactly a hangover, but you will not feel quite right. Maybe we took too much ["at least a teaspoon"] when we took it. But it is pretty violent. Sort of disrupting mental processes . . . .

In a few cases, the individual experience with nutmeg has proved significant. For example, Richard Meltzer took what many might consider an overly large dosage while at Yale. At the high point in the resulting experience, he sat in a coffee shop listening to the juke box and perceived the music as all sounding identical. Meltzer dropped out of Yale, used his tuition money to buy a good stereo and records, and eventually went on to become a vanguard influence in rock music.

STP

Although it is a rare commodity nowadays, STP had a major impact on the psychedelic movement in 1967. Ralph Metzner presents an STP experience in *The Ecstatic Adventure*, that of Ken Green. Metzner described it as a trip "in which a young American yogi shoots himself out of the body with STP, hurtles through incarnations, is attacked by a malevolent spirit and rescued by the power of mantra and guru." At the height of the furor over STP came this early-1967 report by Don McNeil, writing for *The Village Voice* and citing some of STP's characteristics:

> All veterans concur on the overwhelming power of STP. They speak of a maelstrom of relentless energy. "A feeling," said Alpert, "that it's going to do it to you whether you like it or not." The energy seems to manifest itself psychically. "You feel like your body is a conductor for tens of thousands of volts," said a user. "I was desperate for a ground." People tripping on STP physically tremble with the energy sensation. It is a stretching, quivering, shaking experience. Many have emerged from STP with a sudden concern for physical health. "We have need to be strong," said one. "We need protein. The macrobiotic diet is bad news."
>
> The relentless rush of energy is often a frightening experience. "Acid is like being let out of a cage," explained one user. "STP is like being shot out of a gun. There's no slowing down or backing up. You feel like your brakes have given out . . . ."
>
> A key to survival in the STP experience seems to be an ability to surrender to the energy flow of the drug. Resisting the rush or holding back can lead, many report, to an incredibly frustrating uptight experience.
>
> STP seems to lack the disorientation of acid. Although the auditory and visual hallucinations are vivid, a girl explained, "Everything looks like it does

when you're straight. It's like being on the other side of a glass wall." There also seems to be less identity confusion than under LSD. "You know who you are," she said. Many have found that they could easily function—make telephone calls, find cabs—shortly after the peak of the STP experience. These things can be difficult to do after an intense LSD experience.

Another recurring report about STP is a sensation of timelessness. Alpert calls it "a totally NOW orientation." Past and future seem to dissolve in an electric present. As time was lost, Alpert recalled, "I felt that I had lost something human. I felt that I had lost my humanity."

But the most enticing, and clearly the most disturbing, aspect of STP is that, unlike LSD, it seems to have a cumulative effect. It is a long trip to begin with. The direct effects last aobut 14 hours, and a stoned aftermath may continue until asleep.

The next morning, many STP initiates have discovered that they still felt high, or at least "different." It is a mild feeling, but a persistent one. Generally rated a "good" feeling, it seems to last . . . .

Zinberg's Evaluation of MDA

Few studies have been published about MDA's effects. I.S. Turek, R.A. Soskin and Albert Kurland report on one in Vol. 6, No. 1 of the *Journal of Psychedelic Drugs*, in which they describe the subjective effects of 70 mg. of the MDA levo-isomer taken orally by ten subjects, nine of whom had experienced LSD in a similarly controlled setting. Their findings concur with other available reports; they emphasize that, compared to LSD, this compound produces fewer "intuitive experiences involving a sense of ego loss" and "less transcendence of time or space" but more verbal communication.

Changes in perception of the external environment and changes in body awareness—especially "loss of control"—were "either minimal or nonexistent." The team found only a moderate alteration in time perception. Using the Linton-Langs Questionnaire (Modified), they concluded that "seeing new or changed meaning" was a major MDA effect. They said that at least half of their subjects felt that

> the meaning of life was now clearer as a result of the experience and they were able to discern new connections between certain events or experiences that they had not been aware of before . . . . MDA facilitates a state of mind characterized by increased introspectiveness, heightened self-awareness and greater intuitiveness and was associated with emotional states that were described as those of relaxation, acceptance, calmness and serenity. More intense emotional reactions were reported by a few of the subjects. However, they did not feel overwhelmed by, or unable to maintain perspective about, their condition . . . . In some the drug appeared to induce a state of greater openness in which the individual's responsiveness to music was enhanced and the capacity for rapport and empathy increased. For many of the subjects, the experience took on the overtones of deep personal and philosophical-religious meaning.

Most reports agree that MDA evokes little visual imagery, even though Alles saw smoke rings when he first discovered this psychedelic's effects. Like Albert Hofmann, Alles was apparently one of those very sensitive to psychoactivity. Had he not been, a vastly different history may have resulted for this compound cluster.

Alles made an extensive report based almost solely on his first MDA trip, justifying its relevance as a "double-conscious" study. He didn't believe that a large population of users had to be observed to achieve valid results. Norman Zinberg claimed that he made an end-run around this problem as well, after he studied MDA's effects upon experienced trippers (two to fifteen sessions for each of his subjects). All had used marijuana and all drank— "but expressed the classic preference of marijuana users for beer or wine; only one moderate, the rest light imbibers." Zinberg's MDA observations, which appeared in the January-March 1976 issue of the *Journal of Psychedelic Drugs*, present perhaps the finest description yet of the subtle states induced by the archetype of the MDA cluster.

Associated with the Harvard Medical School, Zinberg was interested in "the phenomenology of consciousness change." He chose MDA for use in his study for three reasons: (1) this compound's effects were reportedly not as extreme as those of LSD, (2) it could be obtained in pure form and distributed in known quantities, and (3) users remained capable of expressing their feelings about relationships while the experience was going on. "That suited me well," Zinberg said about this last factor, "because my greatest area of understanding is just there, and not in color/form/perception possibly affected by the drug. This effect also made it likely that users would be interested in talking while tripping."

Zinberg noted that the participants joked in all the sessions that they might have been given a placebo. After the first half-hour to an hour, when MDA's effects became perceptible,

> one person after another would say, "Oh!," and in answer to my questions would describe seeing the sudden clarity of the sky and a feeling of ease and benevolence. Along with this initial "vast tranquilizer" effect came some nausea. Three subjects retched briefly and several described some muscle tightening, especially around the jaw, which also passed after a few minutes ....
>
> None of my subjects had ever had a bad trip. During my observations, there were no periods of panic or hallucination in my terms. Several subjects said that when they closed their eyes or stared at a particular object, delightful visual panoramas occurred which they called hallucinations. These were always reported as pleasant and, seemed to me, to be an exploitation of the subject's capacity to fix on an image and play tricks with their unwavering concentration rather than a hallucination.

For Zinberg, the ability of the users to concentrate their attention in specific areas was a striking quality of the experience:

> Ordinarily people apparently attend to a large volume of stimuli and devote considerable effort to integrating these stimuli into a gestalt. This constant effort at integration shifts focus when the person concentrates on one or

another stimulus. A steady concentration always occurs within an awareness of the whole. The drug allows one to focus on a reduced field of attention so that a particular item stands out .... As nearly as I could learn, no real perceptual changes occur. Rather what happens is a de-automatization of repetitive, usual modes of responding. Subjects reported on color, sound and form, when asked, with complete accuracy, invariably, however, pointing out details that seemed more pertinent now than before. This seemed especially true for colors and the blending and mixing of colors. At times, when they were asked to focus on them, forms and shapes received the same total attention and sense of discovery as did color. In contrast to the impatience with which the subjects waited the hour for the drug to take effect, they now felt almost unaware of time's passage. It was hard to get an answer to the question, "How long have we been here?" When they did answer, they usually thought it to have been longer than it was. This slowing of time continued through the eight to twelve hours of the drug's effects.

The capacity to focus on specific items seems to explain much of what the subjects experience. They could concentrate on inner processes as well as outer perceptions. It was not that particular fantasies were any different, i.e., more primitive, or connected to basic motivation, but that one fantasy or idea was noticed in great detail. It could be thoroughly explored so that the connected affects and ideation which would ordinarily be swept past in the rush of stimuli could receive attention. The introspection thus achieved seemed fresh. Subjects could find things unpleasant such as sand, flies, cold or even the noise of a companion, but no one reported angry or aggressive feelings during the drugged period. However, there was considerable internal interest in previous aggression and meanness that appeared in fantasies or reveries about personal interactions.

Zinberg noted that "people did speak openly of caring for each other," and he had the impression that the experience provided an occasion and an inclination

to say things usually barred from conversation. Despite much talk about origins and memories, no early memories were reported that seemed to have been especially recovered at this time. One person told me how he felt when he met his present girlfriend and how, out of a mixture of anxiety, annoyance and liking, he had picked out the traits and responses that he now loved. A young woman talked about the last time she had seen her mother and of how, out of a mixture of disappointment and longing, she had behaved distantly and now recognized that she did the same thing with her boyfriend. She pointed out how his mouth tightened and his eyebrows came together in an unusual way when she behaved that way, but he never said he was hurt. He responded by saying that he knew she had been thinking of that interaction and that he really knew she loved him and wished he could break through his withdrawal at times like that and tell her what he had been feeling.

This sort of dialogue was typical. The insights did not seem so earth-shaking, although they were spelled out in convincing detail. But it was the repeated insistence on empathic awareness of what the other was thinking that most fascinated me.

Zinberg tried to check out these empathic sensations by speaking separately to individuals having such experiences:

> Not only was such a subject able to describe what others felt, e.g., "A is thinking of sex with B," or "I think C is lost in childhood memories or relationship fantasies with D," but they were also able to say something about the cues that led to these conclusions—the way someone's body was now dripping with sand, the way the lines formed around a person's mouth, or the way somebody looked over there and then looked away. These cues were ones that I had not noticed until they pointed them out to me. However, the intermediate steps of how the cues led to the final, empathic awareness could not be articulated. I would then drift over to the person we had been talking about and asked what s/he had been thinking. 80% of the time my original respondent was correct down to quite fine details. It was remarkable, and it gave me some sense of why some psychedelic users of my acquaintance had become so interested in ESP. I asked particularly if this empathy was based on unusual closeness to a particular individual and usually was told, "No." In fact, it seemed to operate as effectively with people who were not close friends. Certainly it was not bound by sexual interest. While couples who were going together might show particular interest in each other, each could respond to others across sexual lines.

As to questions about sexual aspects of the experience, Zinberg found his subjects' answers "surprisingly uniform":

> Sexual relationships were possible especially as the drug waned, but during the height of the high, people described a greater interest in a general, diffused sensualism than in specific sexuality, such as intercourse or masturbation. (Although two subjects told me that when they had taken the drug alone, and only then, did they become sexually preoccupied and masturbate frequently.) This sensualism showed itself in a wish to touch others or to feel the sand, grass, water, flowers or the like. Again, the desire to touch or pleasure in touching was specifically pan-sexual and often not connected to everyday closeness. Although one of the drug's most potent and consistent effects is the inhibition of the desire to eat, late in the day a single grape or a bit of certain foods or liquids was described as a sensual experience.

Zinberg concluded that a study of the people he had observed

> would show a continuity of basic personality structure both before, during and after drug use. That there is a continuity to the essential personality does not mean, however, that some personality change may not be of great importance in that person's life and extended psychological development. Of all people, psychoanalysts should not make light of the importance of small shifts in personality orientation. Remember Freud's oft-quoted comment that "For psychoanalysis to change neurotic suffering to ordinary human misery is no small event."

MDA and MMDA Compared

In the October-December 1976 issue of the *Journal of Psychedelic Drugs*, Andrew Weil and Alexander Shulgin described first MDA and then

MMDA. Together their reports provide a perspective on the differences between these two closely related compounds.

After more than five years' experience with MDA, Weil had fascinating things to say about this "Love Drug":

> ... effects become apparent in 20 to 60 minutes and persist for about twelve hours .... Some experience initial nausea. Some feel a warm glow spreading through their bodies. Most people become aware of a sense of physical and mental well-being that intensifies gradually and steadily.... effects on human beings are much more interesting than simple stimulation .... Unlike most stimulants, MDA does not increase motor activity. In fact, it suppresses it in a remarkable way, so that people can remain comfortable and content in one position for long periods. This effect is most dramatic in persons who are heavily dependent on coffee and cigarettes .... The combined effects of relaxation and centering greatly facilitate certain kinds of physical activities such as yoga, martial arts, and any disciplines requiring balance and maintenance of posture. For example, I can maintain a headstand longer when I take MDA than normally .... I have also tried things like rock climbing and swimming after taking MDA and again find that my body works in a more coordinated, smoother fashion and that I can do things with it that I usually cannot .... It may become possible to walk barefoot over sharp stones, for instance, and experience no discomfort or injury ....
>
> Participants may feel very loving toward one another, but the feelings are not explicitly sexual because MDA tends to decrease the desire for orgasm. For many people the experience of enjoying physical contact and feeling love with others in the absence of a specific hunger for sex is unique and welcome ....
>
> Habitual users of tobacco feel no need to smoke. Chain smokers of marijuana do not need their weed. Nail biters leave their fingers alone. Compulsive talkers become quiet. Compulsive eaters do not think about food .... There are no hallucinations, illusions, or distortions, simply a great aura of peace and calm and well-being ....
>
> Out of hundreds of experiences with it that I have observed I have seen only two anxiety reactions. The medical potential of the drug is great and quite unexplored. I have noted repeatedly that persons under the influence of MDA, when feeling high, centered, and free of desire, are in a state of complete anergy—that is, they manifest no allergic responses, even to life-long allergens. Asthma disappears; hay-fever disappears; cat allergies go away; there are even no responses to mosquito bites. This effect is temporary and appears to be the physical analog in the body of the mental experience of complete relaxation and lack of anxiety. It might be reproducible without the drug if we could learn to spend more time in that state ....

Shulgin then characterized the closely-allied MMDA:

> The threshold dosage of MMDA in humans is 75 mg (as the hydrochloride salt) and the average effective dose is 150 mg., orally. The first physical symptoms (mydriasis, minor dizziness, fleeting nausea) are apparent at 30-60 minutes. The psychological effects are first noted about 1½ hours following ingestion and are of relatively short duration with peaking in another hour;

these are largely dissipated in yet another two hours. During this period of intoxication, there is a minimum of sensory distortion, but rather a pervasive mood-intensification. In the absence of external stimulation, an accentuation of feelings (both anxiety and euphoria), the spontaneous visualization of images (with eyes closed), a generalized drowsiness and relaxation, and a consistent over-estimation of elapsed time are experienced. The imagery is dream-like in that the subject matter cannot be chosen and it can be voluntarily dispelled by opening the eyes. Eyes-open phenomena, such as color enhancement and distortion of faces and objects, are extremely rare . . . .

The metabolic fate and the kinetics of blood and tissue levels of MMDA, in either experimental animals or in humans, are as yet unstudied . . . . In comparison to most psychedelic drugs, MMDA must be considered to be very mild and produces a state which can be easily manipulated by either the subject or the observer. The duration of action is short, and is followed by physical relaxation which usually leads to an easy and restful sleep . . . .

Naranjo's Psychiatric Distinctions

Differences between MDA and MMDA were further amplified in Claudio Naranjo's *The Healing Journey*, a description of what he observed as one of the earliest to gain access to these semi-synthetics. After using both MDA and MMDA in his practice of psychotherapy, Naranjo concluded that the two operate quite distinctly. He came to consider MDA an "analytical drug," useful primarily for going back into a patient's past. MMDA, on the other hand, was more effective in evoking the feeling of "the eternal now." Here is a quick summation of Naranjo's findings in regard to MDA:

In a first study designed to describe its effects in normal individuals, not one of eight subjects reported hallucinations, visual distortions, color enhancement, or mental imagery, while all of them evidenced other pronounced reactions: enhancement of feelings, increased communication, and heightened reflectiveness, which led to a concern with their own problems or those of society or mankind. Further experiments with MDA in neurotic patients in the context of psychotherapy have confirmed such effects, but here physical symptoms were of frequent occurrence, and visual phenomena were described by most individuals at some point of their experience. Yet the most characteristic feature of the experience of these subjects was one which we will here call age regression . . . .

In the MDA-elicited state the patient simultaneously regresses and retains awareness of the present self. Yet . . . the person more than conceptually remembers the past, as he may vividly recapture visual or other sensory impressions inaccessible to him in the normal state, and he usually reacts with feelings that are in proportion to the event. This is the same process termed "returning" in Dianetics, and which can range all the way from hypermnesia to repetition of a past experience in which not only the old feelings are again felt but physical pain or pleasure and other sensations, as the case may be . . . .

This may occasionally be brought about under the effect of other hallucinogens or without any drug, particularly when sought after through therapeutic maneuvers. Ibogaine, in particular, lends itself well to an exploration of events in a patient's life history for the richness of feeling with which these can be evoked. Yet with MDA regression occurs so frequently and spontaneously that this can be considered a typical effect of this substance, and a primal source of its therapeutic value . . . . In this, the healing process differed from what is observed in most instances of harmaline, MMDA, or even ibogaine therapy . . . .

Author of The Healing Journey, *Claudio Naranjo exchanged LSD for* ayahuasca *with Amazon medicine men and introduced MDA, MMDA, harmine, harmaline, ibogaine and 4-bromo-2,5-dimethoxyphenylisopropylamine into the psychotherapeutic literature.*

Moving on to MMDA, here is how Naranjo distinguished this substance:

MMDA stands with MDA in a category distinct from that of LSD-25 and mescaline as well as from that of harmaline and ibogaine. In contrast to the transpersonal and unfamiliar domain of experience characterizing the action of these two groups of drugs, these feeling-enhancing isopropylamines lead into a domain that is both personal and familiar, differing only in its intensity from that of every day . . . .

In the peak experience that MMDA may elicit, it is possible to speak of both individuality and dissolution, but these are blended into a quite new totality. Dissolution is here expressed in the openness to experience, a willingness to hold no preference; individuality, on the other hand, is implied in the absence of depersonalization phenomena, and in the fact that the subject is concerned with the everyday world of persons, objects, and relationships.

The MMDA peak experience is typically one in which the moment that is being lived becomes intensely gratifying in all its circumstantial reality, yet the dominant feeling is not one of euphoria but of calm and serenity. It could be described as a youthful indifference, or, as one subject has put it, "an impersonal sort of compassion"; for love is embedded, as it were, in calm . . . .

The perception of things and people is not altered or even enhanced, usually, but negative reactions that permeate our everyday lives beyond our conscious knowledge are held in abeyance and replaced by unconditional acceptance.

An unusually large MDA crystal grown in ethanol.

This is much like Nietzsche's *amor fati*, love of fate, love of one's particular circumstances. The immediate reality seems to be welcomed in such MMDA-induced states without pain or attachment; joy does not seem to depend on the given situation, but on existence itself, and in such a state of mind everything is equally lovable . . . .

FORMS AND PREPARATIONS

Over the last decade and a half, there has been much misrepresentation in the black market regarding MDA-like compounds. Recently, providers of these substances seem to have been doing their chemistry homework; the products nowadays aren't bogus very often.

Generally these compounds are distributed as a powder, as clear whitish crystals, or in tablet form. Often the powder or crystals are swallowed in a clear gelatin capsule. The color of the powders varies from white to a brownish hue, the latter color frequently indicating by-products of incomplete synthesis. "Little is known of the effects of ingesting such impurities," comments Jeremy Bigwood. Recalling the dangers posed by PMA, Bigwood suggests sending a sample of any MDA-like compound in question to PharmChem, following the procedure described at the end of Chapter One.

R.E. Schultes

Cohoba *snuff is made from seeds of the* yopo *tree (*Anadenanthera peregrina*), seen here near Boa Vista in Amazonian Brazil.*

CHAPTER SIX

DMT, DET, DPT and Other Short-Acting Tryptamines

It is unfortunate that such a unique and desirable drug as DMT is not freely available and widely used .... Not only are the effects enjoyable, but most users are astonished to learn that a drug can so rapidly produce such profound effects which have such short duration.

— Jeremy Bigwood and Jonathan Ott

HISTORY

The first European observation of psychedelics-use in the New World involved *cohoba* snuff, a powerful mind-alterer made from seeds of the *yopo* tree (*Anadenanthera peregrina*). The main psychoactive components were identified in the early 1950s as DMT (*N,N*-dimethyltryptamine) and 5-methoxy-DMT. These and related compounds are present in other trees, vines and shrubs and even in mushrooms.

This compound cluster exhibits a two-ring, "open-chained," indolic chemical structure, and in contrast to other psychedelics it is all but inactive when taken orally unless accompanied by certain other compounds. Short-acting tryptamines are closely related to neurotransmitters (such as bufo-tenine), to MDA (a major botanical source of the snuffs belongs to the nutmeg family), to tryptophan (an essential amino acid produced in human digestion of proteins) and to psilocybin and psilocin (which are tryptamines of longer duration). DMT, the simplest member, occurs normally in the blood, brain and (in higher concentrations) in the cerebrospinal fluid.

DMT, DET (*N,N*-diethyltryptamine) and DPT (*N,N*-dipropyl-tryptamine) are the compounds in this cluster that have been manufactured and distributed most over the last fifteen years. Compared with the psychedelics already discussed, use of these tryptamines has been limited and irregular until recently. They now appear to constitute a psychedelic grouping of importance in the United States.

Observations of New World Use of Psychoactive Snuffs

The Spanish friar Ramón Paul, who accompanied Columbus on his second voyage to the New World, was the first to record native use of

psychedelics. He watched the Taino Indians of what's now called Haiti snorting "kohhobba" to communicate with the spirit world: "This powder they
draw up through the nose and it intoxicates them to such an extent that
when they are under its influence, they know not what they do." The snuff
was made of seeds from the foot-long pods of a mimosa-like tree that grows
wild only in South America. A specialist in this group of legumes has theorized that by the time of Columbus' second voyage the natives of the West
Indies "may have found it easier to plant the trees than to maintain communication with the mainland for their source of supply."

A 1560 report said that Indians along the Rio Guaviare in Colombia
were accustomed to taking "Yopa . . . . a seed or pip of a tree" together with
tobacco, becoming "drowsy while the devil, in their dreams, shows them all
the vanities and corruptions he wishes them to see and which they take to be
true revelations in which they believe, even if told they will die. This habit of
taking Yopa and Tobacco is general in the New Kingdom." Another chron-
icler wrote in 1599 about Indians chewing "Hayo or Coca and Jopa and
Tobacco," a combination which prompted their "going out of their minds,
and then the devil speaks to them." This account described the *Jopa* as "a
tree with small pods like those of vetches, and the seeds inside are similar but
smaller." In 1741, a Jesuit wrote about *cohoba* use by the Otomac of the
Orinoco region between Colombia and Venezuela: "They have another
abominable habit of intoxicating themselves through the nostrils with certain
malignant powders which they call Yupa which quite takes away their reason,
and they will furiously take up arms . . . ." Describing details of the snuff's
preparation, including addition of lime from snail shells, this priest reported
that "before a battle, they would throw themselves into a frenzy with Yupa,
wound themselves and, full of blood and rage, go forth to battle like rabid
jaguars."

In 1801, the German explorer and naturalist Baron Alexander von
Humboldt (after whom the Pacific current is named), identified the *yopo*
tree botanically. While collecting flora near the Orinoco River, he watched
the Maypure Indians prepare *cohoba* snuff by breaking the pods, moistening
them and allowing them to ferment. When the pods turned black, they were
kneaded with cassava meal and lime from snails into small cakes, which were
eventually powdered. Humboldt noted, "it is not to be believed that the . . .
pods are the chief cause of the . . . effects of the snuff . . . . These effects are
due to the freshly calcinated lime." The lime, in fact, adds nothing to the
snuff's psychoactivity.

Fifty years later, a British explorer and naturalist, Richard Spruce,
made detailed observations of the preparation and use of *yopo* among the
Guahibo of the Orinoco basin, commenting that it was used by all the tribes
of the upper tributaries. He purchased equipment for preparing and snorting
their *niopo* seeds (a grinder, platter, wooden spatula, a container made from
the leg bone of a jaguar and a Y-shaped snuffing tube). The seeds and pods

he collected in 1851 for chemical studies weren't analyzed, however, until 1977.

In 1909, the German anthropologist Theodor Koch-Grünberg described another psychoactive snuff, prepared from a tree bark and inhaled during ritualistic cures by the Yekwanas at the headwaters of the Orinoco:

> This is a magical snuff, exclusively used by witch doctors and prepared from the bark of a certain tree which, when pounded up, is boiled in a small earthenware pot, until all the water has evaporated and a sediment remains at the bottom of the pot. This sediment is toasted in the pot over a slight fire and is then finely powdered with the blade of a knife. Then the sorcerer blows a little of the powder through a reed . . . into the air. Next, he snuffs, whilst, with the same reed, he absorbs the powder into each nostril successively. The *hakudufha* obviously has a strongly stimulating effect, for immediately the witch doctor begins singing and yelling wildly, all the while pitching the upper part of his body backwards and forwards.

Identification of Botanical and Other Sources

In 1916, William Safford determined that the psychoactive principles of *cohoba* snuff did not come from especially powerful tobacco, as was generally thought at the time, but from the beans of *Anadenanthera peregrina* (a member of the pea family, formerly placed in the genus of *Piptadenia,* then *Mimosa* and *Acacia*). In 1938 and 1939, the Brazilian botanist Ducke identified a second kind of psychoactive snuff as coming from another species. He reported that Indians of the upper Rio Negro employed leaves of *Virola theiodora* and *Virola cuspidata* in making a powder they called *paricá*. Ducke was wrong about the leaves; the Indians used sap from the inner bark. However, by pinpointing a species other than the leguminous trees from which *cohoba* is derived, Ducke prompted further investigations into plant psychoactivity where no non-native had previously thought to look.

The brownish snuff described by Ducke was known as *yakee* among the Punave, as *yato* among the Kuripako and as *epená* among the Waiká tribes. His detailed account, published in 1954, described its botany, preparation and shamanistic use by the Barasana, Makuna, Tukano, Kaluyaré, Puhave and other tribes in eastern Colombia. *V. calophylla* and *V. calophylloidea* were then considered the main psychedelic species in use, but *V. theiodora* has since come to be recognized as the most prevalent and highly prized.

Schultes and Hofmann write in their *Plants of the Gods* that *Virola* snuff "is used among many Indian groups in Amazonian Colombia and Venezuela, the Rio Negro, and other areas of the western Amazon of Brazil. The southernmost locality of its known use is among the Paumaré Indians of the Rio Purús in the southwestern Amazon of Brazil." In Colombia, use is usually restricted to shamans, who employ this snuff "ritualistically for diagnosis and treatment of disease, prophecy, divination, and other magico-religious purposes."

Inner bark from the tree represented here by its leaves is the main species of Virolas *used by South American natives as a source of psychoactive tryptamines.*

Among other tribes, especially those known collectively as the Waiká, *epená* may be used individually as well as ceremonially by any male over the age of thirteen or fourteen. Amounts as large as two to three teaspoons are blown into the nostrils through long tubes. Ingestion of large doses is repeated regularly over a two- to three-day period during at least one annual ceremony.

There is no unequivocal archeological evidence showing ancient use of *cohoba* or *epená* snuffs. However, widespread shamanic use and the considerable mythology associated with both botanical sources of DMT suggest that such traditions go far into the past. Snuffing artifacts have been found all over South America, though these implements may have been used for tobacco.

Recently, the Mashco Indians of northern Argentina were reported to smoke and sniff a preparation from *Anadenanthera colubrina* seeds, confirming early Spanish reports of snuffs being made of this species, commonly known as *vilca*. According to one such account from 1571, Incan medicine men made prophecies through inebriation brought about by drinking *chicha* reinforced with *vilca*. *A. colubrina* snuff has since been assayed as having essentially the same psychoactive makeup as *cohoba* and *epená* snuffs.

In 1946, Goncalves deLima, a Brazilian ethnobotanist and chemist, extracted an alkaloid from roots of *Mimosa hostilis*, another member of the pea family, which has been used by natives of eastern Brazil to prepare a potent psychoactive drink. He named this "nigerine"; later it was found to be identical to DMT, first synthesized in 1931 by the British chemist Richard Manske.

In 1954, Stomberg isolated 5-methoxy-DMT* from seeds of *A. peregrina*. Later, DMT, DMT-*N*-oxide and 5-hydroxy-DMT-*N*-oxide were also found in *A. peregrina*. Additional components contributing to psychoactivity have been identified; these also appear in about the same proportions in the *Virola* species used to make *paricá*. However, a Waiká snuff made from *V. theiodora* resin has an unusually high alkaloid content of up to 11 percent, consisting mainly of 5-methoxy-DMT (8 percent) and substantial amounts of DMT.

Testing and Use of Synthetics

The first experiences of pure DMT took place in 1957, when the pharmacologist Stephen Szára, who has long been chief of the National Institute of Drug Abuse's biomedical research branch, injected himself and

---

* This 5-methoxy-DMT compound had already been observed in toads and even in "dream fish" (*Kyphosus fuscus*) found off Norfolk Island in the South Pacific. In order to test the claim by inhabitants that this fish produces "nightmares," Joe Roberts, a photographer for *National Geographic*, broiled and ate some in 1960. The next morning, he reported his experience to have been "pure science fiction": he saw a new kind of car, monuments to mark humanity's first trip into space and so on. A skeptical writer with him had to admit, "I ate a dream fish supper myself. I found it tasty, but strong flavored, like mackerel. I told myself not to dream. But no. I dreamed I was at a party where everybody was nude and the band played, 'Yes, We Have No Pajamas.' "

friends with this compound intramuscularly. He first administered 75 mg. to himself.

The onset of the experience came within three to four minutes. Szára noted trembling, nausea, dilation of the pupils and an elevated blood pressure and pulse rate—accompanied by "brilliantly colored oriental motifs and, later, rapidly changing wonderful scenes." He became euphoric. His attention was "so firmly bound to the visual phenomena" that he was unable to describe them until the experience passed, some forty-five to sixty minutes after its start.

Szára established by further testing that intramuscular injection of 50 to 60 mg. of DMT brought about intense visual displays—with eyes open or closed—within five minutes. These reached peak effects within a quarter of an hour, diminishing and then disappearing totally within half an hour (at the longest, one hour). Subjects became catatonic or lost consciousness when given doses larger than 125 mg.

Albert Hofmann synthesized a series of DMT analogues, but little attention was paid to this work until the mid-1960s.

Ironically, interest began to develop after an adverse experience with DMT. William Burroughs, author of *Naked Lunch* and *Junkie*, had already figured prominently in the drug aspect of the beatnik movement. He had journeyed to Peru in search of *yagé*, and in 1960 he had experimented with stroboscopic machines to produce hallucinations. During the winter of 1960-1961, Allen Ginsberg told Timothy Leary that Burroughs "knows more about drugs than anyone alive" and urged him to initiate a correspondence. Burroughs' second letter to Leary was dated May 6, 1961:

Dear Dr. Leary:
    I would like to sound a word of urgent warning with regard to the hallucinogen drugs with special reference to D-Dimethyltryptamine. I had obtained a supply of this drug synthesized by a chemist friend in London. My first impression was that it closely resembled psilocybin in its effects.
    I had taken it perhaps ten times—(this drug must be injected and the dose is about one grain [approximately 65 mg.] but I had been assured that there was a wide margin of safety)—with results sometimes unpleasant but well under control and always interesting when the horrible experience occurred which I have recorded and submitted for publication in *Encounter* . . . .

In *High Priest*, Leary recalls that he and his associates studied Burroughs' letter, deciding to reserve judgment until after further experiments. "We had learned enough to know that set-and-setting determined the reaction, not the drug. Bill Burroughs alias Doctor Benway had inadvertently taken an overdose [about 100 mg.] of DMT and was flung into a space-fiction paranoia."

Jeremy Bigwood and Jonathan Ott, writing in the November 1977 issue of *Head* magazine, noted that during his period of terror Burroughs had been "gulping down some of his 'metabolic regulator' apomorphine as an antidote." Then they pointed out the significant results of later tests:

Were it not for Timothy Leary, Richard Alpert, and Ralph Metzner, the terror drug would have been excluded from the Psychedelic Age. Although these three had heard nothing but negative reports about the effects of this compound, undaunted they decided to test the drug on themselves. They discovered that when one observes the rules of "set" and "setting," DMT produces a short but ecstatic experience.

The *Psychedelic Review* recorded a Leary experience of DMT where Ralph Metzner sat nearby taking notes, asking at regular intervals: "Where are you now?" In this collaborative article, Metzner's observations appear in a column opposite Leary's perceptions as recalled later. Immersed in the sight of giant, gold-encrusted, shimmering beetles, he heard a voice off in the distance asking, "WHERE ... ARE ... YOU ... NOW?" Afterward, Leary proposed development of an "experiential typewriter" for recording such rapid, high-intensity experiences. Experimenters were to be trained in pressing keys, each of which represented a particular state of mind that could be recorded on a paper tape and later correlated with the passage of time. A prototype for such a machine was attempted but never reached a functioning state.

This article by Leary and Metzner caused a wave of interest in DMT among many in the counterculture. About this time came the discovery that DMT evaporated onto oregano, parsley leaves or marijuana and then smoked could produce effects similar to those from injections, except that they occurred almost immediately and disappeared more rapidly. Materials for making DMT were legal and could be procured easily then. Methods of synthesizing DMT were published in *The Turn-On Book, The Psychedelic Guide to Preparation of the Eucharist* and several short pamphlets.

Before long, DET was also being smoked: a longer-lasting, still-intense experience without the pronounced visual effects of DMT.

State and federal laws enacted from 1966 to 1969 made DMT illegal. Both DMT and DET were included in Schedule I of the Controlled Substances Act of 1970. Source materials for these compounds were put on a "watch" status as well. Soon supplies dried up, and both DMT and DET became rare items—a situation persisting throughout most of the 1970s. During this period, DMT was identified as a normal constituent of human blood (though its function is as yet obscure), prompting Bigwood and Ott to comment:

> Public Law 91-513 specifically proscribes unauthorized possession of any material which contains DMT in any quantity. Under this law ... any individual human being is guilty of such possession.

In the late 1970s, reports about DPT use began appearing in the psychological literature, both in connection with therapy and in efforts to ease the anxieties of dying patients. This short-acting tryptamine, bearing an even longer side-chain, induced psychedelic experiences of about three-and-a-half hours' duration that often came to an abrupt ending, a feature that appealed to some therapists. Many patients had "peak experiences" under DPT. Some people who administered this compound felt, however, that LSD had more memorable results, even if more tiring due to its longer duration.

DPT and 5-methoxy-DMT are still legal and have been used in certain circles for years. Alan Birnbaum, from the Native American Church of New York, wrote to the DEA about the legal status of several DMT-like compounds. In January 1980, Howard McClain of the Regulatory Control Division responded:

> This is in response to your recent inquiry concerning the control status of the substances 4 hydroxy-N,N-diethyltryptamine, dipropyltryptamine, and methyl ethyl tryptamine. They are not currently listed in the Controlled Substances Act, however, if it becomes evident that these chemicals are abused, they will be placed on Schedule I . . . .

BOTANY

Anadenanthera *Species and Other Members of the Pea Family*

Anadenanthera peregrina, a tree that reaches sixty feet in height and approximately two feet in diameter, grows naturally in and is cultivated throughout about a tenth of South America. Its primary locale is described by Schultes and Hofmann as "the plains or grasslands of the Orinoco basin of Colombia and Venezuela, in light forests in southern British Guiana [now known as Guyana], and in the Rio Branco area of the northern Amazonia of Brazil." It also appears "in isolated savanna areas" where it has been introduced by natives, notably the Rio Madeira region. Apparently this tree was also cultivated in the West Indies until about a century ago.

Another growing area for *Anadenanthera* is slightly smaller and centers in northern Argentina, where the seed snuff is known as *cébil*. Three species native to southern Peru and Bolivia—*A. macrocarpa, A. excelsa* and *A. colubrina*—are the source of *vilca* and *huilca*. All four *Anadenanthera* species seem to be used in making snuffs, usually without other plant additives.

D.V. Siva Sankar's enormous green book *LSD—A Total Study* lists eleven legumes that contain bufotenine and DMT. Of these, the second most widely used is *Mimosa hostilis*. Decoctions made from its root play a part in the ceremonies of the ancient Yurema cult of Brazil. The decoction is known as the "wine of *Jurema*." William Emboden describes this "miraculous drink" as

> a wondrous beverage that gives visions of the spirit world. Intended for priests, warriors, and strong young men, the infusion permits a glimpse into the world where rocks destroy the souls of the dead and the Thunderbird sends lightning from his head and runs about producing thunder . . . . The Pankaruru Indians use a similar brew from the bark of *Mimosa verrucosa* or the *caatinga* shrub under the name *Jurema branca*; it too contains N-N-DMT.

ANADENANTHERA
peregrina

Kathleen L. Harrison

This tree was source of the first psychedelic observed in the New World.

Virolas

At least sixty species of the genus *Virola*, part of the *Myristiceae* (nutmeg) family, are known to exist in the New World, chiefly in the tropical regions of Central and South America. A dozen such species have been assayed as containing DMT-type alkaloids, but they are used for inducing visions and trances only around the western Amazon and in adjacent parts of the Orinoco basin. The most frequently used is *V. theiodora*. Others processed into psychoactive snuffs are *V. calophylla*, *V. calophylloides*, *V. elongata* and *V. cuspidata*. Resins of *V. sebifera* are smoked by some Venezuelan Indians (a few references to smoking have appeared in connection with other *Virolas* as well).

DMT-like compounds appear in the sap of the inner bark—not in the seeds or roots of *Virolas*. The making of *epená* therefore involves stripping *Virolas* of their outer bark. An almost colorless liquid then exudes from the inner bark, quickly turning to blood red (the result of enzyme activity) and

R.E. Schultes: *Harvard Botanical Museum Leaflets*

Stripping the bark from Virola theiodora.

hardening into a shiny, gummy resin. The tryptamines and other indoles
lose potency rapidly unless heated immediately. Natives scrape off the inner
bark and heat it or boil it after soaking the bark for about twenty minutes in
cold water. Once the psychoactive compounds are stabilized, the resin is
usually made into a powder.

Schultes and Hofmann comment in their *Plants of the Gods* on the native jungle lore:

> Indians who are familiar with *Virola* trees from the point of view of their hallucinogenic potency exhibit uncanny knowledge of different "kinds" — which to a botanist appear to be indistinguishable as to species. Before stripping the bark from a trunk, they are able to predict how long the exudate will take to turn red, whether it will be mild or peppery to the tongue when tasted, how long it will retain its potency when made into snuff, and many other hidden characteristics .... there is no doubt about the Indian's expertness in recognizing these differences, for which he often has a terminology.

Several bushes, vines and mushrooms also contain DMT and its chemical relatives. Leaves from *Psychotria viridis*, a bush belonging to the coffee family, and *Banisteriopsis rusbyana*, an ivy-like vine, are often added to the drink called *yagé* made from the Amazonian "visionary vine." The presence of this *ayahuasca* vine in the drink enables tryptamines in the leaves to produce mental effects even after they are swallowed. (Commercial and many psychoactive mushrooms contain DMT and other DMT-like compounds. These appear in tiny amounts, however, and wouldn't be activated when eaten unless catalyzed by something like *ayahuasca*.)

CHEMISTRY

Tryptamine Constituents of the Psychedelic Snuffs

In both *Anadenanthera* and *Virola* snuffs, the active principles are indolic alkaloids, either "open-chained" or "closed-ring" tryptamines. The "closed-ring" group will be covered in the next chapter. The "open-chained" group includes DMT and 5-methoxy-DMT, as well as bufotenine (which at present appears to be non-psychoactive). DMT predominates in the species *Virola calophylla*, but in other species the greatest psychic contribution comes from the very short-acting 5-methoxy-DMT.

Trace amounts of the "open-chained" DMT-*N*-oxide and 5-hydroxy-DMT-*N*-oxide, as well as "closed-ring" tryptamines 2-methyl- and 1,2-dimethyl-6-methoxytetrahydro- β -carboline, are present in both *Anadenanthera* and *Virola* snuffs, adding somewhat to their effects. *Virolas* also contain small quantities of 6-methoxy-DMT and monoethyltryptamine.

Altering the Side-Chains

Here is a chemical family portrait of the major short-acting tryptamines:

$$R_1 \diagup \diagdown \diagup^H \quad CH_2CH_2N(R_2)_2$$

DMT—R_1 = H, R_2 = CH$_3$
DET—R_1 = H, R_2 = CH$_2$CH$_3$
DPT—R_1 = H, R_2 = CH$_2$CH$_2$CH$_3$
5-MeO-DMT—R_1 = OCH$_3$,
R_2 = CH$_3$

A full discussion of this compound-cluster's chemistry and effects appears on pp. 98-108 of Brimblecombe and Pinder's *Hallucinogenic Agents*. Many of these compounds display little psychoactivity; others of special interest are the diallyl, dibutyl and diisopropyl analogues, the last having about twelve times the potency of DMT.

DET and DPT are longer acting and more potent than DMT as a result of altering the CH_3 part of the DMT side-chain to CH_2CH_3 and $CH_2CH_2CH_3$ respectively. Psilocin, a longer-acting tryptamine, differs by addition of a hydroxy group through enzyme action. When it is altered into CY-19 and CZ-74 by manipulations similar to the changes of DMT into DET and DPT, the result, in contrast, is shorter action and less potency.

Analogues that are still legal can be synthesized by substituting equal molar amounts of source materials other than dimethylamine, which yields DMT, or diethylamine, which yields DET. Using dipropylamine as a starter yields DPT, methylethylamine yields methylethyltryptamine, methylpropylamine yields methylpropyltryptamine, ethylpropylamine yields ethylpropyltryptamine, etc.

Processes for synthesizing short-acting tryptamines are fairly simple and don't require much in the way of equipment, but they involve a risk of explosion. Also, purchases of several of the source materials are watched by the DEA. One of these is lithium aluminum hydride ($LiAlH_4$), which is dangerous if it comes in contact with water molecules, as is usually required at the end of these processes. A chemist describes an experiment:

> He placed a gray chunk of it in a stainless steel pot and left it exposed to the air to see what would happen. When nothing appreciable occurred, he got a hammer and banged it—which ignited it.
>
> It then burned white hot right through the stainless steel pot and continued to burn on the floor. Of course, one cannot use water to put it out because it reacts with water causing not only a more vigorous reaction but also releasing hydrogen which, as you know, will explode violently itself when it reaches a certain concentration of O_2. Luckily for him, it was a *small* piece.

PHYSICAL EFFECTS

Native Use of Enormous Amounts

Some Indian tribes, particularly those among the Waikás, use psychoactive snuffs in what Schultes and Hofmann refer to as "frighteningly excessive amounts." *Virola* resins with a DMT content as high as 11 percent are routinely ingested in quantities as large as two or three teaspoonfuls.

William Emboden has described the list of accoutrements associated with snuffing as "endless." There are bones from plovers tied together to form tubes, "which enable friends to blow snuff into each other's nostrils," while "V-shaped bones permit self-indulgence in sternutation. These powerful snuffs blown into the upper nasal passages, or even into the sinuses, induce violent fits of sneezing followed by violent states of hallucination."

Detailed observations and photographs illustrating native uses of psychedelic snuffs are presented in the NIMH's The Ethnopharmacological Search for Psychoactive Drugs. *The caption for this photo: "With a forceful blow the powder entered the nose."*

Natives often practice snuffing daily. In Colombia and Venezuela, Hoffer and Osmond write that the *yopo*-snuffing habit

> was carried on by whole populations. The intoxication produced convulsive movements and distortions of face and body muscles, then a desire to dance and finally an inability to control their limbs. Then a violent madness or deep sleep overtook the user. Then they developed stupor.

The Waikás, however, are the greatest risk-takers, as Emboden notes:

> "Leaves of the Angel of Death" or *bolek-hena* is the name for one such snuff derived from *Justicia pectoralis* variety *stenophylla* of the family Acanthaceae [see plate 58 of his *Narcotic Drugs*]. This red-flowered herb enjoys a considerable popularity among the Waikás . . . . Among these peoples, three curanderos have died from using this potent snuff which seems to contain fairly large amounts of tryptamines in the dried and powdered leaves. Often it is an adulterant of snuffs made from the red bark resin of several species of *Virola*.

Use and Safety of Synthetics in Ordinary Amounts

DET and DPT are more potent than DMT. It seems that increasing the amine side-chain makes the tryptamine more water soluble; with increased absorption, less is needed. Yet even 15 to 20 mg. of DMT is sufficient to give strong effects when smoked. In most of the hospital studies, about 50 mg. of DMT was injected intramuscularly.

When DMT is injected, the onset of effects usually takes two to five minutes, time required for the tryptamine to make its way to the brain. The user becomes ecstatic for ten to fifteen minutes, declining to normal states of mind over the next quarter to half hour. Injected DET displays a similar curve of effects but lasts about three hours. DPT has about the same duration as DET but ends more abruptly.

More often, these tryptamines are smoked because less is needed to feel the effects, which arrive in a matter of only a few seconds. The DMT peak lasts for three to ten minutes, and it's all over in twenty to thirty minutes. DET and DPT, which have more subtle effects than DMT, may take a few minutes to register, although, as Alan Birnbaum writes in regard to DPT, "some people have reported to be immediately immersed in the light on the first toke." DET lasts about an hour when smoked; the most intense part of a DPT experience is over in about twenty minutes.

Long available from chemical supply houses, 5-methoxy-DMT is about five times as strong as DMT when smoked and the shortest-acting of all these compounds. The experience is characterized by a "rush" similar to that from amyl nitrate. There is little in the way of visuals, but intense thoughts and perhaps bodily sensations last for five to ten minutes. Many people don't like it; in his *Psychedelic Chemistry*, Michael Valentine Smith compares its effects to having an elephant sit on one's head.

Short-acting tryptamines are smoked in joints or pipes and often are mixed with marijuana. However, it should be emphasized that these compounds provoke an intense experience and should not be taken, in the words of Bigwood and Ott,

> in the carefree way marijuana often is. Smoking DMT while driving is extremely dangerous . . . . Most users prefer to be sitting down or reclining before and during the trip. The smoking should be carried out in a setting free from unexpected intrusions by visitors, a ringing telephone, etc.

Initiates, after taking a toke, have often started to say they weren't feeling anything and then suddenly become silent in mid-sentence. Some people who have started to smoke a DMT joint while standing have suddenly needed to sit down.

The observable physical changes are pupil dilation, increased pulse rate and blood pressure and, in some instances, dizziness, nausea or tremor. Stephen Szára and his associates examined such effects closely in a series of papers (eleven of these are listed in Brimblecombe and Pinder's bibliography at the end of their tryptamine chapter), concluding that these were minor.

Still, DMT and related compounds may not be the proper psychedelics for those with high blood pressure.

In an article about DMT in *Head* magazine, Bigwood and Ott ask: "Why is DMT not a popular drug today?"

> Probably the most important factor relates to the myth that DMT causes brain damage. Though there is no evidence for this, it appears that some early users became frightened by the rapid onset of the effects, the chemical taste of the smoke, and the potency of the drug, and responded by generating myths. The idea that DMT caused brain damage became entrenched in the counter-culture, and is still parroted today.

The suddenness and intensity with which DMT comes on can be somewhat alarming, so much so that, as Grinspoon and Bakalar remark, the "term 'mind-blowing' might have been invented for this drug." Users report feeling that they were "melting into" or "fusing" with the floor, that their heart was stopping, or that their "life-force" was somehow ebbing away. When the experience is over, the user feels normal again but may worry, more than with other psychedelics, about such physical feelings, particularly if the compound was inadvisably used while alone.

The smell of these substances contributes to such suspicions. "Unfortunately," adds Michael Valentine Smith,

> these compounds taste and smell like burning plastic when smoked and are harder to smoke than hash. There is, however, no evidence for the notion that they are damaging.

Tolerance, Potentiation and MAO-Inhibition

Impressive effects from DMT depend to a large extent on a sufficient amount going to the brain all at once. The peak comes on quickly and is hard to build upon. In this sense, DMT exhibits a threshold phenomenon: if the desired intensity is not reached, extra inhalations a few minutes later won't help. In smoking DMT, it is most efficient for one person to fill a pipe with the amount desired and finish it, the next user repeating this process, rather than for a pipe or joint to go around a circle of users as is often done with marijuana. This procedure also equalizes the concentration of the compound more equal; otherwise, the first user would get the strongest toke.

Once an insufficient amount has entered the brain, it is unlikely that a user could get strong DMT effects; twenty minutes must first elapse. But even if a higher level of experience is not attained, the effects can still be impressive, approximating a very colorful, intense hash high, and can be extended if there is an adequate supply on hand. Residual DET and DPT effects can also be sustained by taking continual pipefuls.

In 1962, Sai-Halasz, who worked with Szára, reported that DMT was potentiated by pretreatment with serotonin antagonists like methysergide; in 1963, he announced that such potentiation could be diminished by pretreatment with monoamine oxidase inhibitors.

Under normal circumstances, DMT, DET and DPT are inactive when taken orally. A gram of DMT, well over thirty times the dose needed to achieve effects from smoking, has been swallowed without perceptible psychoactivity. When these substances pass into the stomach, they are attacked by the enzyme monoamine oxidase, which hacks the molecule apart. In the company of MAO-inhibitors, like the β-carbolines associated with *yagé*, these tryptamines become resistant to quick metabolism and thus remain effective when taken orally.

Walter Anirman, author of *Sky Cloud Mountain*, is one of those who has experimented with the user of DMT in conjunction with LSD. About this synergistic combination, he wrote:

> One inhalation of the concentrated smoke, and the world melts into its patterning constituents. A second inhalation, and the body becomes transfixed with a silence so deep and so startling that within it a tear would fall as a torrent. A third inhalation, and sentience visibly radiates itself from everywhere: plants and animals are transfigured to their sacred essence and pebbles sparkle like self-conscious, magical jewels. But the balance is delicate. The vision can detonate along with the nervous system that falters before it .... Such experiences, though often quite horrible, are no more than a widow's mite in the table stakes of consciousness, for under the guidance of the LSDMT synergy, vast realms of perfect attunement may also occur, and the stellar brilliance of the clear-light void shine from everywhere, from everything, inside and out.

Cerebrospinal Tryptamines

L-tryptophan is an essential amino acid prevalent throughout the animal world. It is the only one that is an indole and is generally considered the basic building block for the indolealkylamines, which include most of the compounds discussed in this book. Neither *l*-tryptophan nor bufotenine, a neurotransmitter, is now considered psychoactive, though bufotenine was once thought to be at higher dosages. However, both are cross-tolerant with LSD, as is DMT, which suggests that their molecules may occupy the same or related receptor-sites in the brain. (DMT is not cross-tolerant with psilocybin or mescaline.)

Over the last thirty years, much attention has gone into seeking a "psychotogen," a chemical manufactured in an abnormal brain and nervous system that causes psychosis. "Most psychedelic drugs cannot possibly play this role," as Grinspoon and Bakalar explain,

> because tolerance develops too quickly for a persistent effect. The main exception is DMT, and it has recently been identified as an endogenous compound in the brains of rats and human beings. The enzyme responsible for its synthesis and the sites where it is absorbed by nerve terminals have also been discovered (Christian et al. 1976; Christian et al. 1977). Both LSD and 5-MeO-DMT seem to displace DMT at those sites, which may also be serotonin receptors.

"Christian *et al.*" refers to Dr. Samuel Christian and his associates at the University of Alabama in Birmingham's Neurosciences Program; in 1975 they identified DMT, 5-methoxy-DMT, 5-methoxy-*N,N*-DMT, *N*-methyltryptamine and tryptamine in human cerebrospinal fluid. In May 1977, Dr. Wolfgang Vogel of the Jefferson Medical College in Philadelphia isolated 5-methoxy-DMT in brain tissue; the Christian team also found DMT there.

If DMT and 5-methoxy-DMT are neurotransmitters, as many researchers think, then an excess of them may be a cause of schizophrenia. Observing dramatic increases of DMT in the spinal fluid of animals and humans "during extreme stress," Dr. Christian hypothesized that the tendency among some people to develop mental aberrations might reflect "a genetic predisposition to excessive DMT production as a response to stress." Later work, reported by L. Corbett, Christian and others in the *British Journal of Psychiatry* (1978, 132: 139-144), indicated that schizophrenics do not have higher levels of DMT in their brains than control subjects. Research in this intriguing area continues.

MENTAL EFFECTS

Effects from Cohoba *and* Epená *Snuffs*

Observing Guahibo Indians in the mid-nineteenth century, Richard Spruce remarked that using *cohoba* snuff eliminated hunger and thirst because "one feels so good" and compared the inebriation to that from Fly Agarics. He noted that the Catauixi used the snuff when they were about to go on a hunt in order to render themselves more alert. Shultes and Hofmann write that this snuff from the *yopo* tree is sometimes, as among the Guahibo, taken as a daily stimulant.

> But it is more commonly employed by *payés* ("medicine men") to induce trances and visions and communicate with the *hekula* spirits; to prophesy or divine; to protect the tribe against epidemics of sickness; to make hunters and even their dogs more alert.

As for *epená* snuff, they declare that this "was employed ritualistically for diagnosis and treatment of disease, prophecy, divination, and other magico-religious purposes." Indians under the effects of this *Virola* resin

> characteristically have faraway dream-like expressions that are, of course, due to the active principles of the drug, but which the natives believe are associated with the temporary absence of the shamans' souls as they travel to distant places. The chants during the incessant dancing performed by shamans may at times reflect conversations with spirit forces. This transportation of the soul to other realms represents to the Waiká one of the most significant values of the effects of this hallucinogen.

Emboden adds an interesting comment on the striking tribal differences in visions produced by *epená:*

Among the Witotos, microscopia, or seeing things and people miniaturized, is a characteristic of the *Virola* syndrome; while for the Waiká macroscopia is a part of the visionary experience. This is probably conditioned in part by the tryptamines and in part by cultural background. Macroscopia is inextricable from the Waiká concepts of *hikura*, the spirit who dwells in the *Virola* tree.

DMT Effects

DMT has been the most studied and used of the short-acting tryptamines. Almost everyone who's had a good lungful has been astonished by the rapidity and vividness of the effects. With eyes open, there appears a "retinal circus," where perception of the external world is overlaid with moving, fascinating, brightly colored patterns. With the eyes closed, wrote Bigwood and Ott,

> the subject becomes aware of swirling patterns, often geometric in shape . . . .
> Many people become ecstatic or euphoric, others become meditative and concentrate on the hallucinations with eyes closed. Sometimes, especially during the initial stages of the inebriation, there can be a slight feeling of paranoia, but this is seldom more than momentary.

When Osmond was first given DMT, he remained silent for some time and then responded with: "My . . . word!" Another user, trying to describe the effects briefly, commented, "I took a puff—and then my arms and legs fell off . . . and the garden of God opened up." Yet another user living in the Virgin Islands had been sent some DMT and assumed it was a new kind of *Cannabis*; she telegraphed the sender: "WHAT REPEAT WHAT WAS THAT?"

Alan Watts said the DMT experience was like "being fired out of the muzzle of an atomic cannon." He later re-evaluated DMT, calling it "amusing but relatively uninteresting" compared to LSD, mescaline, psilocybin and *Cannabis*. Most who have tried DMT find it to be immensely pleasurable but without enduring effects.

More than a few artists have discovered inspiration in the presentation of geometric patterns. In early Canadian research, DMT was used successfully in propelling people who resisted LSD's effects into a psychedelic state.

An example of how DMT's effects may be meaningful, evoking more than a sequence of kaleidoscopic images, comes from Richard Alpert, who was debating with Leary whether the word *ecstasy* should be used in describing LSD and psilocybin trips. Alpert thought it would "just get everybody thinking about orgies." Leary liked the word's derivation from *ex* (or *ek*) + *stasis*—"going out of the static."

At this time, Alpert received a huge, hand-embroidered robe brought by a lama from Tibet. Alpert, though appreciative, didn't know what to do with the robe. He decided to wear it while under DMT, considering this question about *ecstasy*. Alpert went into a meditation room at the top of the big house in the Millbrook estate. The smell of incense from the robe surrounded him as he shot DMT into his thigh and lay down.

I found myself walking down some very wide steps into what seemed like a Roman or Greek scene. Torches lit the stairway of a stone castle. I walked down into an underground grotto, where I looked through a door into a room. Inside was a kidney-shaped indoor swimming pool, and beyond that were groves of trees. Nymph-like figures were diving into the pool, which was surrounded by silver statues. I got the feeling of intense sensuality, of a Dionysian, orgy-like place.

I stood at the door, sure I wasn't going to go into this "Sin City"—not me, afraid of my impulses. But then I noticed that one of the statues was of Timothy, who was laughing. I said, "See, I knew I was right!"

Then, suddenly, I was whisked away in an elevator. It felt like being shot up in the Trade Center Building in New York City.

Then, just as suddenly, it stopped. I found myself in a dome that was luminously white. The light wasn't inside or out—the whole thing was luminous. A more intense light seemed to emanate from the center skylight. There were many people in the room, gathered mainly in the center and looking upward.

I crowded in to see what they were looking at. Finally, I reached the center and could look up. I discovered I was looking up into absolutely clear light. I'm looking directly at the light, and it's totally purifying me.

At the most ecstatic moment in this experience, I heard a laugh. I turned to look, and, at the edge of the crowd, there stood Timothy. I realized that he was telling me that this was "ecstasy" too.

I took off the robe, went down to see Timothy, and said, " 'Ecstasy' is a great word. Let's use it."

More than a few users have had frightening, even terrifying experiences on DMT. Because the transition into the altered state is so rapid and so intense, some people have concluded when they saw religious archetypes arise that they had been lured into a pact with the Devil. On this half-hour trip, some people have felt they might "never come back."

Possibly the best published example of the negative side of the DMT experience comes from Jean Houston, coauthor of *The Varieties of Psychedelic Experience*. In the chapter on "The World of the Non-Human," Houston ("S-6") presents an illustration of bad set and setting and the fearful results under such conditions. "It is best to be in a calm and relaxed state," say Bigwood and Ott: "If one is tense or anxious, it would be unwise to smoke DMT." Houston "had been up for three days and two nights working on a manuscript." The "room where the 'experiment' was to take place was a dirty, dingy, insanely cluttered pesthole." She was told she "would see God." After injecting the DMT, Houston experienced "the most terrifying three minutes" of her life, three minutes that seemed an eternity. Eventually, a "face of God" appeared after she made "a final effort at ultimate visions," and it turned out to be "a very wise monkey." Houston "burst out laughing."

DET Effects

DET doesn't have the visual impact of DMT but does evoke intense, pleasurable states of mind, which last for about an hour when the substance is smoked. Meditating users have noticed that they can lock themselves into a lotus position much more easily than before. The DET experience can be built upon by repeated inhalations, with some users reporting that they have begun to "vibrate" and "raise Kundalini energy." Some users find that their eyes turn backward, as in a state of religious ecstasy. Among those who have experienced DET with religious intensity is Alan Birnbaum:

> DET is the first psychedelic which convinced me that the psychedelic is a Primeval Light Being which is God, the Creator. We had smoked it in a large hookah and it was so clear and so bright—unmistakable—it was a Being.

The most extensive report on the effects of DET was submitted by Böszörményi, Der and Nagy in 1959 in the *Journal of Mental Sciences*. They described trials in thirty normal and forty-one psychiatric subjects who were given 0.7 to 0.8 mg./kg. intramuscularly. They concluded that DET was more satisfactory than LSD or mescaline in increasing communication and facilitating therapy because of its shorter duration of action: "We believe DET to be the best and least noxious psychotogenic agent known thus far."

Some of their subjects began to show an interest in art and renewed their interest in writing. Two began to paint. Several who were professional authors compared their experiences with spontaneous inspiration. A young poet reported: "I felt an enormous drive to write, to put down the marvelous feelings." Böszörményi suggested that the increase in creativity resulted from "the emergence of ancient desires and drives which forced the person to satisfy them by creating."

Here is a fairly typical comment about the effects from DET when smoked:

> DET is like grass, but you get very high and are still functional. There's a little hallucination, and a little color distortion. It's not as intense as DMT, and you can do things behind it—like go to lectures or run around the streets. With DMT and acid you're often astonished, wondering what's happening, whereas with DET you know you're on it.

DPT Effects

DPT has not been very widely used to date, but those who have tried it seem to agree that it does produce psychedelic or "peak" experiences. Much of its application in psychotherapy has taken place in Europe, under the supervision of such specialists as Dr. Hanscarl Leuner, who has just published a book in German on psycholytic therapy. Initial reports in the U.S. have come from the Maryland Psychiatric Research Center, which used this drug in conjunction with therapy at Spring Grove Hospital near Baltimore.

In the January-March 1977 *Journal of Psychedelic Drugs*, five doctors on the Spring Grove team discussed their findings about "The Peak Experience Variable in DPT-Assisted Psychotherapy with Cancer Patients." They expressed the opinion that among the many altered states of psychedelic consciousness, peak experiences "are probably among the most difficult to facilitate . . . [but] we now possess a technology that can evoke peak experiences with sufficient potency and reliability to permit us to study their impact on human behavior." They undertook to test such a possibility with DPT, administering it to thirty-four cancer patients who were expected to live at least three months and who were suffering major psychological stress. The goal was to evoke what William James called the "noetic" quality of peak experiences, about which he had written:

> although so similar to states of feeling, [these] mystical states seem to those who experience them to be also states of knowledge. They are states of insight into depths of truth unplumbed by the discursive intellect.

Collected data indicated "clinical improvement of greater magnitude for the group of peakers than for the group of nonpeakers." The team concluded that a cluster of significant changes on various indexes "strongly suggests that the response to psychotherapy was different for the two groups." They cited "the peakers' improvement in 'Capacity for Intimate Contact,' suggesting the enhancement of a quality of interpersonal openness that might mitigate the isolation and lack of meaningful communication often experienced both by terminally ill patients and their closest family members."

The Spring Grove evaluations were complicated because raters were asked not to speak with the subjects about their DPT experiences. Another problem was that some of these patients later classified as "nonpeakers"

> had experiences during the period of DPT action that they viewed as quite meaningful. For example, the subject in the sample of nonpeakers who scored highest on the peak experience items of the Psychedelic Experience Questionnaire (43 percent total score) described having experienced herself during part of the period of DPT action in a visionary synagogue. Within the experiential sequence recounted, she described feeling led by the hand of a wise old man she called God to the front of the sanctuary, and there given a Torah to carry as a sign that she was accepted, forgiven, and had "come home." Although this sequence might well be classified as a "religious experience" or as an "archetypal experience," it did not entail the sense of ego-transcendence and the unitive state of consciousness defined as intrinsic to the term "peak experience" within the context of this study.

Nonetheless, this team concluded from its experiments with DPT "that peak experiences may constitute an intrinsic element of effective psychotherapy for some persons" and that "rapid therapeutic progress in the course of short-term psychotherapy with cancer patients . . . is indicated by this study." In a comment also pertinent for anyone considering use of DPT, they observed that "when a peak experience does occur, its continuing relevance for daily living may be strongly dependent on the degree to which the associated insights are assimilated or transferred into the everyday self-concept and world view of the patient."

In the October-December 1977 issue of the *Journal of Psychedelic Drugs*, the Spring Grove team reported on a controlled study of DPT-assisted psychotherapy with eighty-six alcoholics. Some of these investigators had earlier "quite encouraging" results using LSD as an adjunct to psychotherapy with chronic alcoholics, but they thought DPT might be a more suitable agent because of its shorter duration and its lack of negative publicity. A year later, the group given DPT "showed an advantage in positive outcome measures"—particularly in regard to Occupational Adjustment and Sobriety—when compared to the two control groups. Those given DPT "may have temporarily experienced a substantial number of peak reactions," the authors wrote, and "may have temporarily experienced a more positive mode of functioning." Later follow-ups, however, revealed few long-term differences among the three groups, a result that "would seem to indicate that the DPT group did not know how to integrate their new modes of functioning into the everyday patterns of their lives."

FORMS AND PREPARATIONS

The short-acting tryptamines, usually seen as crystals, are difficult to identify. However, each has a characteristic smell that is easily recalled by people who have tried them once. Over time, they turn increasingly reddish.

Tryptamines may also appear as an oil put onto various herbs, such as parsley, marijuana or red raspberry leaves. Marijuana is probably the best medium, because it is less harsh on the throat and lungs than parsley and because a lot of users like the combination. Some tryptamine enthusiasts object to mixture with pot on the grounds that marijuana detracts from a tryptamine's clarity. Parsley and other herbs can be converted into more neutral carriers by steeping them in water so as to extract most of their aromatic flavoring and then drying the herb.

Some users prefer to smoke a compound like DMT without any carrier in a small glass pipe. A small amount of the crystals or oil is placed in the bowl and then slowly heated until fumes begin to fill the pipe. As has been mentioned, it is most efficient if each user smokes the entire amount he or she wants and then passes the pipe along.

A regular pipe covered with a fine screen can also be used. As Bigwood and Ott explain, the crystals should not be placed directly on the screen because

> they would be aspirated before they can be vaporized. Instead an herb (preferably non-psychoactive) should be placed on the screen and the DMT added atop the herb.
>
> When smoking DMT-soaked parsley, it is often difficult to gauge the proper dose. The only recourse, other than solvent extraction and isolation, is to use the "bioassay technique." Basically, one should try a small amount of the mixture, increasing the dose ... until the desired effects become apparent.

Jeremy Bigwood

Seen as an oil at the upper right, DMT generally appears mixed with an herb—either loose, bottled or in joints. Many users prefer to smoke it from a glass pipe, such as the one seen at the left.

When smoked, fifteen to thirty milligrams of pure DMT is sufficient to produce hallucinogenic effects. This is a small amount, too small to be easily estimated without some reference. We suggest, if you have some DMT to spare, that you weigh out 15 to 30 milligrams as a reference. We do not recommend measuring doses while inebriated.

Jeremy Bigwood

Banisteriopsis caapi, *the Amazonian "vine of the soul," in cross-
section. This climbing vine, or liana, uses jungle trees for
support and can grow half a foot thick. Natives say the rosette
pattern inside is composed of "hearts," and that the vine is
ready for use when seven or more have developed.*
   Yagé, *a psychedelic drink used by natives and urban dwellers
in northwestern South America, is made from the outer bark of
this vine. Psychedelic constituents are harmaline, harmine and
d-1,2,3,4-tetrahydroharmine.*

CHAPTER SEVEN

Ayahuasca, Yagé *and Harmaline*

One wonders how peoples in primitive societies, with no knowledge of chemistry or physiology, ever hit upon a solution to the activation of an alkaloid by a monoamine oxidase inhibitor.

—Richard Evans Schultes

HISTORY

A seventh psychedelic compound-cluster of importance includes three-ringed molecules that chemists would refer to as harmala alkaloids or β - carbolines. To date, harmaline has been the most significant of these compounds tested: its formal names are 4,9-dihydro-7-methoxy-1-methyl-3H-pyrido-[3,4-b] indole and 7-methoxy-1-methyl-3,4-dihydro- β -carboline. Harmaline and other harmala alkaloids, the principle psychedelics in the "magical" beverage *yagé*, appear throughout the plant world. These substances are also present in cigarettes and even in the human pineal gland.

Chapter Six touched on the occurrence of harmala alkaloids in *cohoba* and *epená* snuffs. Although these three-ringed compounds are widespread in the plant kingdom, their use as a psychedelic is known in only two specific, geographically separate traditions: (1) scraping of the bark of *Banisteriopsis* vines to make a drink in northwestern South America and (2) ingestion of the seeds of Syrian rue (*Peganum harmala*), a wild desert shrub, in the Near East. The Amazonian practices are better documented and colorfully illustrate purgative, healing, visual, telepathic, sexual, artistic and therapeutic potentials in psychedelics.

Harmala alkaloids are little known to the psychedelic subculture in the U.S., although they are legal and are stocked by a number of chemical supply houses. These indolic compounds should be of special psychedelic interest because of the highly specific character of the experiences they produce. Unfortunately, the literature on this compound-cluster and *Banisteriopsis* use in the Amazonian region is somewhat confusing: it describes several barks and leaves as well as a drink, which is made with several different recipes and is activated by at least three chemical compounds. Each form has a number of names, and sometimes the same name is used for both botanicals and beverages. In what follows, *ayahuasca* (EYE-a-wasca) refers to the psychedelic species of *Banisteriopsis, yagé* (yah-Hey) to the drink made from their outer bark and *harmaline* to the primary psychedelic compound in the bark.

Records from South American Explorers

Use of *ayahuasca* for visionary experiences appears to be primeval, to judge from the richness of associated mythology. Pre-Columbian rock drawings are similar to contemporary *ayahuasqueros'* paintings, which are said to represent *yagé* visions (see page 127 of *Plants of the Gods* for a fine example of such a drawing on granite). However, the earliest known record of the practices associated with this botanical wasn't set down until the middle of the nineteenth century.

The author was Richard Spruce, at one time a British schoolteacher, who was among the early explorers to make the perilous journey into the Amazon. Spruce almost died of dysentery and malaria but survived to become one of botany's greatest collectors. In 1851, while exploring the upper Rio Negro of the Brazilian Amazon, he observed the use of *yagé*. In 1853, he came upon it twice in Peru. In his *Notes of a Botanist on the Amazon and Andes*, he described its sources, its preparation and its effects upon himself. Unfortunately, Spruce's experience was characterized mainly by his getting sick.

Spruce's *Notes* didn't appear in print until 1908. (They were edited by Alfred Russel Wallace, who simultaneously with Darwin conceived the theory of evolution.) Spruce suspected that additives were responsible for the psychoactivity of this beverage, although he noted that *Banisteriopsis* by itself was considered mentally active. The samples he sent to England for chemical analysis weren't located and assayed until more than a century later. Examined in 1966, they were still psychoactive.

The first widely read description of *yagé* practices was published in 1858 by Manuel Villavicencio, an Ecuadorian geographer. The experience made him feel he was "flying" to most marvelous places. Describing how natives responded, he reported that natives using this drink were able

> to foresee and answer accurately in difficult cases, be it to reply opportunely to ambassadors from other tribes in a question of war; to decipher plans of the enemy through the medium of this magic drink and take proper steps for attack and defense; to ascertain, when a relative is sick, what sorcerer has put on the hex; to carry out a friendly visit to other tribes; to welcome foreign travelers or, at least to make sure of the love of their womenfolk.

Several early explorers of northwestern South America—Martius, Crévaux, Orton, Koch-Grunberg and others—also referred to *ayahuasca, yagé* and *caapi*, all citing a forest liana but offering little detail. In the early twentieth century, it was learned that the use of *Banisteriopsis* vines for healing, initiatory and shamanic rites extends to Peru and Bolivia.

In 1923, a film of Indian *yagé* ceremonies was shown at the annual meeting of the American Pharmaceutical Association. Other noteworthy

Richard Spruce, long-known to botanists primarily for a 600-page monograph on liverworts, was the first to write about yagé *ingestion. As an important nineteenth-century collector of Amazonian flora, his name is attached to the* Banisteriopsis caapi *species, the most important botanical source of harmala alkaloids.*

publications drawing attention to the effects of this drink came from Rusby and White, who observed *yagé* practices in Bolivia in 1922, from the Russians Varnoff and Jezepezuk, who did Colombian fieldwork in 1925-1926, and from Morton, who in 1931 published Klug's southern Colombian notes about *Banisteriopsis inebrians.*

Identification of the Active Principles

Harmaline was first isolated in 1841, from Syrian rue. Its chemical structure was established in 1919, and it was first synthesized in 1927 by Richard Manske.

In 1923, Fischer assayed *yagé*, isolating an alkaloid that he named *telepathine.* The same year, Barriga-Villalba and Albarracin isolated two alkaloids from this drink; they called these *yajeine* and *yajeinine.* In 1928, Lewin isolated *banisterine.* Shortly afterward, Wolfes, as well as Rumpf and Elger, asserted that all these alkaloids were identical: they were harmaline, an indole derivative earlier found in seeds and roots of *Peganum harmala* (Syrian rue). This conclusion was in doubt for some time, until Chen and Chen, working with clearly identified botanicals, demonstrated that all these substances were harmaline.

Hochstein and Paradies determined in 1957 that results from ingestion of *yagé* (without other botanical additives) came mainly from interaction of three molecules—harmaline, harmine and *d*-1,2,3,4-tetrahydroharmine. These findings have been accepted since then by investigators of this plant family.

Developments over the Last Twenty Years

Considerable interest in this psychoactive complex arose from the 1960s fascination with LSD, and reports that ordinarily would have been restricted to the technical literature received fairly wide circulation. *Psychedelic Review* and *The Psychedelic Reader*, for instance, reprinted Richard Evans Schultes' efforts to straighten out confusion about *yagé*. After collecting plants and searching out rubber sources on the Amazon for over a dozen years, Schultes gave his acccount of *yagé* in lectures to the College of Pharmacy at the University of Texas and in *Harvard Botanical Museum Leaflets*. Republication in more popular periodicals, issued by Leary associates, spread the word about *yagé* and its use for divinatory and prophetic purposes. Schultes reported that the effects upon natives of the upper Rio Negro of Brazil,

> with whom I have taken *caapi* many times, is pleasant, characterized amongst other strange effects by colored visual hallucinations. In excessive doses, it is said to bring on frighteningly nightmarish visions and a feeling of extremely reckless abandon, but consciousness is not lost nor is use of the limbs unduly affected.

Heinz Kusel wrote about "Ayahuasca Drinkers among the Chama Indians" in *Psychedelic Review* #6 (1965). Having spent seven years trading in the Upper Amazon region, he observed that "Indians and low-class mestizos alike visit the *ayahuasquero* . . . when they are ailing, or think they need a general check-up, or want to make an important decision, or simply because they feel like it." Kusel added that for a long while it "never crossed my mind to try the liana myself." Eventually, he drank the brew three times. The first two instances were disappointing. He was glad, though, that he persisted.

> There were two very definite attractions; I enjoyed the unreality of a created world. The images were not casual, accidental or imperfect, but fully organized to the last detail of highly complex, consistent, yet forever changing designs. They were harmonized in color and had a slick, sensuous, polished finish. The other attraction of which I was very conscious at the time was an inexplicable sensation of intimacy with the visions. They were mine and concerned only me. I remembered an Indian telling me that whenever he drank *ayahuasca*, he

had such beautiful visions that he used to put his hands over his eyes for fear somebody might steal them. I felt the same way.

In 1963, the first book having *yagé* as a subject appeared; it undoubtedly increased interest in this brew made from a "vine of the soul." In *the YAGE letters*, the writers William Burroughs and Allen Ginsberg related their search for and use of this "magic" drink. A few anthropologists criticized their descriptions as misleading, and many readers were interested in the book as literature. Nonetheless, it has drawn continuing attention to this psychedelic drink.

Among those fascinated by native use of psychoactive plants was Chilean psychiatrist Claudio Naranjo. Naranjo traveled into the Amazon because he "wanted to go where people ate people." Naranjo took along two contemporary items: a polaroid camera and blotter paper, on which he had drawn stars, moon and sun to mark different dosages of LSD. When he met some natives, he conveyed the idea that he was a "medicine man" and distributed the blotters, inviting the natives to try the star-doses (those of lowest potency) while gazing at the night sky. Upon his return several days later, Naranjo learned that the natives liked his "medicine," considering it very powerful. In exchange, they gave him *ayahuasca*, which influenced his subsequent practice of psychotherapy. He described his using harmaline and harmine in *The Healing Journey* (1967).

Since then, a number of people interested in making scientific observations or hoping to have a *yagé* experience have traveled to South America in search of *ayahuasqueros*. "Sean" roamed around the Amazon basin in a boat called "The Visionary Vine." The brothers Dennis and Terence McKenna recounted an *ayahuasca-psilocybe* experience that lasted allegedly for a month in the jungle; their fascinating speculative volume, *The Inner Landscape*, called attention to *yagé* while considering topics of mind-body interactions.

Bruce Lamb's *Wizard of the Upper Amazon* (1971) presented the romantic turn-of-the-century jungle story of Manuel Córdova-Rios, who became an *ayahuasquero* after being kidnapped at age fifteen by the Amahuaca Indians of Peru. This account details his use of *Banisteriopsis* in hunting, healing and telepathy—including group visions.

In 1972, Marlene Dobkin de Rios issued a study—*The Visionary Vine*— of *yagé's* uses in folk healing in an urban setting in Peru. A professor of anthropology at California State College at Fullerton, de Rios observed that the supply of *ayahuasca* was becoming depleted in the jungles near Iquitos, site of her investigations, and that suppliers had to search much further for it. Although her fieldwork was done largely in a slum section of Iquitos, she saw *ayahuasca* being used throughout the region for religious and magic rituals (to receive a protective spirit or divine guidance from the plant spirit); for diagnosing and treating disease; for divination (to learn an enemy's plans, for instance, or to check on a spouse's fidelity); for "witchcraft" (to prevent harm caused by others' malice or to cause harm to others); and for pleasure.

Appearing in 1963, this City Lights book recounts William Burroughs'
South American search for yagé, which he hoped might be "the ultimate
fix," and similar travels by Allen Ginsberg. Andrew Weil described it
as being "distinguished by a uniformly negative tone and, according to
experts on the region, considerable misinformation."

Her report and other shorter accounts increased worldwide awareness of *yagé* and indicate that some practices that have been associated with it are unlike those common to other psychedelics. For example, *yagé* is the only mind-enhancing concoction that has been absolutely taboo on occasion for women. When a trumpet signalled the start of the puberty rites for the Yurupari, female members of the tribe fled into the jungle to avoid a death penalty for their seeing the ceremony or even the drink. In other regions, it was thought that if a woman set eyes on prepared *caapi*, the vine would be rendered ineffective. More generally, women were allowed to drink *yagé* but were discouraged if they wished to become adepts, which frequently involved a year of regularly drinking *ayahuasca* infusions spiked with tobacco juice.

Yurupari puberty rites also differed from the psychedelic rites of other cultures in that adolescents whipped furiously at each other after drinking brown, bitter *ayahuasca* elixirs until their bodies were bloody with welts. A recent account of such a ceremony, which is little practiced now, can be found in *Plants of the Gods* (pp. 123-124). Interest in harmala compounds arose as well from reports that among the Jivaro headhunting tribes of the upper Amazon—and the Cashinahua of Peru—the "dream" contents of *yagé* experiences were commonly regarded as constituting more important guiding principles than ordinary consciousness.

Andrew Weil is among those who feel that "No drug plant has excited more interest than *yagé*." In *The Marriage of the Sun and Moon,* he remembers being offered this "tiger drug" (so called because it was said to inspire visions of big jungle cats) in the Haight-Ashbury in 1967. Later, he tried to find a more authentic experience in Colombia. Each time he got near it, the result was a "fully debased yagé ritual." He concluded that "Today, alcoholism is replacing the ceremonial use of safer drugs" and that "traditional peoples do not automatically form good relationships with psychoactive plants." In the August 1979 *High Times*, Weil reports on a more recent Colombian trip when he was successful in finding a healer using *ayahuasca*. His "Yagé— The Vine that Speaks" details with ten color photographs how it is prepared and used in treating illnesses.

BOTANY

Botanical understanding of what causes *yagé* effects has been, as Schultes put it, more "fraught with confusion" than is the case with other psychedelics. Schultes and Hofmann described these confusions almost apologetically in 1973, writing that "It is difficult for the nonbotanist to understand our lack of understanding of specific delimitations of drug plants, the use of which has been known for more than a century."

Richard Spruce had set identification efforts off to a bad start by suggesting that *yagé*'s peculiar qualities were from the roots of "painted caapi."

This was a vine he called *Haemadictyon amazonicum,* of which no known other example exists than what he collected (it's since been assigned to the *Prestonia* genus). Although he said that the Indians considered a *Banisteriopsis* vine an essential ingredient, his misdirection was repeated by others. The Colombian chemist Fischer, isolating the first alkaloid in *yagé,* placed it in the *Aristolochia* genus. *Banisteriopsis caapi* first became known as a main source in 1927, after French pharmacologists Perrot and Hamet reviewed this psychoactive complex in terms of its botany and chemistry.

Ayahuasca *and* Yagé

Essential to any *yagé* concoction is bark from specific *Banisteriopsis* vines—generally *B. caapi,* often *B. inebrians* and sometimes *B. quitensis.* *B. caapi* climbs up adjacent tropical forest trees and keeps climbing until its flowers are exposed to direct sunlight. It is so greedy for sunlight that sometimes it eventually kills supporting trees. It is occasionally started in greenhouses, where it has been known to take over the roof, leaving only shadow

R.E. Schultes: *Harvard Botanical Museum Leaflets*

Cultivated Banisteriopsis caapi *shoots near Rio Piraparana, Colombia are shown here branching out in all directions. This vine is often harvested when young; natives prefer it young for some purposes, claiming that the effects of young shoots are different from those of older specimens.*

below. The flowers are small and pink, much like apple blossoms. At its base, the vine often has a diameter of six inches.

Schultes and Hofmann report that South American natives

> often have special names for diverse "kinds" of Ayahuasca, although the botanist frequently finds them all representative of the same species. It is usually difficult to understand the aboriginal method of classification: some may be age forms; others may come from different parts of the liana; still others may be ecological forms growing under varying conditions of soil, shade, moisture, etc. The natives assert that these "kinds" have a variety of effects, and it is conceivable that they may actually have different chemical compositions. This possibility is one of the least investigated yet most significant aspects in the study of Ayahuasca.

Natives distinguish at least six different botanical sources of *ayahuasca*. Two that are said to be the most powerful haven't yet been described botanically or chemically.

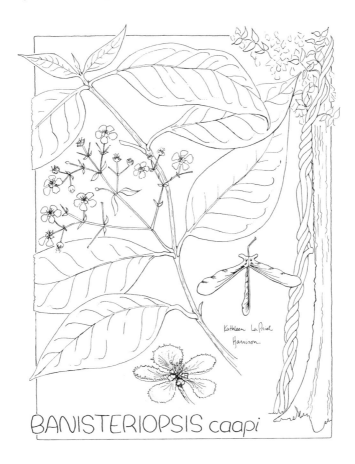

BANISTERIOPSIS caapi

The Admixtures of Yagé

Ayahuasqueros often include at least one additive to *yagé* infusions to enhance states of mind brought about by *B. caapi, inebrians* and *quitensis*. In Colombia, *Daturas* and closely related species of *Brugmansia* are sometimes used; they undoubtedly give this drink added kick but are dangerous. Often tobacco appears; other additives are listed by Schultes and Hofmann:

> *Malouetia tamaquarina* and a species of *Tabermaemontana* of the Apocynaceae; the acanthaceous *Teliostachya lanceolata* var. *crispa* or Toé Negra; *Calathea veitchiana* of the Maranthaceae; the amaranthaceous *Alternanthera lehmannii* and a species of *Iresine*; several ferns including *Lygodium venustum* and *Lomariopsis japurensis; Phrygylanthus eugenioides* of the Mistletoe family; the mint *Ocimum micranthum*; a species of the sedge genus *Cyperus*; several cacti including species of *Opuntia* and *Epiphyllum*; and a member of the genus *Clusia* of the Guttiferae.

The main additives are *Psychotria carthaginensis, P. viridis, Tetrapterys methystica* and *Banisteriopsis rusbyana*. Leaves and stems of the last, known as *oco-yagé* or *chagrapanga*, don't contain the β-carboline alkaloids produced by *B. caapi* and *inebrians*; instead, they have a large amount of *N,N*-DMT, 5-methoxy-*N,N*-DMT, 5-hydroxy-*N,N*-DMT and *N*-β -methyltetrahydro-β -carboline. The other added species contain DMT-type compounds, rendered orally active by the harmala compounds in *ayahuasca*.

Syrian Rue

Harmala alkaloids (or β -carbolines) are manufactured by plants within at least eight botanical families. Except for the *Banisteriopsis* vines, only a small bushy shrub known as Syrian or Asian rue—*Peganum harmala*— is thought to have been used traditionally for psychoactive effects. Known from antiquity, this species belongs to the *Zygophyllaceae* family rather than to the *Malpighiaceae* family to which the *Banisteriopsis* species belong. Preferring desert habitats, it grows some three feet high, has leaves cut into long, narrow segments and produces small, white flowers.

Although Syrian rue was native only to Central Asia and Syria, it now grows wild along the Mediterranean coasts of Europe, Africa and the Middle East. It is esteemed from Asia Minor across to India and northeast Tibet. Its bitter, brown seeds contain β-carbolines identical to those in psychedelic *Banisteriopsis* vines and in about the same proportions.

Syrian rue has been employed in folk medicine as well as being used for dyes in Turkish and Persian rugs. Among Egyptians and a few other peoples, the dried seeds have long been associated with preparation of a love potion (despite the nauseating effects common to most harmala alkaloids). David Flattery has recently brought more attention to this shrub in a published Ph.D. dissertation entitled *Huoma*. He theorizes, almost entirely on linguistic grounds, that *P. harmala* was the "Huoma" or "Soma" of ancient Persia and India (see Chapter Nine for contrasting views).

Syrian rue is the only botanical source of harmala alkaloids other than
ayahuasca *that is known to have been used as a mild-alterer. It has
lately been linked to the "Drink of the Immortals" once known as "Soma."*

During the 1960s, harmala alkaloids were identified in a number of
plants, including tobacco. About 10 to 20 mcg. harman and norharman have
been detected in smoke from a single cigarette, or forty to a hundred times
that found in the tobacco leaf. (See *"Nicotiana* An Hallucinogen?" by Oscar
Janiger and Marlene Dobkin de Rios in the July-September 1976 *Economic
Botany* for a review of these studies.)

CHEMISTRY
Harmalas (β -Carbolines)
This compound-cluster exhibits an extra ring attached to its basic
indolic chemical structure. The resulting three-ring β-carboline system has
an unusually placed methoxy (CH_3O) group, "in marked contrast to the
orientation found in serotonin and the related tryptamines" (Shulgin).

By gentle oxidation, harmaline is converted into harmine, the other
main psychoactive constituent in the botanicals. Upon reduction, harmaline
yields *d*-1,2,3,4-tetrahydroharmine, a third but minor contributor.

Harmaline
(4,9-dihydro-7-methoxy-1-methyl-3H-pyrido-[3,4-b]-indole,
or 7-methoxy-1-methyl-3,4-dihydro- β-carboline)

Harmine   d-*1,2,3,4-Tetrahydroharmine*

Since these molecules have been isolated and synthesized, a number of other β-carboline alkaloids have been developed in the laboratory. Michael Valentine Smith describes the preparation of several analogues in his *Psychedelic Chemistry*. The 6- or 10-methoxy isomer of harmaline, sometimes known as 10-methoxy-harmalan, is about half again as potent by weight as harmaline.

Natural Harmalas in Humans

At least one harmala alkaloid is present in the pineal gland of both humans and several animals. This compound is more abundant in the pineal glands of highly advanced yogis, according to some reports, which has led to speculation that its presence may impart power to the "third eye" in mid-forehead, where the pineal gland lies.

Discussing harmaline's effectiveness in psychotherapy, Naranjo has written:

> I want to mention that this alkaloid is of special interest because of its close resemblance to substances derived from the pineal gland of mammals. In particular, 10-methoxy-harmaline, which may be obtained in vitro from the incubation of serotonin in pineal tissue, resembles harmaline in its subjective effects and is of greater activity than the latter. This suggests that harmaline (differing from 10-methoxy-harmaline only in the position of the methoxy group) may derive its activity from the mimicry of a metabolite normally involved in the control of states of consciousness.

At a 1977 conference in San Francisco, Bo Holmstedt, a pioneer in research on harmala alkaloids from the Karolinska Institutet in Sweden, suggested that similar substrates and enzymes are in the pineal gland for endogenous production of DMT, 5-methoxy-DMT and the N-methyl analogues of harmine and harmaline. Brimblecombe and Pinder, in their *Hallucinogenic Agents* (p. 116), discuss possible metabolism routes by which adrenoglomerulotropine and malatonin, normally present in the pineal body, may be turned into 6-methoxy-harmalan. So far, however, no evidence has conclusively shown that this conversion actually takes place in the human brain.

As with DMT, theories have again been advanced that schizophrenia is associated with increased production of harmala alkaloids. As Shulgin has remarked, consensus among researchers now is that this approach is "a red-herring."

Admixtures

Jeremy Bigwood found in the course of experimentation that DMT could be made orally active in doses of 100 mg. when combined with a sub-threshold dose of harmaline. Many reports from natives indicate that the addition of certain leaves (almost all containing DMT-like substances) makes the *yagé* visions "brighter." Investigators almost unanimously agree that significant potentiation occurs when β-carbolines and short-acting trypt-amines are mixed together.

Although β-carbolines are essential to the psychoactivity of *yagé*, the tryptamines are most important in producing the mental effects. The har-mala alkaloids enable DMT-like substances to become active and prod syner-gistic effects. Schultes and Hofmann, commenting on the expanded length and vividness of results when DMT-like compounds are included, indicate how important in terms of color the presence of monoamine oxidase inhib-itors can be: "Whereas visions with the basic drink are seen usually in blue, purple, or gray, those induced when the tryptaminic additives are used may be brightly colored in reds and yellows."

PHYSICAL EFFECTS

In the preparation of *yagé*, appropriate *Banisteriopsis* vines are gener-ally cut into 6- to 8-inch pieces. The bark is then pounded or shaved off and either soaked in cold water or boiled for hours, sometimes a full day, usually with one or more admixtures. Boiling produces a brown or reddish-brown concoction that's bitter and salty; boiled *ayahuasca* is said to cause nausea to a greater degree than the cold-water infusion. The usual course is to drink a couple of cupfuls, which produce an experience lasting three or four hours. Then, if desired, users drink more *yagé*.

Harmaline, when taken orally by itself, takes a comparatively long time to prompt psychological effects—often about two hours. Potions con-taining both DMT-like and harmala alkaloids, however, take effect rapidly. Spruce noticed responses from *yagé* within two minutes, an unusually quick onset from oral ingestion; others have observed initial effects taking hold within five minutes. Bigwood has contrasted the slow onset of harmaline alone against his *ayahuasca* experiences and his harmaline/DMT experiences:

the latter were "almost identical as far as the time course and visual effect—they both came on quite rapidly."

Purgative Aspects

Andrew Weil found that *yagé's* taste did not cause as much gagging as peyote. However, the nausea in his case was worse:

> Vomiting is the first stage of the effect of yagé. It is not fun, and I say that as someone who likes to vomit in certain circumstances. I held on to a tree and brought up a small quantity of intensely bitter liquid with wrenching spasms. Yagé tastes much worse on the way up than on the way down—so bad that it left me shuddering for a few seconds . . . .
>
> After a few minutes I had to answer another call of nature. The second action of yagé is to purge the intestine. The effect is spectacular and painless. When I went back in, Luis asked me if it had been "a good purge." I told him yes. Eventually, he and Jorge also made trips to the jungle.

At first, Weil could swallow only two cups of *yagé*, though he was encouraged to take more. Eventually he did get another one down. "Luis," he reported, "wanted me to drink more of his brew, but I could not." This element of the *yagé* experience has been treated prominently in accounts from other mind-explorers as well.

In some tribes, stringent dietary procedures are practiced for up to two weeks before ingestion of *ayahuasca*, although many natives use it weekly. Peruvians getting *yagé* from healers commonly abstain from salt, lard, sweets and sometimes sex a day before and a day after taking an infusion. Such procedures help to minimize nausea, but they certainly don't eliminate it. Weil was advised not to eat anything before noon; he hadn't eaten since breakfast the evening he received *yagé* from Luis.

Yagé concoctions are often referred to as a purge, and *ayahuasca* has gained a reputation as "the purgative vine." Harmaline and harmine by themselves also bring about violent diarrhea and vomiting in many users. Naranjo found that about half of his harmaline subjects felt nausea, which he attributed largely to "blocking attempts" to avoid a full psychedelic experience.

Other Physical Side-Effects

Nausea, purges and retching are closely associated with use of β-carbolines, but physical coordination is otherwise hardly impaired. In most accounts, it actually seems enhanced.

When Weil met him, Luis had been preparing *yagé* weekly for curing sessions over a long time, having first drunk it twenty-two years earlier. Weil described Luis as youthful for his age, a typical comment about *ayahuasqueros*, who have been noted for possessing much energy and unusually smooth skin. Weil records much physical movement on the part of this old man:

In the course of the evening Luis drank nine cups of the stuff. Each one sent him to the jungle for further purging, but his animated chanting continued without pause. With each cup he became more energetic. Finally, Jorge helped him into a heavy necklace of jaguar teeth and a fantastic headress of parrot feathers. Then, palm-leaf rattles in his hands, Luis began a stomping, turning dance around the house, all the while uttering the sounds of *yagé* . . . . Luis went out to vomit too but I could barely hear a break in his chanting . . . .

He would dance out the door and we would hear him chanting and singing off into the jungle, circling the house, disappearing into the night. Then he would burst through the doorway in an explosion of feathers and palm leaves, growling like a jaguar.

Aside from the vomiting that frequently accompanies every cupful of the drink, the body's main physical responses include slight increases in blood pressure and heart rate (unless *Daturas, Brugmansias* or other scopolamine-containing substances have been added, which make the *yagé* more dangerous). Some users feel a buzzing in the ears, pricking of the skin at the extremities, giddiness, profuse sweating or tremors. When Schultes first tried *yagé*, he had severe diarrhea the following day.

After taking large amounts of *yagé* natives often become frenzied, displaying agitation for ten or fifteen minutes. More generally, users exhibit lassitude and drowsiness and become withdrawn.

Harmaline is about twice as toxic as harmine in most lab animals; the half-lethal dose (half the animals die) of harmine in dogs and mice is about 200 mg./kg. of body weight. No human deaths have been reported from these compounds. Weil writes:

Luis gives *yagé* to anyone who wants it, to young and old, men and women, sick and well. He says it cannot hurt anyone, and though he gives it to pregnant women, young children and people with high fevers, no one suffers bad effects. Victor and he are both in good shape after taking enormous doses for years . . . . And many of the patients say they are helped. I talked with people in Mayoyoque who say that visits to Luis cured them of various ills.

Healing Qualities

Yagé is known as "the great medicine" in northwestern South America, where it is used for healing much like peyote. Through its assumed intercession with spiritual entities, *yagé* reveals the proper remedies or brings about healing spiritually or magically. In contrast to Western notions of medicine, *yagé* is believed to be curative whether the patient *or* the healer swallows it. "Nature cures the disease," someone said, summing up these processes, "while the healer amuses the patient." Others speak of *ayahuasqueros* "singing the illness away."

In *Visionary Vine*, Marlene Dobkin de Rios outlined many of the procedures used in "curing sessions." In *Wizard of the Upper Amazon*, Manuel Córdova-Rios gave another remarkable account: he continued to use *ayahuasca* medicinally when he returned to city life, seven years after his capture. "My cures," he comments, "for human ailments such as diabetes, hepatitis, leukemia, cancer, paralysis, rheumatism, epilepsy, suicidal depression and the dysfunctions of various internal organs have been called miraculous by some people."

MENTAL EFFECTS

Ayahuasca, yagé and harmala alkaloids prompt a wide range of experiences, which reflect dosage to a considerable degree and the influence of psychoactive additives. Descriptions vary from no psychoactive effects to effects rivaling those of LSD or psilocybin.

Dosage Considerations

Four or five half-foot pieces of bark from a medium-sized vine (an inch or two inches of thickness) are often provided per person in *yagé* brews. Estimates of dosages presented here are rough, being generally based on experiences in the field rather than in the laboratory.

Villalba reported in 1925 that he saw natives use about 20 cm. of the stem, which Hoffer and Osmond estimated as containing about 0.5 gm. of β-carboline alkaloids. "Under its influence," they wrote, "they jumped, screamed, and ran about wildly but continued to take it for days to maintain the state of excitation." They add that Villalba tried the concentrated liquid and had no reaction,

> whereupon he concluded that other white people who had seen visions of the future, of things lost, and visions of distances and illusions, were exaggerating the effect. It is not unusual for people who have not seen, to be sceptical of the claims of others who have.

Michael Valentine Smith suggests in *Psychedelic Chemistry* that harmaline and harmine are both active at about 200 mg. oral dosage. Jeremy Bigwood disputes this, saying that to get effective potentiation from the hydrochloride salts an adult should swallow at least 300 mg. harmaline or 500 mg. harmine. Shulgin puts the "effective dose range" of harmaline at 70 to 100 mg. intravenously or 300 to 400 mg. orally.

The pamphlet *Legal Highs*, published by *High Times* and Level Press, lists chemical houses that supply harmala alkaloids and states as its rough estimate that the equivalent of 100 mg. harmine is "50 mg harmaline, 35 mg tetrahydraharman, 25 mg harmolol or harmol, and 4 mg methoxyharmalan."

Yagé Visions and Their Stages

Shulgin comments that the sense most consistently affected by harmaline is the visual: "There can be vivid images generated, often in the form of meaningful dream-like sequences, and frequently containing subject matter such as wild animals and jungle scenes." Sometimes effects emerge as geometric patterns without much meaning; at other times visions with eyes closed have the character of mundane cartoonery.

A dark, quiet environment is generally preferrable. Pupil dilation is rare, but sharpened night vision is common, as Emboden observes:

> It has been demonstrated to the astonishment of foreigners that an Indian may run through a forest at night under the influence of the drug and not stumble or lose his footing. The vision is remarkably clear and the footing sure.

Ayahuasqueros describe long sequences of dream-like imagery; geometrical patterns; manifestations of spirit helpers, demons and deities; and tigers, birds and reptiles. They see dark-skinned men and women. They experience sensations of flying and of their own death; they see events at a great distance. Many users claim that these visions appear in a spiritually significant progression. Luis told Weil that the stages become increasingly complex with practice and greater dosages: "First come patterns, then plants, then animals, then fantastic architecture and cities. If you are fortunate, you see jaguars." Some claim that the ultimate experience is seeing into the eyes of the "veiled lady."

A few Americans who have experienced *yagé* in the Amazon concur with these views. One young woman, for example, said she "got only plants" until her fourth session. "Amazonian TV," as *yagé* ingestion has been termed, is usually described as beautiful; even the lower-level phantasmagoria is regarded as basically enjoyable. However, more significant experiences are possible. Heinz Kusel was told that the "aesthetic climax of the spectacle" was a vision of "the goddess with concealed eyes (*la diosa con los ojos vendados*), who dwelt inside the twining tropical vine." The first two times he tried *ayahuasca*, Kusel was disappointed. The third time he wasn't:

> The color scheme became a harmony of dark browns and greens. Naked dancers appeared turning slowly in spiral movements. Spots of brassy lights played on their bodies which gave them the texture of polished stones. Their faces were inclined and hidden in deep shadows. Their coming into existence in the center of the vision coincided with the rhythm of Nolorbe's song, and they advanced forward and to the sides, turning slowly. I longed to see their faces. At last the whole field of vision was taken up by a single dancer with inclined face covered by a raised arm. As my desire to see the face became unendurable, it appeared suddenly in full close-up with closed eyes. I know that when the extraordinary face opened them, I experienced a satisfaction of a kind I had never known.

Specificity of Yagé *Visions*

The harmala alkaloids, with and without accompanying DMT-like compounds, have fascinated psychologists and others because of the unusually wide incidence of particular images. Outstanding in this regard are visions of tigers, snakes and naked women (often Negro); the color blue seems to predominate when *ayahuasca* is taken without additives. Although this imagery is not universal, it is common—sometimes frightening—and is closely aligned to the archetypal symbolism that so fascinated Carl Jung. When Naranjo gave harmaline and harmine in psychotherapeutic situations to city dwellers (people who had never been in the jungle), he observed that much of the imagery that was aroused had to do with snakes, panthers, jaguars and other large felines. The recurrence of such images led him to speculate about the action of harmaline on "the collective unconscious."

The anthropologist Michael Harner is one of those claiming to have seen what the Indians are talking about, after having doubted throughout his year of study among the Jivaros of the Ecuadorian Amazon. Four years later, in 1961, he returned and was "turned on" to *yagé* by another tribe. Marlene Dobkin de Rios recounts his experience:

> For several hours after drinking the brew, Harner found himself, although awake, in a world literally beyond his wildest dreams. He met bird-headed people as well as dragon-like creatures who explained that they were the true gods of this world. He enlisted the services of other spirit helpers in attempting to fly through the far reaches of the Galaxy. He found himself transported into a trance where the supernatural seemed natural and realized that anthropologists, including himself, had profoundly underestimated the importance of the drug in affecting native ideology . . . .

Michael Harner and Claudio Naranjo made much of the "constancy" of both *yagé* and harmaline visions in separate essays in *Hallucinogens and Shamanism*. An essentially similar case has been put forth in Furst's *Flesh of the Gods*, where Gerardo Reichel-Dolmatoff writes of the Tukano Indians of the western Amazon region of Colombia. These were the aboriginals Spruce first observed using *yagé*. Koch-Grünberg described their *yagé* practices again half a century later:

> According to what the Indians tell me, everything appears to be larger and more beautiful than it is in reality. The house appears immense and splendrous. A host of people is seen, especially women. The erotic appears to play a major role in this intoxication. Huge multicolored snakes wind themselves around the house posts. All colors are very brilliant . . . .

The Tukanos still live in relative isolation. What caught the eye of Reichel-Dolmatoff was their use of representational paintings on house fronts, rattles and bark loincloths. The natives claimed that these designs were observed during *yagé* inebriation. During 1966-1967 a number of adult males who frequently partook of this brew were offered sheets of paper and a choice of twelve colored pencils. "The men showed great interest in and concentration on this task and spent from one to two hours finishing each drawing."

The colors they selected spontaneously "were exclusively red, yellow, and blue, on very few occasions adding a shade of hazel brown." Certain design elements were regularly repeated. Here's Reichel-Dolmatoff's listing of the Top Twenty:

1. Male organ
2. Female organ
3. Fertilized uterus
4. Uterus as passage
5. Drops of semen
6. Anaconda-canoe
7. Phratry
8. Group of phratries

9. Line of descent
10. Incest
11. Exogamy
12. Box of ornaments
13. Milky Way
14. Rainbow

15. Sun
16. Vegetal growth
17. Thought
18. Stool
19. Rattles
20. Cigar holder

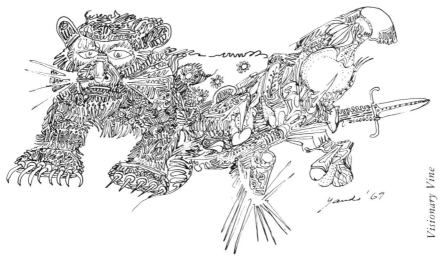

Visionary Vine

A visionary drawing by the Peruvian artist Yando, depicting a feline archetype often attributed to yagé.

"Garden of Eden" and other imagery is more specific to *yagé* than any image pattern is to LSD, mescaline or psilocybin. The near-universality of many *yagé* images suggests that the β-carbolines are a good deal closer than other psychedelics to being a "pure element" in a Periodical Table of Consciousness. These β-carbolines, however, cannot be entirely "pure," as they are accompanied by many negative side-effects.

Auditory Component

Ingestion of *yagé* often results in an enhancement of auditory acuity. To minimize distractions, urban users generally gather in the jungle at night, from about 8:00 p.m. to 2:00 a.m. rather than in someone's home. In *Wizard of the Upper Amazon,* Manuel Córdova-Rios described his frequent *aya-huasca* visions but also stressed the improvement in his sense of hearing, which enlarged his understanding of jungle ways.

As with peyote, *Banisteriopsis* vines are known for "announcing" themselves. Kusel writes:

Once a Campa Indian in my boat, when we were drifting far from shore, was "called" by *ayahuasca*, followed the "call," and later emerged from the forest with a sampling of the fairly rare liana that today is cultivated by the ayahuasquero in secret spots. I myself certainly did not hear the call.

More typically, β-carbolines—like β-phenethlamines and psilocybian molecules—seem to inspire chants and singing. Here are comments from Weil about the two times he took *yagé* with Luis:

From time to time he would pick up a harmonica and turn into a one-man band. He would dance out the door and we would hear him chanting and singing off into the jungle . . . .

Victor and Luis sang and danced all night, periodically going out into the jungle to sing under the trees, then returning to the candle-lit house. Victor congratulated Luis on having made a really strong batch.

Weil's *High Times* article is subtitled "The Vine That Speaks." He substantiates the title in this way:

A yagero's chant is his most precious possession. It comes to him in dreams and stays with him all his life. Until a man receives his chant from the spirit of the vine, he cannot conduct ceremonies. Luis's chant was strangely hypnotic, a mixture of sounds, tunes and words. There were Spanish words, Ingano words and words of a sort I had never heard before. I asked him what one particular word meant. "It is yagé speaking," he answered. "It doesn't mean; it is yagé speaking."

After Córdova-Rios became familiar with *ayahuasca*, he discovered that he could "direct," or at least greatly influence, resulting visions by songs and chants. This technique has been much used by native *curanderos*. Among some tribes, it is even said that "without singing, only visions of snakes appear."

Telepathic Element

Extrasensory perception is fairly prominent in the use of most psychedelics. *Banisteriopsis* vines, throughout their history, have had an unusually high incidence of such effects, as reflected in the name given the first alkaloid isolated ("telepathine"). The reports persist, despite the skepticism of many investigators. Schultes and Hofmann dismiss these claims as "unfounded" in their *Botany and Chemistry of Hallucinogens* (1973). In the *Journal of Psychoactive* [previously *Psychedelic*] *Drugs*, William Burroughs expressed reservations about *yagé* having any exceptional telepathic properties:

medicine men use it to potentiate their powers, to locate lost objects and that kind of thing. But I'm not impressed much by their performance. Everybody has telepathic experiences all the time. These things are not rare. It's just an integral part of life. The faculty is probably increased to some extent by any consciousness-expanding drug.

Flying and long-distance perceptions seem to be characteristic of the telepathic element. Villavicencio, in the first published report about *yagé* use, wrote, "As for myself, I can say for a fact that when I've taken *ayahuasca* I've experienced dizziness, then an aerial journey in which I recall perceiving the most gorgeous views, great cities, lofty towers, beautiful parks, and other extremely attractive objects." Many natives claim not only to see but to travel great distances under the influence of *yagé*, like users of peyote and San Pedro. "Though he had been no farther from his home than Mayoyoque," writes Weil, "Luis says that under yagé he has left his body and visited distant towns and cities, including Florencia and Bogotá."

Writing of *Banisteriopsis caapi* practices observed among the Cashinahua of Peru, the anthropologist Kenneth Kensinger reported that "informants have described hallucinations about places far removed, both geographically and from their own experience." Several,

> who have never been to or seen pictures of Pucallpa, the large town at the Ucayali River terminus of the Central Highway, have described their visits under the influence of *ayahuasca* to the town with sufficient detail for me to be able to recognize specific shops and sights.

Citing an even more convincing instance, Kensinger adds: "On the day following one *ayahuasca* party six of nine men informed me of seeing the death of my *chai*, 'my mother's father.' This occurred two days before I was informed by radio of his death." A similar experience was reported by Manuel Córdova-Rios. After the most intense effects he'd ever had on *yagé*— he had seen his mother dying—he returned to the home of his youth. There he learned that she had died as he had "seen" it at just that time.

Sexual Component

The previous edition of this book mentioned (a) the recurring motif of naked women in *yagé* visions, (b) flagellation in rites-of-passage ceremonies, (c) increased sexual activity in mice given harmala alkaloids and (d) Near Eastern use of Syrian rue as an aphrodisiac. Jeremy Bigwood took exception:

> I'd suggest that you try *active doses* of these alkaloids and attempt sex before writing this section. Or take it from me, harmine, harmaline, *ayahuasca*, DMT/harmaline, etc. are anaphrodisiacs.

The sexual component is thus an ambiguous question at present. Schultes and Hofmann, while disputing claims of extrasensory perception, discuss erotic usage of both *yagé* and Syrian rue in their many writings. Naranjo was impressed by the archtypal sexual imagery evoked by harmaline. Here are additional comments from William Emboden:

> In addition to acting upon the central nervous system, harmine and the related harmaline and harmalol have produced sexual responses in rats under laboratory conditions. Five milligrams of harmine alone produces measurable

sexual activity. This is doubtless one of the reasons why ayahuasca is used in coming of age ceremonies which sometimes involve flagellation and may be heavy in sexual content. Marlene [Dobkin] Rios, who has worked among the Peruvian Amazon tribes, mentioned in her extensive writings on the various uses of ayahuasca that one of the reasons for using the drug is "for pleasurable or aphrodisiacal effects." This was observed earlier by Wiffen in 1915 and Reinburg in 1921. Such phenomena, if not completely ignored, are usually dispatched to an obscure anthropological journal or only obliquely noted. The psychoerotic effects of ayahuasca are well worth more careful documentation and attention.

Psychotherapeutic Potential

In Chapter Nine of *Visionary Vine*, Marlene Dobkin de Rios says that many of the patients at jungle *ayahuasca* sessions go (in the language of Western medicine) "for psychiatric help." She calls "drug healing in the Peruvian jungle .... a very old and honored tradition of dealing with psychological problems that predates Freudian analysis by centuries." Much of the treatment she enumerates is nonverbal. In some places, natives refer to *Banisteriopsis* as "the vine of death"—meaning that it causes one to "die," and then be "born anew."

Some seven years after William Burroughs went out looking for *yagé* (on his first buy he got twenty pounds of it), Allen Ginsberg followed his path to South America. Ginsberg soon had a number of *yagé* sessions. One produced the feeling that he was all covered with snakes; later he felt "like a snake vomiting out the universe." Ginsberg soon learned what was meant by "vine of death." He wrote, "the whole fucking Cosmos broke loose around me, I think the strongest and worst I've ever had." He had fears that he might lose his mind. An epilogue, written by Ginsberg in 1963, puts the experience in perspective:

> Self deciphers this correspondence thus: the vision of ministering angels my fellow man and woman first wholly glimpsed while the Curandero gently crooned human in Ayahuasca trance-state 1960 was prophetic of transfiguration of self consciousness from homeless mind sensation of eternal fright to incarnate body feeling present bliss now actualized 1963.

Transforming experiences interested Naranjo when he gave out harmaline. More than other psychedelics, he found this one to be nonverbal, with mechanisms of psycho-interaction much less clear. Yet—

> Of the group of thirty subjects who were our volunteers, fifteen experienced some therapeutic benefit from their harmaline session, and ten showed remarkable improvement or symptomatic change comparable only to that which might be expected from intensive psychotherapy.

Naranjo summed up the quality of harmaline-aided psychotherapy in this way:

For one sharing the Jungian point of view, it would be natural to think of the artificial elicitation of archetypal experience as something that could facilitate personality integration, and therefore psychological healing. Yet the observation of the psychotherapeutic results of the harmaline experience was not the outcome of any deliberate attempt to test the Jungian hypothesis. These results came as a dramatic surprise . . . even before the recurrence of images became apparent . . . .

It would be hard to offer a simple explanation for the instances of improvement brought about by the harmaline experience. Such improvement usually occurred spontaneously, without necessarily entailing insight into the particulars of the patient's life and conflicts. As in all cases of successful deep therapy, it did involve greater acceptance by the patients of their feelings and impulses and a sense of proximity to their self. Statements like these, however, are not very explicit, and only case histories can adequately illustrate . . . .

The more successful experiences with harmaline have a characteristic spontaneity, and these pose little problem to the therapist. In contrast to experiences of self-exploration at the interpersonal level, it is probably in the nature of an archetypal experience to develop naturally from within, so that the most a person's ego can do is stand by watchfully. Yet such experiences of easy and spontaneous unfoldment of images and psychological events occur only in about every other person, so that it is the business of the psychotherapist to induce them when they will not naturally occur . . . .

Naranjo brought up the issue of intervention because he sees this as a "permanent dilemma in the guidance of harmaline sessions: the balance between stimulation and non-interference." He explains:

Little intervention may well leave a patient to his own inertia and result in an unproductive session; on the other hand, uncalled-for intervention may disrupt the organic development which is characteristic of the more successful harmaline experiences. As a consequence, more tact is needed in conducting these sessions than any other . . . .

Apart from Naranjo's *The Healing Journey*, little has been published about the psychiatric use of harmala alkaloids. Lewin tried harmaline clinically on mental patients in the late 1920s; he wrote a monograph about *Banisteriopsis caapi* as he lay dying. There was no further study until 1957, when Pennes and Hoch gave harmine to hospitalized subjects, mostly schizophrenic. Their results presented in the *American Journal of Psychiatry* indicated that harmaline acted like LSD or mescaline, though the mental effects seemed more clouded. (Hoffer and Osmond describe and criticize this work on pages 476-477 of *The Hallucinogens*.)

While profiling harmaline for the *Journal of Psychedelic Drugs*, Shulgin made an intriguing remark: in psychotherapeutic studies, he wrote, it "has often been used in conjunction with other psychedelic drugs (e.g., MDA, LSD, and mescaline) in which the effects of the latter appear greatly prolonged, and qualitatively modified." He did not elaborate.

FORMS AND PREPARATIONS

Once *Banisteriopsis caapi* and *B. inebrians* take root, they are quite hardy and can attain great heights. Frequently cultivated in South America, they have been grown only rarely in U.S. greenhouses. After the vine has been cut into half-foot to eight-inch pieces, it is pounded to break open the bark, or the bark is scraped off. The bark is then put in water to soak or it is simmered for up to twenty-four hours. When it is boiled, the bark has a light chocolate or reddish color with a slight greenish tinge. Villalba noted in

An ayahuasca *healing session in a jungle clearing.*

1925 that standing *yagé* changed "to a topaz color with a bluish green fluorescence." After six or seven experiences of the cold water infusion, as prepared in the Colombian Amazon, Schultes judged the effects as differing little

> from those from the boiled concoction used in the Putumayo. The intoxication is longer in setting in, and much more of the drink must be taken, but the symptoms of the intoxication and their intensity seem to me to be very similar.

These vines have now become relatively rare in their native jungle growing area, so genuine *yagé* is rarely seen. (Several people who have searched for it report that a decent *ayahuasquero* is hard to find these days; many have given in to "alcohol abuse.")

Harmaline and harmine are both crystalline, the first appearing as yellow and the second as green hydrochloride salts. According to Hoffer and Osmond, both form these salts

> with one equivalent of acid. Harmine crystallizes in needles, melting point 256-257° C., harmaline in platelets, melting point 238° C. Harmine is slightly soluble in water, alcohol, chloroform, and ether. Its hydrochloride salt is freely soluble in hot water. Harmaline is slightly soluble in hot alcohol and dilute acids, and forms blue fluorescent solutions.

Still legal in the U.S., both are currently available at a few chemical supply house at about $5-$10 per dose. If orders are large, however, it is likely that the Drug Enforcement Agency will take an interest.

De l'iboga et de l'ibogaine

This botanical drawing of Tabernanthe iboga, *the major source of ibogaine and related alkaloids, was made in 1901 by Albert Landrin.*

CHAPTER EIGHT
Iboga *and Ibogaine*

Figures and faces materialized from the depths, moving effortlessly on unseen currents. Each was unique, each appeared at a different point in my visual sphere, moved toward me, and attained a peak of aesthetic perfection just as it confronted me from the tiniest distance away. Then it dissolved into light as another, equally beautiful, came into being elsewhere. They were a people suspended in time, adrift in a mind-warp through which I could not reach but clearly saw, for when I stared into the forest, the visionary faces were superimposed on whatever I looked at, and when I withdrew within by closing my eyes, my brain-space became a theater of many dimensions in which my phantom tribe appeared, peered, and passed in wondrous procession.

—Walter Anirman

HISTORY

Ibogaine, the most studied of the alkaloids present in the roots of *Tabernanthe iboga*, is representative of another cluster of indolic molecules that have been included among psychedelics. Ibogaine is a naturally occurring compound of special interest because it comes from an entirely different botanical family than anything discussed above—a contribution to the mystery of psychedelics from equatorial Africa.

Early Reports and Synthesis of Ibogaine

Some commentators credit wild bores with inspiring the practice of ingesting bark from the roots of the "iboga," "éboga," "boga," "libuga," "bocca," "ébogé," "léboga" or "lébuga." After digging up and eating roots of the shrub, boars go into a frenzy and jump around wildly, according to natives. Similar reports have been made about porcupines and gorillas.

The earliest known record of *T. iboga* dates from 1864, when Griffon du Bellay brought specimens to Europe. He stated that when the yellowish root of this plant is eaten,

> it is not toxic except in high doses in the fresh state. In small quantities, it is an aphrodisiac and a stimulant of the nervous system; warriors and hunters use it constantly to keep themselves awake during night watches.

By the 1880s, use of shavings from the root of *iboga* was known to be quite widespread in Gabon and adjacent parts of the Congo. Natives used it during lion hunts to remain awake and alert for up to two days while waiting for the cats to cross their path. According to some residents of Gabon, colonial Germans permitted and possibly encouraged use of *iboga* to suppress fatigue among workers on such projects as the Douala-Yaounde railroad. In 1889 came the first botanical description.

In 1901, Dybowski and Landrin extracted the major alkaloid in the root bark, which they named ibogaine; they found it to be almost as psychoactive in isolation as the entire root. French and Belgian investigators then undertook a flurry of chemical and botanical studies, concluding that it was a stimulant for the central nervous system. M.C. Phisalex suggested that ibogaine contained psychoactivating qualities. Psychoactivity, though evident from native accounts, was not, however, followed up by Western scientists until the mid-1950s. The earliest written report indicating consciousness-changing effects came in 1903 from J. Guien, who commented on the experience of an initiate in a Congo cult:

> Soon all his sinews stretch out in an extraordinary fashion. An epileptic madness seizes him, during which, unconscious, he mouths words, which when heard by the initiated ones, have a prophetic meaning and prove that the fetish has entered him.

Recent Usage

In 1966, Büchi, Coffen, Kocsis, Sonnet and Ziegler published a "total synthesis of iboga alkaloids" (*Journal of the American Chemical Society*, 88: 3099-3109). In 1969, Harrison Pope, Jr. summarized the findings in scores of studies on *Tabernanthe iboga* (pp. 174-184 in the April-June *Economic Botany*). These papers, coming at a time of great interest in psychedelics, stimulated renewed examination of this compound-cluster.

Iboga, like peyote, has become politically significant through its use for religious purposes. Bwiti (male) and Mbiri (female) *iboga*-using groups have apparently unified once-warring tribes in the Congo and Gabon in resistance to Christian and Moslem missionaries. The cults, which have been growing, conduct their ceremonies mainly at night amidst dancing and drumming. As with *yagé*, *iboga* root scrapings are employed to evoke communication with deceased ancestors.

Outside of Africa, very few people have had access to the botanical source or to synthesized ibogaine. People who have tried them have often been impressed; a few have not, considering this cluster merely composed of stimulants like amphetamine. PharmChem has regularly analyzed a small number of genuine samples.

Psychotherapeutic efficacy has been investigated by Claudio Naranjo and described in *The Healing Journey*. He comments on forty sessions he conducted with thirty patients using "either ibogaine or total iboga extract."

Naranjo also discusses ten sessions with a different group of people using *iboga* extracts in conjunction with amphetamine, plus fifty treatments "which I have either witnessed or known indirectly."

BOTANY

The *Tabernanthe iboga* bush, growing to about five feet high, is common in the equatorial underforests in the western part of Africa. It is one of at least seven species of this genus—two of which are known to have been used as mind-alterers (the other is *T. manii*). One of the mysteries about *Tabernanthe*, says Schultes and Hofmann, "is why the Apocynaceae, probably the family richest in alkaloids, should be so sparingly represented in the list of species valued and utilized for their psychotomimetic properties." They suggest that there are

> undoubtably sundry species in this family possessing organic constituents capable of inducing visual or other hallucinations, but either they have not been discovered by aborigines or they are too toxic for human consumption.

Iboga is frequently cultivated in villages of Gabon as a decorative shrub, producing a yellowish- or pinkish-white flower. This flower often grows from the same point with pairs of leaves and branches. The plant yields a small, oval, yellowish-orange fruit—about the size of an olive with an edible sweet pulp—which doesn't contain ibogaine but has sometimes been used as a medicine "for barrenness in women."

The stems, which are said to have a vile odor, contain small amounts of ibogaine and related alkaloids along with large amounts of latex. Roots similar to those of *Rauwolfia* form from a bulbous mass, which can grow to about four inches across. Individual roots branch off from this mass in all directions and may extend as far as 32 inches. The bark from the roots, especially the smaller ones, is preferred by the natives. It is yellowish-brown in its fresh state and turns gray when dried. Alkaloids constitute up to 2.5 percent of the roots and may constitute more than 6 percent of the root bark.

CHEMISTRY

Ibogaine was isolated in 1901 from *Tabernanthe iboga* roots by Dybowski and Landrin and by Haller and Heckel. The most abundant alkaloid in the shrub's root bark, ibogaine exhibts the indole nucleus structure common to most psychedelics. Its stereochemistry (the dotted lines are at angles to the rest of the molecule) was established in the late 1960s:

Ibogaine

Starting in 1942, a number of chemical studies were made of other *iboga* alkaloids, mainly by the French. At least twelve such alkaloids are known; they appear in about the same proportion in both *T. iboga* and *T. manii.* They are all similar in structure to ibogaine. The most important are tabernanthine, ibogamine, coronaridine, voacangine, isovacangine and conopharyngine. Their structures are described in *The Hallucinogens.*

The only study so far on the effects of ibogaine homologues in humans was done by P.B. Schmidt, who in 1967 reported on doses of 0.1 to 1.2 mg./kg. of ibogaine hydrochloride administered orally to twelve subjects. It produced states of inebriation and mild sedation with minor psychic changes. The dosage used by Schmidt may have been insufficient. Chemical references, mainly in French, are listed at the end of Pope's paper in *Economic Botany* (April-June 1969).

PHYSICAL EFFECTS

Moderate doses of ibogaine or *iboga* root bark are stimulating (much like amphetamine) and act as a choline-esterase inhibitor, causing some hypotension and stimulation of digestion and appetite. As with harmala alkaloids, there is no pupil dilation. In larger amounts, these compounds induce nausea and vomiting and put users into a trance where little physical activity is possible. In excessive amounts, *iboga* ingestion has led to convulsions, paralysis and even death brought on by arrest of respiration.

On a number of occasions, leaders of the Bwiti cult have been brought before courts on charges of murder. An instance occurred in November 1950 when it was alleged that they had administered large amounts of *T. iboga* to a young boy for purposes of acquiring a cadaver (there also being the question of panther whiskers mixed in). James Fernandez reports in *Flesh of the Gods* that most such cases of suspected murder involve "women or young people of small body size."

Native *iboga* cults generally use two or three teaspoons for women and three to five for men of the dried, powdered root bark. At this dosage the results are not primarily mental but do excite a substantial activation of motor response, which considerably assists drumming and dancing. Users often feel light, almost as if they are walking above the ground. Naranjo found that a third of his subjects administered ibogaine felt a desire to move or dance during their sessions.

As much as a third to a full kilogram of the root bark has been ingested in some initiation ceremonies. In order to enter the Bwiti cult, an initiate has to see Bwiti, a vision which can only be attained by eating sufficient quantities of *iboga.* The practice has been to start early in the morning, with the root bark being eaten throughout the day "to break open the head" and establish communication with Bwiti and ancestors. The visionary state is usually achieved in the evening, when all members of the Bwiti cult join in a ritual dance. Some candidates almost pass out during the many hours of visions.

Some sleep for several days once the effects have ended, but ordinarily users feel little in the way of after-effects.

The Bwiti cult is fairly puritanical and thus regards manifestations of aphrodisiacal effects as antithetical to the religious purpose of *iboga*. Earlier reports emphasized this component of the experience. According to Adam Gottlieb in his *Encyclopedia of Sex Drugs and Aphrodisiacs*: "It is also used as an aphrodisiac and cure for impotence. Its efficacy as a sex drug is borne out by my personal experience and that of others."

Animal studies with ibogaine have been extensive. When many species are given large amounts, they appear to be frightened and act as though they are hallucinating. Hoffer and Osmond have summarized much of this work in *The Hallucinogens* (pp. 469-470).

In 1905, a Dr. Huchard used doses of 10 to 30 mg. of ibogaine in treating influenza, neuresthenia and depression, and some cardiac disorders. He found that the results were improved appetites, muscle tone and generally improved rates of recovery—along with mild euphoria.

MENTAL EFFECTS

Native Accounts

James Fernandez, writing about *iboga* in Furst's *Flesh of the Gods*, drew on accounts from some sixty users, most of whom spoke of the experience as a journey. As Bwiti initiates, they communed with ancestors, who mostly appeared white (a color identified by natives with the dead). A feeling of levitation is common; rainbow-like halos are taken as a sign that one is beginning to approach the land of one's ancestors and gods.

Fernandez noted similarities in visionary elements: typically, one first saw a crowd of black men who have not eaten *eboka* and were unable to pass to the beyond; then one was met by a relative who is white and guides the user over rivers and other obstacles, traveling on "a journey down a long road that eventually leads to great powers." Often the user meets other ancestors in order of descent, going further and further back in lineage. Sometimes the journey ends in the middle of a rainbow. Time perception was often lengthened, so initiates felt that they had been traveling in the spirit world for several days.

Here is the report from Ndong Asseko, age twenty-two, unmarried and a member of the Essabam clan:

> when I ate *eboka* I found myself taken by it up a long road in a deep forest until I came to a barrier of black iron. At that barrier, unable to pass, I saw a crowd of black persons also unable to pass. In the distance beyond the barrier it was very bright. I could see many colors in the air but the crowd of black people could not pass. Suddenly my father descended from above in the form of a bird. He gave to me then my *eboka* name, Onwan Misengue, and enabled me to fly up after him over the barrier of iron. As we proceeded the bird who was my father changed from black to white—first his tail feathers, then all his

Flesh of the Gods

Toward the end of her initiation and under the influence of a full dose of eboka (Tabernanthe iboga), *an initiate stares intently out of the chapel, waiting for her ancestors to "arrive." Because white is the color of the ancestors, she has been painted all over with* kaolin. *Behind her sits the* nyia-eboka, *her "mother of eboka," who gives her encouragement.*

plumage. We came then to a river the color of blood in the midst of which was a great snake of three colors—blue, black, and red. It closed its gaping mouth so that we were able to pass over it. On the other side there was a crowd of people all in white. We passed through them and they shouted at us words of recognition until we arrived at another river—all white. This we crossed by means of a giant chain of gold. On the other side there were no trees but only a grassy upland. On the top of the hill was a round house made entirely of glass and built upon one post only. Within I saw a man, the hair on his head piled up in the form of a Bishop's hat. He had a star on his breast but on coming closer I saw that it was his heart in his chest beating. We moved around him and on the back of his neck there was a red cross tattooed. He had a long beard. Just then I looked up and saw a woman in the moon—a bayonet was piercing her heart from which a bright white fire was pouring forth. Then I felt a pain on my shoulder. My father told me to return to earth. I had gone far enough. If I went further I would not return.

The aim of the experience is for members to achieve a state of "one-heartedness" *(nlem mvore)* in the early hours of the morning, when the spirits of the initiates and ancestors have mingled. Afterwards, there is a large communal meal.

Modern American Experiences

Only a few people in the U.S. drug subculture have tried ibogaine. But as Walter Anirman, author of *Sky Cloud Mountain*, indicates in his first description of two such trips—the other appears in a chapter entitled "The Lady Iboga"—the results are similar to accounts from Africa:

> I expected to do very little moving later, since I knew from experience that Iboga would thoroughly discoordinate my body, and, indeed, the first effects of the drug were nausea and dizziness. By the time these were intense, I was . . . breathing rapidly, and trying to sit up on the mat; but my legs and head became unbearably heavy and my stomach sagged with pain. . . . Behind the discomfort of my body, however, I was getting the first of Iboga's exuberant hallucinations. My perceptual space melted to a crystalline liquid where shapes shimmered like stains and vivid, piercing sensations pulsed through as pictures from another dimension. I became a continuum of experience in a galactic swirl whose energy first nullified the pain in my body, then penetrated deeper and dissolved my body as well.
>
> Consciousness awoke to its electromagnetic matrix and bedazzled me with lights. My head prismed with colors that resolved themselves into eidetic, omnisensual scenes of long forgotten times. I was ten years old again and running down the railroad tracks near home, off with my boyhood companions into another day of adventures. The tracks became silver cords weaving a Turk's head knot around me, then straightened and became the implacable bars of a crib where I—a diapered baby—howled to be free. The colors turned red, crimson, scarlet, purple; became bright liquids flowing as blood in my sentient tubeways, oozing nourishment through flesh, pulsing with a million aspects of life.
>
> Occasionally, the visionary onslaught would ease for a moment, and I would awaken to my body crumpled on a blanket in a magically unfocusable forest. I managed to sit up several times, hoping to channel the energy more directly along my spine, but could never hold it, and fell over. No sooner was I down than I was off once more, foraging through luxurious strata of psyche, meeting myself in mirrors of mind, abbreviating time to dally with images of yesterday as real in recall as they had been in reality. It was an unending parade, a continuous, extravagant creation, but the flow brooked no impediment. Nothing could be stopped; nothing held for the inquiring mind to examine. Like a volcano, I erupted and bubbled over with marvels, but nowhere could the lava be slowed . . . .

Anirman experienced a "recurring motif" in this "unending flow of encyclopedic images":

> . . . a series of very beautiful, visionary people grew from my mind and moved rhythmically through my seeing. They were lovely to look at. Their

bodies were exquisitely formed; their features highly refined. Dark eyes and black hair accentuated burnished skins, and they were strangely alive, though they appeared to be neither awake nor asleep . . . . Figures and faces materialized from the depths, moving effortlessly on unseen currents. Each was unique, each appeared at a different point in my visual sphere, moved toward me, and attained a peak of aesthetic perfection just as it confronted me from the tiniest distance away. Then it dissolved into light as another, equally beautiful, came into being elsewhere. They were a people suspended in time, adrift in a mind-warp through which I could not reach but clearly saw, for when I stared into the forest, the visionary faces were superimposed on whatever I looked at, and when I withdrew within by closing my eyes, my brain-space became a theater of many dimensions in which my phantom tribe appeared, peered, and passed in wondrous procession.

Naranjo's Psychotherapeutic Findings

In *The Healing Journey*, Claudio Naranjo describes his use of ibogaine in conjunction with psychotherapy. Although he doesn't specify dosages, he declares that archetypes are prominent in the visions and that actions in dreamlike sequences often involve destruction or sexuality. Ibogaine, he claims, elicits a "less purely visual-symbolic experience" than harmaline. He adds:

> With no drug have I witnessed such frequent explosions of rage as with this particular one . . . . With ibogaine, anger is not directed (I would say *transferred*, in the psychoanalytic sense) to the present situation, but, rather, to persons or situations in the patient's past, toward whom and by which it was originally aroused. This is in accord with the general tendency for the person under ibogaine to become concerned with childhood reminiscences and fantasies.

> The salience of animals, primitives, sexual themes, and aggression in ibogaine and harmaline experiences would justify regarding them as drugs that bring out the instinctual side of the psyche. This stressing of man-the-animal contrasts with the effects of the airy or ethereal "psychedelics" . . . .

> Aside from differences in the quality of the ibogaine experience, there are differences in content: a less purely archetypal content, more childhood imagery, and certain themes that appear to be specific to the mental states evoked by the alkaloid—notably fantasies of fountains, tubes, and marshy creatures . . . .

> There is a great difference between the domain of past experience to which MDA facilitates the access and that which is exposed by means of ibogaine. Whereas with the former it is a matter of *events* being remembered, and perhaps reactions or feelings in the face of such events, with ibogaine it is a world of fantasies that the person meets. Parental images evoked by means of ibogaine probably correspond to the child's conception of his parents, which still lies in the subconscious of the adult—but these do not necessarily match the parent's reality. The therapeutic process with ibogaine may be depicted as that of seeing such constructions for what they are and being freed through confrontation with them . . . .

FORMS AND PREPARATIONS

Tabernanthe iboga is grown mainly in Gabon and the Congo, although it can be cultivated in most tropical and semi-tropical areas. Little has been raised in the U.S. It has been propagated successfully in a few greenhouses, as in Berkeley, California.

Natives generally rasp off the root bark and then eat it as a dried powder. Sometimes the powder is mixed with water and drunk as a beverage. *Iboga* is said to be stronger in its fresh state. In a few places, it is taken with other plants, especially with *Alchornea floribunda* (also considered an aphrodisiac), or marijuana.

A small amount of ibogaine has been synthesized for the psychedelic subculture, but this is rare. It is proscribed in Schedule I of the 1970 drug legislation. Its illegal status and the difficult manufacturing process have led most psychedelic chemists to conclude, as Michael Valentine Smith suggests in *Psychedelic Chemistry*, that it isn't worth the trouble.

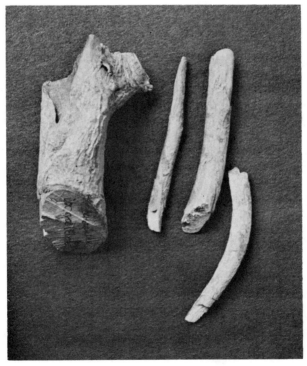

Jeremy Bigwood

Ibogaine and a dozen related alkaloids are found throughout the roots of Tabernanthe iboga, *but the greatest concentration is in the root's bark (up to 6 percent).*

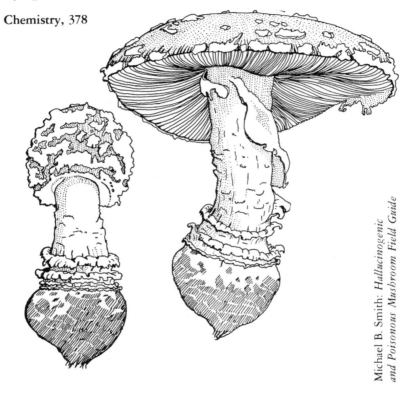

Michael B. Smith: *Hallucinogenic
and Poisonous Mushroom Field Guide*

The Fly Agaric mushroom (Amanita muscaria) *was the earliest fungi species recognized as having psychoactive potential. It was used by shamans in Siberia and in an area along the eastern part of the U.S.-Canadian border and may have inspired the world's earliest religious text, the* Rig-Veda. *Panther Caps* (Amanita pantherina) *contain psychoactive principles similar to those in Fly Agarics, which are drawn here about half natural size.*

CHAPTER NINE

Fly Agaric, Panther Caps and "Soma"

*What I noticed in these visions and what I passed through
are things that I would never imagine even in my thoughts. I can
only mention that from the period when I was first aware of the
notions of life, all that I had seen in front of me from my fifth or
sixth year, all objects and people that I knew as time went on,
and with whom I had some relations, all my games, occupations,
actions one following the other, day after day, year after year, in
one word the picture of my whole past became present in my
sight . . . . If someone can prove that both the effect and the
influence of the mushroom are non-existent and erroneous, then
I shall stop being defender of the miraculous mushroom of
Kamchatka.*

—Joseph Kopéc

HISTORY

"Soma" Identified as the Fly Agaric Mushroom

The earliest religious document is a collection of 1,028 hymns called
the *Rig-Veda*, written by Aryans who swept down into India from the North.
The first of their four *Vedas*, it dates back to at least the second millenium
B.C. and has been described as "the foundation of modern Hinduism." One
hundred and twenty of its verses are devoted to praise of a plant called
"Soma," which is characterized as being "rootless," "leafless," "blossomless"
and "from the mountains."

R. Gordon Wasson first became acquainted with the *Rig-Veda* in 1962.
He puzzled over the identification of "Soma," which had evaded scholars
even though more than a hundred candidates had been proposed. (Most of
the suggestions were ruled out by the passages describing it as "rootless,"
"leafless," etc.) Soon Wasson had a candidate:

> As I entered into the extraordinary world of the Rig-Veda, a suspicion grad-
> ually came over me, a suspicion that grew into a conviction: I recognised the
> plant that had enraptured the poets . . . . As I went on to the end, as I
> immersed myself ever deeper in the world of Vedic mythology, further evidence
> seeming to support my idea kept accumulating. By Jove, I said, this is familiar
> territory!

Wasson concluded that "Soma" was the bright red mushroom species known as the "Fly Agaric" (*Amanita muscaria*). This red mushroom speckled with white is familiar to most people from drawings accompanying fairy tales. It has a notorious history as an inebriating agent used by virtually all of the Siberian tribes—until Russian traders introduced vodka to these peoples in the eighteenth century. This mushroom has the peculiar quality of inebriating up to five people who drink the users' urine.

In a 1968 book entitled *SOMA: Divine Mushroom of Immortality*, Wasson explored the *Rig-Veda*'s evidence. His thesis, that "Soma" is Fly Agaric, has been accepted by many relevant authorities as convincing. Schultes and Hofmann remark that here is "an identification that satisfies all of the many interlocking pieces of direct and indirect evidence—including even a reference in the 'Rig-Veda' to ceremonial urine drinking." Since publication of *SOMA*, Wasson has presented additional, strengthening arguments in "Rejoinder to Professor Brough" (1972) and in "*SOMA* Brought Up-to-Date" (published in 1979 in both the *Journal of the American Oriental Society* and the *Harvard Botanical Museum Leaflet*).

These writings on "Soma" have been of great interest to many people in the drug subculture, many of whom have come to regard the mushroom as psychedelic.

Discovery of Long-Time Use of Fly Agaric in North America

In 1978, Wasson presented a "surprising new discovery" at a mushroom conference in San Francisco, where he and an associate discussed recent evidence that the Fly Agaric mushroom had been used extensively by Indian tribes around the Great Lakes and eastward. He also introduced a current practitioner—Keewaydinoquay, a lively Ojibway woman, then in her sixties, who has been ingesting these mushrooms three to five times a year since the age of fourteen. (See the *Journal of Psychedelic Drugs*, January-June 1979, for these proceedings.)

Ancient ceremonial use of mushrooms was being rediscovered again, the chief clue this time being a letter dated 1626 from a Jesuit in Quebec to his brother in France. The Jesuit described the Indian practices a full century before any published references to Siberian mushroom practices, declaring that "they assure you that after death they go to heaven where they eat mushrooms and hold intercourse with each other."

Fascinated for nearly a half century by Siberian use of *Amanita muscaria* mushrooms, Wasson compared Native American practices and concluded that shamanistic employment of Fly Agaric was "circumpolar in extent" and that the rituals were similar. The only important difference he found was in regard to the "reindeer symbolism" associated with these mushrooms in Siberia; in North America, there is no such symbolism because there are no such animals. Remarkable similarities in practices and beliefs had already been described by the Wassons in *Mushrooms, Russia and History* (1957):

Ray Rogers: *Blotter #3*

Keewaydinoquay, an Ojibway herbalist and university-trained ethno-botanist, first discussed her use of miskwedo *(Fly Agaric mushrooms) publicly in 1978. She had been taking them three to five times a year for more than half a century.*

With our Mexican experiences [with psilocybian mushrooms] fresh in mind, we reread what Jochelson and Bogoras had written about the Korjaks and the Chukchees. We discovered startling parallels between the use of the fly amanita (Amanita muscaria) in Siberia and the divine mushrooms in Middle America. In Mexico the mushroom "speaks" to the eater; in Siberia "the spirits of the mushrooms" speak. Just as in Mexico, Jochelson says that among the Korjaks "the agaric would tell every man, even if he were not a shaman, what ailed him when he was sick, or explain a dream to him, or show him the upper world or the underground world or foretell what would happen to him." Just as in Mexico on the following day those who have taken the mushrooms compare their experiences, so in Siberia, according to Jochelson, the Korjaks, "when the intoxication has passed, told whither the 'fly-agaric men' had taken them and what they had seen." In Bogoras we discover a link between the lightning bolt and the mushroom. According to a Chukchee myth, lightning is a One-Sided Man who drags his sister along by her foot. As she bumps along the floor of heaven, the noise of her bumping makes the thunder. Her urine is the rain, and she is possessed by the spirits of the fly amanita . . . .

Use of *Fly Agaric* in *Siberia*

The earliest report found by the Wassons about Siberian *Amanita muscaria* practices came from a Polish prisoner of war, who wrote in 1658 about the "Ob-Ugrian Ostyak of the Irtysh region" in western Siberia. Published in 1874, it says: "They eat certain fungi in the shape of fly-agarics, and thus they get drunk worse than on vodka, and for them that's the very best banquet."

The first published account of Fly Agaric appeared in 1730, the work of a Swedish colonel who spent twelve years as a prisoner in Siberia. He indicated that the Koryak tribe would buy a mushroom "called, in the Russian Tongue, Muchumor," from Russians in exchange for "Squirils, Fox, Hermin, Sable, and other Furs":

> Those who are rich among them lay up large Provisions of these Mushrooms, for the Winter. When they make a Feast, they pour Water upon some of these Mushrooms, and boil them. They then drink the Liquor, which intoxicates them . . . . Of this Liquor, they . . . drink so immoderately, that they will be quite intoxicated, or drunk with it.

The tribesmen in Siberia did not know about alcohol until after contact with the Russians. Johann Georgi, in a book on Russia published in German in St. Petersburg in 1776, remarked on the differences:

> 'Numbers of the Siberians have a way of intoxicating themselves by the use of mushrooms, especially the Ostyaks who dwell about Narym. To that end they either eat one of these mushrooms quite fresh, or perhaps drink the decoction of three of them. The effect shows itself immediately by sallies of wit and humour, which by slow degrees arises to such an extravagant height of gaiety, that they begin to sing, dance, jump about, and vociferate: they compose amorous sonnets, heroic verses, and hunting songs. This drunkenness has the peculiar quality of making them uncommonly strong; but no sooner is it over than they remember nothing that has passed. After twelve or sixteen hours of this enjoyment they fall asleep, and, on waking, find themselves very low-spirited from the extraordinary tension of the nerves: however, they feel much less head-ache after this method of intoxication than is produced by spiritous liquors; nor is the use of it followed by any dangerous consequences.

The earliest report from someone who had actually eaten a Fly Agaric mushroom appeared in 1837, in Polish. In 1796 or 1797, ill and running a fever, Joseph Kopéc was given a mushroom by an evangelist, who first told him:

> Before I give you the medicine I must tell you something important. You have lived for two years in Lower Kamchatka but you have known nothing of the treasures of this land. Here are mushrooms that are, I can say, miraculous. They grow only on a single high mountain close to the volcano and they are the most precious creations of nature.

Kopéc, wishing "to recover my health and above all to sleep," overcame his fears and ate half a mushroom. Almost immediately he went into a deep sleep, and dreams came one after the other:

I found myself as though magnetized by the most attractive gardens where only pleasure and beauty seemed to rule. Flowers of different colours and shapes and odours appeared before my eyes; a group of most beautiful women dressed in white going to and fro seemed to be occupied with the hospitality of this earthly paradise. As if pleased with my coming, they offered me different fruits, berries, and flowers. This delight lasted during my whole sleep, which was a couple of hours longer than my usual rest . . . .

As a result, Kopéc "started to have confidence" in the *Amanita muscaria's* "supernatural qualities (as my evangelist had taught me to do)." He took a second helping:

Having eaten this stronger dose, I fell soundly asleep in a few minutes. For several hours new visions carried me to another world, and it seemed to me that I was ordered to return to earth so that a priest could take my confession. This impression, although in sleep, was so strong that I awoke and asked for my evangelist. It was precisely at the hour of midnight and the priest, ever eager to render spiritual services, at once took his stole and heard my confession with a joy that he did not hide from me. About an hour after the confession I fell asleep anew and I did not wake up for twenty-four hours. It is difficult, almost impossible, to describe the visions I had in such a long sleep; and besides there are other reasons that make me reluctant to do so. What I noticed in these visions and what I passed through are things that I would never imagine even in my thoughts. I can only mention that from the period when I was first aware of the notions of life, all that I had seen in front of me from my fifth or sixth year, all objects and people that I knew as time went on, and with whom I had some relations, all my games, occupations, actions, one following the other, day after day, year after year, in one word the picture of my whole past became present in my sight. Concerning the future, different pictures followed each other which will not occupy a special place here since they are dreams. I should add only that as if inspired by magnetism I came across some blunders of my evangelist and I warned him to improve in those matters, and I noticed that he took these warnings almost as the voice of Revelation.

Toward the end Kopéc says, "If someone can prove that both the effect and the influence of the mushroom are non-existent and erroneous, than I shall stop being defender of the miraculous mushroom of Kamchatka."

In *SOMA* there are forty-two "exhibits," comprising 105 pages of reports by explorers, travelers and anthropologists on mushroom use in Siberia. Only two of these are from people who tried mushrooms, Kopéc's being one of them. The other says: "These mushrooms contain a very strong poison, and I can say from personal experience that it is highly intoxicating. The natives often use it to get drunk on when they have no alcohol." These remarks were published in Swedish in 1918.

Among the handful of sympathetic observers was Carl von Dittmar, who wrote about the Siberian practices in St. Petersburg in 1900:

Mukhomor eaters describe the narcosis as most beautiful and splendid. The most wonderful images, such as they never see in their lives otherwise, pass before their eyes and lull them into a state of the most intense enjoyment.

Among the numerous persons whom I myself have seen intoxicated in this way, I cannot remember a single one who was raving or wild. Outwardly the effect was always thoroughly calming—I might almost say, comforting. For the most part the people sit smiling and friendly, mumbling quietly to themselves, and all their movements are slow and cautious.

The two firsthand accounts and a few secondhand ones are about the only information on the effects of *Amanita muscaria* on Siberian natives, even though it grew plentifully in Koryak territory. During the off-season a reindeer would often be exchanged for just *one* of these mushrooms. When questioned, natives who had used *Amanita muscaria* said repeatedly and emphatically that they liked it better than alcohol. Alcohol seems to have supplanted use of this mushroom at present, or its use has gone underground.

BOTANY

Poisonous Amanitas

It should first be emphasized that the *Amanita muscaria* and the *Amanita pantherina* (or Panther Cap, a species containing the same psychoactive ingredients, usually in greater concentrations) belong to a genus that is estimated to cause 95 percent of all deaths resulting from mushroom poisoning. Three of their relatives—*A. virosa* (Destroying Angel), *A. verna* and

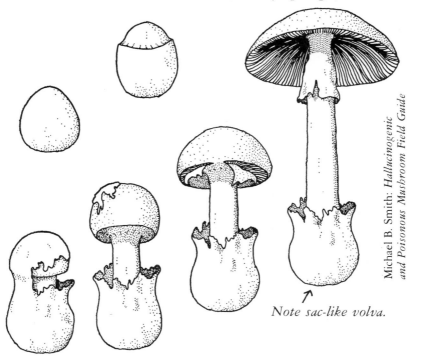

Michael B. Smith: *Hallucinogenic and Poisonous Mushroom Field Guide*

↑
Note sac-like volva.

Stages of development of an Amanita *mushroom.*

Amanita phalloides, *an extremely poisonous mushroom, popularly known as "Death Cap."*

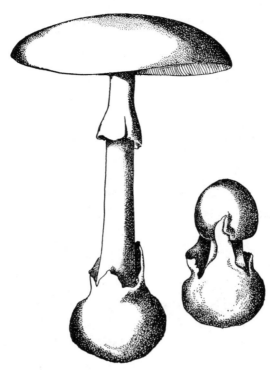

Amanita verna, *another extremely poisonous species.*

especially *A. phalloides* (Death Cap)—contain lethal substances. People usually do not feel these toxins until about two days after they have eaten the mushrooms, by which time pumping the stomach and other medical measures seldom prove effective. The toxins affect the liver and kidneys. Only lately has there been any success in counteracting the virulent poisons by use of dialysis machines and blood transfusions.

Because *Amanita muscaria* and *Amanita pantherina* are similar in appearance to their lethal relatives, it is recommended that one never eat any *Amanita* that is all white.

Fly Agaric and Panther Caps

Fly Agaric and Panther Caps will grow only in "mycorrhizal" relationship with just a few trees—the birch, larch, fir, pine and oak. A symbiotic association between the root cells of these trees (living or dead) and the fungus' mass of underground filaments is necessary if the mushroom is to sprout. "Where these trees are not," Wasson writes, "neither does fly-agaric grow."

This particularity about conditions under which it will grow helped Wasson explain why the "Soma" of the *Rig-Veda* got "lost."

Migrating to India, which for the most part lacks forests of birch, fir, pine and oak, the Aryans were able, Wasson thinks, to find this mushroom growing only in the Himalayas. As they lost their immediate contact with the mushroom, it's not at all surprising, he feels, that the later parts of the *Rig-Veda* speak of "Soma substitutes." The fact that *A. muscaria* grows only in a mycorrhizal relationship may also explain, according to Wasson, why the birch is held in such high regard in many northern lands.

Above Big Sur, California, the Fly Agaric appears in the bright red coloration familiar from countless children's books. In other parts of North America, its color varies considerably—from pink and even white to bright canary yellow. Similar variations occur in Europe and Asia.

After Wasson stirred interest in Fly Agaric, it didn't take long for people to notice that its close relative, the Panther Cap, also has psychoactive effects. The cap for this species comes in yellowish to grayish brown. Like the Fly Agaric, it is usually covered by prominent white "warts" (remains of the "veil" that encloses it when young).

The stem of *A. pantherina* bears a large, lacy ring, or "collar." Appearing at its base is this species' most important distinguishing feature—two or three layers or hoops of tissue attached to the stem (other remnants of the veil, left over from when the stem expands). The Panther Cap, like the Fly Agaric, can be found throughout woodlands—under trees or near stumps. The spores of both are white, so a "spore print" should be taken on dark paper.

Amanita muscaria, *the red, spotted Fly Agaric mushroom familiar from fairy tales, grows near birch, larch, fir, pine and·oak trees.*

Amanita pantherina, *the "Panther Cap," is a close relative that contains the same psychoactive components as Fly Agaric.*

CHEMISTRY

When *Amanita muscaria* was first examined to determine its psycho-active components in 1869, a compound called *muscarine* was isolated. From then until nearly a century later, this compound was believed to be the cause of Fly Agaric's mental effects. More recent studies have shown that muscarine alone raises quite different responses than the mushroom. In fact, this molecule is present in only trace amounts: 0.0002-0.0003 percent of the fresh plant.

Since this mushroom's mental effects are undisputedly strong, other guesses were made, notably *atropine* and *bufotenine*. Such ideas have now been discarded. Modern research into this question began in 1967 with the work in Zurich of the chemist C.H. Eugster and the pharmacologist P.G. Wasser. They discovered that the main psychoactives are *ibotenic acid, muscimol* and *muscazone*, aided possibly by a few other constituents.

Ibotenic acid, considered somewhat toxic, amounts to about 0.03-0.1 percent of the fresh Fly Agaric mushroom. The noticeable differences in the impact of fresh and dried Fly Agaric mushrooms probably results from the transformation of ibotenic acid during the drying process into the more potent and quite stable muscimol.

Taken orally, muscimol displays activity at 10-15 mg.; ibotenic acid is active above 90 mg. The other psychic contributor, muscazone, seems to have considerably less effect.

Muscimol
(3-hydroxy-5-amino methyl isoxazole)

Ibotenic Acid
(α -amino-3-hydroxy-5-isoxazole acetic acid)

The psychoactive principles in *A. muscaria* pass through the human organism in such a way that they are still psychoactive when they emerge in urine. The resulting sequential inebriation quite fascinated the explorers and travelers who first witnessed Fly Agaric use in Siberia. The custom there was described as delicately as anywhere by the English novelist Oliver Gold-smith in 1762:

> The poorer sort, who love mushrooms to distraction as well as the rich, but cannot afford it at first hand, post themselves on these occasions around the huts of the rich and watch the ladies and gentlemen as they come down to pass their liquor, and hold a wooden bowl to catch the delicious fluid, very little altered by filtration, being still strongly tinctured with the intoxicating quality. Of this they drink with the utmost satisfaction and thus they get as drunk and as jovial as their betters.

PHYSICAL EFFECTS

Reports on the experience of Fly Agaric and Panther Cap mushrooms are fairly rare but seem to indicate that somatic sensations vary considerably, a result of dosage differences, the time of year when they are picked (effects seem to decline at the end of the season) and whether they have been dried. *The First Book of Sacraments*, from the Church of the Tree of Life, summarizes the effects brought about by ingestion of Fly Agaric:

> twitching, dizziness and possibly nausea about half an hour after ingestion followed soon by numbness of the feet. At this point a person will frequently go into a half-sleep state for about two hours. He may experience colored visions and be aware of sounds around him but it is usually impossible to rouse him. After this a good-humored euphoria may develop with a light-footed feeling and perhaps an urge to dance. At this time a person often becomes capable of greater than normal feats of strength. Next hallucinations may occur. Objects may appear larger than they are. Sometimes a person may feel compelled to reveal harbored feelings. The post-sleep stage may last three or four hours.

Wasson makes several interesting assertions about the toxicity of *Amanita muscaria.* Its alternate name—Fly Agaric—is said to come from the belief that flies can be killed by means of this mushroom. When Wasson tried the experiment, the flies became temporarily stupified but recovered. Although half of the references pronounce this species "deadly," Wasson claims that there isn't a single firsthand account of lethal poisoning. In fact, he asserts that "most trustworthy observers" testify that, "properly dried, it has no bad effects."

After witnessing a considerable number of Fly Agaric and Panther Cap experiences, Jonathan Ott agrees, but he urges potential users to start with *no more than ¼-½ cup of chopped or sautéed material.* Here are other warnings from Ott:

> The genus *Amanita* possesses at least five species which are potentially lethal. Unless you are very skilled in identification of the *Amanita* species, do not eat an *Amanita* that is all white.
>
> Caution should also be exercised with regard to dosage. These mushrooms are powerful. The effective dose range may be narrow. If it is exceeded, even by a small amount, a dissociative experience may result, even a comatose state or an inability to function. Of course, there are many who desire this type of effect; no doubt it would be alarming to others. There are many unanswered questions concerning the toxicity of these mushrooms. It has been suggested, and there is some evidence to support this, that the toxicity may vary according to location and season.

MENTAL EFFECTS

The Importance of Drying

Impressed by reports about Siberian use of Fly Agaric and feeling this mushroom was the "Soma" of the *Rig-Veda*, Wasson tried self-experimentation:

In 1965 and again in 1966 we tried out the fly-agarics repeatedly on ourselves. The results were disappointing. We ate them raw, on empty stomaches. We drank the juice, on empty stomaches. We mixed the juice with milk, and drank the mixture, always on empty stomaches. We felt nauseated and some of us threw up. We felt disposed to sleep, and fell into a deep slumber from which shouts could not rouse us, lying like logs, not snoring, dead to the outside world. When in this state I once had vivid dreams, but nothing like what happened when I took the Psilocybe mushrooms in Mexico, where I did not sleep at all. In our experiments at Sugadaira there was one occasion that differed from the others, one that could be called successful. Rokuya Imazeki took his mushrooms with *mizo shiru*, the delectable soup that the Japanese usually serve with breakfast, and he toasted his mushrooms caps on a fork before an open fire. When he rose from the sleep that came from the mushrooms, he was in full elation. For three hours he could not help but speak; he was a compulsive speaker. The purport of his remarks was that this was nothing like the alcoholic state; it was infinitely better, beyond all comparison. We did not know at the time why, on this single occasion, our friend Imazeki was affected this way . . . .

Soon after, Wasson noticed with great interest that the Koryaks at the end of the nineteenth century had told Nikolai Sljunin, who wrote a two-volume "Natural History" published in St. Petersburg in 1900, that they thought *fresh* Fly Agaric was poisionous and they refrained from eating the mushrooms until they were dried, either by the sun or over a fire. Wasson was also impressed with a comment in an heroic hymn of the Vogul people. The hero, the "two-belted one," addressing his wife, says: "Woman, bring me in my three sun-dried fly-agarics!"

The drying of this mushroom tremendously affects the strength and nature of the mental experience. "Decarboxylation" of ibotenic acid into muscimol multiplies psychoactivity by a factor of five or six and reduces the undesirable side-effects of fresh *Amanita muscaria*. Those that are fresh may be dangerous or not satisfactorily "bemushrooming." Wasson emphasized how impressively different the results from simple drying can be:

I did not realise this when I went to Japan in the fall of 1965 and 1966, and with Japanese friends tried the fresh fly-agarics. The Rig-Veda had not prepared me for the drying. I had known of course that the Soma plants were mixed with water before being pounded with the pressing stones, but I had supposed that this was to freshen up the plants so that they would be capable of yielding juice when pressed. The desiccation, I thought, was an inevitable consequence of bringing the mushrooms from afar and keeping them on hand. There was nothing to tell me that desiccation was a *sine qua non* of the Soma rite. The reader may think that I should have familiarized myself with the Siberian practice before going to Japan. I agree. Imazeki, who by chance toasted his caps on one occasion before eating them, alone had satisfactory results, insistently declaring that this was nothing like alcohol, that this was far superior, in fact in a different world. Alone among us all, he had known *amrta*, the ambrosia of the Immortals . . . .

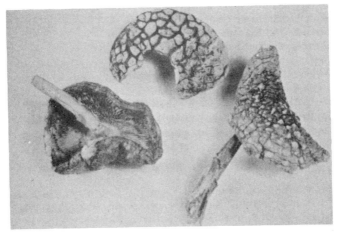

The First Book of Sacraments

Fly Agaric and Panther Cap specimens should be dried before ingestion. This is best done on a drying rack or by suspending them on a wire and leaving them in the sunlight until they resemble those pictured above. Properly dried, these mushrooms retain their psychoactivity for at least a year without marked diminution in potency.

Dosage

Proper dosage depends on many variables. Potency is said to decline, for example, at the end of the season; much variation is exhibited as well between specimens grown in different locales. Reid Kaplan, Wasson's chief colleague in the study of native North American practices, illustrates in his own case how variable this mushroom can be. He failed to feel effects after repeated tries on an empty stomach, with lime, as an enema, etc. These efforts were without any success until he was guided in its use by Keewaydinoquay.

Reports on Siberian tribesmen suggest that they usually take three— one large and two small sun-dried mushrooms, often with reindeer milk or bogberry juice (similar to blueberry juice). However, the Church of the Tree of Life literature on Fly Agaric cautions potential users that "Siberian tribesmen have a far more robust constitution than most of us." It suggests that no one take any more than a single, modest-sized mushroom—at least until its effects are clearly demonstrated.

Jonathan Ott points out that all parts of the Fly Agaric are psychoactive, although the skin of the cap may be the most potent part. Here is his generalized description of a trip resulting from taking dried specimens:

> After oral ingestion, the full effects will begin in about 90 minutes. For me, these are characterized by wavy motion in the visual field, an "alive" quality to inanimate objects, auditory hallucinations and a sense of great mental stillness and clarity. The effects are distinctly different from psilocybin, LSD or mes-

caline, and may last up to eight hours. Side effects often include nausea, slight loss of balance and coordination and drowsiness. Smoking produces a more rapid effect of shorter duration.

The Importance of Mental Set

Andrew Weil writes in *The Marriage of the Sun and Moon* that he was interested in tracking down instances of *Amanita pantherina* ingestion. He pursued some cases reported by Jonathan Ott in the *Journal of Psychedelic Drugs* #8 (1976), among others.

Weil soon found "that they were of two kinds." Some people, he says,

> ate the mushroom by accident. They were foraging for edible species and made a mistake. Thinking the panther was some innocuous edible, they took it home, cooked it and ate it. This mushroom produces an intoxication of rapid onset. Within 15 to 30 minutes, it made all of these people feel very peculiar. . . .
>
> When they began to feel peculiar, all of them decided they had eaten a poisonous species and were about to die. One woman first called her lawyer to change an item in her will, then summoned an ambulance. All of them got sick. All lost consciousness for varying periods of time, from a few minutes to a half hour. All were taken to emergency wards of hospitals, where they uniformly received incorrect medical treatment: large doses of atropine that made their conditions worse. They were admitted to medical wards and discharged in 36 to 48 hours, since it is the nature of the intoxication to subside quickly, usually within 12 hours. Most of these victims said they would never eat mushrooms again. One man said he could not look at mushrooms in the store for months afterward. When told some people ate the mushroom for fun, they shook their heads in disbelief.

Weil found the second kind of *Amanita pantherina* use among people who had already had extensive experience with psychedelics and "believed that nature provides us with all sorts of natural highs just waiting to be picked in the woods":

> When these people felt the rapid effects of *Amanita pantherina*, they welcomed them as signs that the mushroom was really working. None of them got sick. (A few mentioned transient nausea but did not regard it as important.) None of them felt it necessary to summon help. All of them liked the experience and most said they intended to repeat it. Some had already eaten the panther a number of times.

Weil presented this information to groups of physicians; he says they tried hard to come up with some simple, materialistic explanation for the response-difference in the two cases:

> A question they always ask is: "Might there have been a dose difference?" The answer is, yes, there was a dose difference; the people who ate the panther deliberately ate more of it than the people who ate it accidentally.

The Question of "Soma"

R. Gordon Wasson, right in many of his anthropological conjectures about mushrooms, has applied the question of Fly Agaric and other mushrooms to the origins of religious feeling:

> I suggest to you that, as our most primitive ancestors foraged for their food, they must have come upon our psychotropic mushrooms, or perhaps other plants possessing the same property, and eaten them, and known the miracle of awe in the presence of God. This discovery must have been made on many occasions, far apart in time and space. It must have been a mighty springboard for primitive man's imagination.

In the Vedic hymns, wrote Aldous Huxley,

> we are told that the drinkers of soma were blessed in many ways. Their bodies were strengthened, their hearts were filled with courage, joy and enthusiasm, their minds were enlightened and in an immediate experience of eternal life they received the assurance of their immortality.

The hymns of this first book of the *Vedas* undoubtedly vibrate with ecstasy; users are exhalted. "We have drunk the Soma," they say at their height, "we are become Immortals." In Book IX, the god Indra drinks Soma— and it inspires him to create the universe!

Was "Soma," as Wasson repeatedly asserts, the *Amanita muscaria* mushroom?

There is no definitive answer possible, but no candidate more suitable than Wasson's has yet appeared. A recent Ph.D. thesis at the University of California, Berkeley, entitled "Huoma," renews this query, suggesting on the basis of linguistic factors that the plant contained a harmaline compound (which in botanical terms does not fit with Soma's identification).

Although usage isn't widespread, many people report disappointment with *Amanita muscaria*, saying that it's not all that nice, perhaps not even psychedelic. One experimenter noted that after his fourth trip on Fly Agaric he had to re-evaluate Wasson's *SOMA*. His feeling was that ingestion of *Amanita muscaria* was not better than *Cannabis,* opium, *Datura* or betel, all of which were already known in India by the time of the *Rig-Veda*.

Such objections deserve mention, because results for individual users are variable. Some users may get the exaltation described in a few of the above accounts, like those from Joseph Kopéc, Rokuya Imazeki and Johann Georgi. Others have experienced little more than sedative or dissociative effects.

The variable action of this early "psychedelic" in no way denies possible impact. The novelist/essayist Robert Anton Wilson, after examining the conjectures and evidence of Fly Agaric's role in sundry cultures, put the issue squarely: if, as it seems, this mushroom was "the reality behind several of the legendary drugs of early European and Asian mythology," then we might conclude that "this mushroom played a larger role in religious history than any other single factor."

A "belladonna vision" that appears to have been "psychedelic."

Erich Brunkel, from about 1885

CHAPTER TEN

Contrasting Profiles

The nine compound-clusters described thus far, comprising more than a hundred botanicals and synthetics, are the main psychedelics known to date. Other plants—at least 120 from the New World and twenty from the Old World—have suspected or confirmed psychoactivity (Schultes and Hofmann inventory ninety-one, each representing a separate genus, in their 1979 *Plants of the Gods*), and substances isolated from these plants have prompted chemists to synthesize and test new compounds. This chemical work has been outlined in *Psychotropic Substances and Related Compounds*, edited by the late Daniel Efron, who was affiliated with Sandoz, Ciba, Hofmann-La Roche and NIMH. In the first edition (1968), Efron showed 590 molecules and referenced their literature. In 1972, Efron enlarged this book to cover 1,555 compounds (including barbiturates and tranquilizers).

Nonetheless, few plants or compounds other than those in the nine compound-clusters seem eligible for classification as authentic psychedelics. The five to be profiled here—three from plants and two synthetics—have sometimes been proposed as major facilitators of psychedelic experiences.

Belladonna-like Substances

The family *Solanaceae*, made up of more than 2,400 species, is especially noteworthy. Many of its members contain the alkaloids atropine (*dl-*hyoscyamine) and scopolamine (hyoscine). Atropine shows up in mandrake root, henbane and thorn apple; it constitutes just over 4.5 percent of the asthmatic preparation called Asthmador. Schultes and Hofmann claim that there are no reports on the effects of atropine alone "which could explain the addition of belladonna as an ingredient of magic brews in medieval Europe." But Hoffer and Osmond recall several historical incidents that attest to its psychoactivity. One story involved a family of five who in 1963 ate tomato plants that had been grafted onto jimson weed, producing 6.36 mg. of atropine per tomato: "All five developed deliroid reactions of varying intensity and some had to be treated in the hospital several days. This seems to be the first known instance of hallucinogenic tomatoes."

The names *atropine* and *belladona* both relate to this drug complex's effects. The former is derived from *Atropos*—one of the three fates in Greek mythology—as a result of its being used as a poison during the Middle Ages. The latter refers to its ability to dilate the eyes of "beautiful ladies." Both are used nowadays in medicine as an antispasmodic, especially for parkinsonism, with an average dose of atropine being 0.5 mg. Users have survived dosages of more than a gram, but the effects appear toxic in most cases of 10 mg. or more.

385

Atropa Belladonna · Datura Stramonium

Domestic Datura, *a dangerous deliriant.*

Smithsonian Report (Safford, 1916)

Datura meteloides, *a ceremonial deliriant of the ancient Meso-american Zunis and California Indians (two-thirds natural size).*

Probably the more important chemical in most belladonna alkaloids is scopolamine. It appears not only in the already-mentioned sources but also in several tree barks used by natives that are known as *Datura*. Appreciated early on in both hemispheres, it has been used in the Near East to compound the effects of cannabinols and in the Andes to add to mescaline-like effects from the cactus *Trichocereus pachanoi*. In asthmador, scopolamine constitutes 50.4 percent of the mixture. Tim Leary has been quoted as saying he never heard of a good belladonna trip; my own experience has been an exception.

Yohimbe

This "psychedelic stimulant" is derived primarily from the bark of a West African tree called *Pausinystalia* or *Corynanthe yohimbe*, although it is also present in other species of *Corynanthe* and in *Aspidosperma quebran-choblanco* and *Mitragyna stipulosa*. When this alkaloid is brewed as a tea and then drunk, its effects come on within forty-five minutes to an hour. The action is reportedly swifter if taken with 500 mg. vitamin C.

There is an increase in vasodilation and peripheral blood flow, along with stimulation of the spinal ganglia which control erectile tissue, followed by slight "hallucinogenic effects," that last for about two hours. Users may then go off to sleep quite easily.

J.H. of Vancouver, B.C. has written *High Times* to point out that *yohimbe* is a MAO-inhibitor, altering adrenal and other metabolic functions, and thus should be used with caution:

> Anyone with diabetes, kidney or heart disease should not experiment with yohimbe. Moreover, yohimbe should not be used with mescaline, LSD, MDA, MMDA or amphetamines . . . . Avoid chocolate, cheeses, sherry, bananas, pineapples, sauerkraut and other foods containing tryptophans for 12 hours before and after use. The combination may trigger a dangerous rise in blood pressure combined with shortness of breath.
>
> In case of adverse reaction, *get medical help*. Yohimbe is legal, so it's no bust to see a doctor. Sodium amytal is the best antidote for yohimbe poisoning, but let a physician do it. Self-administration of barbs during a panic is mighty dangerous. Most people overdo it.

This bark is generally prepared by boiling so that psychoactive elements are leached out and starting material can be thrown away. Mental effects are fairly mild. Adam Gottlieb comments on *yohimbe's* propensity for produc-ing sexual effects such as erections in males:

> Other pleasurable effects are warm spinal shivers which are especially enjoy-able during coitus and orgasm (bodies feel like they are melting into one another), psychic stimulations, mild perceptual changes without hallucinations, and heightening of emotional and sexual feeling . . . .

Kava-Kava

Kava-kava comes from the root pulp and lower stems of a tall perennial shrub native to the South Pacific islands. It was mentioned by a Swedish

Kava Kava (Steinmetz)

Piper methysticum (kava-kava).

botanist who accompanied Captain James Cook on his first voyage to the Sandwich (Hawaiian) Islands in 1768-1771. In 1886, Louis Lewin examined *kava-kava* in detail.

The plant (*Piper methysticum*) grows best near sea level in areas like the Solomon and Fiji Islands, Samoa, Tahiti and New Guinea. With sufficient sunlight, it can reach twenty feet. The psychic components reside within the root—which after three or four years attains a thickness of three to five inches. The roots in older plants become heavy and knotted, accumulating strength and flavor. After six years, such roots may weigh twenty pounds; after twenty years they may be as heavy as a hundred pounds.

Squibb Handbook

Kava-kava *root: 1, Irregular piece of the root.*
2, Transverse section. 3, Large pith.

When harvested, these roots are scraped and then cut into pieces, which are then either chewed (the Tonga method) or crushed between rocks (the Fiji method). In Norman Taylor's *Narcotics*, there appears a charming account of these preparations—which result in a grayish brown or whitish liquid that most find to be soapy, spicy and numbing to the mouth. In Hawaii, according to Hoffer and Osmond,

> The nobles used it socially for pleasure, the priests ceremoniously and the working class for relaxation. It was given to mediums and seers to enhance their psychic powers. It was used to increase inspiration and to assist contemplation. It seems to have been employed in the way some investigators have tried to use LSD and psilocybin.

Elaborately carved kava-kava *bowl.*

Fijian ceremony. The cup bearer is about to present the cup.

Interestingly, many people in the South Pacific have given up drinking alcohol after being introduced to *kava-kava*. All agree that it leaves no hangover and that it produces a carefree and happy state with no mental or physical excitation. According to Lewin, this is "a real euphoriant which in the beginning made speech more fluent and lively and increased sensitivity to subtle sounds. The subjects were never angry, aggressive or noisy." *Kava-*

kava taken in large amounts regularly has caused drinkers' legs to "become tired and weak, their muscles were controlled poorly; their gait unsteady, and they appeared to be drunk." But the mental changes are usually of a pleasant kind and, many feel, quite magical. A surprising large number of visitors to the Islands are said to have considered *kava-kava* superior to champagne.

If larger quantities are consumed, vision is disturbed, pupils are dilated and walking is difficult. There's a sort of scaling of the skin that develops if *kava-kava* is used frequently and in large amounts.

Kava-kava isn't illegal. It is available in many herb shops and through the mails, notably from advertisers in *High Times*. The fresher it is, the more potent.

Kava-kava's mental action is caused by at least six resinous alpha pyrones: kawain, dihydrokawain, methysticin, dihydromethysticin, yangonin and dihydroyangonin, none of which is water soluble. As a result, they must be emulsified into water or coconut milk, says Adam Gottlieb,

> by prechewing the root as is done in the islands or by adding a little salad oil and lecithin and mixing it up in a blender. To do this mix one ounce of powdered kava-kava, ten ounces of water, two tablespoons of coconut or olive oil and one tablespoon of lecithin granules (available at health food stores) in a blender until it attains a milky appearance. This amount serves two to four persons.

Ketamine

Ketamine, a compound featured in Hitchcock's *Family Plot*, is a non-barbiturate anesthetic that's notable for its lack of harmful side-effects. It's also called Ketalar (ketamine hydrochloride) and has been used for the most part as a child's anesthetic, with intramuscular doses in the range of 9-13 mg./kg. of body weight producing surgical anesthesia within three to four minutes and usually lasting twelve to twenty-five minutes. An intravenous dose of 2 mg./kg. of body weight generally brings about anesthesia within thirty seconds, with the effect lasting five to ten minutes.

When it was given to older people experimentally, some patients gave accounts that sounded like psychedelic experiences of some sort. Soon experimentation revealed that in dosages reduced to about a tenth of the usual amounts, Ketamine produced a "trip" lasting forty-five minutes to an hour. Many users have since testified that lying down quietly while under this drug can lead to a spiritual experience.

The manufacturer Parke-Davis notes that approximately 12 percent of more than 10,000 patients given this drug in 105 separate studies have had unpleasant "emergence reactions":

> THE PSYCHOLOGICAL MANIFESTATIONS VARY IN SEVERITY BETWEEN PLEASANT DREAM-LIKE STATES, VIVID IMAGES, HALLUCINATIONS, AND EMERGENCE DELIRIUM. IN SOME CASES THESE STATES HAVE BEEN ACCOMPANIED BY CONFUSION, EXCITEMENT, AND IRRATIONAL BEHAVIOR WHICH A FEW PATIENTS

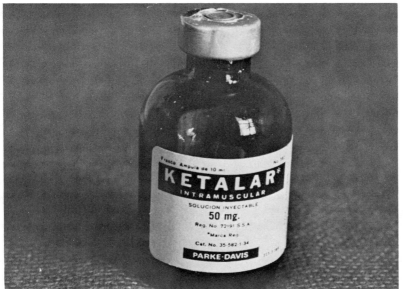

Jeremy Bigwood

Ketamine, distributed as Ketalar, is an anesthetic used for children and the elderly which in lower dosages produces what many consider psychedelic experiences.

RECALL AS AN UNPLEASANT EXPERIENCE. THE DURATION ORDINARILY LASTS NO MORE THAN A FEW HOURS; IN A FEW CASES, HOWEVER, RECURRENCES HAVE TAKEN PLACE UP TO 24 HOURS POST-OPERATIVELY. NO RESIDUAL PSYCHOLOGICAL EFFECTS ARE KNOWN TO HAVE RESULTED FROM USE OF KETALAR . . . .

THESE [EMERGENCE] REACTIONS MAY BE REDUCED IF VERBAL, TACTILE, AND VISUAL STIMULATION OF THE PATIENT IS MINIMIZED DURING THE RECOVERY PERIOD . . . .

People trying low dosages report feeling disconnected from normal, everyday realities. Blood pressure and pulse are often elevated; hypotension and bradycardia have been observed. "Ketamine has a wide margin of safety," observes Parke-Davis' brochure: "several instances of unintentional administration of overdoses of Ketalar (up to ten times that usually required) have been followed by prolonged but complete recovery."

Reactions to low doses are illustrated here by the comments of a friend:

On the way up, there was this music experience. Since I am a musician, he chose the music knowing that I was—and that part of it was incredible. It was OK to keep my eyes open or closed, since it didn't matter. To close my eyes felt better. My perceptions were getting disoriented, and when I closed my eyes a lot of information started to happen. Colors, patterns, cross-connections in sensory perception. Sounds and inner visions got confused.

I got deeper and deeper into this state, until at one point the world disappeared. I was no longer in my body. I didn't have a body.

I reached a point at which I knew I was going to die. There was no question about it, no "maybe I will" or "perhaps I will," and what incredible feelings that evoked!

Then I reached a point at which I felt ready to die. It wasn't a question of choice, it was just a wave that carried me higher and higher, at the same time that I was having what in my normal state I would call the horror of death. It became obvious to me that it was not at all what I had anticipated death to be. Except, I knew it was death, that something was dying.

I reached a point at which I gave it all away. I just yielded, and then I entered a space in which there aren't any words. The words that have been used have been used a thousand times—starting with Buddha. I mean, at-one-with-the-universe, recognizing-your-godhead—all those words I later used to explore what I had experienced.

The feeling was that I was "home." I didn't want to go anywhere, and I didn't need to go anywhere. It was a bliss state of a kind I never experienced before.

I hung out there awhile, and then I came back. I didn't want to come back. The deep state was no longer than half an hour.

When I talked about it to my guide, and shared some words about the experience, he said: "Yeah, what happened and happens to others is that you finally get rid of that heartbreak feeling that we carry from childhood. Finally, that's expunged somehow." That was the feeling: I was rid of my heartbreak. My heart was no longer broken. It was like, "Whew!!!" That was the long-lasting effect—what really lasts and gets supported by similar experiences—not necessarily on any drug at all. That floats, and stays.

In 1978, Marcia Moore and Howard Alltounian published a book about Ketamine, *Journeys into the Bright World.* Another positive account appears in John Lilly's novel-autobiography *The Scientist*, where this compound is referred to as "K." Some users have been highly enthusiastic; a few have been disappointed. Here's a response from someone who saw his Ketamine experience as quite distinct from those induced by other psychedelics:

In regard to my Ketamine experience, I'm not sure—indeed I doubt that anyone could be sure—how to describe it. It has much the same flavor as those described by John Lilly in his autobiographical novel, *The Scientist*, i.e., contact with Beings who seem to be running things here on earth. (I had not read John's book when I took Ketamine and went into that experience without any expectations of the kind of experience it turned out to be. If anything, I anticipated something similar to the effect of other psychoactive substances.) The Beings aspect of the experience was less interesting for me than the total loss of an observer consciousness. Even in my most profound experiences with LSD and mushrooms I retained some kind of ego structure. There was an element of annihilation of the self so total that that which is joined to the One in mystical experience simply disappeared.

Surprisingly, I found myself better able to remember the details of the experience than those I've had with LSD and mushrooms. It was almost as if I had been to the movies. There was story more than concept. Plot is easier to retain than insight. With LSD and mushrooms I have always been able to talk and felt that I might even write if I wanted to, but with Ketamine there was no eye, no writing hand, no world in which such an act could take place.

Ketamine is the only drug that made me sick. I threw up for ten minutes on coming out of it and immediately swore that I would never do it again. Of course, I will.

My experience indicates that it is the most hallucinogenic of the drugs I have taken. It feels like it is giving me access to something more personal and significantly less meaningful than the Ground of Being.

The Ketamine molecule is very similar to that of PCP, an analgesic-anesthetic usually employed in veterinary medicine. PCP is known chemically as phencyclidine or benactazine and has been marketed by Parke-Davis as Sernylan. It has been represented as THC under the name "Hog," "green" and "the Peace Pill." In smoking mixtures, it is often called "Angel Dust." Taken very frequently, PCP sometimes provokes "scattering" or "schizy" effects—and is not recommended. The best reports in the scientific literature come from Domino, Luby and Kovacic (see the extensive bibliography in *PCP*, edited by Ronald Linder). The January-June 1978 issue of the *Journal of Psychedelic Drugs* which is entirely devoted to PCP, presents a dozen views.

Nitrous Oxide

This uncomplicated molecule (N_2O) was produced for the first time two centuries ago—in 1772—by the chemist and political refugee Sir Joseph Priestly. He was also the first person to isolate oxygen. As Priestly tried to determine whether dry carbon dioxide would dissolve iron, he prepared a gas that he named "Dephlogisticated Nitrous Air." He experimented with this gas, soon to be known as nitrous oxide, but never inhaled it.

In 1779, another chemist and social reformer, Thomas Beddoes, opened a Pneumatic Institution in Bristol, England. He hired Humphry Davy (who was later knighted) as his assistant and encouraged him to pursue experiments with N_2O. Davy exposed nitrous peroxide (N_2O_4) to iron, thereby removing three of the four oxygen atoms. The results appeared in Davy's 600-page book, *Researches Chemical and Philosophical, chiefly concerning Nitrous Oxide and its Respiration.* In this, Beddoes described effects:

> there seems to be quick and strong alteration in the degree of illumination of all surrounding objects; and I felt as if composed of finely vibrating strings . . . . immediately afterwards I have often caught myself walking in hurried step and busy in soliloquoy . . . .

Davy, who experimented extensively upon himself with N_2O, introduced it to Samuel Taylor Coleridge, Robert Southey, James Watt (inventor of the steamboat), Peter Mark Roget (author of the famous *Thesaurus*), the potter Josiah Wedgwood (also later knighted) and other luminaries. Before long, patients were flocking to the Pneumatic Institution to be treated with this "gas of paradise." Public feeling about all this ran high as rumors of "strange sexual laboratory procedures and chlorinated Africans pervaded the bustling English seaport." After Davy turned his attention to other things, the Institute deteriorated and soon it closed. Use was confined to "exuberant medical students."

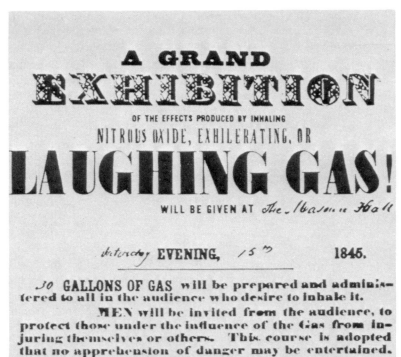

Dentists became interested in the anesthetic properties of nitrous oxide as a result of an accident that occurred during an exhibition of its "laughing gas" properties.

In 1799, having noticed that pain vanished under the influence of this gas, Davy suggested that it be used in surgical operations. This lead was not pursued for another forty-five years. In the 1840s, "laughing gas" appeared in the United States as a form of entertainment. A young dentist named Horace Wells attended a demonstration in Hartford Connecticut in late 1844. The 25¢ admission bought a dose of N_2O, and during the proceedings one of the nitrous oxide sniffers tripped and fell, gashing his leg in the process. To the victim's astonishment, he felt no pain.

Upon questioning the man, Wells was so impressed that he had one of his teeth extracted the next day while under the influence of the gas. He exclaimed: "A new era in tooth-pulling!" Wells was later urged by friends to patent his discovery, but he refused—"No! Let it be as free as the air we breathe!"

Soon the gas was used as an anesthetic in tooth extractions, in childbirth and to some extent in surgery. But it wasn't until the late 1860s that N_2O caught on as a painkiller and use for this purpose spread widely.

At the beginning of this century, attention of a more philosophical nature was directed to this simple compound when William James undertook examination of its properties at Harvard University. Commenting on this nitrous oxide experimentation, James concluded in a much-quoted

A self-portrait of William James from the 1860s.

passage that normal, waking consciousness is but one special kind of consciousness—"parted from it by the filmiest of screens, there lie potential forms of consciousness entirely different." James announced it as his "unshakeable conviction" that with application of "the requisite stimulus," other forms of consciousness "are there in all their completeness.... At any rate, they forbid a premature closing of our accounts with reality."

Even today, no one knows how this molecule of only three atoms causes its anesthetic effect, its hilarity or other more profound effects. For many users, there's no doubt it facilitates access to the "unconscious." Some feel that it also gives access to a state of recognition described by André Breton in *Manifestoes of Surrealism*:

> There is a certain point of the mind from which life and death, the real and the imaginary, the past and the future, the communicable and incommunicable, the high and low, cease being perceived as contradictions.

The tree flower pictured above was described in the mid-sixteenth century by Bernardino de Sahagún as an inebriating substance taken at night with chocolate. It represents the continuing search for psychedelics, having recently been brought from Guatemala by Jeremy Bigwood for chemical investigations.

The sniffer can adjust nitrous oxide dosage easily to whatever level is desired. After stopping sniffing, the effects dissipate rapidly; the gas is removed from the system within five to ten minutes. In contrast to psychedelics described earlier, the effects resist later description. Users retain an impression of the experience rather than a sharp memory.

Danger occurs—as dental experience has established—when users are foolish enough not to breathe oxygen when inhaling nitrous oxide. Earlier in this century, dentists often gave their patients straight N_2O, trying to bring them under it until skin color turned what was known as "Philadelphia blue." The brain, deprived of oxygen too long, can become vegetable. It is a good idea to remember to breathe oxygen regularly. Probably the best practice is to alternate breaths from a nitrous oxide balloon with air.

Users should also avoid inhaling directly from a nitrous oxide aerosol can. Some users have died as a consequence of freezing the throat area because the heat is absorbed as the gas expands. Freon, a similar molecule used as an aerosol propellant, does not have nitrous oxide effects.

Appendixes

Breugal the Elder: detail from "The Alchemist"

Notes on Purity Tests and Precursors

The easiest way for most people to check a psychedelic compound's purity is at a testing station, such as Street Pharmacologist (Box 610233, Miami, FL 33161, 305/446-3585), or PharmChem. PharmChem's analysis is based on thin-layer and gas chromatography and involves comparison with 300 possible psychoactive substances and some 250 possible impurities.

Qualitative findings are available from PharmChem two or three days after a compound's reception—if accompanied by $15 by money order or in cash and an identification code of five numbers and a letter, sent to 3925 Bohannon Dr., Menlo Park, CA 94025. The number to call is (415) 328-6200. Quantitative results are given only to those with DEA licenses.

Chemical test kits advertised by mail order for checking out alleged psychedelics generally rely on the Keller and van Urk-Smith color-change tests. In these, the sample to be examined is poured into a reagent with the resulting color then compared with standards. Albert Hofmann has described these processes as they relate to LSD:

> All derivatives of lysergic acid give characteristic color reactions based on the indole nature of lysergic acid . . . . A solution of traces of a lysergic acid derivative in glacial acetic acid, containing a small amount of $FeCl_3$, when added with concentrated H_2SO_4 develops a brilliant violet-blue color (Keller reaction). In the procedure of van Urk-Smith a solution of p-dimethylamino-benzaldehyde in diluted sulfuric acid containing traces of $FeCl_3$ is mixed with an equal volume of the lysergic acid derivative in tartaric acid solution. A violet-blue color appears. Whereas the Keller reaction is used mainly for qualitative identification, the van Urk-Smith reaction was standardized and can be used for quantitative determinations.

These test kits are mainly useful in determining whether the substance in question is an indole or not. Melting point apparatus is also a rather crude indicator, although valuable as well in finding negative results.

More sophisticated determinations can be made with thin-layer chromatography, a process that is still quite inexpensive. In this technique, the substance to be tested is placed at the bottom of a coated plate and then creeps up through a solvent for ten to fifteen minutes. Various psychoactive components then locate themselves in specific positions and exhibit coloration depending upon the solvent used, and thus can be identified as specific compounds. LSD-25, in a typical reaction, travels about halfway up the gel, where it takes on a bright yellow appearance. The position of iso-lysergic acid diethylamide, by way of contrast, lies right below. Use of different solvents, while assaying the same substance, can be almost as specific as the results derived from equipment costing $40,000-$50,000.

Experience in making thin-layer discriminations is needed, however, since the eventual reading depends upon color distinctions and accurate measurements of resting locations. Gunk from a floor, bits of an eraser, various dyes and even milk have on occasion been thought to have tested out positively by some who have tried color-change tests.   Difficulties in relying on verbal descriptions are evident in *Webster's Third International Dictionary*'s effort at defining *onionskin pink*:

> . . . a light brown that is stronger and slightly redder and darker than alesan; stronger and slightly yellower and darker than blush; lighter, stronger and slightly redder than French beige; and redder, stronger, and slightly lighter than cork . . . .

A few readers of the earlier edition of this book felt that a revision should contain examples of thin-layer chromatography for most psychedelics.   This, however, would require many precise color plates, and is already available in several versions at many university libraries.   Here are examples, in black and white, illustrating typical chromatograms:

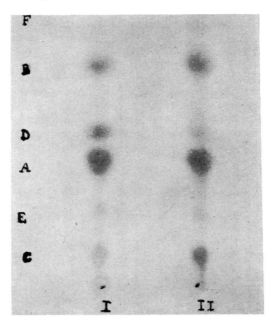

Chromatograms of the alkaloidal extracts of 25 mcg. of Turbina (Rivea) corymbosa *(I), and 25 mcg.* Ipomoea violacea *(II).*

E.G.C. Clark's *Isolation and Identification of Drugs* (The Pharmaceutical Press, London) specifies a method for making "microtests" of a "pedant drop" or "microdrop."   The sulfuric acid-formaldehyde testing of DMT, to illustrate, yields dull orange with a sensitivity of 1.0 mcg. sensitivity, while the ammonium molybdate test yields blue going to green and then yellow with a sensitivity of 0.1 mcg.

When asked about other relevant literature on spot color tests, Carmen Helisten, formerly of PharmChem, recommended the following articles:

Fiorese, F.F., "Immediate Drug Detection on the Spot," *Hosp. Lab. Sci.*, Vol. 9, #4, 1972, p. 240 ff.; Frank, R.S. *et al.*, "Standardization of Forensic Drug Analyses," *J. For. Sci.*, Vol. 19, 1974, p. 163 ff.; Kaistha, K.K., "Drug Abuse Screening Programs:

Detection Procedures, Development Costs, Street Sample Analysis, and Field Tests," *J. Pharm. Sci.,* Vol. 61, #5, 1972, p. 655 ff.; and Velapoidi, R.A. *et al.,* "The Use of Chemical Spot Test Kits for the Presumptive Identification of Narcotics and Drugs of Abuse," *J. For. Sci.,* Vol. 19, 1974, p. 636 ff.

More precise testing is made by column, gas or high performance chromatography equipment, or by use of magnetic resonance or an electron microscope. These methods are all quite expensive and necessitate equipment rarely available outside of industry, universities and crime labs.

In gas chromatography, a sample is introduced into an inert stream of gas flowing through a tube. Through heating, it is broken down into its constituents which are then carried by the gas depending upon how heavy they are. Results are evaluated electronically in terms of nuclear weights and compared with an appropriate standard.

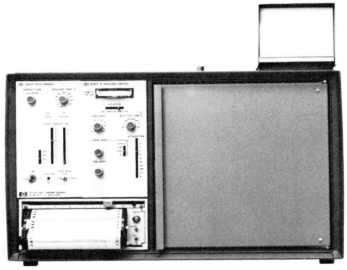

A Hewlett-Packard gas-liquid chromatographic unit, a sophisticated analytical instrument for drug testing.

High-Performance Liquid Chromatography doesn't involve a heating process, which can alter the original substance. Accessibility to this machine and others even more specific is rare, however.

These matters are raised here to indicate how difficult it is to establish the purity of a psychedelic substance with certainty. Bruce Eisner has discussed issues arising from this situation in "LSD Purity: Cleanliness is Next to Godheadliness" (*High Times,* January 1977). He has since remarked that

> The basic nature of the experiences that people were having with LSD had changed from the early- and middle-'60s to the middle-'70s, with a tendency for people to have less visionary or spiritual sessions and more mundane experiences which tended to remain at the level of simple sensory changes .... It became clear to me that a major factor in the quality of LSD reactions was due to the decline in

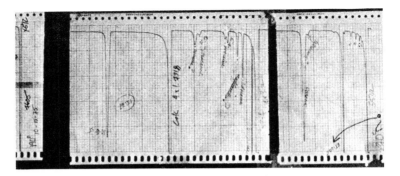

Graph tracings illustrating the output from gas chromatography.

the chemical purity of the substance itself. The deterioration of purity did not refer to chemical adulteration, but rather to the faulty manufacture of LSD by underground chemists, leading to a product which was not chemically pure crystal LSD but LSD mixed with a number of by-products of faulty manufacture. The source of impurities, exposure of LSD crystal to light, heat, moisture, air and combinations of these common environmental conditions deteriorate even the purest LSD into an odd collection of chemicals.

Four factors—set, setting, guide and dosage level—are all explanations in the changing receptivity to LSD in the psychedelic subculture. Pharmaceutical purity, a fifth factor, may play an important part in the overall variability of LSD experiences. At least, this question should be the subject of more thorough scientific research.

As for the synthesizing of psychedelics, Loompanics Unlimited, the publisher of Michael Valentine Smith's 1981 version of *Psychedelic Chemistry*, offers an appropriate warning: "The procedures referred to and described in this work assume a thorough knowledge of advanced lab techniques in organic chemistry, and should not be undertaken lightly by amateurs." At the end of that volume, Richard C. Hall III presents a "DEA Watched List of Chemicals." Many of these substances arouse suspicion only if bought in large or repeated orders, but others "are suspect under any conditions."

A further complication, exposed in a March 1981 *High Times* editorial ("LABSCAM") and an accompanying article ("Anatomy of a Sting"), has been the Drug Enforcement Administration's use of Buckeye Scientific, a Columbus, Ohio chemical supply firm, and other scientific companies to "suck unsuspecting would-be bathtub chemists into a trap that could imprison them for years." That "Buckeye and other DEA snitches," *High Times* declared,

> advertised their set-up scams in *High Times* has brought an embarrassment the magazine will not soon live down .... They recruit would-be chemists to buy raw materials; they deliver the supplies themselves; they allow the carefully cultivated labs to pump out and sell batches of amphetamines, LSD, methaqualone and other bathtub concoctions. Finally, they bust the labs—labs that virtually could not exist without their participation ....

Thoughts on Increasing Intelligence

BY FRANCIS JEFFREY

Timothy Leary has proposed that we think of consciousness and intelligence in terms of an outline of eight dimensions (called "levels," or "circuits" of the brain). The first four dimensions cover mastery of external space-time relationships in the immediate physical/behavioral environment of the human body. The other four dimensions concern access to internal structure and processes.

Leary conjectures that the function of LSD and other psychedelics is to shift our awareness over the continuum of scale and structure represented by these eight levels or circuits. In other words, the brain can be thought of and utilized as a "lens" for focusing on various scales of nature, represented by structures in our CNS—from the largest (physical/behavioral space) down to the smallest (sub-atomic space). *The central idea is that all levels of energy/structure/scale are potentially accessible in consciousness.*

"Circuits of the brain"—as defined by Leary—and "levels of nature"—as defined by science in general—are *imaginary*, or, at best, "relative and fuzzy." A "level" is, in fact, defined by a kind of *stability* which a structure at that level of scale and organization seems to possess. As an example, an individual cell can act as a unicellular organism (as in protozoa). But if this cell is smashed, it will disintegrate into smaller organized units—the next level down on the "scale of nature." *The essence of this observation is that at certain discrete levels, a relatively stable nexus of organization tends to be maintained.*

One of these "islands of stability" in the flux of natural processes is referred to as an *Eigen-state*. The German prefix, *Eigen*, means "characteristic of, or proper to, itself." This *Eigen-state* formulation is applied in all branches of science, ranging from sub-atomic physics (Schrödinger) to behavior/perception theory (von Foerster and Piaget). Existence of an *Eigen-state* implies a "stabilizing mechanism" or a "stabilizing process"—which accounts for the stability by acting to oppose or correct deviations (and perturbations). An *Eigen-state* defines a *nexus* of organization where most of the action is concentrated, and each such nexus is *relatively isolated* from others. This accounts for the "relative and fuzzy" definition of levels.

There is *isolation* between levels, while there is also *coupling* between levels. Effects of psychedelic drugs are explained in terms of a shift in relative *isolation versus coupling* among different pairs of "levels."

The cerebral cortex of the brain is an approximately continuous, homogenous neural medium, which is molded (or "rutted") into preferred tracks of neural transmission by imprinting and by repeated activity (i.e., behavioral learning). Within this system, there exists a relatively discrete series of dimensions ("levels") within which recurrent circular operations stabilize existing patterns: (1) the sensory-motor loop, representing interaction with the physical/behavioral space outside, and (2) an *internal behavior* loop, which operates even in isolation from the outside world and the many intrinsic *Eigen*-behavior loops of the neural substrate and the deeper levels of structure within (i.e., neurons, their interconnections, their internal structures, and their complex channels of interaction with one another).

This defines the levels within the CNS. The relative isolation between levels is maintained by circular operations which stabilize the structure at each level. For each level, there are many entities organized at that level (for example, many neurons) and such entities prefer interaction with other entities *at the same level*. A chemical reaction, for example, in the retina of the eye is almost always interpreted as a signal about the outside world, not as a signal about neurochemistry. Thus *isolation* means that operations at any given level are primarily self-referencing (i.e., they take their own states as inputs for further processing). *Coupling* refers to exceptions to this "self-referential closure."

A general theory of intelligence increase agents:

First, define *intelligence* as "degree of conscious access to one's own structure and processes within." Alternately, define *intelligence* as "a measure of the extent of access to the principles of one's construction and operation." The idea of "intelligence" implies capacity to use this access in order to respond flexibly and creatively to new situations.

Intelligence agents disrupt the cognitive homeostasis of the several *Eigen-states* operating at specific levels of circular operations. This affords access to different *potential Eigen-states*, and to unstable regions intervening in information space. Circular closure (i.e., isolation) is thus diminished, and coupling is increased between certain levels. When this occurs selectively between any two levels, it may result in decreased coupling *within* those levels, and between each of these levels and other levels with which each of them is normally coupled. For example, increased coupling among sub-behavioral (i.e., *internal behavior*) systems may be accompanied by a decrease in coupling at the overt behavior level (i.e., "spaced out").

When coupling between two levels is increased, images of the structure at one level may be translated into the other level. (This assumes that circular operations at each level are not too severely disrupted.) For example, in certain conditions called "imprint vulnerability," the brain copies the external environment.

These notes present the operation of the CNS *with psychedelic substances* as an extension and elucidation of the usual operations of the CNS *without them.* It is hoped it will contribute to a rational understanding and sane use of these potentials, as well as serve as precaution against all-too-frequent abuse, based on ignorance, in both "normal" and un-normal conditions.

Other Literature

The volumes that have been referred to in this book are listed in the index, along with publisher and publishing date. Here, assembled in six groupings, are highlights from other fascinating material that also may be of interest or value to the reader. Publisher's addresses for the most part can be found in *The Literary Market Place (LMP)*, an annual directory carried by most libraries. *Books in Print*, available at bookstores, keeps this story up-to-date.

Writings published before the 1980s are generally accessible only in libraries, used bookstores and private collections. Most universities and colleges have at least a hundred books about psychoactivity in their libraries, and often have much relevant material on microfilm. (The large "Stafford Collection" of psychedelia from the 1960s has been indexed and is open to the public at Columbia University.)

General Treatments of Psychedelics

An easily accessible, recent and fairly inclusive bibliography that shows how extensive the literature is appears on pages 313-334 of Grinspoon and Bakalar's *Psychedelic Drugs Reconsidered*. The Ethno-Pharmacology Society (EPS), which produces a newsletter, can be contacted at 4181 Brisbane Way, Irvine, CA 92715.

Shaman Woman/Mainline Lady: Women's Writings on the Drug Experience (Quill, 1982, edited by Palmer & Horowitz)

The Fabulous Illustrated History of Psychoactive Plants, or Great Grandma's Pleasures, Michael Starks (Lompanics Unltd., 1981)

Changing My Mind, Among Others, Timothy Leary (Prentice-Hall, 1981)

The Whole Drug Manufacturers Catalog, Chewbacca Darth (Prophet Press, 1977)

Development of the Psychedelic Individual, John Curtis Gowan (Creative Education Foundation, 1974)

The Drug Dilemma, Sidney Cohen (McGraw-Hill, 1969)

Confessions of a Hope Fiend, Timothy Leary (Bantam, 1973)

High Times Encyclopedia of Recreational Drugs (Stonehill, 1978)

Sex & Drugs, Robert A. Wilson (Playboy Press, 1973)

The Intelligence Agents, Timothy Leary (Peace Press, 1979)

The Human Encounter with Death, Stanislav Grof & Joan Halifax (E.P. Dutton, 1967)

The Game of Life, Timothy Leary (Peace Press, 1979)

Amazing Dope Tales & Haight Street Flashbacks, Stephen Gaskin (Book Pub. Co., 1980)

Chemical Ecstasy, Walter Houston Clark (Steed & Ward, 1969)

Flashbacks, Timothy Leary (Tarcher, 1983)

Poetic Vision, R.A. Durr (Syracuse U., 1970)

Hallucinogenic Plants, Richard Evans Schultes (Golden Press, 1976)

What Does Woman Want?, Timothy Leary (88 Books, 1976)

Timothy Leary, the Madness of the Sixties and Me, Charles W. Slack (Peter H. Wyden, 1974)

Psychedelic Baby Reaches Puberty, Peter Stafford (Praeger, 1971, Delta Books, 1972)

The Center of the Cyclone, John Lilly (Julian Press, 1972)

Growing the Hallucinogens, Hudson Grubber (20th Century Alchemist, 1973)

Fear and Loathing in Las Vegas, Hunter S. Thompson (Straight Arrow Press, 1973)

Island, Aldous Huxley (Harper & Row, 1963)

The Future of Consciousness: Proceedings of a July 1979 Colloquium (P.E.C., Box 2544, Santa Cruz, CA 95063)

The Politics of Ecstasy, Timothy Leary (G.P. Putnam's, 1968)

The Inner Landscape, Dennis & Terence McKenna (Shambala, 1974)

This Is It, Alan Watts (MacMillan, 1958, Collier Books, 1967)

The Natural Mind, Andrew Weil (Houghton Mifflin, 1972)

Joyous Cosmology, Alan Watts (Pantheon, 1962, Vintage, 1965)

Psychedelic Drugs: Psychological, Medical & Social Issues, Brian Wells (Penguin, 1973)

"The Use of Music in Psychedelic (LSD) Therapy," Helen L. Bonnie and Walter Pahnke, *Journal of Music Therapy,* 1972

Narcotics: Nature's Dangerous Gifts, Norman Taylor (Dell, 1949, Laurel, 1966)

Recreational Drugs, Young, Klein-Beyer and others (Berkeley Books, 1977)

Blotter #3 & #4 (P.E.C., Box 2544, Santa Cruz, CA 95063)

Castaneda's Journey, Richard de Mille (Capra Press, 1976, 1978)

"On the Evolutionary Significance of Psychedelics," Ralph Metzner, *Main Currents in Modern Thoughts* (1964)

The LSD Family

"Owsley & Me," Charles Perry (*Rolling Stone,* Nov. 25, 1982)

The Use of LSD in Psychotherapy (Josiah Macy, Jr. Foundation, 1961)

The Use of LSD in Psychotherapy and Alcoholism (Bobbs-Merrill, 1967)

LSD Psychotherapy, V.W. Caldwell (Grove Press, 1968, Evergreen, 1969)

The Problems and Prospects of LSD (Charles C. Thomas, J.T. Ungerleider, ed., 1968)

Realms of the Human Unconscious: Observations from LSD Research, Stanislav Grof (Esalen & Viking Presses, 1975)

LSD: Man & Society, edited by Debold & Leaf (Wesleyan University Press, 1967)

The Private Sea: LSD & the Search for God, William Braden (Quadrangle Books, 1967, Bantam, 1968)

LSD—The Consciousness-Expanding Drug, edited by David Solomon (G.P. Putnam's Sons, 1964, Berkeley Medallian, 1966)

LSD—A Generation Later: Proceedings of a Colloquium with Albert Hofmann, Oct. 1977 (P.E.C., Box 2544, Santa Cruz 95063)

LSD—My Problem-Child, Albert Hofmann (McGraw-Hill, 1980)

Peyote, Mescaline and San Pedro

Mescal & Mechanisms of Hallucination, Heinrich Kluver (University of Chicago, 1928, 1942, 1966, Phoenix, 1966, 1971)

Miserable Miracle, Henri Michaux (City Lights Books, 1956, 1963)

The Peyote Dance, Antonin Artaud (Farrar, Straus & Giroux, 1976)

Eduardo el Curandero: The Words of a Peruvian Healer, Calderon, Cowan & Sharon (North Atlantic Books, 1982)

Marijuana and Hashish

Marihuana: An Annotated Bibliography Waller, Johnson, Buelke & Turner (Macmillan, 1977)

Marijuana Grower's Guide, Mel Frank & Ed Rosenthal (And/Or Press, 1974, 1978)

Marihuana: Your Legal Rights, Jay Moller (Nolo Press, 1981)

Cannabis in Costa Rica (Institute for the Study of Human Issues, Wm. Carter, ed., 1982)

The Book of Grass, Andrews & Vinkenoog (Grove Press, 1967)

Weed, Jerry Kamstra (Harper & Row, 1974, Bantam, 1975)

How to Grow Marijuana Hydroponically, Patrick Daniel (Sun Magic, 1977, 1978, 1979)

The Marijuana Farmers, Jack Frazier (Solar Age Press)

NORML, 530 Eighth St., S.E., Washington, D.C. 20003, (202) 547-3707

Marijuana: The Cultivator's Handbook, Bill Drake (Wingbow Press, 1979)

How to Grow Marijuana Indoors Under Lights, Murphy Stevens (Sun Magic, 1975)

Marijuana Food, Bill Drake (Simon & Schuster, 1981)

The Marijuana Papers (New American Library, Signet, 1966, David Solomon, ed.)

Roll Away the Stone, Regardie, Crowley, Baudelaire, Ludlow etc. (Llewellyn Pub., 1968)

Marijuana Moonshine, a 60-minute color video cassette on growing marijuana (And/Or, $85)

Psychoactive Mushrooms

"The Mushrooms of Mexico with Psilocybin: A Bibliography," *Botanical Museum Leaflets of Harvard,* March 10, 1963

Florida Mycological Research Center, Box 8104, Pensacola, FL 32505 (478-3912)

Growing Wild Mushrooms, Bob Harris (Wingbow, 1976)

What's In a Mushroom?, Richard Norland (Pear Tree Publications, 1976)

Contrasting Profiles

The Magical and Ritual Use of Herbs: a Magickal Text on Legal Highs, Richard Alan Miller (Organization for the Advancement of Knowledge, 1980)

The Witch's Garden, Harold A. Hansen (Unity Press, 1978)

Laughing Gas, Shedlin & Wallechinsky (And/Or, 1973)

Kava Kava, E.F. Steinmetz (20th Century Alchemist, 1960)

Index

Aaronson, Bernard, 242
Abel, Ernest L., 157, 171
Abramson, Harold, 44, 46-48
absent-mindedness, 159
"acid," 15, 17, 22-25
"Acid Tests," 20
Acorus calamus, 286
Adams, Roger, 186
addiction, 7, 145
adrenolutin, 5
A.E. (George William Russell), 145
Agnew, Kim, 174
Agora Scientific Trust, 49
Aiken, John and Louise, 120, 138, 150
Air Force experimentation, 40
Agaricus bisporus, 245
Agaricus brunnescens, 245
alcohol, iv, 20-21, 62, 188, 215, 221, 223, 300, 339, 372, 374, 391, 392
alcoholism, 7, 69, 80, 88, 330, 356, 370
ALD-52, 67, 100
Aleph compounds, 293
Alice in Wonderland, 114
alkaline phosphatase, 253
Allen, Morse, 233
allergies, 304
Alles, Gordon, 132, 287-289, 290, 296, 299-300
Alltounian, Howard, 394
Alpert, Richard (Ram Dass), 19, 20, 26, 49, 50, 58, 65, 87, 241, 272, 290, 298-299
Alschuler, Al, 87
Altered States of Consciousness (Drug Abuse Council, 1975), 71
Altered States of Consciousness (Doubleday, 1969, Anchor Books, 1972), 83
Amanita muscaria, 1, 225, 227, 368-383
Amanita pantherina, 225, 374, 376-377
Amanita phalloides, 375, 376
Amanita verna, 374, 376
Amanita virosa, 374
"Amazonian TV," 349
American Journal of Psychiatry, The, 203, 355
American Medical Association, 166
American Pharmaceutical Association, 334
American Psychological Association, 81, 150
American Psychiatric Association, 83
American Scholar, The, 17
aminization, 282
amphetamine, 23, 61, 78, 132, 134, 281, 296-297, 362, 388
amotivational syndrome, 191, 194
analgesics, 74, 199-200, 392-399
Anadananthera peregrina, 264, 308-309, 311, 313, 316-317, 319
Anderson, Arthur, 104

Anderson, Chester, 42
Anderson, Edward S., 104, 123, 126, 128, 132, 135
Andes, 118-119
anesthetics, 392-399
"Angel Dust," 395
Anhalonium williamsii, 126
Anirman, Walter, 324, 359, 365, 383
Anslinger, Harry J., 166-169, 173-174, 178, 203
antibacterial action, 136-137, 200
aphrodisiacs, 342, 353-354, 359, 363, 367, 388
apomorphine, 314
archetypes, 348-351, 355, 363-365, 366
architects, 83, 149-150
Archives of General Psychiatry, 84
Argyreia nervosa, 98-99
Argyreia genus, 98-100
Ariocarpus fissuratus, 129
Ariocarpus retusus, 129
Army experimentation, 40, 44, 47-49, 289
Art and Science of Cannabis Cookery, The (Level Press), 221
arthritis, 73
ARTICHOKE, Project, 46, 233
Art of the Huichol Indians (Fine Arts Museums of San Francisco/Harry N. Abrams, 1978), 140-141, 144, 149
Asian rue, 342-343
Asseko, Ndong, 363-364
asthma, 136, 190
Asthmador, 385, 388
Atharva-Veda, 157
Athens study, University of, 191
atropine, 378, 382, 385-386
auditory effects, 145-146, 275-276, 391
ayahuasca, 305, 319, 332-357
ayahuasqueros, 334, 336-337, 347, 349, 356
Ayurveda, 283
ayurvedic medicine, 286
Aztecs, 95, 103-104, 227, 273-277

badoh negro, 96
Bakalar, James, 1, 56, 323, 324
Banisteriopsis, 332-335, 342, 345, 352-354
Banisteriopsis caapi, 245, 332, 340-342, 355, 356
Banisteriopsis inebrians, 335, 340, 356
Banisteriopsis quitensis, 340, 342
Banisteriopsis rusbyana, 319, 342
Baroff, Ralph, 176
Barron, Frank, 25, 49, 86, 240, 242
Bateson, Gregory, 44
Baudelaire, Charles, 162

409